Jesus' Parables for Disciples

Over 100 Stories, Analogies, and Figurative Sayings

for Personal Devotional Use, Small Groups or
Sunday School Classes, and Sermon Preparation for Pastors and Teachers

JesusWalk® Bible Study Series

by Dr. Ralph F. Wilson
Director, Joyful Heart Renewal Ministries

Additional books and reprint licenses are available at:
www.jesuswalk.com/books/parables.htm

Links to audio recordings of each lesson at:
www.jesuswalk.com/parables/parables.htm

Free Participant Guide handout sheets are available at:
www.jesuswalk.com/parables/parables-lesson-handouts.pdf

JesusWalk® Publications
Loomis, California

Copyright © 2023, Ralph F. Wilson. All rights reserved. May not be copied or reproduced without explicit permission.

Paperback
   ISBN: 9798397567015

Library of Congress subject heading:
   Jesus Christ – Parables

Suggested Classifications
   Library of Congress: BT375.3
   Dewey Decimal System: 226.8

Published by JesusWalk® Publications, P.O. Box 565, Loomis, CA 95650-0565, USA.

JesusWalk is a registered trademark and Joyful Heart is a trademark of Joyful Heart Renewal Ministries.

Unless otherwise noted, all the Bible verses quoted are from the New International Version (International Bible Society, 1973, 1978), used by permission.

2023-06-07

Preface

Jesus constantly framed his teachings in figurative terms. Mark tells us, "He did not say anything to them without using a parable." Why? Partly to veil his teachings so his enemies couldn't use them against him and partly to make them memorable for his disciples to ponder and pass on.

Indeed, one of Jesus' prime means of discipling was to use parables, analogies, and figures of speech of all kinds to capsulize Kingdom truths. Contained in these stories and analogies is a vast domain of teaching designed to change lives.

My goal in this study is to help form you as a follower, a disciple of Jesus by helping you understand these same parables that Jesus used to form the first disciples – and to help you apply them in your life today.

Ralph F. Wilson, detail of 'The Sower (after Millet)' (2023), original watercolor, 10 x 14 inches, private collection. Inspired by Jean-Francois Millet's 1850 painting.

This study is different. Most books on the parables cover 25 to 35 of the best-known teaching parables such as the Good Samaritan, the Prodigal Son, and the Sower, but exclude many others. They look mainly at parables that contain "stories," but tend to exclude figurative analogies such as the Parable of the Vine and the Branches and the Parable of the Good Shepherd and the Sheepgate.

It comes down to definitions. You can define a parable as a *story* that illustrates a spiritual truth; that's how the English dictionary defines it. But when you consider the Greek and Hebrew words that describe figurative speech (Greek *parabolē* and Hebrew *māshāl*), you find that a truly biblical definition of *parabolē* is *much* broader than just stories. A biblical definition would include stories and allegories, of course, but also comparisons, similitudes, and maxims of all kinds.

Rather than see the essence of a parable in terms of a *story*, we should look at a parable in terms of *comparison* – sometimes in stories, other times in similes, metaphors, and simple analogies. They are illustrations that illuminate spiritual truths by comparing them with commonly observed situations and objects.

The effect of adopting a truly biblical definition is significant. Now, instead of two or three dozen parables, we find more than 100 stories, analogies, and sayings that Jesus used to train his disciples -- much truer to the breadth and depth of Jesus' own training of his disciples.

This series of 12 lessons is designed to explore essentially all of Jesus' parables, analogies, and sayings. We'll also survey three of Jesus' powerful *acted parables*. Some we'll examine in detail, others more briefly. Our guiding principle is how central a parable or analogy is to Jesus' mission of building disciples for the Kingdom. (A few additional parables and analogies are included in an appendix for the sake of completeness.)

Each parable or analogy is placed in its context and historical setting, then mined for the gold that Jesus' intended for his first disciples – and for us today.

I invite you on a 12-week internship with the Master as we take a deep dive into *Jesus' Parables for Disciples*.

Pastor Ralph
Loomis, California
September 1, 2023

Table of Contents

Preface	3
Table of Contents	5
Reprint Guidelines	11
References and Abbreviations	12
Introduction to Jesus' Parables	14
1. Parables about God's Love	**22**
1.1 Searching for the Lost	22
Parable of the Lost Sheep (Luke 15:3-6a, §172; Matthew 18:12-14, §133)	23
Parable of the Lost Coin (Luke 15:8-10; §172)	25
Parable of the Lost Son or the Prodigal Son (Luke 15:11-32; §173)	27
1.2 The Father's Forgiveness and Mercy	33
Parable of the Two Debtors (Luke 7:41-43, 47, §83)	33
Parable of the Unmerciful Servant (Matthew 18:23-35, §136)	34
2. Parables about Israel's Unbelief	**41**
2.1 Israel's Barrenness, Pride, and Disobedience	43
Parable of the Barren Fig Tree (Luke 13:6-9; §162)	43
2.2 Rejection of the Messiah by Israel	45
Analogy of the Hen and Chickens (Matthew 23:37, §211; Luke 13:34, §167)	45
Parable of the Wedding Banquet (Matthew 22:1-10, §205, cf. §170)	46
Parable of the Great Banquet (Luke 14:15-24, §170, cf. Matthew 22:2-10, §205)	46
2.3 Excluding Israel from Messiah's Kingdom	55
Parable of the Wicked Tenants (Matthew 21:33-46; Mark 12:1-12; Luke 20:9-19, §204)	55
3. Parables about Repentance	**62**
3.1 Uncleanness is Internal not External	63
Analogy of Cleansing the Cup (Matthew 23:25-26, §210; Luke 11:39-41, §154)	63
Analogy of the Whitewashed Tombs (Matthew 23:27-28, §210)	65
Analogy of the Defiling Heart of Man (Mark 7:14-23; Matthew 15:10-11, 15-20, §115)	65
3.2 Repent before Judgment Comes	69
Parable of the Guilty Defendant (Matthew 5:25-26, §22; Luke 12:57-59, § 161)	69
Parable of the Wise and Foolish Builders (Matthew 7:24-27, §43; Luke 6:47-49, §78)	72

Parable of the Narrow and Wide Gates (Matthew 7:13-14, §40) ... 74
3.3 Discipleship Requires Obedience ... 77
Parable of the Two Sons (Matthew 21:28-31, §203) ... 77
3.4 Discerning Sin in Our Lives ... 79
Parable of the Speck and the Beam (Matthew 7:3-5, §36; Luke 6:41-42, §76) ... 79
Parable of the Good Eye (Matthew 6:22-23, §33; Luke 11:34-36, §153) ... 81

4. Parables about Final Judgment ... 84
4.1 Role Reversal at Judgment ... 84
Parable of the Rich Man and Lazarus (Luke 16:19-31, §177) ... 85
4.2 Separation of the Righteous and Wicked ... 90
Parable of the Sheep and the Goats (Matthew 25:31-46, §229) ... 90
Parable of the Weeds or Tares (Matthew 13:24-30, §96; 36-43, §100) ... 95
Parable of the Net (Matthew 13:47-50, §102) ... 99
4.3 Grace Triumphs over Judgment ... 102
Parable of the Laborers in Vineyard (Matthew 20:1-16, §190) ... 102

5. Parables about Readiness for Christ's Return ... 107
5.1 Signs of Impending Return ... 107
Parable of the Weather Signs (Luke 12:54-56, §160) ... 107
Parable of the Budding Fig Tree (Matthew 24:32-33; Mark 13:28-29; Luke 21:29-31; §220) ... 108
Analogy of Lightning (Luke 17:24, §184; Matthew 24:27, §218) ... 109
Analogy of the Vultures Gathering (Luke 17:37, §184; Matthew 24:38, §218) ... 110
5.2 Watchfulness and Obedience Needed ... 111
Parables of the Watching Servants (Mark 13:34-37, §222; Luke 12:35-38; §158) ... 112
Parable of the Burglar (Luke 12:39-40; Matthew 24:43-44; §158) ... 116
Parable of the Wise and Foolish Virgins (Matthew 25:1-13; §227) (Also known as the Parable of the Ten Maidens; Ten Virgins; Ten Bridesmaids) ... 118
5.3 Faithful Service in the Master's Absence ... 122
Parable of the Wise and Faithful Steward (Matthew 24:45-51, §226; Luke 12:42-46; §§158-159) ... 122

6. Parables about Salvation ... 128
6.1 Analogies of Salvation ... 128
Analogy of Spiritual Birth (John 3:3-7) ... 129
Analogy of the Wind of the Spirit (John 3:8) ... 130
Analogy of Lifting the Bronze Serpent (John 3:14-15) ... 131
Parable of the Bread of Life (John 6:35) ... 131
Parable of Water for Eternal Life (John 4:10, 13-14) ... 132

Table of Contents

Parable of Streams of Living Water (John 7:37-39) — 133
Saying of the Camel and the Needle (Matthew 19:23-24; Mark 10:24-25; Luke 18:24-25; §189) — 135

6.2 Parables of Jesus' Death and Resurrection — 137
Acted Parable of the Bread and the Wine (Matthew 26:26-29; Mark 14:22-25; Luke 22:15-20; §236) — 137
Acted Parable of Baptism (Mark 1:4-8; Matthew 28:19-20; Mark 16:15-16) — 139
Analogy of the Kernel of Wheat (John 12:24) — 140
Analogy of the Rooms in the Father's House (John 14:2-4) — 141
Parable of the Woman in Childbirth (John 16:21) — 142

6.3 Setting People Free — 143
Analogy of a House Divided (Matthew 12:25-26; Mark 3:24-26; §86; Luke 11:17-18, §149) — 143
Parable of Binding the Strong Man (Matthew 12:29; Mark 3:27, §86; Luke 11:21-22, §149) — 144
Parable of the Empty House (Matthew 12:43-45, §88; Luke 11:23-26, §150) — 147

7. Parables about the Nature of Christ's Kingdom — 150

7.1. Small but Expanding — 151
Parable of the Mustard Seed (Matthew 13:31-32; Mark 4:30-32; Luke 13:18-19; §97) — 151
Parable of the Yeast or Leaven (Matthew 13:33, §98; Luke 13:20-21, §164) — 152
Parable of the Seed Growing by Itself (Mark 4:26-29, §95) — 154

7.2 John the Baptist and Jesus the Messiah — 156
Parable of the Bridegroom's Guests (Matthew 9:14-15; Mark 2:18-20; Luke 5:33-35; §54) — 156

7.3 The Old and the New — 157
Parable of the Unshrunk Cloth (Matthew 9:16; Mark 2:21; Luke 5:36; §54) — 158
Parable of the Wineskins (Matthew 9:17; Mark 2:22; Luke 5:37-39; §54) — 158

7.4 The Flock of the Kingdom — 162
Parables of the Good Shepherd and the Sheep Gate (John 10:1-18) — 162

8. Parables about Responding to the Kingdom — 171

8.1 Receptivity to the Kingdom — 172
Parable of the Sower (Matthew 13:1-9, 18-23; Mark 4:3-9, 13-20; Luke 8:4-8, 11-15; §§90, 93) — 172
Saying: Pearls before Swine (Matthew 7:6, §37) — 181

8.2 Forcible Nature of Discipleship — 182
Parable of the Narrow Door (Luke 13:23-27, §165) — 182

8.3 The Priority of Discipleship — 185
Analogy of Foxholes and Nests (Matthew 18:19-20, §49; Luke 9:57-58, §138) — 185
Analogy of the Dead Burying the Dead (Matthew 18:21-22, §49; Luke 9:59-60, §138) — 186
Analogy of Looking Back from the Plow (Luke 9:61-62, §138) — 186

8.4 Counting the Cost of Discipleship — 187

Parable of the Tower-Builder (Luke 14:28-30, §171) ... 187
Parable of the Warring King (Luke 14:31-32, §171) ... 188
Parable of Taking Up One's Cross (Matthew 16:24-25; Mark 8:34-35; Luke 9:23-24; §123; and Matthew 10:37-39, §62; Luke 14:25-27, §171) ... 189

8.5 Ultimate Prize of the Kingdom ... 194
Parable of the Hidden Treasure (Matthew 13:44, §101) ... 194
Parable of the Pearl of Great Price (Matthew 13:45-46, §101) ... 195

9. Parables about Disciple Character ... 198
9.1 Humility ... 198
Parable of the Pharisee and Tax Collector (Luke 18:9-14, §186) ... 199
Parable of Becoming Like Little Children (Matthew 18:3-4, §129) ... 203
Parable of Welcoming Little Children (Matthew 19:13-15; Mark 10:13-16, Luke 18:15-17; §188) ... 204
Parable of Places at the Table (Luke 14:7-11, §169) ... 206

9.2 Avoiding Hypocrisy ... 208
Analogy of the Yeast of the Pharisees (Matthew 16:5-6, 11-12; Mark 8:14-15, §120; Luke 12:1, §154) ... 208

9.3 Abiding ... 211
Parable of the Vine and the Branches (John 15:1-8) ... 211
Parable of Eating Jesus' Flesh (John 6:53-58) ... 220
The Analogy of the Yoke (Matthew 11:28-30, §68) ... 221

10. Parables about Disciple Values ... 224
10.1 Careful Discernment ... 224
Analogy of the Wolf in Sheep's Clothing (Matthew 7:15-16a, §41) ... 225
Analogy of the Tree and Fruit (Matthew 7:16-20, §41; Luke 6:43-44; §77; Matthew 12:33-35, §86) ... 225
Analogy of the Treasure Chest of the Heart (Luke 6:45, §77) ... 226
False Prophets vs. Imperfect Leaders ... 229
Parable of the Unjust Steward (Luke 16:1-13; §174) ... 229

10.2 Trust and Money ... 235
Parable of the Rich Fool (Luke 12:16-21, §156) ... 235
Parable of the Two Masters (Luke 16:13, §174; Matthew 6:24, §34) ... 238
Parable of the Birds and the Lilies (Matthew 6:25-34, §35; Luke 12:22-31, §157) ... 241

10.3 Faithful Prayer ... 242
Analogy of Asking a Father for Bread (Matthew 7:9-11, §38; Luke 11:11-13, §148) ... 242
Parable of the Friend at Midnight (Luke 11:5-10, §147) ... 243
Parable of the Unjust Judge (Luke 18:1-8, §185) ... 246

Table of Contents

    Analogy of the Faith of a Mustard Seed (Matthew 17:19, §127; Luke 17:6, §180)   249

11. Parables about Disciple Practices   251
11.1 Humble Service   251
  Acted Parable of Washing the Disciples' Feet (John 13:4-17)   251
  Parable of the Dutiful Servant (Luke 17:7-10, §181)   256
11.2 Service in the Kingdom   259
  Parable of the Talents (Matthew 25:14-30, §228)   259
  Parable of the Minas or Pounds (Luke 19:12-27; §195)   259
11.3 Showing Love and Mercy   270
  Parable of the Good Samaritan (Luke 10:30-37; §144)   270

12. Parables about Caring for the Lost   277
12.1   A Heart for the Lost   277
  Analogy of the Doctor and the Sick (Matthew 9:12; Mark 2:17; Luke 5:31; §53)   278
  Analogies of the Lost Sheep (Matthew 9:36; 10:5-6; 15:24; John 10:16)   280
12.2 Workers in the Harvest   282
  Analogy of the Harvest and the Laborers (Matthew 9:37-38, §58; Luke 10:2, §139)   282
  Analogy of Fields White for Harvest (John 4:35)   284
  Analogy of the Sowers and Reapers (John 4:36-38)   284
  Analogies of the Sheep and Wolves, Serpents and Doves (Matthew 10:16, §58; Luke 10:3, §139)   285
12.3 Witnessing to the Lost   287
  Analogy of Sparrows (Matthew 10:29-30, §60; Luke 12:6-7, §155)   287
  Analogy of Fishers of Men (Matthew 4:18-20; Mark 1:16-18; §11; Luke 5:10-11, §17)   288
  Analogy of the Savorless Salt (Matthew 5:13, §20; Mark 9:50; Luke 14:34-35, §171)   288
  Analogy of the City on a Hill (Matthew 5:14; §20)   290
  Analogy of the Lamp under a Bushel (Matthew 5:15, §20; Mark 4:21; Luke 8:16-17, §94; Luke 11:33; §153)   290
12.4 Teaching the Kingdom   293
  Parable of the Scribes of the Kingdom (Matthew 13:51-52, §103)   293

Appendix 1. Participant Handouts   297
Appendix 2. List of Jesus' Parables and Analogies   298
Appendix 3. A Vocabulary for Parables and Analogies   302
  Hebrew and Greek Words for Parable   302
  An English Vocabulary for Parables   302

Appendix 4. Miscellaneous Parables, Analogies, and Sayings — 305
  1. Light and Darkness — 306
    Analogies of Walking in Light and Darkness (John 9:4; 11:9-10; 12:35-36a) — 306
    Analogy of the Light of the World (John 8:12; 9:5; 1:4-9) — 307
  2. Jesus — 307
    Saying: Physician, Heal Yourself (Luke 4:23-24, §10) — 307
    Analogy of the Temple of Jesus' Body (John 2:18-22) — 308
    The Parable of the Sign of Jonah (Matthew 12:38-42, §87; Luke 11:29-32, §152) — 309
    Analogy of the Slave and the Son (John 8:34-36) — 310
    Analogy of the Bridegroom's Friend (John the Baptist, John 3:29-30) — 311
  3. Jesus' Enemies — 312
    Analogy of the Children in the Marketplace (Matthew 11:16-19, §65; Luke 7:31-32, §82) — 312
    Parable of Rescuing from a Well (Matthew 12:9-14, §70; Luke 14:2-5, §168) — 313
    Saying of the Blind Leading the Blind (Matthew 15:14, §115; Luke 6:39, §76) — 313
    Analogy of the Brood of Vipers (Matthew 12:34, §85; 23:33, §210) — 314
    Analogy of the Den of Robbers (Matthew 21:13; Luke 19:46, §198; John 2:16) — 314
  4. The Kingdom — 314
    Analogy of Peter the Rock (Matthew 16:18, §122; John 1:42) — 314
    Analogy of the Keys of the Kingdom (Matthew 16:19, §122) — 315

Appendix 5. The Great Messianic Banquet — 316

Appendix 6. Slavery in Jesus' Day — 319

Reprint Guidelines

Copying the Handouts. In some cases, small groups or Sunday school classes would like to use these notes to study this material. That's great. An appendix provides copies of handouts designed for classes and small groups. There is no charge whatsoever to print out as many copies of the handouts as you need for participants.

www.jesuswalk.com/parables/parables-lesson-handouts.pdf

All charts and notes are copyrighted and must bear the line:

"Copyright © 2023, Ralph F. Wilson. All rights reserved. Reprinted by permission."

You may not resell these notes to other groups or individuals outside your congregation. You may, however, charge people in your group enough to cover your copying costs.

To copy the book (or the majority of it) for your congregation or group you are requested to purchase a reprint license for each book. A Reprint License, $2.50 for each copy, is available for purchase at

www.jesuswalk.com/books/parables.htm

Or you may send a check to:

Dr. Ralph F. Wilson
JesusWalk Publications
PO Box 565
Loomis, CA 95650, USA

The Scripture says,

"The laborer is worthy of his hire" (Luke 10:7) and "Anyone who receives instruction in the word must share all good things with his instructor." (Galatians 6:6)

However, if you are from a third world country or an area where it is difficult to transmit money, please make a small contribution instead to help the poor in your community.

References and Abbreviations

BDAG	Walter Bauer and Frederick William Danker, *A Greek-English Lexicon of the New Testament and Other Early Christian Literature* (Third Edition; based on previous English editions by W.F. Arndt, F.W. Gingrich, and F.W. Danker; University of Chicago Press, 1957, 1979, 2000)
Beasley-Murray, *John*	George R. Beasley-Murray, *John* (Vol. 36, Word Biblical Commentary; Word, 1987)
Brown, *John*	Raymond E. Brown, *The Gospel According to John* (The Anchor Bible, volumes 29 and 29A; Doubleday, 1966)
DJG	Joel B. Green, Scot McKnight, and I. Howard Marshall (editors), *Dictionary of Jesus and the Gospels* (InterVarsity Press, 1992)
DJG2	Joel B. Green, Jeannine K. Brown, and Nicholas Perrin (editors), *Dictionary of Jesus and the Gospels, Second Edition* (IVP Academic, 2013)
Dodd, *Parables*	C. H. Dodd, *The Parables of the Kingdom* (Revised Edition; Charles Scribner's Sons, 1961)
ISBE	Geoffrey W. Bromiley (general editor), *The International Standard Bible Encyclopedia* (fully revised from the 1915 edition; Eerdmans, 1979-1988)
Edersheim, *Life and Times*	Alfred Edersheim, *The Life and Times of Jesus the Messiah* (2 volume edition; Eerdmans, 1969, reprinted from the third edition, 1886)
France, *Mark*	R.T. France, *The Gospel of Mark* (New International Greek Testament Commentary; Eerdmans, 2002).
France, *Matthew*	R.T. France, *The Gospel of Matthew* (New International Commentary on the New Testament; Eerdmans, 2007)
Green, *Luke*	Joel B. Green, *The Gospel of Luke* (The New International Commentary on the New Testament; Eerdmans, 1997)
Grudem	Wayne A. Grudem, *Systematic Theology: An Introduction to Biblical Doctrine* (Zondervan, 1994, 2000)
Hunter	Archibald M. Hunter, *Interpreting the Parables* (Westminster Press, 1960)
Jeremias, *Parables*	Joachim Jeremias, *The Parables of Jesus* (Second Revised Edition; Charles Scribner's Sons, 1954, 1963, 1972)
KJV	King James Version (Authorized Version, 1611)

References and Abbreviations

Liddell-Scott	Henry George Liddell and Robert Scott, *A Greek-English Lexicon* (revised and augmented throughout by Sir Henry Stuart Jones with the assistance of Roderick McKenzie; Oxford, Clarendon Press, 1940)
Marshall, *Luke*	I. Howard Marshall, *Commentary on Luke* (New International Greek Testament Commentary; Eerdmans, 1978)
Metzger	Bruce M. Metzger, *A Textual Commentary on the Greek New Testament* (United Bible Societies, 1971)
Morris, *John*	Leon Morris, *The Gospel According to John* (New International Commentary on the New Testament; Eerdmans, 1971)
Morris, *Matthew*	Leon Morris, *The Gospel According to Matthew* (Pillar Commentary series; Eerdmans, 1992)
Moulton and Milligan	James Hope Moulton and George Milligan (*The Vocabulary of the Greek Testament Illustrated from the Papryi and other Non-Literary Sources* (London, 1929)
NASB	New American Standard Bible (The Lockman Foundation, 1960-1988)
NIDNTT	Colin Brown (editor), *New International Dictionary of New Testament Theology* (Zondervan, 1975-1978)
NIV	New International Version (Biblia [International Bible Society], 1973, 1978)
NJB	New Jerusalem Bible (Darton, Longman & Todd Ltd., 1985)
NKJV	New King James Version (Thomas Nelson, 1982)
NLT	New Living Translation (Tyndale House Foundation, 1996, 2004, 2015)
NRSV	New Revised Standard Version (Division of Christian Education of the National Council of Churches of Christ, USA, 1989)
Snodgrass, *Stories*	Klyne R. Snodgrass, *Stories with Intent: A Comprehensive Guide to the Parables of Jesus* (Eerdmans, 2008)
Strack and Billerbeck	Hermann L. Strack and Paul Billerbeck, *Commentary on the New Testament from the Talmud and Midrash* (München: German, 1926; English, 1956).
TDNT	Gerhard Kittel and Gerhard Friedrich (editors), Geoffrey W. Bromiley (translator and editor), *Theological Dictionary of the New Testament,* (Eerdmans, 1964-1976; translated from *Theologisches Wörterbuch zum Neuen Testament,* ten volume edition)
Thayer	Joseph Henry Thayer, *Greek-English Lexicon of the New Testament* (Associated Publishers and Authors, n.d., reprinted from 1889 edition)

Introduction to Jesus' Parables

As we begin our study of Jesus' parables, we need to specify exactly what we mean by "parable."

What Is a Parable?

The simplest definition of a parable might be stories intended to convey spiritual truths. Indeed, that is how "parable" is usually defined in English.

But some of Jesus' most powerful parables are short, just a verse or two – hardly long enough to develop into a real narrative. Instead, they set up contrasts that compare well-known practices and situations with spiritual truths. For example,

> "He told them still another parable: 'The kingdom of heaven is like yeast that a woman took and mixed into a large amount of flour until it worked all through the dough.'" (Matthew 13:33)

It's short. A simple comparison. There is hardly a story line, just a common situation with a spiritual comparison. But Matthew refers to it as a "parable."

The Greek word is *parabolē* – "a narrative or saying of varying length, designed to illustrate a truth especially through comparison or simile, comparison, illustration, parable, proverb, maxim."[1] Notice that this is much broader than the usual definition of our English word "parable"[2] The New Testament *parabolē* follows the breadth of the Hebrew noun *mashal* that includes an even wider range of stories, sayings, and comparisons both long and short. (For more on this, see Appendix 3. A Vocabulary for Parables and Analogies.)

One's definition of "parable" is important. Some scholars count about 30 parables. Others over 60.[3] Rather than focusing narrowly on the so-called "teaching parables," I'll be exploring over 100 of Jesus' stories, analogies, and sayings. (See Appendix 2. List of Jesus' Parables and Analogies.) Of course, I will be spending more time on parables and analogies central to Jesus' disciple-making ministry, and less on the others.

---

[1] *Parabolē*, BDAG 759, 2a.
[2] Parable, "A usually short fictitious *story* that illustrates a moral attitude or a religious principle" (*Merriam-Webster Collegiate Dictionary*, 11th Edition). Blomberg defines a parable as "A metaphor or simile often extended to a short narrative; in biblical contexts almost always formulated to reveal and illustrate the kingdom of God" (Craig L. Blomberg, "Parable," ISBE 3:655). Dodd says it is "a metaphor or simile drawn from nature or common life, arresting the hearer by its vividness or strangeness, and leaving the mind in sufficient doubt about its precise application to tease it into active thought" (Dodd, *Parables*, p. 5). Snodgrass summarizes this way: "In most cases a parable is an expanded analogy used to convince and persuade" (Snodgrass, *Stories*, p. 9).
[3] Garwood P. Anderson, "Parables," DJG2 651.

Introduction to Parables

I've decided to be comprehensive, if not exhaustive. Why? Because many of these more obscure analogies convey powerful truths – and my goal here is to train modern-day disciples by means of the parables and analogies Jesus used. (I have pulled 14 parabolic sayings out of the lesson text itself, but for the sake of completeness included them in Appendix 4. Miscellaneous Analogies and Sayings.)

Parables in John's Gospel

Some scholars insist that John's Gospel doesn't contain any true parables.[4] Indeed, the Greek noun *parabolē* does not occur in John at all. It is true that the figures of speech in John may differ some from those in the Synoptic Gospels. However, it is wrong to say that John contains no true parables. Hunter identifies about thirteen.[5] Brown concludes:

> "We must recognize that the illustrations and figures found in both John and in the Synoptics come under the name *mashal*. The most we can say is that the allegorical element receives more emphasis in John."[6]

Parables in John often tend to be extended metaphors, reflections on a comparison, with less of a story line. However, I see them as true parables in spite of the differences.

Thus, I have included from John's Gospel such important parables as the Parable of the Vine and the Branches (Lesson 9.3) and the Good Shepherd and the Sheepgate (Lesson 7.4), as well as many shorter parables and analogies.

The scope of this will encompass all the narratives and sayings of Jesus that would be covered by the Greek definition of *parabolē* that we saw above.

> "A narrative or saying of varying length, designed to illustrate a truth especially through comparison or simile, comparison, illustration, parable, proverb, maxim."[7]

Categories of Parables

Some scholars classify parables into various precise categories.[8] I'll often use the term "parable" broadly, but I'll focus on three simple categories:

1. Sayings, short pithy maxims.

---

[4] Snodgrass (*Stories*, pp. 22-23) says, "In the technical sense there are no parables in John. They are *meshalim* such as the Door to the Sheepfold or the Good Shepherd," but nothing like the Synoptic forms.

[5] A. M. Hunter, *Parables*, pp. 78-79.

[6] Brown, *John*, 2:668-669.

[7] *Parabolē*, BDAG 759, 2a.

[8] Snodgrass (*Stories*, pp. 9-15) classifies parables into 7 categories: (1) aphoristic sayings; (2) similitudes (double indirect), extended similes that lack plot development; (3) interrogative parables (double indirect) that contain questions to draw in the hearer; (4) double indirect narrative parables, analogies dealing with two different realms and with two levels of meaning; (5) juridical parables that include an accusatory element; and (6) single indirect narrative parables. sometimes called "example stories"; and (7) "How much more" parables.

2. Analogies, any kind of comparison that lacks a plot, such as metaphors and similes.
3. Parables, stories that usually include some narrative element. But I also use it for a few one-verse figures of speech that are popularly known as parables.

I've also included some Acted Parables that involve deliberate comparisons but are acted out (Bread and Wine, Baptism, Washing the Disciples' Feet).

The Nature of the Kingdom

Many of the parables in the Synoptic Gospels are designed to teach the disciples about the nature of the Kingdom of God. The Jews had been expecting Messiah to come, overthrow the Roman oppressors, and set up David's kingdom on earth. So, Jesus must explain a number of things about the spiritual nature of the Kingdom he brings, often through parables. You'll see some that begin, "The kingdom of God is like ...."

Incidentally, for "Kingdom of God" (Mark and Luke), Matthew substitutes "Kingdom of heaven," since he is writing for Jewish readers who sought by this euphemism to avoid using the word "God." But there is no difference in meaning between the two.

Jesus' Purpose in Teaching via Parables

Why did Jesus' teach in parables? It is complicated. I believe that parables are designed to both (1) clarify truth to those who are seeking after it, and (2) obscure truth for those who are spiritually dull. Let me explain.

1. Parables Are Intended to Clarify Truth to the Spiritually Hungry

Jesus concludes the Parable of Sower (Lesson 8.1) with the words:

"He who has ears to hear, let him hear." (Mark 4:9)

He wants the spiritually hungry, who have "ears to hear," to understand his teachings.

"The secret of the kingdom of God has been given to you." (Mark 4:11)

Clearly, parables were designed to reveal the secrets or mysteries[9] of the Kingdom. They compared spiritual truths to familiar objects, people, and situations so that the disciples could understand better what Jesus was saying.

Bare theological statements are uninteresting, boring. But when their meaning is fleshed out in a story or comparison, people are drawn in and begin to understand the nuances Jesus is seeking to convey. Parables function as memory capsules that enable the disciples to recall and refresh their memories of Jesus' teaching.

---

[9] *Mystērion*, "secret," here, "the unmanifested or private counsel of God, (God's) secret," the secret thoughts, plans, and dispensations of God (BDAG 661, 1a).

But parables could sometimes be frustrating for the disciples and difficult for them to understand. On one occasion they tell him with some relief: "Now you are speaking clearly and without figures of speech"[10] (John 16:29).

2. Parables Are Intended to Hide Truth from the Spiritually Dull

On the other hand, parables are meant to obscure the truth to those who are not spiritually hungry, who are only looking for ways to oppose Jesus.

> "¹¹ The secret of the kingdom of God has been given to you. But to those on the outside everything is said in parables ¹² so that,
>
>> 'They may be ever seeing but never perceiving,
>> and ever hearing but never understanding;
>> otherwise they might turn and be forgiven!'" (Mark 4:11-12)

Jesus explains that the reason he uses parables is *for the purpose*, "so that" (verse 12a), the blind Israelites won't understand.

Jesus quotes from Isaiah 9, as do other New Testament writers.[11] Each time the verse is quoted in the New Testament, it is to remind the readers that though Isaiah was called to preach to the Jewish people, most would not listen because they had dull hearts. They don't have ears tuned to hear spiritually. (For more on this, see my exposition of the Parable of the Sower, Lesson 8.1.)

It is possible to hear the gospel many times, but each time you fail to respond positively, your heart becomes that much more calloused and less able to understand the next time. Gospel hardening is a normal effect when the gospel is preached to fallen mankind. Some will seek the light, but the majority will not. Even when Jesus himself preaches the gospel, few follow the way, as he says in the Parable of the Narrow and Wide Gates (Lesson 3.2):

> "Enter through the narrow gate. For wide is the gate and broad is the road that leads to destruction, and many enter through it. But small is the gate and narrow the road that leads to life, and only a few find it." (Matthew 7:13-14)

At first, the religious leaders of Jesus' day heard him with curiosity. But after a while, they listened only to trick him, trip him up, and formulate charges against him so they could have him arrested. Jesus' preaching hardened people's hearts.

In other words, Jesus speaks in parables "in order that" spiritually dull people won't really understand what he is saying. Perhaps, this is a way of applying his directive "Do not cast your pearls before swine" (Matthew 7:6; Lesson 8.1). Through parables, Jesus can

---

[10] "Figures of speech" (NIV, NRSV), "figurative speech" (ESV), "proverb" (KJV) is *paroimia*, "a brief communication containing truths designed for initiates, veiled saying, figure of speech," in which especially lofty ideas are concealed (BDAG 780, 2).

[11] Matthew 13:14-15; Luke 8:10; Mark 4:12, as well as Acts 28:26-27 and Romans 11:8.

communicate with the people who are eager to listen, while others won't understand enough to cause immediate trouble. Furthermore, the parables encapsulate nuggets of Kingdom truth that can be remembered, pondered, and communicated to others.

A Long History of Allegorizing Jesus' Parables

Now let's consider how to interpret Jesus' parables. For over a thousand years, the parables were commonly interpreted as allegories, where each element was spiritualized to represent something else. For example, Origen (185-254 AD) and later Augustine (354-430 AD) saw the Parable of the Good Samaritan (Luke 10:25-37, Lesson 11.3) as symbolizing Christ healing the wounds caused by sin. Every element corresponded to something else.

Wounded traveler	Adam
Jerusalem	Paradise
Jericho	The moon that waxes, wanes, and dies; human mortality
Robbers	The devil and his angels
Priest	The Law
Levite	The Prophets
Samaritan	Christ
Wounds	Disobedience, vices, and sin
Oil and wine	Comfort and exhortation
Donkey	The Lord's body that bears our sins
Inn	The Church
Two Denarii	Knowledge of the Father and the Son
Innkeeper	The Apostle Paul
Promised Return	Christ's Second Coming

If this all sounds outlandish, it is! But allegorizing was *the* traditional method of interpretation until the Reformers, who sought the "plain meaning" of Scripture. In spite of that, allegorizing still lives today. I once attended a church that considered allegorizing the high priest's garments was leading the congregation to "deeper truth." The problem with allegorizing is that you lose all the restraints of the actual text – context, history, and use of words. You can make a parable mean anything you want it to mean, if you have an active enough imagination.

Introduction to Parables

Seeking Rules of Interpretation

While Luther and Calvin sought to return to the plain meaning of Scripture in the fifteenth and sixteenth centuries, it wasn't until the beginning of the twentieth century that interpreters began to work out rules of interpretation for parables. German Bible scholar Adolf Jülicher (1857-1938) insisted that, in keeping with classical Greek usage, each parable could have only one point of comparison, rather than several, as in an allegory. In reaction to the unbridled allegorization of parables in the Church, he also insisted that Jesus didn't use allegories.[12] Since his time, we can see that, though he was on the right track, he overstated the situation.[13]

While there is no one set of rules that can be applied rigorously to interpret all parables, Anderson gives us a helpful structure to consider, in terms of (1) allegory, (2) the single point, (3) eschatology, (4) structure, (5) literary context, and (6) polyvalence (that is, bearing multiple senses and resisting a singular determinate meaning).[14] We'll keep these in mind as we consider at each parable in the pages that follow, but we need to consider three in this introduction – allegory, the single point, and the first-century context.

Allegory. For the most part, Jesus' parables are not typical allegories like Pilgrim's Progress, where each element corresponds to something else. As mentioned, allegorization led the Church astray for many, many centuries. However, a couple of Jesus' parables actually do indeed have allegorical features. In the Parable of the Wicked Tenants (Lesson 2.3) it is rather clear that the vineyard owner represents God, the vineyard is Israel, the tenants are the Jews and Jewish leaders, the owner's representatives are the prophets, and the owner's son is Jesus. There are occasional allegorical elements here and there in other parables.[15] However, *for the most part*, Jesus' parables are not allegories.[16]

The Single Point. Along with Jülicher's insistence that Jesus' parables were not intended as allegories, he taught that each parable has only a single point of comparison (whereas an allegory would have several). That is helpful, but not entirely the case. Indeed, a few parables may have more than one point. The Parable of the Good Samaritan (Lesson 11.3), for example, teaches both that (1) our neighbor might be an enemy, and (2) loving means doing practical good to our fellow man. The Parable of the Lost Son (Lesson 1.1) has points about the Father's

---

[12] Adolf Jülicher, *Die Gleichnisreden Jesu* (1888, 1899).
[13] Brown, *John*, 1:390-391. A. Jülicher at the end of the last century "maintained that allegory was an artificial, literary device, and was never used by a rustic preacher like Jesus who spoke in simple parables. The Christian exegetes were the ones who interpreted Jesus' one-point parables as if they were allegory.... In "Parable and Allegory Reconsidered," NovT 5 (1951), 36-45 (NTRE Ch XIII), we have tried to show that, although Jülicher's theory continues to have a considerable following, it is really a gross oversimplification.... He was wrong in drawing a sharp distinction between parable and simple allegory in Jesus' own preaching."
[14] Garwood P. Anderson, "Parables," DJG2, pp. 660-662.
[15] The Parable of the Sower (Lesson 8.1) and the Parable of the Weeds or the Tares (Lesson 4.2).
[16] "Parables are allegorical, some more than others." (Snodgrass, *Stories*, p. 16).

love, as well as the older son's resentments. We'll consider them in due course. But, *usually*, parables have only one point. We shouldn't look for more.

First Century Context. It is vital that we understand the historical and cultural context in which Jesus is speaking. Snodgrass cautions, "If we are after the intent of Jesus, we must seek to hear a parable as Jesus' Palestinian hearers would have heard it."[17] We'll be watching for this as we examine each parable. Only after we understand parables in their own context, can we accurately apply them to our lives in the present day.

Parables and Storytellers

As we study the parables, we need to understand the longer parables as a product of a storyteller's art. In our culture, stories appear in print or on the screen as fixed, completed. But in an oral culture it is more fluid.

If you've done some public speaking, you know that audiences differ. Some are less spiritually-attuned; others are more responsive. As you get a feel for the audience, you vary your message some – and your choice of illustrations – in order to reach that particular group. Jesus' parables are like that. Some seem almost identical in the Synoptic Gospels. But others vary from one Gospel to the other. They can be found in different contexts and even use different words to express the same idea, such as in the Parable of the Guilty Defendant (Lesson 3.2). We must remember that the disciples heard Jesus' parables hundreds of times over three years – in many different villages and contexts. No wonder we see variations between the Synoptic Gospels.

Gospel Parallels

Long ago when I was a college student, I was required to purchase a copy of Throckmorton's *Gospel Parallels* for my "Bible as Literature" class. I still have that thin volume, though the cloth binding is frayed around the edges and the pages covered with notes. As a long-time student of the Gospels, I have given it a lot of use! It helpfully compares the texts of Matthew, Mark, and Luke in side-by-side columns.

If you are a teacher or pastor, I encourage you to get a volume for your ongoing studies. Since many of the parables are given in two or three Gospels with (usually) minor differences, being able to compare them side-by-side is useful. To make this easy for you, I have included in the headings the section number (§) of the passages as found in Burton H. Throckmorton, Jr. (ed.), *Gospel Parallels: A Comparison of the Synoptic Gospels*, a classic since 1949, commonly used in Bible schools and seminaries. You can find this in various editions and Bible translations in "used" condition for about $10 US. All of the Throckmorton editions display identical section numbers.

---

[17] Snodgrass, *Stories*, p. 25.

In my discussion of the parables, I generally ignore slight variations in the Synoptic accounts and only comment on the more striking differences. Often, I'll follow Luke's account, since I wrote extensively on the parables in *Disciple Training in Luke's Gospel* (JesusWalk Publications, 2010, 2020). I've also drawn on parables covered in other studies: *Jesus and the Kingdom of God: Discipleship Lessons* (JesusWalk, 2010), *Sermon on the Mount: the Jesus Manifesto* (JesusWalk, 2011), and *John's Gospel: A Discipleship Journey with Jesus* (JesusWalk, 2015).

That's enough of an introduction. Now let's get into the Scriptures themselves and delight in the parables that Jesus teaches his disciples.

1. Parables about God's Love

With a bit more than 100 parables, analogies, and sayings of Jesus, where do you begin? I'd like to start on an up-note with some of Jesus' winsome parables that teach us about God – his love, his heart for the lost, his forgiveness, and his mercy. Here are the parables we'll be considering in this lesson.

1.1 Searching for the Lost

- Parable of the Lost Sheep (Luke 15:3-6a; Matthew 18:12-14)
- Parable of the Lost Coin (Luke 15:8-10)
- Parable of the Lost Son or the Prodigal Son (Luke 15:11-32)

1.2 The Father's Forgiveness and Mercy

- Parable of the Two Debtors (Luke 7:41-43, 47)
- Parable of the Unmerciful Servant (Matthew 18:23-35)

Remember Jesus' chief purpose here – to train his disciples. So as his modern-day disciples let's see what we can learn from these parables.

Alfred Usher Soord, 'The Lost Sheep' (1900). Original is oil on canvas, 275 x 182 cm., St. Barnabas Church, Homerton, East London.

1.1 Searching for the Lost

Welcoming and Eating with Sinners (Luke 15:1-2)

In Luke's Gospel, the Parables of the Lost Sheep, the Lost Coin, and the Lost Son (or the Prodigal Son) are a series, set in a context of complaining and murmuring over Jesus' choice of friends.[1]

> "[1] Now the tax collectors and 'sinners' were all gathering around to hear him. [2] But the Pharisees and the teachers of the law muttered, 'This man welcomes sinners and eats with them.'" (Luke 15:1-2)

---

[1] In Matthew, the context of the Parable of the Lost Sheep (Matthew 18:12-13) is found among Jesus teaching about little children, then the "little ones" who believe in Jesus (Matthew 18:1-10). Jesus concludes the parable with the words, "In the same way your Father in heaven is not willing that any of these little ones should be lost" (Matthew 18:14).

1. Parables about God's Love

A crowd is gathering to hear Jesus teach, but over to the side some Pharisees and teachers of the law are complaining, murmuring, muttering. They are the strict observers of every part of the Mosaic law, as well as the oral law, and look down on the common people who aren't as strict as they. They are really upset that Jesus makes a practice of warmly welcoming[2] and eating with society's outcasts – tax collectors and sinners.[3] In fact, one of his own disciples, Matthew/Levi is an ex-tax collector, who, at his conversion, had invited Jesus and his disciples to a great banquet at his house, along with all of his unsavory friends (Luke 5:27-32). When criticized on that occasion, Jesus had remarked:

"It is not the healthy who need a doctor, but the sick.
I have not come to call the righteous, but sinners to repentance." (Luke 5:31-32)

(We'll consider this passage and others in Lesson 12, Parables on Caring for the Lost.).

Jesus responds to the Pharisees' criticism with three parables about joy at finding something or someone that is lost, parables that help his hearers understand better the Father's heart and his value system.

Parable of the Lost Sheep (Luke 15:3-6a, §172; Matthew 18:12-14, §133)

"³ Then Jesus told them this parable: ⁴ 'Suppose one of you has a hundred sheep and loses one of them. Does he not leave the ninety-nine in the open country and go after the lost sheep until he finds it? ⁵ And when he finds it, he joyfully puts it on his shoulders ⁶ and goes home.'" (Luke 15:3-6a)

The Hebrews had been a shepherd people as far back as Abraham, Isaac, and Jacob. Though the economy had broadened considerably since then, sheep were still a solid part of agrarian life in Jesus' world. Sheep were raised for wool, for meat, and for sacrifices in the temple in Jerusalem. A hundred sheep would be a fairly normal size for a small sheep farmer.[4] Many families might keep a few sheep, but this farmer focuses his living on this considerable herd of sheep.

In Jesus' parable, the farmer is probably counting his herd at evening, as was customary. He finds one missing. No doubt he leaves the ninety-nine with a helper or in a sheep pen, and then goes off looking for the lost sheep until he finds it. He looks in the thickets and gullies, he climbs a hill or two looking. No doubt he has done this before and knows where sheep are likely to hide.

---

[2] The verb "welcomes" (NIV, NRSV), "receives" (ESV, KJV) is *prosdechomai*, "receive," here, "receive in a friendly manner" (BDAG 877, 1a).
[3] The Pharisees followed the Rabbinical dictum: "Let not a man associate with the wicked, not even to bring him to the law" (*M. Ex.* 18:1 (Luke 65a), cited by Strack and Billerbeck II, 208; cf. I, 498f).
[4] Jeremias, *Parables*, p. 133.

There is no blame directed toward a straying sheep; the emphasis Jesus is making in this parable is seeking out something which is lost, finding it, and celebrating the discovery as a joyful event. We could read other things into the parable[5] – but to do so would be to miss the point Jesus is making. Israel is not the lost sheep here, but the tax collectors and sinners – they are the lost sheep of the house of Israel that Jesus is sent to (Matthew 10:6; 15:24; see Analogies of the Lost Sheep in Lesson 12.1). When the shepherd finds the stray sheep, he joyfully carries it on his shoulders back to the flock.[6]

Rejoicing over Sinners Repenting (Luke 15:6b-7)

> "[6b] Then he calls his friends and neighbors together and says, 'Rejoice with me; I have found my lost sheep.' [7] I tell you that in the same way there will be more rejoicing in heaven over one sinner who repents than over ninety-nine righteous persons who do not need to repent." (Luke 15:6b-7)

It's time for a party, a celebration. The shepherd calls his friends and says, "Come on over for something to eat and drink. We're celebrating finding my sheep that was lost on the hills."

What does the parable mean? In this context, the lost sheep is a sinner and the ninety-nine sheep represent the righteous. This is Jesus' answer to the Pharisees who were grumbling about Jesus' welcoming tax collectors and sinners.

God rejoices, angels rejoice, when a sinner repents! There is a celebration for every victory, for every person who was in jeopardy and is now rescued.

It doesn't help this parable to identify the shepherd as Jesus, though Jesus is clearly the Good Shepherd in the Parables of the Good Shepherd and the Sheep Gate (Lesson 7.4). Rather, Jesus presents a situation familiar to his listeners – a shepherd with a missing sheep – just as the woman in the Parable of the Lost Coin is any woman who has lost a coin. Matthew 18:10-14 contains a very similar parable in the context of teaching his disciples. It concludes:

> "In the same way your Father in heaven is not willing that any of these little ones should be lost." (Matthew 18:14)

Having said that the parable itself is not about Jesus but any caring shepherd, as we *apply* the parable to our lives, it's inevitable that we think about Jesus searching for the lost, as in the case of Zacchaeus's salvation, Jesus says: "The Son of Man came to seek and to save what was lost" (Luke 19:10). Jesus' redemption is no mass salvation, but one-by-one, person-by-person, name-by-name. Jesus is on a search-and-rescue mission. That's what the Kingdom of God is really like. Seeking the lost is Jesus' mission. We'll see further use of images of the shepherd

---

[5] Psalm 119:176; Isaiah 53:6; Jeremiah 50:6; Ezekiel 34:8, 11, 16, 31; Matthew 10:6; 15:24; 18:10-14; 1 Peter 2:25.

[6] I've heard some foolishness about the shepherd having to break a sheep's legs, but I've never seen it in any reputable source. The parable isn't about having to correct the sheep, but about the joy the shepherd has in finding his missing sheep.

1. Parables about God's Love   25

caring for the sheep in the Parables of the Good Shepherd and the Sheep Gate (Lesson 7.4) and Analogies of the Lost Sheep (Lesson 12.1).

Parable of the Lost Coin (Luke 15:8-10; §172)

Jesus continues in Luke with a similar parable that has the same point – rejoicing when something that is lost is found.

James J. Tissot, 'The Lost Drachma' (1886-94), gouache on gray wove paper, Brooklyn Museum, New York.

> "8 Or suppose a woman has ten silver coins and loses one. Does she not light a lamp, sweep the house and search carefully until she finds it? 9 And when she finds it, she calls her friends and neighbors together and says, 'Rejoice with me; I have found my lost coin.' 10 In the same way, I tell you, there is rejoicing in the presence of the angels of God over one sinner who repents." (Luke 15:8-10)

A woman's entire fortune consists of ten silver coins. The coin is probably a drachma, about the same value as a denarius, which was a day's wages. The ten silver coins might represent the woman's dowry, we're not sure. But one thing we know for sure: for a poor peasant woman that lost coin was extremely valuable. She couldn't afford to lose it!

Palestinian homes often didn't have any windows. So in order to search diligently, the woman lights a dim oil lamp with a sputtering wick. She holds the lamp high. Then she gets down on her knees and uses the lamp to light beneath the tables and shelves. No luck. Now she sweeps the house – maybe the coin is covered in the dust of the dirt floor. Finally, she spots the glint of the silver coin in the flickering light. She reaches for it and holds it between her fingers.

She is so elated that she rushes out and calls to her friends and neighbors to whom she had earlier expressed her worry over the missing coin. Come on over! We're celebrating! I found my lost coin!

The meaning is similar to the Lost Sheep. The lost coin represents a lost sinner. And the party represents God's joy in a sinner repenting and coming to him.

A Matter of Focus

How we view these parables has a lot to do with how we view the Church's mission. Is our job to take care of the needs of the righteous who have gathered into our congregations? Certainly. But what about the lost who seldom or never attend? What about the husband of the faithful wife who stays at home to watch sports? What about those in our churches who seem to drop out of regular attendance? Who goes and searches for them until they find them and discover the reason for their straying?

What about the people who now live in the community that surrounds the church building? Once church people lived there, but now the neighborhood has changed. Who will seek after them? What about the Muslims? The Hindus? The agnostics? The younger generation that has fallen away? What about their spiritual welfare? What about their children? What about the lost?

Who is seeking the lost? Or have we gotten like the Pharisees, with a sense of superiority, blaming the lost for their sinful lifestyles and not caring at all about their eternal plight?

These two parables and the next (the Lost Son) reveal God as a Searching Father, looking for the lost, actively seeking them, and rejoicing when they are found.

"There is rejoicing in the presence of God over one sinner who repents." (Luke 15:10)

An essential part of God's character is grace, extending favor and mercy to the undeserving. In Jesus, we see an active program of seeking out the hurting and oppressed, the blind and the imprisoned (Luke 4:18-19). This is the message of the cross, the message of grace, the message of active love.

One important part of this series of lessons are three to five Discussion Questions in each lesson. We learn by reflecting on what we have been taught, processing it, and thinking through its implications. Don't skip this step or you will have gained head knowledge without heart knowledge! I encourage you to write out your own answer to each question, perhaps in a journal. If you are studying with others, discuss it. If you are studying online, click on the web address (URL) following the question and read others' answers or post your own. (Note: You'll need to register on the Forum before you can post your own answers.
http://www.joyfulheart.com/forums/instructions.htm)

Q1. (Luke 15:1-10) What do the Parables of the Lost Sheep and the Lost Coin teach disciples about God's heart? In what way do these parables represent a contrast to the murmuring of the Pharisees? How should a disciple implement Jesus' value of seeking the lost in his or her own community?
https://www.joyfulheart.com/forums/topic/2175-q1-lost-sheep-and-lost-coin/

1. Parables about God's Love

Parable of the Lost Son or the Prodigal Son (Luke 15:11-32; §173)

Now we come to a favorite – the Parable of the Lost Son or Prodigal Son, found only in Luke. The context is still the murmuring of the Pharisees and scribes about Jesus associating with sinners and tax collectors (Luke 15:1-2). In response, Jesus has told two stories about rejoicing when the lost is found – the Parables of the Lost Sheep and the Lost Coin. Now he tells a third parable.

Giving the Younger Son His Share (Luke 15:11-12)

"[11] Jesus continued: 'There was a man who had two sons. [12] The younger one said to his father, "Father, give me my share of the estate." So he divided his property between them.'" (Luke 15:11-12)

Bartolomé Esteban Murillo, a detail from 'The Return of the Prodigal Son' (1667-70), National Gallery of Art, Washington, DC, oil on canvas, 236.1 x 261 cm. Full image.

The three characters are introduced at once: a man with two sons – a common enough occurrence. What was very *uncommon* was the youngest's request to inherit his share of the estate prior to his father's death – *and* the father's willingness to grant his request.

The father is depicted as a wealthy farmer with servants and lands. His sons would have enjoyed privileged status in the community. But the youngest isn't satisfied with his lot. He wants everything that will be his, and he wants it now!

Inheritance laws in Israel were designed to favor the older son, giving him a double share, probably with the purpose of keeping a family's land holdings together and preserving the family farm intact.[7] If there were four sons, the older son would receive two shares, with each of the other three sons one share apiece. Typically, the older son would be the executor and assume the role as family head after his father's death. Sometimes an older son would decide *not* to split up the family holdings between the brothers (Luke 12:13).

Dividing up a father's estate before his death was known[8] but frowned upon.[9] But if this were to happen, the father would continue to enjoy the usufruct, that is, "the right to utilize and enjoy the profits and advantages of something belonging to another so long as the property is not damaged or altered."

---

[7] Numbers 27:8-11; 36:7-9; Deuteronomy 21:17.
[8] *Tobit* 8:20-21.
[9] *Sirach* 33:20-24.

Squandering Wealth in Wild Living (Luke 15:13)

"Not long after that, the younger son got together[10] all he had, set off for a distant country and there squandered his wealth in wild living." (Luke 15:13)

So long as his father is alive, his sons have a responsibility to support their father each with his share of the family wealth, but the younger son ignores this and spends it all on himself, squandering it.[11] His focus is on "wild living" (NIV)[12] – wine, women,[13] and song. The money might have lasted for a few years, but then he is broke – a destitute foreigner in a strange land.

Reduced to Feeding Swine (Luke 15:14-16)

His friends desert him, his Ferrari is repossessed, he is evicted from his penthouse apartment. He is out on the street.

"[14] After he had spent everything, there was a severe famine in that whole country, and he began to be in need. [15] So he went and hired himself out to a citizen of that country, who sent him to his fields to feed pigs. [16] He longed to fill his stomach with the pods that the pigs were eating, but no one gave him anything." (Luke 15:14-15)

There is a prolonged famine that puts everyone, even average farmers, on the edge of survival. Where the prodigal son might have gotten a job in normal times, now few are hiring. Crops have failed, and, in the agrarian economy of the first century, the landless are out of luck.

The son eventually finds a job, but the job requires him to feed carob pods[14] to swine – and he can't even eat the pods he is feeding the pigs. Only the very poor would eat such food.[15]

Not only is his food almost non-existent, his job of feeding swine is considered abhorrent, since swine are unclean animals for Jews. For a Jewish man, nothing could be lower! There isn't even anyone to help him by giving alms. Jesus says, "no one gave him anything" (Luke 14:16b). He is in a "far country" and "the practice of almsgiving was little observed among the

---

[10] The younger son's share of the estate may have been partly in land, but the phrase, "got together all he had," indicates that he sold what he needed to and turned his share into cash. The Greek word, *synagō*, here has the sense "turn into cash" rather than its normal meaning "gather together" (Marshall, *Luke*, p. 607).

[11] The Greek word is *diaskopizō*, "scatter, disperse," and in our passage, "waste, squander" (BDAG 236, 2).

[12] The Greek adverb is *asōtōs*, "wastefully, prodigally" (BDAG 148), from the noun *asōtia*, "wastefulness" then "reckless abandon, debauchery, dissipation, profligacy" (BDAG 148, see Ephesians 5:18; Titus 1:6; 1 Peter 4:4). The English word "prodigal," which we often use to name this parable, comes from a Latin word *prodigere*, "to drive away, squander."

[13] His brother protests to the father that the prodigal brother has wasted all his inheritance on prostitutes (Luke 15:30).

[14] These are the pods of *Ceratonia siliqua*, a Palestinian tree.

[15] Rabbi Acha (about AD 320) remarks, "When the Israelites are reduced to carob pods, then they repent" (Lv. R. 35 (Luke 132c); SB II, 213-215, cited by Marshall, *Luke*, p. 609).

1. Parables about God's Love

Greeks and Romans."[16] The picture Jesus paints is of a man reduced to the lowest of the low. There is no direction to go but up.

> "[17] When he came to his senses, he said, 'How many of my father's hired men have food to spare, and here I am starving to death! [18] I will set out and go back to my father and say to him: Father, I have sinned against heaven and against you. [19] I am no longer worthy to be called your son; make me like one of your hired men.' [20] So he got up and went to his father." (Luke 15:17-20a)

He begins to compose a confession to say to his father. His apology includes four essential points:

1. He confesses sin against God – expressed in Jewish fashion as "against heaven" – for his moral failures and sinful lifestyle.
2. He confesses sin against his father for squandering property that legally and morally should have been conserved to support his father.
3. He renounces any legal claim to sonship. Though he is a son by birth, his father would need to use his older brother's resources to support him, since his father has already divided the property. He recognizes that he has no legal claim to the rights of sonship.
4. He asks to be hired as a servant at the estate. While his father no longer legally owns the estate, he is still running it, and will do so as long as he is physically able.

The Prodigal has worked out what he will say and how he should say it.

The Father's Compassion (Luke 15:20b-21)

> "[20b] But while he was still a long way off, his father saw him and was filled with compassion for him; he ran to his son, threw his arms around him and kissed him. [21] The son said to him, 'Father, I have sinned against heaven and against you. I am no longer worthy to be called your son.'" (Luke 15:20b-21)

I love verse 20: "But while he was still a long way off, his father saw him." The father has been longing for his son's return for many years. His eyes often turn to the road coming into the estate. This afternoon he glances up to the road as he has thousands of times before.

Far down the road is the figure of a man coming towards the house. The father recognizes his son's characteristic walk when he is far off. The old man gets up and begins to run to his son.

On the one side is the son, rehearsing his speech, afraid that his father will not receive him, moving at an uncertain pace toward the house. And on the other side is the father running, running, his robes blowing behind him as he hurries to his son whom he has longed for.

---

[16] Green, *Luke*, p. 581.

This is no stiff, awkward meeting. The father throws his arms around his son in a happy embrace and kisses him as a sign of welcome and love. The son begins his rehearsed speech about sin and lack of worthiness, but the father stops him.

Kill the Fatted Calf (Luke 15:22-23)

The father turns to the servants who have tagged along after the running father:

> "²² Quick! Bring the best robe and put it on him. Put a ring on his finger and sandals on his feet. ²³ Bring the fattened calf and kill it. Let's have a feast and celebrate." (Luke 15:22-23)

What is necessary now is a proper celebration of the father's joy.

- **The best robe**. He honors the son who has dishonored himself.
- **A ring**. He lavishes on the boy a sign of his love and wealth.[17]
- **Sandals on his feet**. His boy is destitute, barefoot. The father is quick to clothe him and care for his needs. Sandals were the sign of a freeman as opposed to a slave.
- **The fatted calf**. A man of the father's station would have a calf that had been specially fed in order to be ready for a special occasion such as this.

Dead and Alive Again (Luke 15:24)

The father calls for a feast and a celebration.

> "'For this son of mine was dead and is alive again; he was lost and is found.' So they began to celebrate."[18] (Luke 15:24)

The father expresses his joy in extravagant language. Dead, lost. That is the way it had seemed from the father's perspective. But now his son for whom he had despaired of hope was now alive and found! So far, this falls in line with the previous parables – losing, finding, and celebrating.

The Older, Stay-at-Home Brother

There is a second part of the parable that we must ponder if we want to understand Jesus' whole teaching in this passage. The parable so far has been about sinners being found. Now Jesus parable turns to those who are trying to live righteous lives.

---

[17] The ring might also represent authority, especially if it were a signet ring, but we are not told this. Marshall (*Luke*, p. 610) argues that the ring is a symbol of authority, especially of royal authority, and cites 1 Maccabees 6:15; Josephus, *Antiquities* 12:360; and Esther 3:10; 8:8. However, I disagree. That all rings represent authority seems to me to be stretching the evidence.

[18] "Celebrate" (NIV, ESV, NRSV), "make merry" (KJV) is *euphrainō*, "to be glad or delighted, enjoy oneself, rejoice, celebrate" (BDAG 414-415, 2).

1. Parables about God's Love

The unfairness of the father receiving the undeserving son bothers the older son. Grace sticks in his craw. Sibling rivalry is on display.

Hearing the Celebration (Luke 15:25-30)

"²⁵ Meanwhile, the older son was in the field. When he came near the house, he heard music and dancing. ²⁶ So he called one of the servants and asked him what was going on. ²⁷ 'Your brother has come,' he replied, 'and your father has killed the fattened calf because he has him back safe and sound.'[19] The older brother became angry and refused to go in. So his father went out and pleaded with him." (Luke 15:25-28)

The older son remains adamant. He begins to blame his father.

"²⁹ Look! All these years I've been slaving[20] for you and never disobeyed your orders. Yet you never gave me even a young goat so I could celebrate with my friends. ³⁰ But when this son of yours who has squandered your property with prostitutes comes home, you kill the fattened calf for him!" (Luke 15:29-30)

The elder brother's attitude reminds me of Jonah. God calls Jonah to go to Nineveh, the capital city of Assyria, Israel's greatest enemy, to call them to repentance. And when they repent, instead of rejoicing at their salvation, Jonah is angry that God would forgive Israel's enemy.

Everything I Have Is Yours (Luke 15:31-32)

In the parable, the father remonstrates with his son.

"'My son,' the father said, 'you are always with me, and everything I have is yours.'" (Luke 15:31)

We can be angry with God, too. Perhaps because we haven't really gotten to know the Father, to enjoy his best blessings and glory in his bounty. Perhaps our religion, like the Pharisees', has been reduced to joyless duty. The father explains,

"But we had to celebrate and be glad, because this brother of yours was dead and is alive again; he was lost and is found." (Luke 15:32)

The father ends with an explanation of the idea that concludes each of the "Lost" Parables: The lost is found! We must celebrate!

This parable has a personal application we must learn from. But, as mentioned, it has a larger meaning. The father is God. The younger son represents Jewish sinners. The older son

---

[19] "Safe and sound" is Greek *hygiainō*, "to be in good physical health, be healthy" (BDAG 1023, 1).

[20] "Served" (ESV, KJV), "slaved" (NIV), "worked like a slave" (NRSV) is *douleuō*, "perform the duties of a slave, serve, obey (BDAG 259, 2aα). He could have used a milder word *diakoneō*, "to serve," but he uses the stronger word that refers directly to slavery.

stands for the self-righteous Pharisees who can't accept the concept of grace, God's love for undeserving sinners. This parable and all the "Lost" Parables include a strong warning to the Jewish leaders. Sadly, they rejected God's purpose for them (Luke 7:30) and turned the nation away from the Messiah God sent to save them.

As we probe for meaning, we need to pause. We get into difficulty when we try to press any parable. Parables are only illustrations Jesus is using to make a point, but no illustration has complete correspondence on every point, as would a full allegory.

Let's consider some implications.

1. God does not prevent us from sinning and rebelling. We have **freedom** to do so.
2. **Repentance** is necessary for us to return to God. Without repentance we act as if we have a right to something. Repentance recognizes and confesses our moral bankruptcy and changes direction. Repentance is a strong theme here, since Jesus mentions it in each of these three parables (Luke 15:7, 10, 17-19).
3. Even though he loves us immensely, God waits patiently until we "come to our senses." We can't talk, pursue, or persuade people into repenting. It is a **conviction** they must come to by themselves with the help of the Holy Spirit (John 16:8). Of course, the Holy Spirit can work strongly through anointed preaching and witnessing, but without the Holy Spirit's work, such preaching can come across as judgmental.
4. The sinner is morally bankrupt and has absolutely **no claim** on the Father, only the Father's love.
5. God our Father is ready to show **abundant mercy**. The son deserves nothing, but the father heaps upon him the privileges of sonship. These are not due to merit but to mercy. Part of the charm of this story is the utter graciousness of the father contrasted with the stinginess and jealousy of the older son.

If this is the way my Father in heaven feels towards the wayward and sinful – full of compassion and mercy – so must I nurture his attitude toward the lost around me. As a disciple I must not be proud or self-righteous, but boast only of the grace of God. It is not a matter of fairness toward sinners, but of love. And we, if we are older brothers, need to learn both to seek the lost like our Father seeks and to celebrate what our Father celebrates.

> **Q2. (Luke 15:11-32) What does this parable have in common with the Parables of the Lost Sheep and Lost Coin? What does the parable tell us about our Father's way of operating and his values? In what ways does the older son hold his father's values? In what ways does he lack them? What should disciples learn from this parable to equip them for ministry?**
> https://www.joyfulheart.com/forums/topic/2176-q2-lost-son/

1. Parables about God's Love

1.2 The Father's Forgiveness and Mercy

The Parables of the Lost Sheep, Lost Coin and Lost Son show us a Father who is searching, seeking out his lost children. This leads us to consider two parables that further illustrate the Father's forgiveness and mercy.

Parable of the Two Debtors (Luke 7:41-43, 47, §83)
Also known as the Parable of the Two Cancelled Debts

The Parable of the Two Debtors, found only in Luke, is tucked into the midst of a larger account of the anointing by a sinful woman (Luke 7:36-50). I'll recap it briefly.

Jesus has been invited to dinner by a somewhat hostile, well-to-do Pharisee named Simon. Simon doesn't invite Jesus because he wants to be a disciple, but rather because he believes that hosting a famous rabbi will enhance Simon's reputation as a social power in town – and perhaps provide an opportunity to trip up the Healer.

'Anointing by a sinful woman' unknown artist. If you know the artist, please let me know so that I can give appropriate credit.

Somehow, a woman of the town, a known sinner, comes to the house to see the famous guest. Weeping, she begins to wet Jesus' feet with her tears and anoint them with an expensive perfume that fills the house with its fragrance. Simon thinks to himself that Jesus can't be much of a prophet, if he doesn't know the kind of woman this is. Jesus knows Simon's thoughts.

First, Jesus asks permission to speak, and then tells a short parable to make a point. The story recalls the appreciation one would feel to be absolved of the crushing and fearful load of debt to a moneylender, one who has the power to throw non-payers into debtor's prison.

> "⁴¹ 'Two men owed money to a certain moneylender. One owed him five hundred denarii, and the other fifty. ⁴² Neither of them had the money to pay him back, so he canceled the debts of both. Now which of them will love him more?'
>
> ⁴³ Simon replied, 'I suppose the one who had the bigger debt canceled.'
>
> "You have judged correctly," Jesus said." (Luke 7:41-43)

Five hundred denarii might amount to a year and a half's wages. Fifty denarii might amount to one month's wages. The purpose of the parable, of course, is to point out that the person who is forgiven the greater debt would be expected to have greater gratitude to the creditor than the one forgiven less.

Jesus uses the parable to contrast Simon's lack of warmth in welcoming his guest with the woman's extravagant expression of love with her kisses and anointing (verses 44-46). The point is:

"Therefore, I tell you, her many sins have been forgiven — for she loved much. But he who has been forgiven little loves little." (Luke 7:47)

The woman came to Jesus with overflowing thankfulness because she knew he had forgiven her many sins. I am guessing she had been to Jesus' meetings and heard his promises of God's love and forgiveness. But Simon had no sense of thankfulness or love toward Jesus at all.

In this instance, the parable itself isn't the center of the teaching; rather it prepares the hearers for Jesus' public declaration of forgiveness of the woman's sins.[21]

> Q3. (Luke 7:41-43, 47) According to Jesus' Parable of the Two Debtors, do you think the woman was saved *prior to* the dinner or *during* the dinner? How effusive is your love for Jesus? How should we as disciples express our gratitude for salvation?
> https://www.joyfulheart.com/forums/topic/2177-q3-two-debtors/

Parable of the Unmerciful Servant (Matthew 18:23-35, §136)

(Also known as the Parable of the Unforgiving Servant, Ungrateful Servant, or Wicked Servant)

The parable begins with the words:

"The kingdom of heaven is like ...."

Jesus is trying to help his disciples distinguish the nature of his heavenly kingdom from what they expected – that the Messiah would restore David's physical kingdom and free the Jews from their oppressors.

Indeed, several parables begin this way.[22] In Lesson 7 I have grouped several of these parables to be considered together. But we will consider this parable here under the theme of God's love and forgiveness.

Harold Copping (British illustrator, 1863-1932), "The Parable of the Unmerciful Servant."

---

[21] For a full exposition of the larger passage, see http://www.jesuswalk.com/luke/025-anointing.htm

[22] "Like a man who sowed good seed..." (Matthew 13:24 = Mark 4:26); "Like a mustard seed..." (Matthew 13:31 = Mark 4:30 = Luke 13:18); "Like yeast that a woman took..." (Matthew 13:33); "Like a treasure hidden in a field" (Matthew 13:44); "Like a net that was let down into the lake..." (Matthew 13:47); "Like the owner of a house..." (Matthew 13:52); "Like a king who wanted to settle accounts with his servants" (Matthew 18:23); "Like a landowner to went ... to hire men to work in his vineyard" (Matthew 20:1); "Like a king who prepared a wedding banquet for his son" (Matthew 22:2).

1. Parables about God's Love 35

A Massive Debt (Matthew 18:24-27)

Peter has just asked Jesus a question:

> "²¹ 'Lord, how many times shall I forgive my brother when he sins against me? Up to seven times?' ²² Jesus answered, 'I tell you, not seven times, but seventy-seven times.'" (Matthew 18:21-22)

Now Jesus illustrates his answer with a parable.

> "²³ Therefore, the kingdom of heaven is like a king who wanted to settle accounts[23] with his servants. ²⁴ As he began the settlement, a man who owed him ten thousand talents was brought to him." (Matthew 18:23-24)

It is obvious in this parable that this king is powerful and fabulously wealthy. From time to time the king would audit his books to make sure he wasn't being cheated by his underlings. His bookkeeper finds an unpaid debt of 10,000 talents. A "talent" (*talanton*, the denomination of money referred to in the Parable of the Talents, Lesson 11.2) was first a weight, then a unit of coinage. In general, one Tyrian talent would be worth about 6,000 denarii,[24] a denarius being the average amount that a laborer might earn for one day's work. If you calculate that a day laborer working six days per week might earn $150 to $200 USD, here's how you might calculate this administrator's debt:

$$10,000 \text{ talents} = \$15 \text{ to } \$20 \text{ million USD}$$

Considering the sums involved, I would guess that the debtor here is probably a provincial governor or perhaps a tax farmer who had agreed to remit to the king a specific amount of taxes for a tax district.[25] It is a staggering debt!

Foreclosure and Slavery (Matthew 18:25)

Alas, the debtor couldn't pay – not even a portion!

> "Since he was not able to pay, the master ordered that he and his wife and his children and all that he had be sold to repay the debt." (Matthew 18:25)

---

[23] "Settle accounts" (NIV, ESV, NRSV), "take account" (KJV) is *synairō*, used here in a commercial sense as "settle accounts, cast up accounts" (BDAG 964). Also in verse 24 as "reckoning/reckon," "settle/settlement." "Accounts" is the common noun *logos*. We often see *logos* used in the sense of, "word, message." But here (and in Matthew 18:23) it is used in a special sense as "computation, reckoning" (BDAG 603, 2b).

[24] "At 6,000 drachmas or denarii to the Tyrian talent, a day laborer would need to work 60,000,000 days to pay off the debt. Even assuming an extraordinary payback rate of 10 talents per year, the staggering amount would ensure imprisonment for at least 1,000 years" (*Talanton*, BDAG 988).

[25] Josephus tells of an occasion when Ptolemy Ephinanes, King of Egypt (reigned 203-181 BC), asked principal men in his empire to bid for the position of tax farmer or tax collector for the provinces of Celesyria, Phoenicia, Judea, and Samaria. They bid 8,000 talents – and were accused by Ptolemy of conspiring to bid too low. Whoever bid successfully for such a contract would be instantly liable to the king for a debt of 8,000 talents (Josephus, *Antiquities*, 12.4.4).

Perhaps he had collected the taxes, but then invested them in some scheme that had failed miserably – or perhaps they had been stolen by bandits during transfer to the king, or even lost when a ship went down. We don't know.

In ancient times, there were two main remedies for unpaid debt: either (1) sale of the person's goods to pay the debt, or (2) debtor's prison, or both.

Debtor's prison was not a punishment so much as a means to induce the debtor's relatives and friends to collect money to pay his debt in order to bring about his release. But in light of the immense size of this administrator's debt, there is no way his family could be induced to pay even a portion to get him out of debtor's prison. Nor would the sale of the debtor's estate cover such a massive debt. Nevertheless, his property and lands ae seized to be sold for what the king can get out of them and the administrator and his family are ordered sold into slavery – a common fate for those who couldn't pay a debt.[26] (For more, see Appendix 6. Slavery in Jesus' Day.)

Mercy (Matthew 18:26-27)

The administrator's case is hopeless, so he does the only thing he can do. He begs.

> "[26] The servant fell on his knees[27] before him. 'Be patient with me,' he begged, 'and I will pay back everything.' [27] The servant's master took pity on him, canceled the debt and let him go." (Matthew 18:26-27)

The administrator doesn't ask for mercy. Rather he asks for time. He requests the king's patience and rashly promises to "pay back everything." The king knows that such a promise of repayment is both impossible and silly. And he realizes that even if he gains a pittance from the sale of the administrator's estate and the value of his family as slaves,[28] it won't even make a dent in the massive debt owed. So the servant's master takes pity[29] on him, cancels the entire

---

[26] Jewish law prohibited sale of a man except for theft, and sale of the wife was forbidden, so this parable was cast in a non-Jewish context (Jeremias, *Parables*, p. 211, citing *Sota* 3.8; *Tos Sota* 2.9).

[27] *Proskyneō*, "to express in attitude or gesture one's complete dependence on or submission to a high authority figure, (fall down and) worship, do obeisance to, prostrate oneself before, do reverence to, welcome respectfully." Frequently used to designate the custom of prostrating oneself before persons and kissing their feet or the hem of their garment, the ground, etc. The Persians did this in the presence of their deified king and the Greeks before a divinity or something holy (BDAG 883, b). The KJV "worshipped" expresses a chiefly British, now archaic, use of the term, "to honor a human being."

[28] Jeremias (*Parables*, p. 211) notes that the average value of a slave was 500 to 2,000 denarii, citing *b Qid* 18a (Bar.); *B.Q.* 4.5.

[29] Took pity" (NIV), "out of pity for him" (ESV, NRSV), "was moved with compassion" (KJV) is *splanchnizomai*, "have pity, feel sympathy, with or for someone" (BDAG 938), from *splanchnon*, "the viscera, inward parts, entrails," considered in ancient times as the center of the emotions.

1. Parables about God's Love

debt,[30] and releases him.[31] (verse 27). The king's compassion wipes out the entire obligation. The administrator is clear of his immense debt! He is free!

The Tiny Debt (Matthew 18:28-30)

In a happy daze, the administrator begins to leave the palace grounds. Now the plot thickens.

> "[28] But when that servant went out, he found one of his fellow servants who owed him a hundred denarii. He grabbed him and began to choke him. 'Pay back what you owe me!' he demanded.
>
> [29] His fellow servant fell to his knees and begged him, 'Be patient with me, and I will pay you back.' [30] But he refused. Instead, he went off and had the man thrown into prison until he could pay the debt." (Matthew 18:28-30)

The man sees one of his fellow government servants, one whom he has loaned 100 denarii, worth about 100 days' work, perhaps $15,000 to 20,000 in US currency. It is a considerable sum, but nothing compared to the debt our administrator has just been forgiven, that is, $15 to $20 million USD. It a mere 0.1% of the amount!

Yet in anger the man grabs the fellow servant violently and begins to choke him. He demands immediate payment. When the fellow servant asks for patience and promises to pay it in full – which was probably just possible with such a sum – the man refuses and has him thrown into debtor's prison until the debt is paid in full.

His action might be understandable and perhaps even legal, but in light of the mercy he has just received, it is grossly inappropriate.

The King's Wrath (Matthew 18:31-34)

But others have seen the ugly incident.

> "[31] When the other servants saw what had happened, they were greatly distressed[32] and went and told their master everything that had happened.
>
> [32] Then the master called the servant in. 'You wicked servant,' he said, 'I canceled all that debt of yours because you begged me to. [33] Shouldn't you have had mercy[33] on your fellow servant just as I had on you?'" (Matthew 18:31-33)

---

[30] "Cancelled the debt" (NIV), "forgave the debt" (NRSV, KJV) is two words, *daneion*, "loan" (BDAG 212) and *aphiēmi*, here, "to release from legal or moral obligation or consequence, cancel, remit, pardon" (BDAG 156, 2).

[31] The word "let him go" (NIV), "released" (NRSV), "loosed" (KJV) is *apolyō*, a legal term meaning, "to grant acquittal, set free, release, pardon a prisoner" (BDAG 117, 1).

[32] *Lypeō*, "become sad, sorrowful, distressed" (BDAG 604, 2a).

[33] *Eleeō*, "to be greatly concerned about someone in need, have compassion/mercy/pity" (BDAG 315).

The king recalls the man to his throne room. Livid with rage, he shouts that he is "wicked."[34] He has forgiven the man an astronomical sum. Why couldn't his debtor have the common decency to do the same for a relatively small sum? To refuse to do so was an insult to the king's own mercy.

> "In anger his master turned him over[35] to the jailers to be tortured, until he should pay back all he owed." (Matthew 18:34)

This is more than debtor's prison. This is the kind of active torture[36] reserved for the king's enemies. In Jesus' day people would have nodded sadly. Though torture was prohibited by Jewish law as inhumane, scourging was commonly used by the Romans to interrogate prisoners. Jeremias observes:

> "Torture was regularly employed in the East against a disloyal governor, or one who was tardy in the delivery of the taxes, in order to discover where they had hidden the money, or to extort the amount from their relations or friends. The non-Jewish practice in legal proceedings ... is drawn upon to intensify the frightfulness of the punishment."[37]

Jesus intends this parable to stick in his disciples' memories.

Jesus' Warning (Matthew 18:35)

But then Jesus says something unexpected and terrible.

> "This is how my heavenly Father will treat each of you unless you forgive your brother from your heart." (Matthew 18:35)

Jesus refers to God as "my heavenly Father" in an intimate and formal title. Forgiveness "from your heart" is in contrast to forgiveness with one's lips only.[38] The forgiveness must be genuine.

The Lord's Prayer (Matthew 6:12, 15)

Jesus is quite serious about forgiveness! Consider the fifth petition of the Lord's Prayer, and Jesus' subsequent commentary on it:

---

[34] *Ponēros*, "pertaining to being morally or socially worthless, wicked, evil, bad, base, vicious, degenerate" (BDAG 853, 1aα).

[35] *Paradidōmi*, "hand over, turn over, give up a person," as a technical term of police and courts, "hand over into [the] custody [of]" (BDAG 762, 1a).

[36] "Jailers to be tortured" (NIV), "to be tortured" (NRSV), "tormenters" (KJV), is *basanistēs*, "guard in a prison, frequently under orders to torture prisoners, oppressive jailer," in our verse, "merciless jailer" (BDAG 168). The word is closely related to *basanos*, "severe pain occasioned by punitive torture, torture, torment" (BDAG 168).

[37] Jeremias, *Parables*, pp. 212-213.

[38] Matthew 15:8, quoting Isaiah 29:13.

"Forgive us our debts, as we also have forgiven our debtors." (Matthew 6:12)

Three Greek words are used in relationship to sin in the Lord's Prayer in Matthew and Luke. Christians from different traditions use different words as they recite the Lord's Prayer – "debt," "trespass," and "sin."[39] But they amount to the same thing.

This prayer, "Forgive us our debts, as we forgive our debtors" is a sort of trick prayer. It is a prayer Jesus uses to teach his disciples the elements of praying aright. The Greek word *hōs*, is a conjunction marking a point of comparison, meaning "as."[40] Jesus teaches us to ask God to forgive us "as" we forgive others. In other words, if we forgive others only a little and hold grudges, we are asking God to forgive us only a little and bear a grudge against us.

Then Jesus clarifies this point:

> "For if you forgive men when they sin against you, your heavenly Father will also forgive you. But if you do not forgive men their sins, your Father will not forgive your sins." (Matthew 6:14-15)

How could it be plainer?

Love and Forgiveness

If we are to know and understand God, we must love. He is filled with grace; so must we be. We must know and understand forgiveness. If we reject this part of God, we reject the essence of who He is (1 John 4:16-21). So when Jesus puts it so bluntly – you must forgive in order to be forgiven (Matthew 6:14-15) – we dare not reject this truth.

Some ask: Isn't this a sort of "works righteousness"? If you are required to do something before you can be forgiven, then isn't this righteousness by works? No.

To be free you must let go of unforgiveness. Is that meritorious so as to earn heaven? No, not any more than repentance from sin is meritorious. We don't earn heaven by repentance or by forgiving. But we must let go of our bondage to sin and hate if we want to receive something better. (For more on forgiveness, read my article, "Don't Pay the Price of Counterfeit Forgiveness," www.joyfulheart.com/maturity/forgive.htm)

My dear friend, I know that it can sometimes be very, very hard to forgive. Sometimes it seems impossible. So here is a place to start. Pray this kind of prayer. "Lord, I know I should forgive so-and-so, but I can't seem to be able to. So I ask you to make me *want* to forgive. Soften

---

[39] "Debt" (Matthew 6:12), Greek *opheilēma*, 1. "debt = what is owed, one's due." 2. in a religious sense debt = sin (as Aramaic *hobah* in rabbinical literature) (BDAG 743). "Trespass" (Matthew 6:14-15, KJV), Greek *paraptōma*, "in imagery of one making a false step so as to lose footing: a violation of moral standards, offense, wrongdoing, sin" (BDAG 770).[39] *Paraptōma* is a compound word from *para-* "beside or near" + *piptō* "to fall." Thayer defines it as "a lapse or deviation from truth and uprightness; a sin, misdeed" (Thayer 485). "Sin" (Luke 11:4), Greek *hamartia* "sin. The action itself as well as its result, every departure from the way of righteousness…" (BDAG 43-44). Literally, "a failing to hit the mark" (Thayer 30).

[40] *Hōs*, BDAG 1103-1106.

my heart, I pray. In Jesus' name and with his power. Amen." Don't keep bitterness. Start somewhere to rid yourself of it, and you'll be set free indeed.

Q4. (Matthew 18:23-35) In the Parable of the Unmerciful Servant, where do you see justice? Where do you see grace? Where do you see greed? Where do you see unforgiveness? What lessons from this parable are disciples to incorporate into their lives?
https://www.joyfulheart.com/forums/topic/2178-q4-unmerciful-servant/

We've been studying Jesus' parables that talk about the Father's seeking and joy in finding the lost. A parable about forgiveness that engenders love in the recipient. And a parable about the need to forgive. Jesus is teaching us what his disciples are called to be – sons of the Father!

Prayer

Father, forgiveness is so hard, especially when the people who hurt us are close to us. Help us to learn to forgive, to will to forgive those who sin against us. Help us to love like You do. To love the lost like You do, and to seek them with the passion of our Lord Jesus Christ. In His holy name we pray. Amen.

2. Parables about Israel's Unbelief

Jesus tells a number of parables about the Jewish nation – God's desires for it, its rejection of Jesus, and its exclusion from the Kingdom. In addition, he hints that the Gentiles will come to faith.

Some have built entire theologies about the place of the people of Israel during the End Time. I have no desire to do that here, only to recount what Jesus taught his own disciples through parables. However, I believe it is important not to identify the modern State of Israel with the Jewish nation in the New Testament. When the Kingdom of God ultimately comes with the Presence of Jesus, his Kingdom will far transcend any human government or territory.

Jesus gave a number of parables to help his disciples understand the perilous place of the Jewish nation in their day, as well as the blindness and deceit of its leaders. Alas, these parables tell a tragic tale.

Harold Copping (1863-1932), 'The Parable of the Fig Tree,' watercolor.

2.1 Israel's Barrenness, Pride, and Disobedience

- Parable of the Barren Fig Tree (Luke 13:6-9)
- Analogy of the Hen and Chickens (Matthew 23:37; Luke 13:34)

2.2 Rejection of the Messiah by Israel

- Parable of the Wedding Banquet (Matthew 22:1-10)
- Parable of the Great Banquet (Luke 14:15-24, cf. Matthew 22:2-10)

2.3 Excluding Israel from Messiah's Kingdom

- Parable of the Wicked Tenants (Matthew 21:33-46; Mark 12:1-12; Luke 20:9-19)

While most of these parables apply to the Jewish nation in Jesus' time, there is much we disciples can learn from them that is applicable in our lives today.

The "Jewish Nation" in the Time of Jesus

Before we begin, let's take quick look at the governance of Palestine in Jesus' day. Of course, there wasn't really a "Jewish nation" by that time. The whole region was part of the Roman Province of Judea. After Pompey the Great brutally conquered Jerusalem in 63 BC, Rome ruled Palestine through puppet kings, eventually through Herod the Great from 37 to 4 BC. But soon after Herod's death, Rome ruled Judea and Samaria directly under a Roman Prefect – during Jesus' ministry this was Pontius Pilate (ruled 26-36 AD). Other areas where Jesus ministered were ruled by Herod's sons, not as full official kings but "tetrarchs," puppet rulers under Rome. Herod Antipas (ruled 4 BC to 39 AD) governed Galilee and Perea as a client king of Rome.

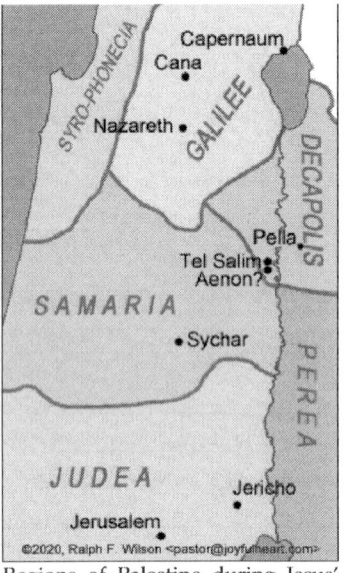

Regions of Palestine during Jesus' Ministry. Larger map.

Jewish Religious Leaders

In order to keep good order, the Romans and Herod allowed the Jewish religious leaders to administer many of the laws through the Great Sanhedrin in Jerusalem and the local sanhedrins in the various towns. The High Priest (Caiaphas in Jesus' day), more a political appointee rather than a spiritual leader, was selected by Herod Antipas. The Great Sanhedrin or Council had 70 members, sometimes called "rulers" or "elders." Some of these were Gamaliel, Joseph of Arimathea, and Nicodemus. Members were usually from one of two groups: the Sadducees and the Pharisees. The Sadducee party that included the high priest and many other priests didn't believe in angels, spirits, or resurrection on the Last Day.

The Pharisee party, which *did* believe in these things, taught strict observance of both the Torah and the oral law, a series of man-made rules designed as a "hedge" around the Mosaic law, sometimes called "the tradition of the elders" (Matthew 15:2-6). Pharisees developed the practice of fasting on Mondays and Thursdays to intercede for the nation as a whole.[1] Pharisees far exceeded the requirements of the law in this regard. They scrupulously tithed or gave one tenth of everything they acquired, even down to the herbs in their garden (Luke 11:42).

Indeed, the Pharisees put on a show of holiness. They flaunted their piety by praying loud, long, pious prayers in the synagogues and street corners (Matthew 6:5-8). They loved to be publicly honored (Matthew 23:5-12). They cultivated a reputation for righteousness, but inside they were anything but holy (see Lesson 3.1).

---

[1] Marshall, *Luke*, p. 221; J. Behm, TDNT 4:924-935.

2. Parables about Israel's Unbelief

Jesus warns his disciples against the leaven or yeast of the Pharisees – hypocrisy (Matthew 13:33, Lesson 7.1) – pretending strict holiness, but at the same time filled with judgmentalism, pride, and plots to kill the Son of God.[2]

In the Gospels you also see local "rulers" who were in charge of local synagogues and synagogue courts. Some local synagogue leaders, such as Jairus, came to believe in Jesus; others, like the "rich young ruler," resisted his ministry.

Another group of leaders is variously called "lawyers," "teachers of the law," or "scribes." These were the trained Bible scholars who had studied under learned Rabbis, and typically had disciples studying under them (as Saul studied under Gamaliel). These were the nation's recognized Bible experts.

With few exceptions, the Jewish leadership of Jesus' day came to see Jesus as a threat, turned against the Messiah God had sent to save his people, and eventually had him killed.

Jesus didn't have much good to say about the religious leaders of his time. He refers to them metaphorically as "a brood of vipers" (Matthew 12:34, see Appendix 4.3), and their sale of sacrifices and money changing in the temple, "a den of robbers" (Matthew 21:13; John 2:16; see Appendix 4.3).

2.1 Israel's Barrenness, Pride, and Disobedience

Parable of the Barren Fig Tree (Luke 13:6-9; §162)
(Not to be confused with the Cursing of the Fig Tree or the Parable of the Budding Fig Tree, Lesson 5.1)

With that introduction to the Jewish nation and its leaders, let's begin with Jesus' Parable of the Barren Fig Tree, found only in Luke. It occurs in the context of Jesus talking about the importance of repentance – not of sinners in particular, but of Israelites in general – "Unless you repent, you too will all perish" (Luke 13:5).

"⁶ Then he told this parable: A man had a fig tree, planted in his vineyard, and he went to look for fruit on it, but did not find any. ⁷ So he said to the man who took care of the vineyard,

N.C. Wyeth, 'The Barren Fig Tree,' from an oil painting, one of a set of six Christmas cards on Jesus' parables published 1923.

---

[2] Matthew 6:1-8; Mark 7:6; 12:13-17; Luke 6:41-42; 13:10-17. Many of the "woes" against the scribes and Pharisees are prefaced in Matthew 23 with the phrase, "you hypocrites."

'For three years now I've been coming to look for fruit on this fig tree and haven't found any. Cut it down! Why should it use up the soil?'

[8] 'Sir,' the man replied, 'leave it alone for one more year, and I'll dig around it and fertilize it. [9] If it bears fruit next year, fine! If not, then cut it down.'" (Luke 13:6-9)

A landowner looks for fruit on his fig year for three years straight and doesn't find any. The first year, he is hopeful. The second year he is disappointed. The third year, he is disgusted. "Cut it down," he tells his gardener. "It's just wasting space[3] in my garden."

But the gardener isn't quite ready to give up on it. He prescribes cultivation and more fertilizer. Loosen the soil around the roots to let air in. Fertilize with "dung, manure"[4] to provide organic material that might give it a growth spurt. One more year. And then if it doesn't do anything, then if it doesn't bear any fruit, then I'll cut it down.

The key to the meaning of the parable lies in the identity of the fig tree. Fig trees (*Ficus carica*) are common in Israel, and, along with vineyards, were seen as a sign of prosperity and peace: "Every man will sit under his own vine and under his own fig tree" (Micah 4:4; cf. 1 Kings 4:25; Zechariah 3:10). But this fig tree isn't prosperous. It is in trouble. It no longer bears fruit.

Israel is often typified as a vine or vineyard, but here the unproductive fig tree likely refers to the nation of Israel.[5] God might be seen as the owner and perhaps Jesus is the Gardener, still trying to minister to Israel so that they turn again to God and produce spiritual fruit. (I don't allegorize the three days as referring to the Trinity, but rather as a common literary motif signifying a pattern of occurrences.[6])

Placed in the context of repentance, Jesus is calling Israel to repent – or else experience judgment like the catastrophes he has just commented on – the slaughter of Galileans and the fall of the tower in Siloam (Luke 13:1-4). Judgment is imminent, but there is still time to repent while Jesus is still with them.

John the Baptist's message was similar. Unless people begin "to bear fruit in keeping with repentance," judgment will come.

---

[3] "Use up" (NIV, ESV), "waste" (NRSV), "cumbereth" (KJV) is the verb *katargeō*, "to cause something to be unproductive, use up, exhaust, waste" (BDAG 525, 1).

[4] "Fertilize" (NIV), "put on manure" (ESV, NRSV), "dung" (KJV) is two words, the verb *ballō*, "put, place, apply" (BDAG 163, 3a), and the noun *kopion*, "dung, manure" (BDAG 559, 1).

[5] In these verses Israel is represented by fig trees or figs: Hosea 9:10; Jeremiah 8:13; 24:1-8; Micah 7:1

[6] "Three is the minimum number necessary to establish a pattern of occurrences. A single event can be pure chance; a pair can be mere coincidence; but three consecutive occurrences of an event serve as a rhetorical signal indicating special significance" (Leland Ryken, et al. (eds.), *Dictionary of Biblical Imagery* (InterVarsity Press, 2000), p. 866). Examples include: Elijah stretching himself over the widow's child (1 Kings 17:21); the temptations of Jesus (Matthew 4:3-8); Jesus' prayers in Gethsemane (Matthew 26:39, 42, 44); Peter's vision (Acts 10:9-16); Peter's denial (Matthew 26:34); Jesus' restoration of Peter (John 21:15-17).

2. Parables about Israel's Unbelief 45

> "The ax is already at the root of the trees,
> and every tree that does not produce good fruit will be cut down
> and thrown into the fire." (Luke 3:9)

Jesus gives this as a parable of mercy, but also as a call to Israel to repent. How can we extend the lesson to ourselves? Though we are saved by grace, not by works, God is looking for productivity in our lives. Why?

> "For we are God's workmanship, created in Christ Jesus to do good works, which God prepared in advance for us to do." (Ephesians 2:10)

Fruitfulness, both in character and in good works and ministry, is important to God,[7] and he will examine our works and reward them (1 Corinthians 3:12-15). Moreover, fruitfulness is a by-product of spiritual health. We'll study more about fruit and fruitfulness in Jesus' Parables of the Wicked Tenants (Lesson 2.3), the Tree and Fruit (Lesson 10.1), and the Vine and the Branches (Lesson 9.3).

> **Q5. (Luke 13:6-9) What caused Israel's barrenness in Jesus' time? What keeps the fruit of the Holy Spirit (Galatians 5:22-23) from growing and maturing in our lives? What can we disciples learn from the Parable of the Barren Fig Tree?**
> https://www.joyfulheart.com/forums/topic/2179-q5-barren-fig-tree/

2.2 Rejection of the Messiah by Israel

Jesus told some parables about Israel rejecting God's call. These stories call forth in me a sorrow. It shouldn't have to be this way! If only the Jews would open their eyes and listen! If only people today would open their hearts to the Lord who is active in their midst!

Analogy of the Hen and Chickens (Matthew 23:37, §211; Luke 13:34, §167)

In Jesus' Analogy of the Hen and Chickens, given during Holy Week, you can sense his affection for Israel.

> "³⁷O Jerusalem, Jerusalem, you who kill the prophets and stone those sent to you, how often I have longed to gather your children together, as a hen gathers her chicks under her wings, but you were not willing. ³⁸Look, your house is

Altar Mosaic of Hen and Chickens, Church of Dominus Flevit, Mount of Olives, Jerusalem. Larger image.

---

[7] Matthew 7:19-20; 12:33; 21:43; Luke 8:15; 20:10; John 15:2, 16.

left to you desolate. [39] For I tell you, you will not see me again until you say, 'Blessed is he who comes in the name of the Lord.'" (Matthew 23:37-39)

The hen covering her chicks with her wings is a protective gesture. Jesus loves Israel deeply, but as he had experienced again and again over his three years of ministry, "you were not willing." "He came to that which was his own, but his own did not receive him" (John 1:11). How very sad!

Parable of the Wedding Banquet (Matthew 22:1-10, §205, cf. §170)

(Sometimes known as the Parable of the Marriage Feast. Not to be confused with the Parable of the Places at the Table, Lesson 9.1)

Parable of the Great Banquet (Luke 14:15-24, §170, cf. Matthew 22:2-10, §205)

Now we'll examine a pair of parables with a number of similarities:
1. The Parable of the Wedding Banquet (Matthew), and
2. The Parable of the Great Banquet (Luke).

"The kingdom of heaven is like a king who prepared a wedding banquet for his son." (Matthew 22:2)

"A certain man was preparing a great banquet and invited many guests." (Luke 14:16)

We'll them together. Jesus taught constantly over a period of three years, so it is likely that his stories varied from one telling to another, as he sought relevance to a particular crowd's needs and understanding. So it is with the Parable of the Great Banquet in Luke and the Parable of the Wedding Banquet in Matthew.[8]

Pieter Breugel the Younger, 'The Peasant Wedding Banquet' (1568), Kunsthistorisches Museum, Vienna. Larger image.

This pair of parables has many similarities. But each also has its own tone, is told under different circumstances, and conveys its own unique point or purpose. I think Luke's Parable of the Great Banquet is about evangelism to the unworthy and sinners in the face of Jewish rejection. Matthew's Parable of the Wedding Banquet, on the other hand, is more about God's

---

[8] This parable is also preserved in *Gospel of Thomas*, 64, in form somewhat similar to Luke's account.

2. Parables about Israel's Unbelief

judgment of rejecting Israel. Some scholars might conflate these into a single parable, but I think they should be considered related but distinct parables.

Similarities and Differences

The parables have obvious similarities. In both parables a wealthy master holds a great feast, but his invited guests refuse to come when informed that the hour has come. To replace them, servants scour the entire area for other guests.

But there are also differences, since Jesus applies this parable differently to different audiences.

Wedding Banquet (Matthew 22:1-10)	**Great Banquet (Luke 14:15-24)**
Occasion: Chief priests and Pharisees discuss arresting Jesus in the temple, but are afraid of the people.	Occasion: Supper discussion at Pharisee's house about the great eschatological banquet at the End and inviting guests to a dinner who can't pay you back.
"The kingdom of heaven is like...."	A commentary on those will feast in the kingdom of God.
A king.	A certain man.
Banquet for son's wedding.	Great banquet.
Invited guests pay no attention to servant.	Invited guests make flimsy excuses.
Invitees mistreat and kill the servants. The king sends his army, kills them, and burns their city.	
Servants invite guests both good and bad.	Servants invite the poor, the crippled, the blind and the lame of the town, and countryside, and "compel them to come in."
Man not wearing a wedding garment is severely punished.	

These comparisons should give us some things to look out for as we study this pair of parables.

Come, Everything is Ready

In both parables the master prepares a "great banquet" with many guests invited. Neither is a small, intimate gathering.

> "He sent his servants to those who had been invited to the banquet to tell them to come." (Matthew 22:3)

"At the time of the banquet he sent his servant to tell those who had been invited, 'Come, for everything is now ready.'" (Luke 14:17)

While it may seem strange in light of invitation practices in the twenty-first century, in the first century world, the invitation would be two-fold: (1) the initial invitation some days or weeks ahead of time, and (2) the actual summons to the meal when it is ready.[9]

Once the host finds out how many guests have accepted his initial invitation, he is able to determine how many animals are to be killed and cooked.[10] Both a wedding feast for a king's son and a "great banquet" would involve a large number of guests.

Not to appear at a banquet to which one had previously agreed to attend was a grave breach of social etiquette, an insult to the host. In a society where one's social standing was determined by peer approval, this was an act of social insult as well. A whole series of guests to reject the final summons could be seen as a conspiracy to discredit the host entirely.

Excuses, Excuses (Luke 14:18-20)

In Matthew's parable, the invitees make no excuses, "but they paid no attention and went off..." (Matthew 22:5a). But in Luke's parable, the invitees make lame excuses.

"But they all alike began to make excuses. The first said, 'I have just bought a field, and I must go and see it. Please excuse me.' Another said, 'I have just bought five yoke of oxen, and I'm on my way to try them out. Please excuse me.'
Still another said, 'I just got married, so I can't come.'" (Luke 14:18-20)

The rejection is unanimous. The first claims to have just bought a field that he must inspect. What? He bought it sight unseen? The second has just purchased five pairs of oxen and must try them out. No one buys five pairs of oxen without testing them first! The first two invitees are men of wealth. Purchasing property is a wealthy man's luxury. Five yoke of oxen are for an estate; one or two pairs of oxen would be adequate for a small farm.[11]

The third excuse, that the guest has just been married, is also fake. When he accepted the invitation, he would have known of his wedding plans. That was the time to politely decline. But to back out at the last minute is an act of calculated rudeness.

Both parables indicate the master's anger. In Matthew's account, the king sends an army to destroy the city of those who ignored his invitation. (More about that in a moment.) In

---

[9] Such a practice is attested both in Jewish and Roman settings. Esther 6:14; *La.* R 4:2; Strack and Billerbeck I, 880f; Philo, *Opif* 78; Terence, *Heaut.* 169f; Apuleius *Met.* 3:12, cited by Marshall, *Luke*, pp. 587-588.

[10] A chicken or two would suffice for 2 to 4 guests, a duck for 5 to 8, a kid for 10 to 15, a sheep for 15 to 35 people, or a calf for 35 to 75 people (Kenneth E. Bailey, *Through Peasant Eyes* (Eerdmans, 1980), p. 94, cited by Green, *Luke*, p. 558, fn. 151).

[11] Jeremias, *Parables*.

2. Parables about Israel's Unbelief

Luke's parable, the master's anger prompts the vow: "I tell you, not one of those men who were invited will get a taste of my banquet" (Luke 14:24).

Luke: Compel Them to Come In (Luke 14:21-24)

The last-minute rejection presents a serious problem to the host. How would it look for an important man to have an empty banquet? The host's hall must be full. He will *not* be made a fool of. He *will* have a full house!

So, in both parables, the rejection of the master's invitation prompts a command to broadly invite everyone who can be found in the entire area. This time the goal is not to select people of the appropriate social class or those who might deserve to be invited. Rather, the goal is to fill the banquet hall with warm bodies.

In Luke's parable, the servant is proactive and has already followed through on his master's desire to fill the banquet hall.

Eugène Burnand, detail of 'Invitation to the Feast' (1899), oil on canvas, 470x220 cm., Kunstmuseum Winterthur, Switzerland (full painting)

> "²¹ The servant came back and reported this to his master. Then the owner of the house became angry and ordered his servant, 'Go out quickly into the streets and alleys of the town and bring in the poor, the crippled, the blind and the lame.'¹² ²² 'Sir,' the servant said, 'what you ordered has been done, but there is still room.'" (Luke 14:21-22)

Now the master widens the scope of the search.

> "²³ Go out to the roads and country lanes and *make them come in, so that my house will be full.* ²⁴ I tell you, not one of those men who were invited will get a taste of my banquet." (Luke 14:23-24)

The first sweep of the town included both the "broad, main streets or public squares" and the "narrow streets, lanes, alleys."¹³ The second sweep was outside the town in the rural areas, the "road, highway"¹⁴ and "fences, hedges."¹⁵ Inside the town would be the poor, the beggars,

---

¹² The list of guests to be invited is identical to the list Jesus had suggested to his Pharisee host in Luke 14:13 – those who could not repay him by inviting him in return – the poor, the crippled, the blind, and the lame.
¹³ *Rhumē*, Marshall, *Luke*, p. 590.
¹⁴ *Hodos*, BDAG 690-692.
¹⁵ *Phragmos*, BDAG 1064.

the indigent. But outside the town would be the vagabonds and sojourners, those who were shunned and unwelcome in the towns.

Note the phrase, "Compel them to come in!" It was a custom to politely refuse to come until pressed to – like politely refusing to take a second helping at a meal until the host says, "Oh, but you must!" The Greek word used is *anankazō*, "compel, force," of inner and outer compulsion, and then weakened, "strongly urge/invite, urge upon, press."[16] The rich man hasn't sent out soldiers to sweep the area, round up everyone, and march them to his house. But he has instructed his servants not to take "No" for an answer and to encourage and strongly urge everyone they meet to accept this invitation.

Matthew: Invite Anyone You Find – both Good and Bad (Matthew 22:8-14)

While Luke's emphasis is on the diligence of the search, Matthew's emphasis seems to be on the quality of the guests.

> "⁸ Then he said to his servants, 'The wedding banquet is ready, but those I invited did not deserve to come. ⁹ Go to the street corners and invite to the banquet anyone you find.' ¹⁰ So the servants went out into the streets and gathered all the people they could find, **both good and bad**, and the wedding hall was filled with guests." (Matthew 22:8-10)

Notice the phrase describing these invitees, "both good and bad." Jesus is setting us up for the punch line of this version of the parable. Now the king enters the banquet hall and surveys the motley group of guests present for his son's wedding.

> "¹¹ But when the king came in to see the guests, he noticed a man there who was not wearing wedding clothes. ¹² 'Friend,' he asked, 'how did you get in here without wedding clothes?' The man was speechless.
>
> ¹³ "Then the king told the attendants, 'Tie him hand and foot, and throw him outside, into the darkness, where there will be weeping and gnashing of teeth.'
>
> ¹⁴ "For many are invited, but few are chosen." (Matthew 22:11-14)

You wouldn't expect last-minute guests to a wedding to have "wedding clothes," that is, their very best expensive garments, designed both to honor the king and to show off their high status. After all, many of these new guests were poor people; some were vagabonds.

Some have speculated that people were given wedding clothes upon entry, but some neglected to put them on. It sounds "fair," but there is no indication from any ancient literature that this was the practice. Rather, I think the text means that some dressed in their best, even though it was humble, and fixed themselves as best they could. But one man didn't bother to dress up at all. Rather, he came dirty and disheveled – an insult to both the king and his son.

---

[16] *Anankazō*, BDAG 60.

2. Parables about Israel's Unbelief

The king demands an explanation. The man has no excuse. He is speechless. So the king orders him to be thrown out of the well-lit banqueting hall into the darkness of night outside.

Weeping and Gnashing of Teeth (Matthew 22:13)

Two of Jesus' other parables talk about gathering all together both good and bad, with the angels sorting out the good from the bad at the End Time – The Parable of the Net (Lesson 4.2) and the Parable of the Weeds or Tares (Lesson 4.2). The final judgment looks at the deeds and the hearts as only God can.

Jesus intends this darkness to be interpreted as hell, for he adds that "there will be weeping and gnashing of teeth," an indication of deep anguish upon the realization that it is too late to do the right thing (Psalms 112:10). Judgment has already been given. The phrase "weeping and gnashing of teeth" is also present in Jesus' teaching that at God's great banquet in the kingdom of heaven the evildoers and unbelievers will be excluded[17] (See Appendix 5. The Great Messianic Banquet).

To those who live in democracies this may seem harsh, but in Jesus' day there were no democracies. The king's word was law; you didn't insult the king. Jesus' hearers understood well enough; they didn't quibble about the king's constitutional authority to punish evildoers.

Many Are Called, but Few Are Chosen (Matthew 22:14)

These parables use the verb "call" (*kaleō*) a number of times in the sense of "invite" – five times in Matthew and twelve times in Luke. Matthew concludes the parable with an epigram:

"For many are called, but few are chosen."[18] (Matthew 22:14, ESV)[19]

This sums up the message of this parable, but also the two that precede it in Matthew – the Parables of the Two Sons (Lesson 3.3) and the Wicked Tenants (Lesson 2.3, which we'll consider in a minute). The "many" and the "few" speak of a weeding process, whereby many invited to the feast will not actually attend. We see this many/few theme in several other parables: The Parables of the Narrow Door (Lesson 8.2), the Narrow and Wide Gates (Lesson 3.2), the Net (Lesson 4.2), and the Weeds or Tares (Lesson 4.2).

---

[17] Luke 13:28; Matthew 8:12; 13:42, 50; 24:51; 25:30; Revelation 22:15.

[18] "Chosen" is *eklektos*, "'pertaining to being selected, chosen,' generally of those whom God has chosen from the generality of mankind and drawn to himself" (BDAG 306).

[19] This saying is inappropriately added to many Greek texts of Matthew 20:16 (C D W Θ f¹, ¹³ Byz). Metzger (*Textual Commentary*, p. 41) observes, "Although it is possible that the words ... had been accidentally omitted from an ancestor of ℵ B L Z 085 owing to homoeoteleuton, the Committee regarded it as much more likely that they were added here by copyists who recollected the close of another parable (22:14, where there is no significant variation of reading)." The Committee gave the text without the addition an {A} confidence rating, "virtually certain."

So that you don't get confused, note that Paul uses the term "called" *differently* than Jesus. Jesus uses it as "invited" as in our parable. Paul uses the term as meaning "chosen."[20] The Greek word can bear both meanings.[21] Paul doesn't disagree with Jesus at all; he just uses different words to explain it.

An Allegory

In interpreting parables we need to be careful not to over-allegorize, that is, to find a corresponding meaning for each and every detail of the story. But these parables are clearly allegories. This pair of parables has three points of correspondence.

1. The host is God the Father, inviting his people Israel to the great messianic banquet (Luke 14:15).[22] (See Appendix 5. The Great Messianic Banquet.)

2. The rich and socially elite who reject at the last minute the host's invitation are the Pharisees and Jewish religious establishment who reject John the Baptist and Jesus, who begin to plot against Jesus and eventually render the ultimate insult of having Jesus executed as a common criminal.

3. The poor and downtrodden are the common people who "heard him gladly" (Mark 12:37, KJV).[23] Perhaps those inside the town are the Jews, while those in the outlying areas are the Gentiles. Beyond this level of allegory, I don't believe we should go.

In addition, as we'll see in a moment, Matthew' king sending an army to kill the "murderers" and burn their city (Matthew 22:7) is a prophetic allegory of the siege and destruction of Jerusalem in 70 AD.

Common Themes

As I meditate on both parables, I am impressed with a number of themes:

1. Lame Excuses. I am sorry to say that in the lame excuses of the original guests I hear some of my own shallow excuses for not doing God's will. We may be able to convince ourselves that what we are doing is noble, but way too often our excuses are an insult to God. It is his mercy that we are not consumed!

2. Rejection and Insult. We feel badly when we are rejected, but what about the Father? Think of his grieving and broken heart, his anger and mercy. I recall the verses at the beginning of John's Gospel that express this:

---

[20] Morris, *Matthew*, p. 553.
[21] "Called" (ESV, NRSV, KJV), "invited" (NIV) is *klētos*, "pertaining to being invited, called, invited to a meal" (BDAG 549). Depending on the context it can mean "call, invite," "summoned to court," "invoked," or even, "called out, chosen" (Liddell-Scott 960, meanings 2, 4).
[22] Isaiah 25:6; Matthew 8:11-12; Luke 13:28-30; 22:30; Revelation 19:9.
[23] Matthew 21:46; Luke 19:48.

2. Parables about Israel's Unbelief

> "He came to that which was his own, but his own did not receive him. Yet to all who received him, to those who believed in his name, he gave the right to become children of God – children born not of natural descent, nor of human decision or a husband's will, but born of God." (John 1:11-13)

This parable is a bittersweet reminder of rejection, but also of mercy.

3. Mercy and grace. There's a clear theme of grace and mercy, especially in Luke's parable. Those who are not worthy to come to the host's table – the poor, lame, crippled, blind – are now invited. They represent you and me. We are unworthy to eat at our Host's table, but we have been invited and cleansed. How true it is: "Blessed is the man who will eat at the feast in the kingdom of God" (Luke 14:15b). This is God's mercy, pure and simple.

4. Evangelism and the Lost. A fourth, and closely related theme, is evangelism. The poor, lame, crippled, and blind are now sought out. They are not just invited, but they are sought out and urged, compelled, to accept the invitation. These would include the poor and oppressed among the Jewish people, but also the Gentiles. You and I are the servants who bring a marvelous invitation of acceptance and forgiveness.

5. Delaying the meal until the house is full. The Host has prepared food for a large number of guests, and he won't be satisfied until his house is completely full. This reminds of two other verses:

> "The Lord is not slow in keeping his promise, as some understand slowness. He is patient with you, not wanting anyone to perish, but everyone to come to repentance." (2 Peter 3:9)

> "And this gospel of the kingdom will be preached in the whole world as a testimony to all nations, and then the end will come." (Matthew 24:14)

6. Judgment. Those who reject the invitation – for whatever reason – will not taste of the Master's banquet. We bear good news, but do so with humility and sadness, realizing that contained within the very message are the seeds of judgment if they reject. We are not damning people by telling them the Good News. Actually, the Good News is their only hope – they are already under God's judgment for their sins. It is only that deliberately rejecting the invitation invites greater judgment, and that saddens us.

7. Judgment on the Jewish Nation Those who reject the invitation are replaced with those who will come to his feast. As mentioned, those who reject the invitation are the Pharisees and Jewish rulers who, by and large, rejected Jesus and his message and were responsible for his death. In Luke we read:

> "I tell you, not one of those men who were invited will get a taste of my banquet.'" (Luke 14:24)

In Matthew the rejection of the servant's invitation is much stronger.

> "⁵ They paid no attention and went off.... ⁶ The rest seized his servants, mistreated them and killed them. "(Matthew 22:5-6)

Jesus allegorizes the mistreatment and killing of the prophets God sent to Israel as he does in the Parable of the Wicked Tenants (Lesson 2.3), which we'll consider in a moment. There the punishment is explicit:

> "He will bring those wretches to a wretched end." (Matthew 21:41a)

In Matthew's Parable of the Wedding Banquet, the punishment is also explicit:

> "The king was enraged. He sent his army and destroyed those murderers and burned their city." (Matthew 22:7)

As mentioned above, I believe this is an allegory of the siege and destruction of Jerusalem in 70 AD. Jesus prophesies this at the Triumphal Entry and later reiterates it to his disciples in the temple (Luke 21:5-6)

> "⁴³ The days will come upon you when your enemies will build an embankment against you and encircle you and hem you in on every side. ⁴⁴ They will dash you to the ground, you and the children within your walls. They will not leave one stone on another, because you did not recognize the time of God's coming to you." (Luke 19:43-44)

More on the fall of Jerusalem in the Parable of the Wicked Tenants (Lesson 2.3) below.

8. Feasting in the Kingdom of God. Finally, both versions of the parable are clearly alluding to the Great Messianic Banquet that we outline in Appendix 6. The Jews in Jesus' day looked forward to sitting down with Abraham, Isaac, and Jacob in the Kingdom of God, what Christians refer to as the Marriage Supper of the Lamb (Revelation 19:7).

> **Q6. (Matthew 22:1-10; Luke 14:15-24) Who do the excuse-makers represent? What are the potential results of excusing ourselves from carrying out God's will as we know it?**
> **https://www.joyfulheart.com/forums/topic/2180-q6-excuses/**

> **Q7. (Matthew 22:1-10; Luke 14:15-24) In Jesus' Parables of the Wedding Banquet (Matthew) and the Great Banquet (Luke), who are the people represented by those recruited from the streets and lanes of the city? From the highways and hedges? Who do the servant-recruiters represent? How diligent are you and your church in recruiting those who are of a lower class than others in your congregation? What keeps you from this**

2. Parables about Israel's Unbelief

Kingdom task? How might your church fulfill it?
https://www.joyfulheart.com/forums/topic/2181-q7-compel-them-to-come-in/

2.3 Excluding Israel from Messiah's Kingdom

We'll examine one final parable among those that deal with Israel's apostasy and rejection of Jesus – the Parable of the Wicked Tenants.

Parable of the Wicked Tenants (Matthew 21:33-46; Mark 12:1-12; Luke 20:9-19, §204)
(Also known as the Parable of the Wicked Husbandman or Bad Tenants)

If Matthew's Parable of the Wedding Banquet (Lesson 2.2) portends terrible judgment of an army destroying the king's enemies and their city, the Parable of the Wicked Tenants goes even farther. This parable occurs in all three Synoptic Gospels, but we'll be following Matthew's version here.

Planting a Vineyard (Matthew 21:33)

Jesus begins his story with a familiar hallmark of Israelite agriculture, a vineyard. While a number of parables include allegorical elements, this parable seems more allegorical than most, with each element representing something else.

> "Listen to another parable: There was a landowner[24] who planted a vineyard. He put a wall around it, dug a winepress in it and built a watchtower. Then he rented[25] the vineyard to some farmers[26] and went away on a journey." (Matthew 21:33)

The vineyard and fig tree are almost proverbial for abundant blessing. The phrase, "each man under his own vine and fig tree" is repeated over and over in the Old Testament.[27] The vineyard sometimes refers metaphorically to Israel:

---

[24] "Landowner" (NIV, NRSV), "master of a house" (ESV), "householder" (KJV) is *oikodespotēs*, "master of the house, householder" (BDAG 695).

[25] "Rented" (NIV), "let out" (ESV), "let forth" (KJV), "lease" (NRSV) is Greek *ekdidōmi*, "let out for hire, lease."

[26] "Tenants" (ESV, NRSV), "farmers" (NIV), "husbandmen" (KJV) is the plural of *geōrgos*, which can refer either to the owner of a farm, or, in this case, to one who does agricultural work on a contractual basis, "vinedresser, tenant farmer" (BDAG 196).

[27] 1 Kings 4:25; 2 Kings 18:31; Isaiah 34:4; 36:16; Joel 1:12; 2:22; Micah 4:4; Haggai 2:19; Zechariah 3:10.

'The Killed Vintners,' Codex Aureus of Echternach (1030-1040 AD), illuminated gospel book, Germanic National Museum, Munich. Larger image.

"The vineyard of the Lord Almighty is the house of Israel..." (Isaiah 5:1-7).[28]

Jesus seems to intend the vineyard in this parable to represent Israel. Matthew and Mark note that the landowner dug a wine press so the harvest could be processed on-site, and built a tower or elevated shaded platform where a worker could be stationed day and night during the growing season to watch for animals that might ruin the crop.[29]

Seeking Fruit from the Tenants (Matthew 21:34-36)

Once planted, a new vineyard might take three or four years to establish a good harvest, but then it would keep producing for many years, a quarter of a century or longer, before it began to decline. For the absentee landlord, this vineyard is an investment that would pay dividends each year for the rest of his life. Like today, tenant farmers were usually paid by allowing them to keep a portion of the harvest, with a fixed percentage going to the owner. But these tenants didn't want to share.

"³⁴ When the harvest time approached, he sent his servants to the tenants to collect his fruit. ³⁵ The tenants seized his servants; they beat[30] one, killed another, and stoned a

---

[28] See also Isaiah 27:2; Jeremiah 12:10; and Micah 7:1.

[29] Isaiah 5:2; 27:2-3.

[30] "Beat" (*derō*) means to literally "to skin, flay," colloquially, "to beat, whip," "cudgel, thrash" (BDAG 218-219; Liddell-Scott, p. 380). "Treat shamefully" (Luke and Mark: NIV, ESV, cf. KJV), "insult" means "to dishonor, shame," perhaps subject to public ridicule (*Atimazō*, BDAG 148-149). It is an especially grievous offense in the honor-shame oriented Semitic society. "Wound" (Mark and Luke) is Greek *traumatizō*, from which we get our word "traumatize" (BDAG 1014).

2. Parables about Israel's Unbelief

third. ³⁶ Then he sent other servants to them, more than the first time, and the tenants treated them the same way." (Matthew 21:34-36)

It's pretty clear to the disciples whom he is referring to. In their presence Jesus had rebuked the scribes and Pharisees:

"You approve of what your forefathers did; they killed the prophets, and you build their tombs. Because of this, God in his wisdom said, 'I will send them prophets and apostles, some of whom they will kill and others they will persecute.'" (Luke 11:48b-49)

"O Jerusalem, Jerusalem, you who kill the prophets and stone those sent to you." (Luke 13:34a)

The ruling class in Jerusalem is doing the same as their ancestors – killing the prophets who were sent to Israel to correct them and to turn their hearts and praises to God as his fruit from his vineyard. So, in Jesus' parable, the tenants represent the unbelieving rulers, while the vineyard is the nation of Israel itself, God himself the owner.

Sending His Son to the Tenants (Matthew 21:37-39)

But in Jesus' parable this rebelliousness does not stop with killing only the prophets.

"³⁷ Last of all, he sent his son to them. 'They will respect my son,' he said. ³⁸ But when the tenants saw the son, they said to each other, 'This is the heir. Come, let's kill him and take his inheritance.' ³⁹ So they took him and threw him out of the vineyard and killed him." (Matthew 21:37-39)

The owner's son deserves respect.[31] Instead, he is thrown out of the vineyard and slain. Of course, in this thinly-veiled allegory, the son is the Son of God whose death takes place outside the city walls on Golgotha.[32]

The Tenants' Punishment (Matthew 21:40-41)

Here, Jesus asks a rhetorical question, to which his hearers reply.

⁴⁰ "'Therefore, when the owner of the vineyard comes, what will he do to those tenants?' ⁴¹ 'He will bring those wretches to a wretched end,' they replied, 'and he will rent the vineyard to other tenants, who will give him his share of the crop at harvest time.'" (Matthew 21:40-41)

While "kill" in verses 38 and 39 means "to deprive of life, kill," the verb in verse 41 "put to a wretched end" (NIV), "put to a miserable death" (ESV, NRSV), "miserably destroy" (KJV) is

---

[31] "Respect" (NIV, ESV, NRSV), "reverence" (KJV) is *entrepō*, "have regard for, respect," show deference to a person in recognition of special status (BDAG 341, 2).

[32] "Kill" is Greek *apokteinō*, literally, "to deprive of life, kill" (BDAG 114, 1a).

a stronger, more final verb meaning "to perish, destroy, put an end to, abolish," then "to kill, put to death."[33]

Prophetic Allegory of the Fall of Jerusalem in 70 AD

I think of the utter destruction of Jerusalem by the Romans in 70 AD, the end of the Jewish nation – even as a self-governing kingdom under the Romans. At the fall of Jerusalem, the temple was destroyed, the city was burned, the walls were pulled down, and perhaps a million or more people were killed during the siege of the city, with another 97,000 people enslaved, many of them dying in the arena as gladiators to entertain the Romans.[34] This crushing destruction was terrible evidence of the wrath of God upon his rebellious people.

The listeners must understand something of what Jesus means in this parable. The key idea of a vineyard probably tipped them off that Israel was the subject. Perhaps the plots swirling around Jesus and the people's belief that he was the Messiah contributed to their understanding. Even Jesus' enemies "knew he was talking about them" (Matthew 21:45).

The Cornerstone (Matthew 21:42; Psalm 118:22-23)

Now Jesus teaches how the Old Testament prophets had predicted this, using a series of references to the "stone." "Stone" and "Rock" are often used as titles of God in the Old Testament.[35] First, Jesus quotes Psalm 118:22-23:

> 'The stone the builders[36] rejected
> has become the capstone;[37]
> the Lord has done this,
> and it is marvelous in our eyes'?" (Matthew 21:42)

---

[33] "Kill" is *apokteinō* (BDAG 114, 1a). *Apollumi*, BDAG 114-115, 1aα; Thayer 64, 1aα.

[34] Josephus, *Wars of the Jews*, 6.9.3 [420].

[35] Genesis 49:24; Deuteronomy 32:4-5; Psalm 18:2; 31:2-3; 61:2-3; 71:3; 89:26; 92:15; 144:1; Isaiah 8:14; 26:4; 44:8; 51:1.

[36] "Builders" is a participle of the Greek verb *oikodomeō*, "build," construct a building. It is also used in a transcendent sense for building up the Christian church (Matthew 16:18; Romans 15:20; 1 Peter 2:5) (BDAG 696, 1bβ).

[37] The exact role of the stone in this passage has been disputed. "Cornerstone" (ESV, NRSV), "head of the corner" (KJV) points to the first stone placed in a building, from which all the others are aligned. Others consider it to be the "capstone" (NIV) above the door or the porch. Whichever the word refers to, the point is that while it was rejected by the builders, it ultimately was placed by God in the key position of the entire building. Jeremias (*Parables*, p. 274) asserts that according to the agreed testimony of the Syriac translation of Psalm 118.22, Symmachus, Testimony of Solomon, Tertullian, Aphraates, Prudentius, and Synagogue poetry, the reference is "the stone which crowns the building, or, more precisely, the key stone of the structure probably set above the porch" (BDAG 542).

2. Parables about Israel's Unbelief

This passage was *not* interpreted messianically in Jesus' time,[38] but here Jesus declares it as definitely messianic in intent. The builders, of course, are the leaders of the Jewish nation. "Rejected" is *apodokimazō*, "to reject (after scrutiny), declare useless."[39] The rulers didn't just make a quick judgment error on the spur of the moment. This word indicates that they had a chance to examine the "stone" carefully and then reject it after due reflection.

Now Jesus pronounces terrible judgment on Israel.

> "Therefore I tell you that the kingdom of God will be taken away from you and given to a people who will produce its fruit." (Matthew 21:43)

We'll come back to this judgment in a moment. But first, let's see Jesus' other references to the Stone – a title of Yahweh in the Old Testament and of Jesus' in the New Testament.

The Stumbling and Crushing Stone (Matthew 21:44 = Luke 20:18)

Having established Psalm 118:22 as messianic, Jesus connects it with two other messianic verses about the stone.

> "He who falls on this stone will be broken to pieces, but he on whom it falls will be crushed."[40] (Matthew 21:44[41] = Luke 20:18)

The Stone that people stumble or fall on in verse 44a is a reference to Isaiah's prophecy about the Lord Almighty (Yahweh of the hosts or armies):

> "He will be a sanctuary; but for both houses of Israel he will be
> a **stone** that causes men to **stumble**, and a **rock** that makes them **fall**.
> And for the people of Jerusalem he will be a trap and a snare. (Isaiah 8:14)

The stone that crushes in verse 44b is seen in a passage from the Prophet Daniel that *was* understood as messianic by the Jews of Jesus' day.

> "While you were watching, a rock was cut out, but not by human hands. It struck the statue on its feet of iron and clay and **smashed** them.... In the time of those kings, the God of heaven will set up a kingdom that will never be destroyed, nor will it be left

---

[38] I am relying heavily for the history of Messianic interpretation on the scholarship of Joachim Jeremias, *lithos*, TDNT 4:272-273. He observes that a Messianic understanding of this passage is first found in the writings of Rashi who died in 1105 AD (TDNT 4:273, note 4).

[39] *Apodokimazō*, BDAG 110, a.

[40] "Falls" is the common Greek verb *piptō*. "Broken to pieces" (NIV, NRSV, ESV), "broken" (KJV) is Greek *synthlaō*, "crush (together), dash to pieces," to crush in such a way that an object is put in pieces (BDAG 972). "Crushed" (ESV, NRSV, NIV), "grind to powder" (KJV) is *likmaō*, "crush" (BDAG 596), sometimes used in the sense of "winnow."

[41] A few early Greek manuscripts omit verse 44 (D it sy^a). Most include it. However, the text is found undisputed in Luke 20:18. Metzger (*Textual Commentary*, p. 47) observes that most modern scholars regard Matthew 21:44 as an interpolation from Luke 20:18. However, the Committee included it in their text with a {C} "considerable degree of doubt" confidence level.

to another people. It will **crush** all those kingdoms and bring them to an end, but it will itself endure forever." (Daniel 2:34, 44-45)

Judgment upon Israel

Now let's examine Jesus' sad and decisive judgment on Israel.

> "Therefore I tell you that the kingdom of God will be taken away from you and given to a people who will produce its fruit." (Matthew 21:43)

The fruit the son in the parable was sent to collect represents the faith and righteousness due to the God of Israel. But though Jesus has called them to repentance, the Jewish leaders reject the Son of God and kill him. Then God rejects them and transfers the Kingdom of God to others – namely, the Gentiles, as we see in the Book of Acts. I can't over emphasize how important this verse is to understanding the relationship of the Kingdom of God to the Gentiles. Here is the progression.

1. **Abraham**. God reveals himself and makes a covenant with Abraham and his descendants forever.
2. **Moses.** God sets up his laws for Israel and establishes his throne room in their midst – first in the ark in the Holy of Holies of the tabernacle and later in the Jerusalem temple.
3. **Jesus.** God sends his Messiah "to the lost sheep of the house of Israel." He restricts his disciples from going to other peoples during his three years of ministry.
4. **The Cross**. This represents both the final rejection of Israel of their Messiah as well as the atonement of the sins of the whole world.
5. **Resurrection and Ascension**. In the Great Commission, the disciples are now instructed to "go and make disciples of all nations" (Matthew 28:19), to "go into all the world and preach the good news to all creation" (Mark 16:15).
6. **Holy Spirit**. On Pentecost, the Holy Spirit falls on people from all nations. Jesus commands his disciples: "You will receive power when the Holy Spirit comes on you; and you will be my witnesses in Jerusalem, and in all Judea and Samaria, and to the ends of the earth" (Acts 1:8).

Is There Any Future for Israel?

When you read Romans 9, 10 and 11 (and I encourage you to do that today), you catch Paul's struggle with the question of Israel's rejection of the Messiah and God's rejection of them as his Chosen People.

> "I have great sorrow and unceasing anguish in my heart." (Romans 9:2)

> "My heart's desire and prayer to God for the Israelites is that they may be saved." (Romans 10:2)

2. Parables about Israel's Unbelief

Paul employs the agricultural figure of grafting – the olive tree, of course, represents Israel.

> "If you [Gentiles] were cut out of an olive tree that is wild by nature, and contrary to nature were grafted into a cultivated olive tree, how much more readily will these, the natural branches, be grafted into their own olive tree!" (Romans 11:24)

There *is* hope for Israel!

> "[25] I do not want you to be ignorant of this mystery, brothers, so that you may not be conceited: Israel has experienced a hardening in part until the full number of the Gentiles has come in. [26] And so all Israel will be saved." (Romans 11:25-26a)

How will God do this in the End Time? Some say the Jews will be saved during the Tribulation, but that is mere speculation. We don't know the details. But we do know that ultimately, God will keep his promise to Israel and restore them to being his people – along with the Gentiles. Come soon, Lord Jesus!

> **Q8. (Matthew 21:33-46) Who do the servants sent to collect the landowner's share of the crop represent? What happened to Israel who rejected God's servants and Son who were sent to them? This is a parable about resisting those whom God sends to us to help us. Have you ever seen a church reject a pastor or leader that God sends to help them? Why is supporting our pastors and leaders important to God's plan for the church? (Hebrews 13:7, 17). In the Beatitudes, how does Jesus encourage those who are rejected and persecuted? (Matthew 5:10-12)?**
> https://www.joyfulheart.com/forums/topic/2182-q8-wicked-tenants/

We've studied Jesus' parables about the nation of Israel, who as a whole refused to repent and believe the Gospel. In the next lesson, we'll examine a series of Jesus' parables about repentance and the need for it.

Prayer

Lord, when we see the judgment brought about by the rebellious leaders of Israel, we think of the rebellion we sometimes find in our own hearts. Lord, forgive us and our grandiose plans for greatness. Help us to recognize You when You come in our midst. And help the Jewish people who, by and large, are still blind. Have mercy! In Jesus' name, we pray. Amen.

3. Parables about Repentance

John the Baptist came as a prophet calling on people to reform their lives – to repent of their sins so they can begin to live in a new way, preparing for the coming Kingdom of God. Thousands came to the lonely places along the Jordan where he was baptizing, lining the bank of the river. Thousands also came to be baptized as a sign of their repentance – a mikvah, a baptism of cleansing from their uncleanness and sins. (More on this in Lesson 6.1).

Jesus began his ministry with the same message as that of his reformer-cousin John the Baptist. Jesus announced:

> "The time has come. The kingdom of God is near. Repent and believe the good news!" (Mark 1:15; cf. Matthew 3:2 = Matthew 4:17)

A number of Jesus' parabolic teachings center on repentance. There is no salvation without repentance!

Harold Copping,(1863-1932) 'John the Baptist,' watercolor.

3.1 Uncleanness is Internal not External

- Analogy of Cleansing the Cup (Matthew 23:25-26; Luke 11:39-41)
- Analogy of Whitewashed Tombs (Matthew 23:27-28)
- Analogy of the Defiling Heart of Man (Mark 7:14-23; Matthew 15:10-11, 15-20)

3.2 Repent before Judgment Comes

- Parable of the Guilty Defendant (Matthew 5:25-26; Luke 12:57-59)
- Parable of the Wise and Foolish Builders (Matthew 7:24-27; Luke 6:47-49)
- Parable of the Narrow and Wide Gates (Matthew 7:13-14)

3.3 Obedience Required

- Parable of the Two Sons (Matthew 21:28-31)

3.4 Discernment

- Parable of the Speck and the Beam (Matthew 7:3-5; Luke 6:41-42)
- Parable of the Good Eye (Matthew 6:22-23; Luke 11:34-36)

3.1 Uncleanness is Internal not External

As we begin examining Jesus' parables about repentance, we need to consider three analogies in which Jesus taught about the nature of uncleanness and cleansing. These parables answer the question: Why do we need to repent? What do we need to repent of?

Analogy of Cleansing the Cup (Matthew 23:25-26, §210; Luke 11:39-41, §154)

In Matthew, this brief saying is in the context of a series of woes on the Pharisees.[1] In Luke, it is given during a dinner at the home of a Pharisee.

Ritual Rinsing of Hands before Meals

> "When Jesus had finished speaking, a Pharisee invited him to eat with him; so he went in and reclined[2] at the table. But the Pharisee, noticing that Jesus did not first wash before the meal, was surprised." (Luke 11:37-38)

The word translated "wash" is Greek *baptizō*, which means "dip, immerse," used in the New Testament in a ceremonial sense. Here it means, "wash ceremonially for the purpose of purification, wash, purify." It is also used of baptism: "plunge, dip, wash, baptize."[3]

The Pharisees took ritual cleansings very seriously. For example, at the wedding at Cana that Jesus attended, six stone water jars were present, "... the kind used by the Jews for ceremonial washing, each holding from twenty to thirty gallons" (John 2:6).

We teach our children to wash their hands thoroughly before eating in order to prevent diseases. But the Pharisees didn't wash in order to get rid of germs. They washed as required by the "tradition of the elders" in order to cleanse their hands from spiritual defilement that might be taken into the body. Mark describes the custom:

> "³ (The Pharisees and all the Jews do not eat unless they give their hands a ceremonial washing, holding to the tradition of the elders. ⁴ When they come from the marketplace they do not eat unless they wash. And they observe many other traditions, such as the washing of cups, pitchers and kettles.)

---

[1] In Luke it is the first of six woes against the Pharisees. As you'll see, the Analogy of Cleansing the Cup (Lesson 3.1) and the Analogy of the Defiling Heart of Man (Lesson 3.1) have a very similar context. To me they bear the marks of the same teaching being given on similar but different occasions. We'll follow Luke's version for the Analogy of Cleansing the Cup.

[2] The phrase "reclined at the table" (NIV, ESV), "took his place at the table" (NRSV), "sat down to meat" (KJV) is a single verb, *anapiptō*, "to recline on a couch to eat, lie down, recline" (BDAG 70, 1).

[3] *Baptizō*, BDAG 164, meanings 1 and 2.

⁵ So the Pharisees and teachers of the law asked Jesus, 'Why don't your disciples live according to the tradition of the elders instead of eating their food with 'unclean' hands?'" (Mark 7:3-5)

"The tradition of the elders" was not part of the Bible, but was known as the "oral law," a series of rules designed by the pious as "a hedge around the law," a kind of fence to keep people from violating the core of the law itself. Observe the "oral law," they reasoned, and you aren't in danger of breaking the actual laws in the Torah.

Many organizations have holiness rules. For example, "Don't dance," is a rule designed to prevent illicit sex. "Don't drink," is a rule designed to keep a person from drunkenness. And so on. Rules aren't bad; all families have family rules to keep the household running smoothly. But it is possible to so enshrine our rules that we miss the point entirely.

In the case of the Jews, the actual hand washing didn't involve soap or scrubbing, but rather dribbling some water over the hands. It was an act of spiritual cleansing, ritual cleansing, not really physical cleansing.[4]

Outer vs. Inward Cleansing

When Jesus and his disciples don't participate in the ritual of "hand washing" at the table that day, their Pharisee host shows surprise.[5] He probably remarks to Jesus about this failure and is met with a sharp response.

> "Then the Lord said to him, 'Now then, you Pharisees clean the outside of the cup and dish, but inside you are full of greed and wickedness.'" (Luke 11:39)

It was an insult to the host, surely. But Jesus is trying to make a vital point to save these Jewish leaders from their purely external understanding of purity.[6]

I have used the same ceramic coffee mug for about 40 years, given to me by my church secretary when I pastored in Los Angeles. It's a wonder that it hasn't broken in all these years. The outside of the cup looks fine, but the inside is stained with coffee from yesteryear. Disclaimer: Every once in a while, I soak the inside in bleach to remove the stains – but not often enough! It is dark with coffee stains. Gross!

---

[4] Stephen Westerholm, "Clean and Unclean," *DJG*, p. 129.

[5] "Surprised" (NIV), "astonished" (ESV), "amazed" (NRSV), "marvelled" (KJV) is *thaumazō*, "to be extraordinarily impressed or disturbed by something" (BDAG 444, 1aγ).

[6] "Jesus is saying that their practice of cleansing the outside of a cup and dish is just external. Apparently, the cleanliness of the outside of the pottery was distinguished from, and considered more important for ritual purposes than, the inside" (Westerholm, "Clean and Unclean," *DJG*, p. 130).

3. Parables about Repentance

Jesus uses cups and dishes as an analogy regarding the Pharisees' character. They are very concerned with outward purity and observance, but their hearts are full of greed[7] and wickedness.[8]

> "Blind Pharisee! First clean the inside of the cup and dish, and then the outside also will be clean." (Matthew 23:26)

Jesus calls the Pharisees, "blind" – "foolish people!"[9] This is obvious! Jesus calls on the Pharisees to see the obvious – that cleaning must include the outside *and* the inside. The inside is the real person.

Analogy of the Whitewashed Tombs (Matthew 23:27-28, §210)
(Also known as Analogy of the Whitewashed Sepulchers)

Matthew continues in the "woes" against the Pharisees along a very similar line:

> "27b You are like whitewashed tombs, which look beautiful on the outside but on the inside are full of dead men's bones and everything unclean. 28 In the same way, on the outside you appear to people as righteous but on the inside you are full of hypocrisy and wickedness." (Matthew 23:27-28)

Just prior to Passover, the Jews would whitewash the tombs and graveyards around Jerusalem with lime-plaster to make them visible. That way, pilgrims to the festival wouldn't accidentally defile themselves by touching a dead person's grave, and thus have to go through ritual cleaning all over again.[10] The whitewashed tomb comment is similar to his saying about the cup: the outside looks clean, but what is inside defiles.[11]

Analogy of the Defiling Heart of Man (Mark 7:14-23; Matthew 15:10-11, 15-20, §115)

A similar but distinct analogy is found in both Matthew and Mark in the context of Jesus' disciples eating with unwashed hands, as we just saw in the Analogy of Cleansing the Cup

---

[7] "Greed" (NIV, ESV, NRSV), "ravening" (KJV) is *harpagē*, "robbery, plunder," here, "the inner state of mind that leads to seizure, greediness, rapacity" (BDAG 133, 3).

[8] "Wickedness" is *ponēria*, "state or condition of a lack of moral or social values, wickedness, baseness, maliciousness, sinfulness" (BDAG 851).

[9] "Foolish people" (NIV), "You fools" (ESV, NRSV, KJV) is the adjective *aphron* (in the vocative): "pertaining to lack of prudence or good judgment, foolish, ignorant" (BDAG 159).

[10] Morris, *Matthew*, p. 585; France, *Matthew*, pp. 875-876.

[11] Luke concludes this teaching in a different way. "But give what is inside the dish to the poor, and everything will be clean for you" (Luke 11:41). Jesus turns the analogy of dishes that are dirty and clean to dishes that bear food that can be given to the poor. He is saying, if you want to cleanse the inside of the dish (which is a metaphor for the inner man), then give food from inside that dish to those who are hungry – a very powerful metaphor indeed.

(Lesson 3.1 above). Let's examine Mark's version of the Analogy of the Defiling Heart of Man. Jesus speaks to the crowd:

> "[14] Listen to me, everyone, and understand this. [15] Nothing outside a man can make him 'unclean' by going into him. Rather, it is what comes out of a man that makes him 'unclean.'" (Mark 7:14-15)

On the surface it's a kind of riddle. Later, when they were alone....

> "[15] Peter said, 'Explain the parable (*parabolē*) to us.' [18] 'Are you so dull?' he asked. 'Don't you see that nothing that enters a man from the outside can make him "unclean"? [19] For it doesn't go into his heart but into his stomach, and then out of his body.' (In saying this, Jesus declared all foods 'clean'.)"[12] (Mark 7:15-19)

Jesus is referring to the alimentary or digestive tract that his followers had a basic understanding of:

1. Eat with mouth.
2. Digest in stomach, intestines, etc.[13]
3. Defecate (literally, "goes out into the latrine").[14]

Inner Depravity

Mark and Matthew spell out the nature of this inner uncleanness.

> "[20] What comes out of a man is what makes him 'unclean.' [21] For from within, out of men's hearts, come evil thoughts, sexual immorality, theft, murder, adultery, [22] greed, malice, deceit, lewdness, envy, slander, arrogance and folly. [23] All these evils[15] come from inside and make a man 'unclean.'" (Mark 7:20-23)

Matthew's and Mark's lists vary slightly. Several of these defiling acts relate to infractions of the Ten Commandments.

---

[12] Notice that Mark observes parenthetically here that in this teaching "Jesus declared all foods 'clean.'" In other words, foods unclean to the Jews (pork, etc.) don't defile a person spiritually. Romans 14:14.

[13] "Stomach" (NIV, ESV, NRSV), "belly" (KJV) is *koilia*, "the cavity of the body," here more specifically, "the organ of nourishment, the digestive tract in its fullest extent: 'belly, stomach.'" Even the last part of the alimentary canal is *koilia* (BDAG 550, 1a).

[14] "Out of his body" (NIV), "is expelled" (ESV), "into the sewer" (NRSV), "goeth out into the draught" (KJV) reflect two key words: *ekporeuomai*, "go out" and *aphedrōn*, "toilet, latrine" (BDAG 155). Thayer (p. 88) sees *aphedrōn* as of Macedonian origin, "the place into which the alvine discharges are voided; a privy, sink." "Privy" (Liddell-Scott, p. 287).

[15] "Evils" is the plural of *ponēros*, "wicked, evil, base, worthless, vicious, degenerate" (BDAG 851, 1aα).

3. Parables about Repentance

- Evil thoughts.[16]
- Sexual immorality or fornication.[17]
- Theft[18] (Exodus 20:15)
- Murder[19] (Exodus 20:13)
- Adultery[20] (Exodus 20:14).
- Greed or covetousness[21] (Mark; Exodus 20:17).
- Malice or wickedness[22] (Mark).
- Deceit[23] (Mark).
- False witness (Matthew, Exodus 20:16).[24]
- Lewdness or licentiousness[25] (Mark).
- Envy[26] (Mark; Exodus 20:17).
- Slander.[27]

---

[16] "Evil thoughts" (NIV, ESV, KJV), "evil intentions" (NRSV) is two words: the adjective *kakos*, "pertaining to being socially or morally reprehensible, bad evil" (BDAG 501, 1b) and the plural noun *dialogismos*, "reasoning," here, "thought, opinion, reasoning, design ... evil machinations" (BDAG 232, 2).

[17] "Sexual immorality" (NIV, ESV), "fornication/s" (NRSV, KJV) is *porneia* (from which we get our word "pornography"), "unsanctioned sexual intercourse," a broad word that covers all kinds of sexual sins, "unlawful sexual intercourse, prostitution, unchastity, fornication" (BDAG 854, 1).

[18] "Theft/s" is *klopē*, "theft, stealing" (BDAG 550), from *kleptō* (from which we get our word "kleptomaniac"), "to steal."

[19] "Murder/s" is *ponos*, "murder, killing" (BDAG 1063).

[20] "Adultery/adulteries" is *moixeia*, "adultery" (BDAG 656).

[21] "Greed" (NIV), "coveting" (ESV), "covetousness" (KJV), "avarice" (NRSV) is *pleonexia*, "the state of desiring to have more than one's due, greediness, insatiableness, avarice, covetousness" (BDAG 824).

[22] "Malice" (NIV), "wickedness" (ESV, NRSV, KJV) is *ponēria*, "state or condition of a lack of moral or social values, wickedness, baseness, maliciousness, sinfulness" (BDAG 851).

[23] "Deceit" is *dolos*, "taking advantage through craft and underhanded methods, deceit, cunning, treachery" (BDAG 256).

[24] "False testimony" (NIV), "false witness" (ESV, NRSV, KJV) is *pseudomarturia*, "false witness" (BDAG 1097). This is specifically lying in a court of law.

[25] "Lewdness" (NIV), sensuality" (NRSV, "licentiousness" (NRSV), "lasciviousness" (KJV) is *aselgeia*, "lack of self-constraint which involves one in conduct that violates all bounds of what is socially acceptable, self-abandonment" (BDAG 141).

[26] "Envy" (NIV, ESV, NRSV) is literally, "an evil eye" (KJV), using *ponēros*, "wicked, evil, bad, base worthless, vicious, degenerate" (BDAG 851). "An evil eye" is "one that looks with envy or jealousy upon other people" (cf. Matthew 6:23), by metonymy for "envy, malice", but the meaning "stinginess, love for one's own possessions" is upheld for all the New Testament passages (BDAG 744).

[27] "Slander" (NIV, NRSV, ESV), "blasphemy" (KJV) is *blasphēmia* (from which we get our word "blasphemy"), "speech that denigrates or defames, reviling, denigration, disrespect, slander" (BDAG 178, a).

- Arrogance or pride[28] (Mark), the opposite of humility.
- Folly or foolishness (Mark).[29]

Jesus concludes: "These are what make a man 'unclean'" or "defile" him (Mark 7:20).[30] As we see in the Sermon on the Mount, the Pharisees emphasized the outward act, but Jesus says that God looks at the inner person, the heart (Matthew 5:21-22).

All this recalls what Jeremiah said long, long ago about the nature of man.

"The heart is **deceitful**[31] above all things and beyond cure.[32]

Who can understand it?" (Jeremiah 17:9)

There is an underlying selfishness deep down in us that is deceitful, devious, conniving. Paul bemoans our state:

"I know that nothing good[33] lives in me, that is, in my sinful nature (KJV, "flesh," *sarx*)." (Romans 7:18)

There is something twisted about our nature that gives us what John Wesley called "a bent to sinning." Jesus, too, knew this:

"24 Jesus on his part did not entrust himself to them, because he knew all people 25 and needed no one to bear witness about man, for he himself knew what was in man." (John 2:24-25, ESV)

We've spent considerable time looking at three of Jesus' analogies about the corruption of the inner person.

1. Analogy of Cleansing the Cup
2. Analogy of Whitewashed Tombs
3. Analogy of What Defiles a Man

---

[28] "Arrogance" (NIV), "pride" (ESV, NRSV, KJV) is *hyperēphania*, "a state of undue sense of one's importance bordering on insolence, arrogance, haughtiness, pride" (BDAG 1033).

[29] "Folly" (NIV, NRSV), "foolishness" (ESV, KJV) is *aphroyunē*, "the state of lack of prudence or good judgment, foolishness, lack of sense," moral and intellectual (BDAG 159).

[30] The word is *koinoō*, "to make common or impure, defile,' in the cultic sense (BDAG 552, 2a).

[31] "Deceitful" (ESV, NIV, KJV), "devious" (NRSV) is 'āqōb, used twice in the Old Testament as "uneven, bumpy ground" (Isaiah 40:4) and then "tough, crafty" (heart), in Jeremiah 17:9 (Holladay 281). "Insidious, deceitful" (BDB 784).

[32] "Beyond cure" (NIV), "desperately sick" (ESV), "perverse" (NRSV), "desperately wicked" (KJV) is 'ānaš, "be sick" (BDB 60); 1. "incurable" (Isaiah 17:11), 2. "calamitous" (Jeremiah 17:16) (Holladay 22). The basic meaning of the word is "to be sick" (2 Samuel 12:15) but most frequently it is used to describe a wound or pain which is incurable.... In Jeremiah 17:9 it describes the desperate spiritual state of the heart in terms of illness" (TWOT #135).

[33] "Good" is the adjective *agathos*, "pertaining to meeting a relatively high standard of worth or merit, good" (BDAG 3, 2aα).

Now we know *why* repentance is so vital for Jesus' disciples, those who would follow after him. We are corrupt. We need inner cleansing and we are unable to cleanse ourselves.

> **Q9. (Mark 7:14-23; Matthew 15:10-11, 15-20) What does Jesus teach about the heart of man? What does Jeremiah 17:9 tell us about the heart of man? Why do we try to look good on the outside, but resist letting Jesus change us on the inside? Why is repentance necessary for an outwardly "moral" person in order to be saved?**
> https://www.joyfulheart.com/forums/topic/2183-q9-defiled-hearts/

3.2 Repent before Judgment Comes

Now we'll look at three parables Jesus told about the need to get things right before judgment comes, before it is too late.

Parable of the Guilty Defendant (Matthew 5:25-26, §22; Luke 12:57-59, § 161)

Alcoholics Anonymous, a movement that helps men and women get free from addictions, has formulated a process of repentance in their Twelve Steps. Here are two that stand out to me:

> Step 4. Made a searching and fearless **moral inventory** of ourselves.
>
> Step 9. Made **direct amends** to such people wherever possible, except when to do so would injure them or others.

The Twelve Steps were written by people strongly influenced by Jesus' teaching. In the Sermon on the Mount, Jesus tells his disciples that if you are worshipping and remember that your brother has something against you, go, reconcile to your brother first before you offer worship to God. Repent of what is wrong in your life now. Don't put it off. "First go and be reconciled to your brother; then come and offer your gift." (Matthew 5:24). In other words, "Make amends." Don't put off repentance for what you know is wrong.

To help illustrate this, Jesus tells the Parable of the Guilty Defendant. Where it appears in Luke, Jesus introduces it with the words.

> "Why don't you judge for yourselves what is right?" (Luke 12:57)

"Right" is *dikaios*, "that which is obligatory in view of certain requirements of justice, right, fair, equitable."[34] In other words, don't wait for someone to take legal action against you before you do the right thing. Figure out for yourself what is the right thing and take care of it, rather than wait for a judge to make a ruling against you.

---

[34] *Dikaios*, BDAG 247, 2

In the Sermon on the Mount the brief parable about civil litigation over a debt follows Jesus' command to reconcile to your brother before worshipping God.

> "²⁵ Settle matters[35] quickly with your adversary[36] who is taking you to court. Do it while you are still with him on the way, or he may hand you over to the judge,[37] and the judge may hand you over to the officer,[38] and you may be thrown into prison.[39] ²⁶ I tell you the truth, you will not get out until you have paid the last penny." (Matthew 5:24-26)

The assumption of the parable is that in this case the adversary is in the right and you are in the wrong, for Jesus wouldn't tell us to be reconciled with someone by denying the truth. The situation in Jesus' parable is this: You owe someone a great deal of money, but you won't or can't pay up. So your creditor takes you to court. The case is black and white. You are sure to lose in court and then be sentenced to debtor's prison until your friends pay off your debt ("to the last penny") so that you can be released.

Scales of Justice

We don't have debtor's prisons today, but they were common in Western jurisprudence until recently. On the surface they seem stupid: If a person is in prison, he can't work to repay his debt. But what happened was that when you were thrown into debtor's prison, your family and friends would come up with the money in order to get you out. Then you have to live the rest of your life with your family glowering at you, never letting you forget the hardship you have caused them. (More on this in the Parable of the Unmerciful Servant, Lesson 1.2.)

A smart man, Jesus says, will settle out of court if he has a losing case. An intelligent man, Jesus says, will come to an agreement satisfactory to his creditor. A wise man, Jesus says, will appeal to his creditor for mercy, since if your case goes before the judge, it is sure to go against you.

---

[35] "Settle matters" (NIV), "come to terms" (ESV, NRSV), "agree" (KJV) is the present active participle of *eunoeō*, "be well-disposed, make friends" (BDAG 409). "To wish (one) well, to be well disposed, of a peaceable spirit" towards anyone (Thayer, p. 260).

[36] "Adversary" (NIV, KJV), "accuser" (ESV, NRSV) is *antidikos*, "one who brings a charge in a lawsuit, accuser, plaintiff" (BDAG 88, 1).

[37] "Judge" (Matthew) is *kritēs*, "one who has the right to render a decision in legal matters, a judge" (BDAG 570, 1a). "Magistrate" (Luke) is *archōn*, "one who has administrative authority, leader, official" (BDAG 140, 2).

[38] In Matthew, "officer" (NIV, NRSV, KJV), "guard" (ESV) is *hypēretēs* (loanword in rabbinical literature; frequently as technical term for a governmental or other official) one who functions as a helper, frequently in a subordinate capacity, helper, assistant" (BDAG 1035). Perhaps "deputy" is a good translation. In Luke, "officer" is *praktōr*, a technical term designating certain officials. Here a court functionary who is under a judge's orders, something like a "bailiff" or "constable," who is in charge of a debtor's prison (BDAG 859).

[39] "Prison" is *phylakē*, "the place where guarding is done, prison" (BDAG 1067).

3. Parables about Repentance

If the person you owe money to is already taking you to court, Jesus says in the Luke version, do your best[40] to put together a payment plan before it goes to the judge! Otherwise, the court will rule, turn you over to a bailiff who will put you in debtor's prison, until every last bit is paid. The texts specify the smallest, thinnest Greek and Roman coins.[41]

Settle Your Debt before Judgment

What does the parable mean? Some have tried to make it an allegory where the adversary is the devil and the judge is God. But the devil isn't given that kind of power or prominence in other passages about the Last Judgment. Rather the devil himself is judged first (Revelation 20:10, 14-15).

Rather than an allegory, this parable has a single point: If you know that judgment will surely go against you, you are a fool not to try to settle the case ahead of time. The implication is: Recognize your sins and make haste to repent and seek mercy before Judgment Day or you'll pay for them completely at the Judgment. Get right with God now! Repent now! Later will be too late!

Q10. (Matthew 5:23-26) Why did Jesus tell the Parable of the Guilty Defendant? How do people we have wronged and to whom we have not kept our promises get in the way of us worshipping God properly? In what ways is it hypocritical not to address these matters to the best of our ability?
https://www.joyfulheart.com/forums/topic/2184-q10-guilty-defendant/

---

[40] In Luke, "try hard" (NIV), "make an effort" (ESV, NRSV), "give diligence" (KJV) is *ergasia*, "engagement in some activity or behavior with sustained interest, practice, pursuit" of something (BDAG 390, 1). "Settle" (NIV), "come to terms" (ESV, NRSV), "agree" (KJV) is *apallassō*, "free, release," here, "to settle a matter with an adversary, come to a settlement, be quit of" (BDAG 96, 3).

[41] "Last penny" (NIV, ESV, NRSV), "uttermost farthing" (KJV) is two words, *eschatos*, "last" and (in Matthew and Luke) *kodrantēs*, (Latin loanword, *quadrans*), "quadrans, penny" = two lepta. It was the smallest Roman coin (BDAG 550). In Mark, *leptos*, "small copper coin, 1/128 of a denarius, something between a penny and a mill (BDAG 592, 2).

Parable of the Wise and Foolish Builders (Matthew 7:24-27, §43; Luke 6:47-49, §78)

(Also known as the Parable of the House on the Rock.)

The Parable of the Wise and Foolish Builders appears at the end of blocks of Jesus' teaching known respectively as the Sermon on the Mount (Matthew 5:3-7:27) and the Sermon on the Plain (Luke 6:20-49).[42]

This parable reminds me of the English fable of the Three Little Pigs, about shoddy construction and the big bad wolf who threatens to blow the house down.

Sandcastle. Photo credit: Unsplash/CC0 public domain.

Heedless Followers (Luke 6:46-47)

Jesus is surrounded by hundreds or thousands of people listening. I'm sure that after his meetings, people would come up and tell him that they want to be his followers. But how many of these hearers would actually put into practice his teachings? Only a fraction. So he exhorts them to both listen to his words *and* put them into practice. He asks:

> "Why do you call me, 'Lord, Lord,'[43] and do not do what I say? (Luke 6:46)

Most fail to put Jesus' teachings "into practice."[44] They may call themselves disciples, "hearers, followers," but they aren't following.

> "I will show you what he is like who comes to me and hears my words and puts them into practice." (Luke 6:47)

Jesus tells a parable to describe them.

---

[42] The accounts are similar, but curiously, use some different Greek words in the telling, demonstrating to me that they draw from different traditions of Jesus' sayings.

[43] The Greek word for "lord" is *kyrios*, "one who is in charge by virtue of possession, owner." The word is also used of the owner of a slave and as a designation of God himself (BDAG 576). When pious Jews read the Bible, they felt the divine name Yahweh too holy to pronounce for fear that they might break the Third Commandment. So they substituted the Hebrew word *adonai*, "Lord," in its place whenever they read it. Thus, when Jesus' followers are calling him "Lord, Lord," they are speaking to him with extreme reverence and respect, bordering sometimes on worship.

[44] "Puts them into practice" (NIV), "does them" (ESV, KJV), "acts on them" (NRSV) is the present active participle of *poieō*, "make, product" something, "do," here, "to carry out an obligation of a moral or social nature, do, keep, carry out, practice, commit" (BDAG 839, 3a).

3. Parables about Repentance

Digging Deep Foundations with the Shovel of Obedience (Luke 6:48)

Building a good foundation requires the wisdom to spend adequate time to construct an adequate foundation. Matthew's version of the parable contrasts the builders as "foolish" and "wise" builders.[45] Here's Luke's account of the person who puts Jesus' words into practice.

> "He is like a man building a house, who dug down deep[46] and laid the foundation[47] on rock."[48] (Luke 6:48a)

Bedrock is typically covered with dirt. The diligent builder takes the time and effort to dig down all the way to a rock substrate. It's more work, but the house stands when disaster strikes.

As I write, my home state of California is going through a series of "atmospheric rivers" of moisture resulting in lots of rain. Rain is expected today again. With the ground saturated, there is flooding. On television we see houses being flattened by the flood waters or floating downstream. It looks just like Jesus' parable.

> "When a flood came,[49] the torrent[50] struck[51] that house but could not shake[52] it, because it was well built.[53] But the one who hears my words and does not put them into

---

[45] Matthew differentiates the men with the words "wise" and "foolish" (as in the Parable of the Ten Virgins). "Wise man" is two words: *anēr*, "man" and *phronimos*, "sensible, thoughtful, prudent, wise" (BDAG 1066). "Foolish man" is two words: *anēr*, "man" and *mōros*, "foolish, stupid" (BDAG 663, a).

[46] "Dug down deep" (NIV), "dug deep" (ESV, NRSV, KJV) is the aorist active indicative of two verbs: *skaptō*, "dig into the ground, dig" (BDAG 926); and *bathunō*, "make deep," intransitive, "go down deep" (BDAG 162).

[47] "Laid the foundation" is two words: the aorist active indicative of the very common *tithēmi*, "put, place, lay" and the noun *themlios*, "the supporting base for a structure, foundation" (BDAG 448-449, 1b), in verses 48 and 49.

[48] "Rock" is *petra*, "bedrock or massive rock formations, rock" as distinguished from stones (BDAG 809, 1a).

[49] "Flood" is *plēmmura*, "the overflowing of a body of water, high water, flood" (BDAG 826). "Came" (NIV), "arose" (ESV, NRSV, KJV) is the aorist middle participle of the very common verb *ginomai*, "be, become," here, "come into being as an event or phenomenon from a point of origin, arise, come about, develop" (BDAG 197, 3a).

[50] "Torrent" (NIV), "stream" (ESV, KJV), "river" (NRSV) is *potamos* (from which we get our word "hippopotamus"), "river, stream." It can refer to "the mountain torrents or winter torrents which arise in ravines after a heavy rain and carry everything before them" (BDAG 856, a).

[51] "Struck" (NIV), "broke against" (ESV), "burst against" (NRSV), "beat vehemently upon" (KJV) is the aorist active indicative of *prospessō*, "to break into pieces upon striking against something," here, "to break in force against, burst upon" (BDAG 884, 2).

[52] "Shake" is the aorist active infinitive of *saleuō*, "shake, cause to waver/totter" (BDAG 911, 1).

[53] "Well built" (NIV, ESV, NRSV), "founded upon a rock" (KJV) is two words: the perfect passive infinitive of *oikodomeō*, "to construct a building, build" (BDAG 696, 1a); and the adverb *kalōs*, "fitly, appropriately, in the right way, splendidly" (BDAG 505, 1). The KJV "founded upon a rock," represents a major textual variant of the Byzantine text (A C (D) L W Θ Ψ *f*[1, 13]). Metzger's committee prefers the "well built" (P[75] B L W Ξ) with a {B} confidence rating ("some degree of doubt") (Metzger, *Textual Commentary*, p. 142).

practice is like a man who built a house on the ground[54] without a foundation. The moment the torrent struck that house, it collapsed[55] and its destruction was complete."[56] (Luke 6:48b-49)

Jesus' pre-ministry profession was as a carpenter, one who specialized in building houses. He abhorred shoddy work for he had seen houses collapse.

Because of the earthquakes we have in California, there are strict building codes that specify foundations of a certain width and depth. Embedded bolts are required to attach the mudsill to the foundation wall. In addition, in earthquake-prone areas, building codes require metal tie-downs or straps anchored in concrete that fasten the structure to the foundation. When a 6.5 or 7.0 earthquake ripples down the fault zone, it is soon apparent which houses are fastened to foundations. As I write, Turkey is recovering from a massive earthquake of 7.8 on the Richter scale. Many buildings today are rubble because of shoddy workmanship, and contractors and building inspectors who didn't follow the building codes are being jailed.

My dear friend, how firmly anchored is your life to the Rock Jesus? How carefully have you put his teachings into practice? Are you a serious, conscientious follower? Or a slipshod, enthusiastic believer who never gets around to anchoring his life in Jesus? Torrents do come to our lives. Earthquakes do bounce us around. Maybe you've just had a serious trembler in your life. It's not too late to found your life solidly on Jesus and his teachings.

> **Q11. (Matthew 7:24-27; Luke 6:47-49) Why does Jesus focus the Parable of the Wise and Foolish Builders on "putting into practice" rather than in "believing"? How can you help young Christians move from believing to true discipleship?**
> https://www.joyfulheart.com/forums/topic/2185-q11-wise-and-foolish-builders/

Parable of the Narrow and Wide Gates (Matthew 7:13-14, §40)

Repentance means changing one's heart, turning in a new direction. Jesus tells a parable about choosing between narrow and broad gates (*pulē*,[57] Matthew 7:13-14), which we'll

---

[54] "Ground" (NIV, ESV, NRSV), "earth" is *gē*, "earth, ground" (BDAG 196, 6a). Matthew uses *ammos*, "sand," here of a sandy subsoil (BDAG 54).

[55] "Collapsed" (NIV), "fell" (ESV, NRSV, KJV) is *sympiptō*, "to fall together in a heap, fall in, collapse" (BDAG 959, 1). Matthew uses *piptō*, "fall," here, of something that, until recently, has been standing (upright), "fall (down), fall to pieces." Of structures, "fall, fall to pieces, collapse, go down" (BDAG 115, 1bβ).

[56] "Destruction" (NIV), "ruin" (ESV, NRSV, KJV) is *rhēgma*, "the event of reduction to a ruined state, wreck, ruin, collapse," literally, "breaking" (BDAG 904). Matthew: "Fell with a great crash" (NIV), "great was the fall of it" (ESV, KJV) uses *ptosis*, "state or condition of falling, fall" (BDAG 896). "Complete" (NIV), "great" (ESV, NRSV, KJV) is *mega*, "great."

[57] "Gate" is *pulē*, "gate, door," literally of gates of cities (BDAG 897, b).

3. Parables about Repentance

consider here. A similar Parable of the Narrow Door (*thura*,[58] Luke 13:23-27) we'll consider in Lesson 8.2.

The Parable of the Narrow and Wide Gates found in the Sermon on the Mount is short, just two verses, without much context. It is a curious parable, actually a command that uses comparisons.

> "[13] Enter through the narrow gate.
> For wide is the gate and broad is the road that leads to destruction,
> and many enter through it.
> [14] But small is the gate and narrow the road that leads to life,
> and only a few find it." (Matthew 7:13-14)

This parable is a study in contrasts

Narrow gate	Wide gate
Hard/narrow way	Broad/easy way
Few	Many
Life	Destruction

Jesus presents two figures, first a gate,[59] then a road.[60]

Two gates. As you enter my rural property from the main road you see two gates. To the left is a narrow pedestrian gate about 42 inches wide (about 1.05 meters) leading to a trail through the woods. To the right is a wide 12-foot gate (3.7 meters) that swings open for a car to go up the driveway. To go to the house, you'd have to go through our pedestrian gate single file, but a lot of people could walk through the wide gate simultaneously. Jesus talks about the two gates with words describing simple dimensions: narrow[61] (KJV "strait") and wide.[62]

Two roads. The other figure is two roads. It is easy to visualize the broad roadway of a multilane freeway and the narrow road of an off-ramp. Jesus describes these, however, with words suggesting how you might *feel* on such a road.

1. "Broad" (NIV, KJV), "easy" (NRSV, ESV) is the adjective *euruchōros*, "pertaining to ample room, broad, spacious, roomy."[63]

---

[58] "Door" is *thura*, "door" of habitable quarters (BDAG 462, 1bβ).

[59] "Gate" is *pulē*, "gate, door," literally of gates of cities (BDAG 897, b).

[60] "Way" is *hodos*, "way, road, highway" (BDAG 591).

[61] "Narrow" (NIV, NRSV, ESV), "strait" (KJV) is the adjective *stenos*, "in reference to dimension, "narrow" (BDAG 942). "Strait" is an archaic English word that means, "strict, rigorous," then "narrow" (*Merriam-Webster's 11th Collegiate Dictionary*).

[62] "Wide" (NIV, ESV, NRSV, KJV) is the adjective *platus*, "pertaining to great extent from side to side, broad, wide" (BDAG 823).

[63] *Euruchōros*, BDAG 412.

2. "Narrow" (NIV, KJV), "hard" (ESV, NRSV) is *thlibō*, "to cause something to be constricted or narrow, press together, compress, make narrow."[64]

The few, the many.[65] We live in an age of polls that tell us what "most" people believe. We tend to adopt an unspoken attitude that, if a lot of people are doing something or believing something, then it can't be that bad. So many people can't be wrong. But it is this very myth of the majority that Jesus warns his disciples against. His disciples must be willing to take the "road less traveled."[66] As a parent I remember saying thousands of times, something like, "Just because everybody else is doing it doesn't make it right."

Lemmings have a reputation of following one another over a cliff. It's not true – fortunately.

The two destinations. Jesus also talks about two destinations. The wide gate and broad road lead to destruction. The noun refers to "annihilation both complete and in process, ruin," here of eternal destruction as punishment for the wicked.[67] Whenever we see the word in the New Testament it seems to promise a terrible end.[68] I don't expect that the masses know they're headed for hell; they just don't think much about it. They merely follow the bulk of humanity along a well-traveled road, as Paul puts it, "when you followed the ways of this world ... gratifying the cravings of our sinful nature and following its desires and thoughts" (Ephesians 2:1-3).

The other destination is life, fulfillment, eternal life[69] in the Kingdom of God! Blessing! In contrast to those on the broad highway, those who take the narrow gate and the rougher dirt road have chosen it for a purpose. They know where they want to go and take steps to get there. As the psalmist wrote:

"[19] Open for me the gates of righteousness;
I will enter and give thanks to the Lord.

---

[64] *Thlibō*, BDAG 457, 2.
[65] "Many" is the adjective *polus*, "pertaining to being a large number, many, a great number of" (BDAG 847, 1aα). "Few" is the adjective *oligos*, "pertaining to be relatively small in number, few" (BDAG 702, 1b).
[66] The phrase is from a well-known poem, "The Road Not Taken" (1916) by Robert Frost. It begins, "Two roads diverged in a yellow wood..." and concludes: "Two roads diverged in a wood, and I – I took the one less traveled by...."
[67] *Apōleia*, BDAG 127, 2.
[68] Acts 8:20; Romans 9:22; Philippians 1:28; 3:19; 2 Thessalonians 2:3; 1 Timothy 6:9; 2 Peter 2:1; 3:7, 16; Revelation 17:8, 11.
[69] "Life" is *zōe*, "life," here, "transcendent life," here, of life in the blessed period of final consummation (BDAG 430, 2bβ).

[20] This is the gate of the Lord
through which the righteous may enter."
(Psalm 118:19-20)

"Few there be that find it" (KJV, vs. 14b). "Finding" something presupposes searching earnestly. Jesus has just taught, "Seek and you shall find" (Matthew 7:7-8). The way is clear only to those who search for it, for at times it doesn't not seem well-trodden, though many saints have walked that way.

Q12. (Matthew 7:13-14) Why is "seeking" necessary to "find" the narrow gate? Why do you think Jesus concludes this brief parable with the phrase, "and only a few find it"? How is this parable designed to strengthen disciples to be willing to go against the flow, to be different from others in the culture?
https://www.joyfulheart.com/forums/topic/2186-q12-narrow-and-wide-gates/

3.3 Discipleship Requires Obedience

Parable of the Two Sons (Matthew 21:28-31, §203)
(Not to be confused with the Parable of the Prodigal Son or Lost Son)

The Jewish leaders have increasingly rejected Jesus. He weeps over them in his love (Luke 19:41). But it is important that Jesus' disciples see through the surface hypocrisy of the Pharisees and other seemingly pious Jewish leaders.

Jesus tells the Parable of the Two Sons during Holy Week. He is in the temple where the chief priests and elders question his authority. Jesus tells them he will answer them if they can answer one question:

"John's baptism – where did it come from? Was it from heaven, or from men?" (Matthew 21:25)

The chief priests and elders are on the spot. If they acknowledge John the Baptist as heaven-sent, they'll be asked why they didn't follow him. If they repudiate John, the people will turn against them. So they refuse to answer. Jesus replies by telling this parable.

"[28] 'What do you think? There was a man who had two sons. He went to the first and said, "Son, go and work today in the vineyard."

[29] "I will not," he answered, but later he changed his mind and went.

[30] Then the father went to the other son and said the same thing. He answered, "I will, sir," but he did not go.

> ³¹ Which of the two did what his father wanted?'
>
> 'The first,' they answered." (Matthew 21:28-31a)

At first glance, it seems like a pretty obvious story of a seemingly faithful son who doesn't follow through on his word, and a rebellious son who changes his mind and ends up obeying his father.

But Jesus isn't just telling the parable to teach his disciples the importance of repentance and obedience. The parable is an indictment of the Jewish leaders who had rejected John the Baptist, the prophet whom God had sent to them. It becomes clear as Jesus continues:

> "³¹ᵇ I tell you the truth, the tax collectors and the prostitutes are entering the kingdom of God ahead of you. ³² For John came to you to show you the way of righteousness, and you did not believe him, but the tax collectors and the prostitutes did. And even after you saw this, you did not repent and believe him." (Matthew 21:31b-32)

The sad truth is that the Jewish leaders saw a move of God but rejected it – and despised those who were converted in this revival. They not only prevent others from repentance, but they miss out themselves (Luke 11:52). Jesus says of them:

> "The Pharisees and experts in the law rejected God's purpose for themselves, because they had not been baptized by John." (Luke 7:30)

This can happen in traditional churches today. Leaders must recognize when God is moving, repent of their sins of unbelief, traditionalism, and lifeless faith, and get on board rather than try to stop the move of God.

However, even more this parable speaks to me of the importance of actual obedience to discipleship. It's easy to say, "I'll do it." But true disciples actually follow through. Yes, we often struggle and begin with fits and starts, and begin again. But we follow through. Obedience is the result of true repentance and the mark of a true disciple of Jesus.

Q13. (Matthew 21:28-31) Which son represents the tax collectors and prostitutes? Why do you think so? Why is it harder to actually obey, rather than just mouth the words? How is the lesson of this parable similar to the lesson of the Parable of the Wise and Foolish Builders? (Matthew 7:24-27) Why is actual obedience essential to true discipleship?
https://www.joyfulheart.com/forums/topic/2187-q13-two-sons/

3. Parables about Repentance

3.4 Discerning Sin in Our Lives

We've been considering parables about repentance. But for us to repent, we need to discern our sins truly. Jesus tells two parables along this line. In Lesson 10.1 we'll consider several other parables about a different kind of spiritual discernment by disciples.

Parable of the Speck and the Beam (Matthew 7:3-5, §36; Luke 6:41-42, §76)
(Also known as the Parable of the Mote and the Beam)

Judgmentalism and hypocrisy go hand in hand. Jesus addresses both judgmentalism and hypocrisy in the Parable of the Speck and the Beam, found in both Matthew's Sermon on the Mount and Luke's Sermon on the Plain.

It powerfully illustrates the need for both humility and repentance in us before we presume to criticize or minister to others. Matthew and Luke's versions are quite similar. Here's the context in Matthew. Jesus has just brought up the topic of judgmentalism.

> "Do not judge, or you too will be judged. ² For in the same way you judge others, you will be judged, and with the measure you use, it will be measured to you." (Matthew 7:1-2)

Now the parable.

> "³ Why do you look at the speck of sawdust in your brother's eye and pay no attention to the plank in your own eye? ⁴ How can you say to your brother, 'Let me take the speck out of your eye,' when all the time there is a plank in your own eye? ⁵ You hypocrite, first take the plank out of your own eye, and then you will see clearly to remove the speck from your brother's eye." (Matthew 7:3-5)

Domenico Fetti, detail of 'Parable of the Mote and the Beam' (ca. 1619), oil on wood, 24 x 17 in., Metropolitan Museum of Art, New York City.

This parable has to do with two kinds of objects in one's eye:

- One object is **tiny**. "Speck" (ESV, NIV, NRSV), "mote" (KJV) is *karphos*, "a small piece of straw, chaff, or wood, to denote something quite insignificant, speck, splinter, chip."[70]

---

[70] *Karphos*, BDAG 510.

- One object is **large.** "Plank" (NIV), log" (ESV, NRSV), "beam" is *dokos*, "a piece of heavy timber, such as a beam used in roof construction or to bar a door, beam of wood."[71]

Jesus is using humor – very small speck vs. very large timber – to make his point. Jesus is speaking in hyperbole, "extravagant exaggeration,"[72] used here to make a point.

A speck in your eye is annoying, makes your eye water, and affects your ability to look at anything else very long, since your eye is so irritated. Sometimes you need to ask another person to get the speck out. They have to get your head in a position with enough light for them to see so they can carefully remove it. Specks are so small.

Here's the situation. One person with a beam, plank, or timber in his eye is trying to see well enough to remove a speck from someone else's eye. The point is this: until we take the time to deal with our own sins and weaknesses, we're in no position to help someone else get rid of sin in his own life. The reason we're in no position to help is that we can't see clearly. The Pharisees were the self-appointed correctors of everyone else in society. But though they scrupulously kept the letter of the oral interpretation of the law, too often they missed the spirit or purpose of the law. On other occasions, Jesus rebuked them sharply for their hypocrisy:

"You blind guides! You strain out a gnat but swallow a camel." (Matthew 23:23-24)

Here's hyperbole again, the camel is compared to a gnat, just as the beam is compared to a speck. The Pharisees just don't "get" it. (In Appendix 4.3, we consider the saying, "the blind leading the blind.") Jesus' point is that the accusers' sins are much greater than the sins they see in others.

Psychologists have a term for this kind of distortion in perception. They call it "projection," where you project onto others your own sins and weaknesses.

It works this way. A person struggling with sexual temptation, for example, will loudly and harshly denounce someone else who has fallen in that area. In the 1990s, for example, one prominent televangelist harshly denounced another televangelist for his sexual failures. A few months later it came out that the first televangelist was struggling with his own temptations and was seen coming out of a hotel room with a prostitute.

Trying to correct someone else's failings without dealing first with your own sins results in a harsh and judgmental attitude that is unchristlike – and ineffective in producing change in the other person. Certainly, we are not to close our eyes to sin in the Body of Christ, especially by leaders (1 Timothy 5:19-20), but we are to not to rush to judgment. We are to look with eyes of mercy and forgiveness, quick to redeem and come to the aid of a fallen brother, rather than to stomp upon him further.

---

[71] *Dokos*, BDAG 256.
[72] Hyperbole, *Merriam-Webster's 11th Collegiate Dictionary*.

3. Parables about Repentance

Jesus doesn't say we aren't to help our brothers and sisters get rid of their irritating and debilitating sins. But we are to deal with our own glaring sins *first*, so we can see well enough to help them, rather than overreact. Then when we see the sins of others, we'll do so with mercy rather than judgmental self-righteousness. Paul says,

> "Brothers, if someone is caught in a sin, you who are spiritual should restore him gently. But watch yourself, or you also may be tempted." (Galatians 6:1)

There is a reason that the spiritual members should seek to restore others. Presumably, they've already dealt with their own sinfulness and are able to restore "gently"[73] rather than harshly. Jesus' classic parable about this contrast is the Parable of the Pharisee and the Tax Collector (which we examine in Lesson 9.1); the Pharisee is self-righteous while the tax collector is humble and repentant.

Q14. (Matthew 7:3-5) What is humorous about the Parable of the Speck and the Beam? How can we get to a place where we can see with clear spiritual eyes? Why does Paul insist that "spiritual" members correct sinning Christians with gentleness? What does judgmentalism have to do with hypocrisy?
https://www.joyfulheart.com/forums/topic/2188-q14-speck-and-beam/

Parable of the Good Eye (Matthew 6:22-23, §33; Luke 11:34-36, §153)
(Also known as the Parable of the Single Eye and the Lamp of the Body)

Spiritual blindness is also the point of Jesus' Parable of the Good Eye. It occurs in Matthew as part of the Sermon on the Mount and in Luke as part of a discourse with the crowds. It is a difficult parable for us to understand, so we'll take a bit of time with it.

Since Luke's version is a bit longer, we'll follow his narrative. Jesus has just taught about putting a lamp out in the open to shed light, rather than hiding it. (See the Analogy of the Lamp and the Bushel, Lesson 12.3.) Jesus' message is not given in a corner but spread abroad for all. However, reception of his truth is dependent upon the character of the recipient, which he explores in a this parable.

The Eye as the Window of the Soul (Luke 11:34)

Jesus begins the parable by saying,

---

[73] "Gently" (NIV), "a spirit of gentleness" (ESV, NRSV), "a spirit of meekness" (KJV) is two words: *pneuma*, "spirit" and *prautēs*, "the quality of not being overly impressed by a sense of one's self-importance, gentleness, humility, courtesy, considerateness, meekness" in the older favorable sense (BDAG 861).

> "Your eye is the lamp of your body. When your eyes are good, your whole body also is full of light. But when they are bad, your body also is full of darkness." (Luke 11:34)

We're used to thinking of lamps in terms of witness, lighting the house so others can see (Lesson 12.3). But here Jesus switches the metaphor. Instead of lighting others, the body's eyes are seen as lenses that transmit light into the body itself.

The reason this is difficult for us is that it isn't a scientific concept but a spiritual one. It is how they looked at things in first century Palestine. The shining light is Jesus, but his light comes into our life only if we have open eyes (hearts) to see and believe the truth. Then we are filled with the inner "glow" of spiritual life.

It all depends upon the health of our spiritual eyes. The word describing the "good eye" means "single, without guile, sincere, straightforward," that is, without a hidden agenda.[74] The description of bad eyes uses the Greek word *ponēros*. In the physical sense it means "in poor condition, sick," and in the ethical sense, "pertaining to being morally or socially worthless, wicked, evil, bad, base, worthless, vicious, degenerate."[75]

Healthy spiritual eyes allow the full light of Christ's presence and truth to flood into us. But sick, wicked, selfish spiritual eyes, like the Pharisees had, keep us in darkness. What can blind us? Sin. Money. Self-interest. Fear of losing our position.

Psychologists tell us that we all have a filtering system that enables us to concentrate on the important stimuli that we receive, while at the same time ignoring or filtering out all of the unimportant stimuli going on at the same time. Marketers tell us that we see hundreds or thousands of advertising messages each day. To keep our sanity, we filter most of them out. Sometimes men filter out the nagging of their wives, and wives filter out the abusive language of their husbands. We are capable of shutting ourselves into our own little world even in the midst of powerful stimuli of noise and motion and light. Filtering mechanisms are necessary.

When Light Is Darkness (Luke 11:35-36)

The real question, then, is what have we set our filters to filter out? Is our filtering system tuned to God's truth? Does it let in that which is true and good and wholesome, or is it set to admit the perverse, hateful, and obscene? Jesus' admonition is squarely to us disciples:

> "See to it, then, that the light within you is not darkness. Therefore, if your whole body is full of light, and no part of it dark, it will be completely lighted, as when the light of a lamp shines on you." (Luke 11:35-36)

---

[74] *Haplous*, BDAG 104. "The word-group is most used to express such positive values as free from inner discord, innocent, upright, pure. So when this idea of singleness and simplicity is applied to the physical eye, it probably means healthy vision, in contrast to "double vision" (Marshall, *Luke*, p. 489).
[75] *Ponēros*, BDAG 851, 1.

3. Parables about Repentance

Is your spiritual ear tuned to the negatives or to the positives? To good thoughts or to sinful thoughts. Is your spiritual ear sensitive enough to hear God's voice clearly? Or have you been filtering out God for so long that it is a habit? How do you even know what is right and good, and what is not?

I think of that prayer chorus:

> "Open our eyes, Lord, We want to see Jesus,
> To reach out and touch Him, And say that we love Him;
> Open our ears, Lord, And help us to listen.
> Open our eyes, Lord, we want to see Jesus."[76]

We need exposure to the full strength of Jesus' Light and Spirit to change us and give us true discernment. The Pharisees saw Jesus perform miracles and exorcisms, but they discerned them through their unhealthy, sick, self-protecting, wicked spiritual eyes, and saw Jesus as their enemy rather than their Friend. We can't afford to misinterpret Jesus. We must know him as He is!

We've been studying a series of Jesus' parables that explore the need for discernment of our sins followed by repentance, for actually applying what we have learned from our Master. This is often difficult. Introspection can be agonizing. No wonder some people avoid it and make fun of it. But true discernment, repentance, and putting into practice Jesus' teachings is the only way to grow as a disciple. We walk together on the journey, along the narrow road with Jesus that leads to the Kingdom of God!

Prayer

Father, without the Holy Spirit to bring us to truth, we can be so deceived, so blind to our own inward and outward sins! Forgive us. Help us to be quick to repent. Please help us to actually put into practice what Jesus teaches us. In His holy name, we pray. Amen.

---

[76] Words and music by Robert M. Cull, "Open Our Eyes, Lord" (John 12:20), © 1976 Maranatha! Music.

4. Parables about Final Judgment

In many Christian circles it is not fashionable to talk about hell and judgment. We'd rather be positive than negative, we say. We want to draw people to Christ by love, rather than by fear.

I get that. But the truth is that Jesus our Master taught at some length about judgment. And to be his true disciples, we need to study this area of his teachings. It is part of the gospel. And, like it or not, fear is a powerful motivator to find safety and salvation.

'Last Judgment' (5th century), mosaic, Church of Sant'Apollinare Nuovo, Ravenna, Italy

4.1 Role Reversal at Judgment
- Parable of the Rich Man and Lazarus (Luke 16:19-31)

4.2 Separation of the Righteous and Wicked
- Parable of the Sheep and Goats (Matthew 25:31-46)
- Parable of the Weeds or Tares (Matthew 13:24-30, §96; 36-43)
- Parable of the Net (Matthew 13:47-50)

4.3 Grace Triumphs over Judgment
- Parable of the Laborers in Vineyard (Matthew 20:1-16)

Many of Jesus' parables touch on final judgment – I can think of at least 13 parables beyond those we'll cover in this lesson.[1] But let us consider the parables that display Jesus' teaching on judgment with clarity.

4.1 Role Reversal at Judgment

A continuing theme in Jesus' teaching is that in the Kingdom, roles will be reversed.

"The last will be first, and the first will be last." (Matthew 20:16)

---

[1] Other parables that touch on judgment include Parables of the Unmerciful Servant (Lesson 1.2), Barren Fig Tree (Lesson 2.1), Marriage Feast (Lesson 2.2), Great Banquet (Lesson 2.2), Wicked Tenants (Lesson 2.3), Guilty Defendant (Lesson 3.2), Wide and Narrow Gates (Lesson 3.2), Wise and Faithful Steward (Lesson 5.3), Talents (Lesson 11.2), Minas or Pounds (Lesson 11.2), Narrow Door (Lesson 8.2), Vine and the Branches (Lesson 9.3), and Rich Fool (Lesson 10.2).

4. Parables about Final Judgment

The saying occurs in three instances in the Synoptic Gospels, each time summarizing Jesus' teaching on those occasions:

- Rich Young Ruler (Matthew 19:30 = Mark 10:31, §189)
- Parable of the Laborers in the Vineyard (Matthew 20:16, §190, Lesson 4.3)
- Parable of the Narrow Door (Luke 13:30, §165, Lesson 8.2)

Those who seem to be a "success" in this life, will not necessarily succeed in the life to come, and vice versa. We see it again capsulized in one of the most intriguing of Jesus' parables on judgment – the Parable of the Rich Man and Lazarus.

Parable of the Rich Man and Lazarus (Luke 16:19-31, §177)
(Also known as the Parable of Dives and Lazarus)

Where the Parable of the Rich Man and Lazarus appears in Luke, Jesus has been teaching about materialism and money. His audience includes his disciples (verse 1) as well as "the Pharisees who loved money." He tells a story that contrasts one who is extremely rich with one who is extremely poor.

Fedor Andreevich Bronnikov, detail, 'Parable of Lazarus' (1886), oil on canvas, original dimensions 127×84.5 cm,

Portrayal or Parable?

Before we get into the parable however, we need to ask ourselves: Is this a *portrayal* of an actual situation or a *parable*, a story for the sake of comparison? Is the Parable of the Rich Man and Lazarus a divinely inspired portrayal of heaven? It seems different, for example, from the lush word pictures in the Book of Revelation.[2]

In a parable, the story doesn't have to be about real people or even real situations. But to achieve its teaching goal, a parable must be striking and memorable, so that as the story or comparison is retold and remembered. The hearers must be able to imagine the situation. The story doesn't have to be true in all its particulars, but the popular mind needs to be able to relate to its stereotyped characters, in this case, the rich man, the poor man, and Father Abraham.

In America, we have our own fables of heaven – a whole series of jokes that have St. Peter at the pearly gates deciding who should enter heaven and who should go to hell. Lawyers, especially, don't do well in this genre of jokes. You don't stop the joke teller because his

---

[2] Many scholars believe that Jesus is drawing upon a popular Jewish folk-tale that had roots in Egypt about a rich man and poor man whose lots after death are completely reversed (Marshall, *Luke*, pp. 633-634; Jeremias, *Parables*, p. 183).

portrayal is inadequate, or leaves out the great white throne judgment (Revelation 20:11). You accept the semi-mythical props of the story and listen for the punch-line.

Jesus is not trying to make a joke here – the subject is deadly serious. Nor do I think Jesus is trying to teach his disciples the details of the after-life in this parable. I believe he is using a popular story genre to make a spiritual point. As Snodgrass puts it:

> "We must remember that parables are vignettes, not systems, and certainly not systematic theologies."[3]

Contrasting the Rich Man and Lazarus (Luke 16:19-21)

In this parable, Jesus begins by painting a quick portrait of the rich man – a very, very rich man.

> "There was a rich man who was dressed in purple and fine linen and lived in luxury every day." (Luke 16:19)

A purple wool mantle was costly, since purple dye was extremely expensive, extracted from murex sea or rock snails. A finely-woven linen tunic was considered the height of luxury. "Feasted sumptuously" (ESV) suggests that no expense was spared at his banquets.[4] The rich man is not named, though he is sometimes called Dives, the Latin word for "rich man."

Eugene Burnard, 'Rich Man' in *The Parables* (1908), Conté crayon and charcoal.

Next, Jesus swiftly sketches a portrait of an extremely poor man lying at the rich man's impressive gate.[5]

> "21 At his gate was laid a beggar named Lazarus, covered with sores 21 and longing to eat what fell from the rich man's table. Even the dogs came and licked his sores." (Luke 16:20-21)

Lazarus (short for Eleazar, which means "He whom God helps") is a miserable beggar, covered with numerous ulcerated sores licked by dogs. In Jesus' culture dogs were not pets, but were considered unclean. The wild street dogs that scavenge the garbage are licking

---

[3] Snodgrass, *Stories*, p. 429.
[4] "Lived in luxury" (NIV), "feasted sumptuously" (ESV, NRSV), "fared sumptuously" (KJV) is two words: *euphrainō*, "be glad or delighted, enjoy oneself, rejoice, celebrate" (BDAG 415, 2; used of celebrations in the parables of the lost sheep, coin, and son; and the parable of the rich fool); and the adverb *lamprōs*, "splendidly, sumptuously" (BDAG 585), "magnificently" (Thayer 371).
[5] *Pylōn*, "gateway, entrance, gate," especially of the large, impressive gateways at the entrance of temples and places (BDAG 897, 1).

4. Parables about Final Judgment

Lazarus's open wounds. The picture of Lazarus is one of abject misery. Lazarus is lying at a suitable place for begging, next to the rich man's gate, hoping that the food scraps will be thrown his way at the end of the meal. He isn't hoping for crumbs, but "pieces of bread which the guests dipped in the dish, wiped their hands with, and then threw under the table."[6]

The scene is set in three short verses. The very rich man and the sick, miserable poor man.

Abraham's Bosom (Luke 16:22)

Now the story Jesus begins to get interesting. Ears perk up.

> "The time came when the beggar died and the angels carried him to Abraham's side." (Luke 16:22)

Jesus pictures angels carrying Lazarus to Abraham. "Side" (NIV, ESV), "bosom" (KJV) is Greek *kolpos*, "bosom, breast, chest." The ancient banqueting practice of reclining at the table would have one's head on someone's breast. So this puts Lazarus in the place of honor at the right hand of Abraham at the banquet in the next world.[7]

Jesus is drawing on a common Jewish belief of the time known as the Bosom of Abraham, the place where the righteous, especially Jewish martyrs, would go in the after-life, comforted by Abraham and the other patriarchs. The idea is found in Jewish papyri and apocryphal literature in the intertestamental period.[8] (See Appendix 5. The Great Messianic Banquet).

Again, I don't think Jesus is teaching us the nature of heaven or hades in this parable. But all Jesus' hearers know the images and are ready for the story.

The Rich Man in Hell (Luke 16:22b-26)

In contrast to Lazarus's bliss in the Bosom of Abraham, Dives is in torment in hell.

> "22b The rich man also died and was buried. 23 In hell, where he was in torment, he looked up and saw Abraham far away, with Lazarus by his side. 24 So he called to him, 'Father Abraham, have pity on me and send Lazarus to dip the tip of his finger in water and cool my tongue, because I am in agony in this fire.'" (Luke 16:22b-24)

The rich man is in "hell." The Greek word used here is *Hades*, the place of the dead, and in Jewish thought, the intermediate place of the dead prior to the final judgment.[9] He is in

---

[6] Jeremias, *Parables*, p. 184.
[7] *Kolpos*, BDAG 556-557.
[8] For example, "For if we so die, Abraham and Isaac and Jacob will welcome us, and all the fathers will praise us" (4 Maccabees 13:17). Wikipedia article, "Bosom of Abraham"; Kaufmann Kohler, "Abraham's Bosom," *Jewish Encyclopedia* (1906).
[9] *Hades*, BDAG 19; Jeremias, *Parables*, p. 185. Though Greek *gehenna* is usually used to refer to the place of final punishment, in Jewish literature torment can be a feature of the intermediate state as well as of the final state of the wicked (Marshall, *Luke*, p. 637, cites 1 Enoch 22; Wisdom 3:1; 4 Maccabees 13:15; 2 Clement 17:7; 10:4).

torment,[10] parched with thirst, suffering. "I am in agony[11] in this fire" (verse 24). He still views Lazarus as a slave who can be ordered around at his whim.

> "²⁵ But Abraham replied, 'Son, remember that in your lifetime you received your good things, while Lazarus received bad things, but now he is comforted[12] here and you are in agony. ²⁶ And besides all this, between us and you a great chasm[13] has been fixed, so that those who want to go from here to you cannot, nor can anyone cross over from there to us.'" (Luke 16:25-26)

The die has been cast; the outcome is irreversible.

God's Word Is Sufficient Warning (Luke 16:27-31)

But Dives doesn't quit. He has another appeal.

> "²⁷ He answered, 'Then I beg you, father, send Lazarus to my father's house, ²⁸ for I have five brothers. Let him warn them, so that they will not also come to this place of torment.'
> ²⁹ Abraham replied, 'They have Moses and the Prophets; let them listen to them.'
> ³⁰ 'No, father Abraham,' he said, 'but if someone from the dead goes to them, they will repent.'
> ³¹ He said to him, 'If they do not listen to Moses and the Prophets, they will not be convinced even if someone rises from the dead.'" (Luke 16:27-31)

In the context, the rich man proposes that Lazarus should rise from the dead to warn his brothers. But Luke's post-resurrection readers will immediately think of Jesus, and how even his manifest resurrection was not enough to sway the Pharisees from their hardened opposition to the truth that was clearly before them. Marshall notes, "The rich man knows from personal experience that his family do not take seriously what the law and the prophets say. Something more is needed."[14]

What's the Point?

Of course, Jesus is saying that riches don't count for anything after we die, but that isn't the thrust of this parable. I think he is making several points.

1. In the Kingdom, the worldly wealthy and the poor in spirit reverse places.
2. If we close our eyes to the truth we are given, then we are doomed.

---

[10] *Basanos*, "severe pain occasioned by punitive torture, torture, torment" (BDAG 168).
[11] *Odynaō*, "to undergo physical torment, suffer pain" (BDAG 692, 1).
[12] *Parakaleō*, "come alongside," here, "comfort, encourage, cheer up" (BDAG 764, 4).
[13] "Chasm" (NIV, NRSV, ESV), "gulf" (KJV) is *chasma*, "chasm" (literally a "yawning"), from *chaskō*, "yawn, gape" (BDAG 1081).
[14] Marshall, *Luke*, p. 639.

4. Parables about Final Judgment

3. Wealth without active mercy for the poor is great wickedness.

As you may recall, this parable follows Jesus' teaching on money and materialism – the Parable of the Unjust Steward (Lesson 10.1), and serving Mammon (Lesson 10.2).

Jesus condemns the Pharisees for their love of money combined with their lack of mercy for the poor. Remember his comment about their scrupulous tithing?

> "Woe to you Pharisees, because you give God a tenth of your mint, rue and all other kinds of garden herbs, but **you neglect justice and the love of God**. You should have practiced the latter without leaving the former undone." (Luke 11:42)

It isn't their piety that he is condemning here, but what they *are not* doing – showing mercy to the poor, seeking justice for the downtrodden. It is ironic that the Pharisees who prided themselves on being such Bible scholars missed the spirit of the Old Testament – mercy and justice.

What Are We Doing for the Poor?

In a sense, the Parable of the Rich Man and Lazarus teaches a similar lesson to that of The Parable of the Unjust Steward (Luke 16:1-9, Lesson 10.1). We can use our money in a way that secures for us secure eternal damnation or in a way that secures us friends in eternal habitations who will welcome us. But there's more.

William Barclay titles this passage, "The Punishment of the Man Who Never Noticed."[15] Lazarus was at his door and he didn't notice. Who is at our door that we don't notice?

- Needy emigrants who avoid the social welfare system for fear of being deported?
- Divorced moms with kids who are living below the poverty level, but are too ashamed to ask for help?
- Families where the breadwinner is sick or shiftless or missing?
- The homeless in our streets who can't afford the increasing cost of housing?
- The poor in third world countries who are out of sight and out of mind?

The Parable of the Sheep and the Goats (Matthew 25:31-46) teaches a similar lesson about neglecting mercy, as we'll see below (See Lesson 4.2).

Wealth in itself is not bad. After all, Abraham was wealthy. But wealth brings with it responsibilities, a certain stewardship.

> "From everyone who has been given much, much will be demanded; and from the one who has been entrusted with much, much more will be asked." (Luke 12:48b, Lesson 5.3)

---

[15] William Barclay, *The Gospel of Luke* (Revised Edition; Daily Study Bible Series; Westminster Press, 1975), pp. 212-217.

We will give an accounting for how we handle the wealth God has given us. Hunter concludes:

> "If a man (says Jesus) cannot be humane with the Old Testament in his hand and Lazarus on his doorstep, nothing – neither a visitant from the other world nor a revelation of the horrors of Hell – will teach him otherwise. Such requests for signs are pure evasions."[16]

Q15. (Luke 16:19-31). What was the Rich Man's sin that landed him in hell? Since it isn't stated explicitly, what must it be? In hell, what is the Rich Man's attitude towards Lazarus? What is the main point of the Parable of the Rich Man and Lazarus? What are you and your church doing to aid the very poor in your area? In the world?
https://www.joyfulheart.com/forums/topic/2189-q15-rich-man-and-lazarus/

4.2 Separation of the Righteous and Wicked

Jesus tells three parables that illustrate the separation of the righteous from the wicked at the End Time – the Parables of the Sheep and the Goats, the Weeds or Tares, and the Net. We'll look at them each in turn.

Parable of the Sheep and the Goats (Matthew 25:31-46, §229)
(Also known as the Parable of the Judgment of the Nations.)

This parable found only in Matthew appears in the context of several other parables about the End Time. It follows the Parable of the Talents.

Jesus begins by setting the scene with himself – the Son of Man – seated on a throne of judgment.

> "When the Son of Man comes in his glory, and all the angels with him, he will sit on his throne in heavenly glory." (Matthew 25:31)

Son of Man is the title Jesus used for himself, a reference to the "son of man" in Daniel's messianic prophecy that unfolds in Yahweh's throne room (Daniel 7:13-14)

Of course, this glorified Son of Man is Jesus himself! In our parable he is called "King" in verses 34, 40. The phrase, "comes in glory," of course, refers to Christ's Second Coming.[17] This will be a manifestation of God's Shekinah glory as seen in Exodus and in Revelation.[18]

---

[16] Hunter, *Parables*, p. 84.
[17] Mark 8:38, cf. Matthew 16:26-27; Luke 9:26-27; 2 Thessalonians 1:7, 10.
[18] Exodus 24:17; Deuteronomy 4:24; Hebrews 12:29; Psalm 18:8; 50:3; Isaiah 29:6; 30:30; Revelation 1:14; 2:18; 19:12.

4. Parables about Final Judgment

"³² All the nations will be gathered before him, and he will separate the people one from another as a shepherd separates the sheep from the goats. ³³ He will put the sheep on his right and the goats on his left." (Matthew 25:32-33)

Let's look at the elements of these verses one by one.

"All the nations" uses the noun *ethnē* (from which we get our word "ethnic"), "a body of persons united by kinship, culture, and common traditions, 'nation, people.'"[19] In other words, this judgment is not just of Israel or believers, but of all peoples, those about whom the Great Commission was given – "Go and make disciples of all nations" (Matthew 28:19).[20]

"As a shepherd separates the sheep from the goats" (verse 32b). The King on his throne puts the sheep on his right and the goats on his left (verse 33). The place of honor, of course, is at a person's right hand.[21]

The Israelites were a shepherd people who raised both sheep and goats. In their culture, one wasn't considered "good" and the other "bad." Both were eligible to be used for sacrifices (Leviticus 3:7, 12). Even the Passover sacrifice could be a lamb or a kid.[22] Sheep and goats were pastured together and cared for by the same shepherd. Both sheep and goats were milked. Both could be slaughtered for food. The sheep's wool and goat's hair were used for various kinds of textiles. Goat skins were used as containers – wineskins, for example. The only difference I can see is that Israel was often referred to in the Old Testament as "sheep," but never "goats."

There are occasions when a shepherd would commonly separate the sheep from the goats[23] because goats are naturally more aggressive than sheep. Lonnie Oldag, who raises herds of both goats and sheep in Alabama tells me, "When you don't separate them, the goats beat up on the sheep. So I separate them so my sheep don't get beat up."[24] That makes sense to me. When the sheep and goats are confined in a sheepfold for protection at the end of the day, the goats would be routinely separated from the sheep as a practical measure in order to protect them and help them settle down better for the night.

Jesus is saying that at the Last Judgment, the saved will be separated from the lost like a shepherd separates the sheep from the goats. We see this same separation on the Last Day in

---

[19] *Ethnē*, BDAG 276, 1.
[20] Also Matthew 24:14, 30; Mark 11:17; Luke 24:47.
[21] Hebrews 1:3; 12:2; 1 Peter 3:22; Acts 7:55-56.
[22] Exodus 12:4 uses the term *śeh* for the Passover sacrifice, which could refer to either a sheep or a goat (TWOT #2237; Jacob Zallel Lauterbach, "Passover Sacrifice," *Jewish Encyclopedia* (1906).
[23] Some academics have suggested a separation on cold nights night, since the goats are more susceptible to the cold than the sheep, though this is disputed (*Morris*, Matthew, p. 636; Jeremias, *Parables*, p. 206; Snodgrass, *Stories*, p. 550; France, *Matthew*, pp. 961-962, fn. 88).
[24] Lonnie J. Oldag, Rolling "O" Farm, Hackleburg/Phil Campbell, Alabama. https://www.youtube.com/watch?v=UhYiIdl8qis

the Parable of the Net (Lesson 4.2), Parable of the Weeds or Tares (Lesson 4.2), and the Parable of the Wise and Foolish Virgins (Lesson 5.2).

Characteristics for Separating (Matthew 25:34-46)

Now the King addresses those on each side of him.

> [34] "Then the King will say to those on his right, 'Come, you who are blessed by my Father; take your inheritance, the kingdom prepared for you since the creation of the world. [35] For I was hungry and you gave me something to eat, I was thirsty and you gave me something to drink, I was a stranger and you invited me in, [36] I needed clothes and you clothed me, I was sick and you looked after me, I was in prison and you came to visit me.'
>
> [37] Then the righteous will answer him, 'Lord, when did we see you hungry and feed you, or thirsty and give you something to drink? [38] When did we see you a stranger and invite you in, or needing clothes and clothe you? [39] When did we see you sick or in prison and go to visit you?'
>
> [40] The King will reply, 'I tell you the truth, whatever you did for one of the least of these brothers of mine, you did for me.'
>
> [41] Then he will say to those on his left, 'Depart from me, you who are cursed, into the eternal fire prepared for the devil and his angels. [42] For I was hungry and you gave me nothing to eat, I was thirsty and you gave me nothing to drink, [43] I was a stranger and you did not invite me in, I needed clothes and you did not clothe me, I was sick and in prison and you did not look after me.'
>
> [44] They also will answer, 'Lord, when did we see you hungry or thirsty or a stranger or needing clothes or sick or in prison, and did not help you?'
>
> [45] He will reply, 'I tell you the truth, whatever you did not do for one of the least of these, you did not do for me.'
>
> [46] Then they will go away to eternal punishment, but the righteous to eternal life." (Matthew 25:34-46)

In this parable, the separation is based on how people treated Jesus when they saw him in need. The occasions are:

- Feeding him when hungry,
- Inviting him into one's home when he had no place to live,
- Clothing him when he had no clothes.
- Visiting him when he was in prison.

Both groups deny seeing Jesus in need. "When did we see you" in need? they ask.

4. Parables about Final Judgment

"The King will reply, 'I tell you the truth, whatever you did for one of the least of these brothers of mine, you did for me.'" (Matthew 25:40, cf. vs. 45)

In other words, Jesus is saying that the way they treated "these brothers of mine" is the way they treated Jesus himself. In some way, Jesus is present in "these brothers."

Who are "these brothers of mine"?

The key question that determines how you interpret the Parable of the Sheep and the Goats turns on whom you identify as "these brothers of mine."[25] There have been primarily four interpretations over the history of the Church.

1. **All needy persons.** This is the final judgment of all persons (Universal).
2. **Needy Christians.** This is the judgment of Christians (Ecclesiastical).
3. **Jesus' Own Disciples**, and, by extension, **Christian missionaries.** Nations will be judged on how they treat Christian missionaries who spread the faith (Missionary).
4. **Jews.** People are judged on how they treat the Jews during the tribulation (Dispensationalist).[26]

Among these, "all needy persons" and "Jesus' own disciples" seem most likely.

All Needy Persons. In the Old Testament especially, God is also closely identified with the needy *in general*.

"He defends the cause of the fatherless and the widow,
and loves the alien, giving him food and clothing." (Deuteronomy 10:18)

"A father to the fatherless, a defender of widows,
is God in his holy dwelling." (Psalm 68:5)

"He who is kind to the poor lends to the Lord. (Proverbs 19:17a)

One objection to the "least brothers" being all needy persons might be that the parable might be seen to teach salvation by works. However, you could argue that people showed mercy *because* they had been saved, not *in order to* be saved.

Jesus' Own Disciples. On the other hand, there are good reasons to see "least brothers" as Jesus' own disciples (which is an extension of the "missionary" interpretation above). Jesus' disciples might well be imprisoned for their faith (Luke 21:12). Indeed, Jesus uses the term "brothers" to refer to his disciples (Matthew 12:50; 28:10). And Jesus also uses the term "little ones" to refer to disciples (Matthew 10:40-42; 11:25). Moreover, Jesus is closely identified with his disciples:

---

[25] "One of the least of these brothers of mine" (NIV), "one of the least of these my brothers" (ESV, cf. KJV), "one of the least of these who are members of my family" (NRSV) is several words, including: *elachistos*, "pertaining to the lowest in status, least" (BDAG 314, 1); the plural of *adelphos*, "brother." The plural can also mean "brothers and sisters" (BDAG 18, 1 and 2a).

[26] Snodgrass, *Stories*, pp. 551-552.

"For where two or three come together in my name, there am I with them." (Matthew 18:20)

This seems to parallel "whatever you did for one of the least of these brothers of mine, you did for me" (Matthew 25:40).

So which is it? Who are the "the least of these my brothers"? Are the righteous those who show mercy to Jesus's disciples? Or those who show mercy to any in need? Scholars argue both sides.[27]

However, in the final analysis, it may not make a great deal of practical difference whether the "least brothers" are needy people in general or Jesus' disciples in particular. Those who are given eternal life are those who do the will of God from the heart (Matthew 7:21; 12:50) towards the needy, whoever they are. That is the point of Jesus' parable.

What does the parable teach us? That we will be judged by how love and compassion show up in our behavior, motivated by the Holy Spirit who has come to live inside us when we receive Christ. Jesus said, "By their fruits you shall know them" (Matthew 7:16, Lesson 10.1).

Q16. (Matthew 25:31-46) What are the "sheep" complimented for? What are the "goats" condemned for? Is this salvation by works? If no, why not? How does Jesus identify himself with "the least of these my brothers"? Why did Jesus tell this parable to his disciples? What do modern-day disciples need to learn from it? How should this parable motivate missions to aid immigrants, the poor, and the homeless?
https://www.joyfulheart.com/forums/topic/2190-q16-sheep-and-goats/

---

[27] Snodgrass weighs the arguments and concludes: "'These least brothers of mine' must be understood generally of those in need" (*Stories*, p. 557). On the other hand, Morris concludes: "[Jesus' brothers as his disciples] is the probably the way that we should understand the words, but that does not give the follower of Jesus license to do good deeds to fellow Christians, but none to outsiders. Such an attitude is foreign to the teachings of Jesus" (Morris, *Matthew*, p. 639). France agrees that the description "these my smallest brothers and sisters" probably refers to Jesus' disciples, but observes that both groups did not know that their actions were directed toward Jesus. "They have helped or failed to help not a Jesus recognized in his representatives, but a Jesus incognito. As far as they were concerned it was simply an act of kindness to a fellow human being in need, not an expression of their attitude to Jesus" (*Matthew*, pp. 958-959).

4. Parables about Final Judgment

Parable of the Weeds or Tares (Matthew 13:24-30, §96; 36-43, §100)
(Also known as the Parable of the Wheat and the Tares.)

Another parable about separation at the Last Judgment is the Parable of the Weeds or Tares, found only in Mathew's "parables chapter."[28] It follows the Parable of the Sower (Lesson 8.1) and draws on some of the same images of sowing seed and reaping a harvest.

Farmers in Jesus' day would be quite familiar with a common weed we know as Bearded Darnel (*Lolium temulentum*). So Jesus uses it in a teaching parable.

> "24 The kingdom of heaven is like a man who sowed good seed in his field. 25 But while everyone was sleeping, his enemy came and sowed weeds among the wheat, and went away. 26 When the wheat sprouted and formed heads, then the weeds also appeared." (Matthew 13:24-26)

Bearded Darnel (*Lolium temulentum*)

"Weeds" (NIV, NRSV, ESV) or "tares" (KJV, NASB), "darnel" (NJB) is the plural of Greek *zizanion*, "a troublesome weed in grainfields, darnel, cheat."[29] Bearded darnel

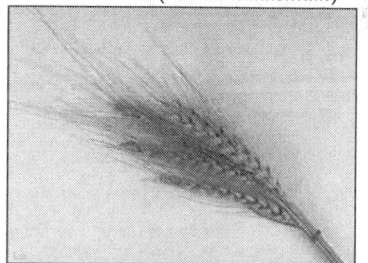

Common Wheat (*Triticum aestivum*)

is a vigorous grass closely resembling wheat or rye, a serious weed of cultivation until modern sorting machinery enabled darnel seeds to be separated efficiently from seed wheat.[30]

If darnel seeds are not separated from the wheat grain, the flour can be infected with the mold ergot, producing vomiting, malaise, and even death.[31] Darnel still grows today as a hated weed in grain fields, waste places, moist farm fields, and along roadsides.[32]

In Jesus' parable, the wheat field has been planted and growing for a number of weeks before the seed-head emerges. Some sharp-eyed servant sees that many of the plants are actually darnel, not wheat.

I am sure that a small amount of seed grain was mixed inadvertently with darnel seed as a matter of course. Darnel was a pesky weed. It was something that farmers just had to deal

---

[28] A brief version of the parable is also found in the apocryphal *Gospel of Thomas* 57.
[29] *Zizanion*, BDAG 429.
[30] Wikipedia article, "*Lolium temunlentum*," cites Armand Marie Leroi, *The Lagoon: How Aristotle Invented Science* (Bloomsbury, 2014). pp. 296–297. Referenced 13 Jan 2022.
[31] R.K. Harrison, "Weeds," ISBE 4:1045.
[32] Only when the seedhead appears can it be easily distinguished, and when ripe, wheat will appear brown, while darnel is black (Wikipedia article, "*Lolium temulentum*," citing Walter de Gruyter in Heinrich W. Guggenheimer (ed.), *The Jerusalem Talmud* (2000), vol. 1, part 3, p. 5).

with, often by repeated weeding while the crop was growing.[33] But as the servant sees so much darnel among the wheat, he panics. Something is seriously wrong. He runs to his master.

> "27 The owner's servants came to him and said, 'Sir, didn't you sow good seed in your field? Where then did the weeds come from?'
>
> 28 'An enemy did this,' he replied.
>
> The servants asked him, 'Do you want us to go and pull them up?'
>
> 29 'No,' he answered, 'because while you are pulling the weeds, you may root up the wheat with them. 30 Let both grow together until the harvest. At that time I will tell the harvesters: First collect the weeds and tie them in bundles to be burned; then gather the wheat and bring it into my barn.'" (Matthew 13:27-30)

While the darnel can be identified by careful observation once the seed heads appear, normal weeding wouldn't suffice in this case. To pull up the darnel sewed maliciously in the entire field would be so pervasive that pulling it all up will disturb the wheat roots and ruin the whole crop. Waiting and separating the wheat from the weeds at the end of the growing season is the best course of action in this case. Then they would burn all the collected darnel plants so its seeds wouldn't escape and contaminate future crops.

Explanation of the Parable

By the time Jesus comes to this parable in Matthew 13, he has told several parables – the Parable of the Weeds here, as well as the Parable of the Mustard Seed and the Parable of the Yeast (both in Lesson 7.1). Only now do the disciples have a chance to question him privately.

> "36 Then he left the crowd and went into the house. His disciples came to him and said, 'Explain[34] to us the parable of the weeds in the field.'
>
> 37 He answered, 'The one who sowed the good seed is the Son of Man. 38 The field is the world, and the good seed stands for the sons of the kingdom. The weeds are the sons of the evil one, 39 and the enemy who sows them is the devil. The harvest is the end of the age, and the harvesters are angels.'" (Matthew 13:36-39)

While a typical parable will have only a single point of comparison, or perhaps two, the Parable of the Weeds seems to be a sort of allegory. Jesus identifies seven points of comparison.

Sower	Son of Man, Jesus' exalted title
Field	The world

---

[33] Jeremias, *Parables*, p. 225.
[34] "Explain" (NIV, ESV, NRSV), "declare" (KJV) is *diasapheō*, "to clarify something that is obscure, explain," literally, "make clear" (BDAG 236, 1). From *dia-* (distribution) + *saphēs*, "clear," *saphēnizō*, "make clear or plain" (Liddell-Scott, p. 1586).

4. Parables about Final Judgment

Good seed	The "sons of the kingdom," that is, the genuine believers.
Weeds	The "sons of the evil one,"
Enemy	The devil
Harvest	The End of the Age
Harvesters	The angels

Jesus has identified the characters in the drama. Now he puts the plot into action.

"⁴⁰ As the weeds are pulled up[35] and burned in the fire, so it will be at the end of the age. ⁴¹ The Son of Man will send out his angels, and they will weed out of his kingdom everything that causes sin and all who do evil. ⁴² They will throw them into the fiery furnace, where there will be weeping and gnashing of teeth. ⁴³ Then the righteous will shine like the sun in the kingdom of their Father. He who has ears, let him hear.'" (Matthew 13:36-43)

Evil continues on up to the Last Judgment. Only then are true believers separated from the false, and reward and punishment executed.

Fiery Punishment and Gnashing of Teeth

This parable uses a couple of concepts about hell that are common to Jewish teaching of the period as well as to the New Testament – weeping and gnashing of teeth and the fiery nature of eternal punishment.

"Weeping and gnashing of teeth" is a stock phrase describing the terror and eternal regret of those who are being punished.[36] Gnashing of teeth would be a response to extreme pain, found in a number of parables.[37] The fiery nature of the punishment is also common both in New Testament parables[38] and Jewish apocalyptic literature of the time.

---

[35] "Pulled up" (NIV), "gathered" (ESV, KJV), "collected" (NRSV) in verse 40 is the present passive indicative of *sullegō*, "to gather by plucking or picking, collect, gather (in), pick" (BDAG 956). In verse 41 the future active of the same verb is translated "weed out" (NIV), "gather" (ESV, KJV), "collect" (NRSV).

[36] "Weeping" is *klauthmos*, "weeping, crying." With the article and "gnashing of teeth," "the article indicates the unique and extreme character of the action" (BDAG 546).

[37] "Gnashing of teeth" is two words: the plural of *odous/odontos*, "teeth"; and the noun *brugmos*, "gnashing" of teeth striking together." Danker notes that chattering of teeth would be because of cold, grinding of teeth because of pain (BDAG 184). Those who suffer such are: unbelieving Jews excluded from the final feast in the Kingdom (Matthew 8:12), unrighteous in the Parable of the Weeds (Matthew 13:49-50, Lesson 4.2), the servant in the Parable of the Wise and Faithful Steward (Matthew 24:51, Lesson 5.3), evildoers in the Parable of the Narrow Door (Luke 13:27-28, Lesson 8.2), the guest lacking a wedding garment in the Parable of the Wedding Feast (Matthew 22:13, Lesson 2.2); the wicked servant in the Parable of the Talents (Matthew 25:30, Lesson 11.2).

[38] The fiery image of punishment may have sprung from Daniel's companions Shadrach, Meshach, and Abed-nego punished by being thrown into "a blazing furnace" (Daniel 3:6, 11, 15, 17, 19-23, 26), probably a smelting furnace. Chaff is burned "with unquenchable fire" in John the Baptist's vision of the punishment of the

A final judgment and assignment of the wicked to hell are not popular topics in our secular world. They are jeered at as remnants of a medieval understanding of God. Much more popular is a forever-forgiving God who is completely non-judgmental. Of course, the Bible's teaching of the forgiveness and grace of God must be understood along with its teaching of sure punishment for those who don't repent of their sins. Disciples of Jesus need to adopt Jesus' world view of a final judgment and punishment of the unbelievers.

The Parable of the Weeds is sung every Thanksgiving in many American churches in the hymn "Come, Ye Thankful People Come" (1844) by Henry Alford. You can see the parable clearly, especially in verses 2 and 3:

"All the world is God's own field, fruit as praise to God we yield;
Wheat and tares together sown are to joy or sorrow grown;
First the blade and then the ear, then the full corn shall appear;
Lord of harvest, grant that we wholesome grain and pure may be.

For the Lord our God shall come, and shall take the harvest home;
From the field shall in that day all offenses purge away,
Giving angels charge at last in the fire the tares to cast;
But the fruitful ears to store in the garner evermore."

Applying the Parable of the Weeds or Tares

The Parable of the Weeds or Tares is a fearful parable and easy to misinterpret. Historically, the parable has been interpreted in terms of how to deal with sin in the Church – specifically rooting out heretics. The problem with this interpretation, however, is that Jesus specifies that "the field is the world" (Matthew 13:38a).

---

wicked (Matthew 3:12). The "goats" (in the Parable of the Sheep and the Goats (Lesson 4.2) are assigned "the eternal fire prepared for the devil and his angels" (Matthew 25:41). In his teaching of one's hand causing a person to sin, Jesus describes hell as "where the fire never goes out" ... "where 'their worm does not die and the fire is not quenched'" (Mark 9:43, 48). In Jesus' Parable of the Rich Man and Lazarus (Lesson 4.1), the rich man is in hell, "in torment," and asks that Lazarus "cool my tongue, because I am in agony in this fire" (Luke 16:23-24). In the Book of Revelation: Those who worship the beast and bear his mark "will be tormented with burning sulfur in the presence of the holy angels and of the Lamb. And the smoke of their torment rises for ever and ever" (Revelation 14:10-11). The beast (Antichrist) and the false prophet are "thrown alive into the fiery lake of burning sulfur" (Revelation 19:20). Those condemned before the Great White Throne Judgment are "thrown into the lake of fire. The lake of fire is the second death" (Revelation 20:13-14). On the Last Day, the unrighteous "will be in the fiery lake of burning sulfur. This is the second death" (Revelation 21:7-8).

4. Parables about Final Judgment

Jesus seems to have given the parable to answer the question: If the Kingdom is already present in the world, how can we explain the presence of evil. Isn't the Messiah supposed to bring an end to evil and usher in the Kingdom of God? Judgment will come, but it will be a delayed judgment that will take place "at the end of the age" (verse 40).[39]

The parable also teaches that all evil in the world cannot be attributed to God – that there is an enemy.

Parable of the Net (Matthew 13:47-50, §102)
(Also known as that Parable of Drawing in the Net or of the Dragnet)

A third parable about separation of the righteous and wicked at the Last Judgment is Jesus' Parable of the Net. It is found towards the end of Mathew's "parables chapter" (Matthew 13), following the Parables of the Weeds (Lesson 4.7), the Hidden Treasure (Lesson 8.5), and the Pearl of Great Price (Lesson 8.5).

> "⁴⁷ Once again, the kingdom of heaven is like a net that was let down into the lake and caught all kinds of fish. ⁴⁸ When it was full, the fishermen pulled it up on the shore. Then they sat down and collected the good fish in baskets, but threw the bad away." (Matthew 13:47-48)

Harold Copping (1863-1932), 'The Drag Net' (1907-1925) from *The Copping Bible pictures: scripture pictures* (Abingdon Press/Westminster Press, 1907-1925). Larger image.

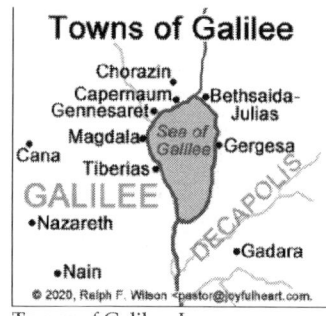

Towns of Galilee. Larger map.

No doubt, Jesus told this parable on the shores of the Sea of Galilee where entire village economies were based on catching fish with large nets. In addition to Capernaum, there were Bethsaida ("house of fishing") and Magdala (Migdal Nunaya, "bulwark of the fishes") or Tarichaea ("salting installation for fish," the Greek name of Magdala). Fishermen would sell their fish fresh in the local markets. The rest they would salt and dry for export as far as Spain.[40]

Fishing Nets

Fishermen have fished the waters of Galilee for thousands of years. Occasionally people would fish with a hook and line (Matthew 17:24-27), but commercial fishing took place with nets and teams of fishermen to handle them. They primarily used two types of nets:

---

[39] Snodgrass, *Stories*, pp. 212-213.
[40] *Great People of the Bible and How They Lived* (Reader's Digest Association, 1974), p. 439.

Casting net. Poorer fishermen who didn't own boats could use casting nets along the shore. The casting net was thrown out over the water. Weights at the edge would pull the net to the bottom, catching any fish that might be under it. The net opening was 10 to 20 feet (3 to 6 meters) in diameter. The fisherman would wade out to the net, and gather it in, bringing any fish to shore.[41]

Seine net or drag net.[42] These were large vertical wall-like nets that could be attached to the shore or to another boat. A boat could drag the other end out into the water in a semicircular arc and then back to the shore again, pulling in as many fish as it could. Then a team of fishermen on both ends of the net would pull it into the boat or onto the shore. One might dive in the center of the net to disentangle it from any rocks or obstructions on the bottom as the net dragged across.[43] This is the net described in the parable.

You can imagine the need for mending the nets. Disentangling fish from the nets sometimes broke the fibers, as did debris from the lake bottom, or the strain of too many fish. The hours were rugged. The best deepwater fishing was at night, then the mornings would be given to mending the nets, sorting fish, and perhaps using casting nets along the shore if their night's labors hadn't netted enough fish (Matthew 4:18; Mark 1:16).

Sorting the Fish

With that background, let's examine the parable again.

"*47 Once again,[44] the kingdom of heaven is like a net that was let down into the lake and caught all kinds of fish. 48 When it was full, the fishermen pulled it up on the*

---

[41] The Greek word *diktyon*, a generic term "net," but in the New Testament only of "fishnet" (BDAG 250. Carl G. Rasmussen, "Net," ISBE 3:524). When used with Greek *amphiblēstron* ("throwing"), it indicated "a circular casting-net used in fishing, casting-net," with the verb *ballō*, "throw out a casting-net" (Matthew 4:18; Mark 1:16) (BGAD 55). The verb is *amphiballō*, "cast," a technical term for the throwing out of the circular casting-net (Mark 1:16).

[42] This net is sometimes indicated by the Greek word *diktyon* and in our passage by *sagēnē*, "seine, dragnet" (BDAG 910).

[43] Another way to use this kind of net was to take it into deep water, often at night and sometimes with another boat, and lay out the floats at the top of the net in a long line across the water. Fish might be driven into the net by the splashes of the fisherman. Then the ends would be pulled together surrounding a school of fish, and they would be pulled on board the boat (Gary M. Burge, "Fishers of Men: The Maritime Headquarters of Jesus' Headquarters in Galilee," *Christian History*, Summer 1998, p. 36). Burge calls this a "trammel net," though I would guess that the sophisticated kind of net he describes hadn't been developed in the first century.

[44] "Once again" indicates that this parable also explained the nature of the Kingdom as had previous parables.

shore. Then they sat down and collected the good fish in baskets,[45] but threw the bad away."[46] (Matthew 13:47-48)

The dragnet brings in all kinds of fish – both marketable fish and fish nobody would buy. The "good fish" would include tilapia (especially Saint Peter's Fish, *Tilapia galilea*), three species of carp (especially *Barbus longiceps* and *B. canis*), and Kinneret sardine (*Acanthobrama terraesanctae*).[47] The "bad fish" would have been catfish (*Clarias lazera*). Since catfish don't have scales, they aren't Kosher for Jews (Leviticus 11:9),[48] and thus would have been thrown away.[49] The fresh "good" fish would go to market in buckets or baskets.

Fiery Judgment

Using the illustration of sorting good fish from bad, Jesus explains judgment at the End of the Age.

> "[49] This is how it will be at the end of the age. The angels will come and separate the wicked from the righteous [50] and throw them into the fiery furnace, where there will be weeping and gnashing of teeth." (Matthew 13:49-50)

The point of comparison here is the sorting into good and bad categories. In the parable, the fishermen do the sorting; in the application God's angels do the sorting. While I doubt that the bad fish were burned along the shores of Galilee, Jesus makes a point that the wicked will be thrown into a fiery furnace, such as we just saw in the Parable of the Weeds (Lesson 4.2).

Interpretation

The meaning of the Parable of the Net seems pretty straightforward. There will be a final judgment at the End of the Age where the righteous are recognized and the wicked are

---

[45] "Collected" (NIV), "sorted" (ESV), "put" (NRSV), "gathered" (KJV) is *sullegō*, "to gather by plucking or picking, collect, gather (in), pick" something (BDAG 956). "Baskets" (NIV, NRSV), "containers" (ESV), "vessels" (KJV) is *angos* "a container primarily for liquids or wet objects, vessel, container" (BDAG 9). "Vessel, receptacle" to hold liquids, such as wine, milk. "Vat," "pitcher," "bucket, pail," "wine-bowl," "cinerary urn," "sarcophagus" (Liddell-Scott, p. 7).

[46] "Threw away" (NIV, ESV), "threw out" (NRSV), "cast away" (KJV) is two words: the verb *ballō*, "throw" (BDAG 163, 1b), and the adverb *exō*, "outside, out" (BDAG 354, 2a). Also used of bad salt (Matthew 5:13; Luke 14:35) and dead branches (John 15:6).

[47] Mendel Nun, *The Sea of Galilee and Its Fishermen in the New Testament* (Israel: Kinnereth Sailing Co., 1989); Mendel Nun, "Cast Your Net upon the Waters: Fish and Fishermen in Jesus' Time," *Biblical Archaeology Review* (19:6, Nov/Dec 1993); R. K. Harrison, "Fish," ISBE 2:309.

[48] An archaeological study of fish bones in 30 sites from around Judea found catfish and shark bones in villages and cities from the late Bronze Age through the Hellenistic period (first century BC). However, by the second century AD, most Jews were avoiding catfish. (Yonatan Adlera and Omri Lernau, "The Pentateuchal Dietary Proscription against Finless and Scaleless Aquatic Species in Light of Ancient Fish Remains," *Tel Aviv*, Vol. 48, 2021, Issue 1, pp. 5-26).

[49] Mendel Nun, "The Kingdom of Heaven is Like a Seine," *Jerusalem Perspective*, 1 Nov 1989.

punished. Like the Parable of the Weeds (Lesson 4.2), judgment is not immediate, but it is sure. The disciples, who were hoping that Jesus Messiah would destroy evil and set up the ancient Kingdom of God in their lifetime, were wrong. Judgment will be delayed, but will surely come at the End of the Age.

> **Q17. (Matthew 13:47-50)** What is similar about the Parable of the Weeds and the Parable of the Net? What belief are these two parables meant to counter? How does a belief in the ultimate triumph of righteousness encourage Christians?
> https://www.joyfulheart.com/forums/topic/2191-q17-weeds-and-net/

4.3 Grace Triumphs over Judgment

Judgment is a pretty heavy topic for us. Fortunately, Jesus told one parable about judgment that is lighter, and a bit humorous when you think about it. We'll end this lesson with the Parable of the Laborers in the Vineyard.

Parable of the Laborers in Vineyard (Matthew 20:1-16, §190)
(Also known as the Parable of the Workers in the Vineyard, or Vineyard Workers)

'Laborers in the Vineyard,' Codex Aureus of Echternach (1030-1040 AD), illuminated gospel book, Germanic National Museum, Munich. Larger image.

Jesus' Parable of the Laborers in the Vineyard follows immediately after the encounter with the Rich Young Ruler and Jesus' radical teaching that salvation is impossible to man, but requires an act of God (Matthew 19:16-30, Lesson 6.2). Jesus turns the world's wisdom upside down. He concludes the teaching in Matthew with words we just looked at:

"Many who are first will be last, and many who are last will be first." (Matthew 19:30)

4. Parables about Final Judgment

Then he proceeds to tell another parable that shows just how radical the Kingdom of God really is, just how much it breaks all human rules and expectations – the Parable of the Laborers in the Vineyard.

Bringing in the Grape Harvest (Matthew 20:1-7)

> "¹ For the kingdom of heaven is like a landowner[50] who went out early in the morning to hire men to work in his vineyard. ² He agreed to pay them a denarius for the day and sent them into his vineyard." (Matthew 20:1-2)

Jesus paints a picture of a landowner at the end-of-summer grape harvest, just before the cold sets in. When the grapes are ripe, they must be harvested immediately while they are at their peak. In a large vineyard, this requires a lot of men working at the same time to cut the grapes. The custom was for day laborers to stand in the village marketplace waiting for someone to hire them. You may have observed the parking lot at Home Depot (a large building products store chain in the US), where each morning you might see many day laborers waiting to be picked up by a contractor for a job.

The landowner in our story goes to the marketplace early in the morning to hire workers. He agrees to pay them the going wage for a day's labor – one denarius. It's fair. They accept. And off they go for a day's work cutting grapes.

There is lots of work to be done. The landowner comes back to the market several times to get more workers.

> "³ About the third hour he went out and saw others standing in the marketplace doing nothing. ⁴ He told them, 'You also go and work in my vineyard, and I will pay you whatever is right.' ⁵ So they went.
>
> He went out again about the sixth hour and the ninth hour and did the same thing. ⁶ About the eleventh hour he went out and found still others standing around. He asked them, 'Why have you been standing here all day long doing nothing?'
>
> ⁷ 'Because no one has hired us,' they answered.
>
> He said to them, 'You also go and work in my vineyard.'" (Matthew 21:3-7)

The first group hired at dawn is promised one denarius, what was considered a fair day's wages. The others assume he will pay a fair wage, but it isn't stated.

Hiring Time	Promised wages
Early morning (about 6 am)	1 denarius, a normal day's wages
Third hour (about 9 am)	"Whatever is right"

---

[50] "Landowner" (NIV, NRSV), "householder" (KJV), "master of a house" (ESV) is *oikodespotēs*, "master of the house, householder" (BDAG 695). The word occurs in several parables (Matthew 13:27, 52; 20:1-2; 21:33; 24:43; Luke 12:39; 13:25; 14:21).

Sixth hour (about noon)	No mention of wages
Ninth hour (about 3 pm)	Same
Eleventh hour (about 5 pm)	Same

Paying Outrageous Wages (Matthew 20:8-15)

So far, the story is intriguing, but normal. Now it takes a radical turn. A regular employee might be paid less often, but according to the Torah, day laborers must be paid daily, at the time they finish their shift. (Deuteronomy 24:14-15). The men line up and the foreman pays them in cash, starting with the men most recently hired.

> "8 When evening came, the owner of the vineyard said to his foreman,[51] 'Call the workers and pay them their wages, beginning with the last ones hired and going on to the first.'
>
> 9 The workers who were hired about the eleventh hour came and each received a denarius. 10 So when those came who were hired first, they expected to receive more. But each one of them also received a denarius." (Matthew 20:8-10)

When the day-long workers see the men who had worked only an hour or two receive a full day's pay, they perk up. The landowner is paying big bonuses! But when it comes to them, they receive only full day's wages like everyone else. They are angry!

> "11 When they received it, they began to grumble against the landowner. 12 'These men who were hired last worked only one hour,' they said, 'and you have made them equal to us who have borne the burden of the work and the heat of the day.'" (Matthew 20:11-12)

The angry workers sound like children. "It isn't fair!" But the landowner doesn't accept that accusation.

> "13 He answered one of them, 'Friend, I am not being unfair to you. Didn't you agree to work for a denarius? 14 Take your pay and go. I want to give the man who was hired last the same as I gave you. 15 Don't I have the right to do what I want with my own money? Or are you envious because I am generous?'" (Matthew 20:13-15)

The landowner diagnoses their anger with precision. His response is variously translated:

"Are you envious because I am generous?" (NIV, NRSV)

"Do you begrudge my generosity? (ESV)

"Is thine eye evil, because I am good?" (KJV)

---

[51] "Foreman" (NIV, ESV), "manager" (NRSV), "steward" (KJV) is *epitropos*, "manager, foreman, steward" (BDAG 385, 1).

4. Parables about Final Judgment

In many cultures the term "evil eye" denotes a magical influence or curse, but not in the Bible.[52] Rather, here an "evil eye" is descriptive of envy, jealousy, and lack of generosity.[53] The full-day workers envy those who worked one hour for full pay. They are greedy. They want more! The landowner's generosity[54] is scorned.

The First Will Be Last (Matthew 20:16)

Jesus concludes this parable with the same words that ended Matthew chapter 19:

> "So the last will be first, and the first will be last." (Matthew 20:16)

Affairs in God's Kingdom operate on different rules than earthly kingdoms.

This isn't an easy parable. Snodgrass designates this as one of the three most difficult parables to interpret.[55] Some see the early morning workers as the Jews who have been faithful, worked hard, and – compared to the Gentiles – deserve salvation, but I think that misses the point. Rather, Jesus is teaching that God, represented by the landowner, operates on the basis of generosity, not fairness. This is grace – unearned and undeserved – even though that offends people who demand absolute fairness, a fair wage for a day's work. This is a parable of outrageous grace.[56]

To conclude, if we demand fairness from God, then we are lost, since "all have sinned and fall short of the glory of God" (Romans 3:23). It doesn't matter that some are better than others. Fairness demands absolute justice and justice requires that sin must be punished.

This parable teaches that God is generous. He doesn't give us salvation based on what we deserve, but out of his own generosity. Praise God!

Q18. (Matthew 20:1-16) What does the Parable of the Laborers in the Vineyard teach us about God's generosity? About grace? What in our heart rises up to demand recognition and fairness when we feel we are overlooked and taken for granted? How much of

---

[52] France, *Matthew*, p. 262, fn. 25, citing F.C. Fensham, *Neot* 1 (1967), 51-58.

[53] The Greek text refers to the "evil eye" (*ponēros*, "evil" and *opthalmos*, "eye,"), that is "one that looks with envy or jealousy upon other people" (*opthalmos*, BDAG 744, 1). Used in Sirach 14:10; Matthew 6:23; Mark 7:22; Proverbs 28:22; 22:9; see Snodgrass, *Stories*, p. 376.

[54] "Generous" (NIV, NRSV), "generosity" (ESV), "good" (KJV) is *agathos*, "good," here, pertaining to meeting a high standard of worth and merit, "good," in context, "kind, generous" (BDAG 3, 2aα).

[55] Snodgrass, *Stories*, p. 362. He places it alongside other difficult parables: the Unjust Steward and Matthew's account of the Wedding Banquet.

[56] While salvation is by grace – free of charge or any goodness on our part – rewards for service are different. We'll discuss this with the Parables of the Talents and Minas in Lesson 11.2.

this is a godly sense of fairness and how much is pride?
https://www.joyfulheart.com/forums/topic/2192-q18-laborers-in-the-vineyard/

Judgment is a subject that Christians often avoid talking about, perhaps in reaction to the fire and brimstone preaching of a former era. Nevertheless, salvation from terrible judgment is an important backdrop to understand and appreciate Christ's amazing salvation.

Prayer

Lord Jesus, you have saved us from the awesome judgment and punishment that we deserve for our sins. You have cleansed and forgiven us and set us on your Way. Thank you. Help us to both be humbly appreciative and to help other lost souls to find your Way. In your holy name, we pray. Amen.

5. Parables about Readiness for Christ's Return

A number of parables are included in Jesus' teaching about his return. Rather than provide a comprehensive study of Jesus' teaching about his Second Coming, I will try to restrict myself to the teaching in and adjacent to his parables on the subject.

Here are the analogies and parables we'll consider.

5.1 Signs of Impending Return

- Parable of the Weather Signs (Luke 12:54-56)

Charles Haslewood Shannon, 'The Wise and Foolish Virgins' (1919-1920), oil on canvas, 111x178 cm, National Museums Liverpool, Walker Art Gallery.

- Parable of the Budding Fig Tree (Matthew 24:32-33; Mark 13:28-29; Luke 21:29-31)
- Analogy of Lightning (Luke 17:24; Matthew 24:27)
- Analogy of the Vultures Gathering (Luke 17:37, Matthew 24:38)

5.2 Watchfulness and Obedience Needed

- Parables of the Watching Servants (Luke 12:35-39; §158; Mark 13:34-37)
- Parable of the Burglar (Luke 12:39-40; Matthew 24:43-44)
- Parable of the Wise and Foolish Virgins (Matthew 25:1-13)

5.3 Faithful Service in the Master's Absence

- Parable of the Wise and Faithful Steward (Matthew 24:45-51; Luke 12:42-46)

5.1 Signs of Impending Return

Jesus uses a number of brief parables to point to signs of his Second Coming. We won't spend long on any of them, but we need to explore them briefly. We begin with two parables about being observant of nature's signs that portend future events.

Parable of the Weather Signs (Luke 12:54-56, §160)

First, a parable about amateur weather forecasting:

> "He said to the crowd: 'When you see a cloud rising in the west, immediately you say, "It's going to rain," and it does. And when the south wind blows, you say, "It's going to be hot," and it is.'" Hypocrites! You know how to interpret the appearance of the earth and the sky. How is it that you don't know how to interpret this present time?" (Luke 12:54-56)

Palestine has fairly predictable weather patterns, with prevailing winds blowing from the Mediterranean east across Palestine. Thus, a rain cloud in the west will blow east and bring rain. The Israelites were used to this pattern. But when the winds shifted and a south wind began, they knew it would be hot, blowing across the sweltering sands of the Negev desert bringing intense heat to Judea and Galilee, called a "simoon."

You can understand signs of change in the weather, Jesus says, but you are dull when it comes to understanding signs of change in spiritual things. The Messiah, the Son of God, is present in their midst. A huge sea change in salvation history is occurring before their eyes, and they are too blind to see it!

Parable of the Budding Fig Tree (Matthew 24:32-33; Mark 13:28-29; Luke 21:29-31; §220)

Next, Jesus told a similar parable about observing the signs.

> "He told them this parable: "Look at the fig tree and all the trees. When they sprout leaves, you can see for yourselves and know that summer is near. Even so, when you see these things happening, you know that the kingdom of God is near." (Luke 21:29-31)

Some commentators have made a lot out of the fig tree as being representative of Israel (as it is in the Parable of the Barren Fig Tree, Lesson 2.1). I don't see any reference to Israel here, since Jesus adds in Luke, "and all the trees" (verse 29). The spring budding happens to all deciduous trees as an indicator of summer coming.

Both Matthew and Mark end the saying with great clarity: The kingdom "is near, right at the door." The word "near" is common to the parables in all three Gospels, close in point of time, as an experience or event.[1]

---

[1] "Near" (NIV, ESV, NRSV), "at hand" or "nigh" (KJV) is the adverb *engus*, pertaining to being in close in point of time, near," and then, by extension, "close as an experience or event, close" (BDAG 271, meanings 2a and 3).

5. Parables about Readiness for Christ's Return

Previous to this in Luke, Jesus has given a number of signs that *do not* indicate Christ's imminent coming – wars, rumors of wars, etc.[2] The final signs, however, will be signs in the heavens (vs. 25a), signs on the earth (vs. 25b), and heavenly bodies shaken (vs. 26a). Only then will they "see the Son of Man coming in a cloud with power and great glory" and begin to rejoice (vs. 27).

This parable is a simple "this-is-similar-to-that" kind of expression. When you see the new leaves beginning to come out in the spring, it is a sign that summer is near. Just so, when you see these last signs taking place (Luke 21:25-28), you know that the final breaking through of the Kingdom of God at hand, followed by the Last Judgment.

Both the Parable of the Weather Signs and the Parable of the Budding Fig Tree basically are saying the same thing: stay alert to the signs you are seeing.

Analogy of Lightning (Luke 17:24, §184; Matthew 24:27, §218)

Now we move to two similar analogies that tell us about the suddenness and wide visibility of Christ's coming. First, the Analogy of Lightning.

> "For as lightning that comes from the east is visible[3] even in the west, so will be the coming of the Son of Man." (Matthew 24:27)

> "For the Son of Man in his day will be like the lightning, which flashes and lights up the sky from one end to the other."[4] (Luke 17:24)

Lightning can be seen at great distance and lights up a huge area, a radius of 150 to 200 miles or more. Since lightning often starts tens of thousands of feet above the earth, the normal horizon caused by the earth's curvature doesn't limit its view nearly as much as if it took place at ground level. It "lights up the sky from one end to the other" (Luke 17:24b). When Jesus comes, he won't appear to just a few or in secret. He will be visible to all. "Every eye will see him" (Revelation 1:7), believer and unbeliever alike.

---

[2] (1) False christs (Luke 21:8), (2) wars (vss. 9-10), (3) natural disasters (vs. 11a), (4) great signs (vs. 12b), (5) persecution and witness (vss. 12-15), (6) betrayal and hatred (vss. 16-17), Jerusalem trampled by Gentiles (vss. 20-24).

[3] "Is visible" (NIV), "shines" (ESV, KJV), "flashes" (NRSV) is *phainō*, "to shine," here, "appear, be or become visible, be revealed" (BDAG 1047, 2a).

[4] The word translated lightning is Greek *astrapē*, "lightning" and the word translated "flashes" is the verbal form of this root, *astraptō*, "to flash, gleam" (BDAG 146). A closely-related word *astron* means "star, constellation" which has found its way into the English language with such words as "astronomy." The third word translated "lights up" (NIV) or "shineth" (KJV) is Greek *lampō*, "to emit rays of light, shine, flash, gleam" (BDAG 585-586).

Analogy of the Vultures Gathering (Luke 17:37, §184; Matthew 24:38, §218)
(Also known as the Parable of the Vultures and the Carcass)

Jesus uses another analogy in his teaching of his Second Coming. While this analogy may seem grizzly and gross to some, it sounds to me like a popular saying in Jesus' culture – a maxim like our proverb: "Where there's smoke, there's fire."

Jesus has been teaching his disciples about the suddenness of Christ's coming like lightning, like the days of Noah and Sodom, the danger of Lot's wife looking back, one will be taken and another left (Luke 17:22-36). Now, in Luke, the disciples ask a question.

> "'Where, Lord?' they asked.
> He replied, 'Where there is a dead body,[5] there the vultures will gather.'" (Luke 17:37)

Matthew gives the saying without the disciple's question.

> "Wherever there is a carcass,[6] there the vultures will gather." (Matthew 24:28)

. The KJV rendering of "eagles" seems somehow grander: Eagles seem more glorious than vultures. But "eagle" here probably refers to the vulture.

Eight species of eagles and four species of vultures appear in Palestine, most probably described by the same words (Hebrew *neser*, Greek *aetos*). In the Near East, both eagles and vultures ate carrion, hunted prey, and were considered unclean animals.[7] The Eurasian Griffon Vulture (*Gyps fulvus*), for example, found in Israel and the Negev, has a wingspan of 7.5 to 9 feet (2.3 to 2.8 meters), and has been recorded as circling on thermals as high as 2,250 feet (690 meters) above the earth.

This brief analogy may be difficult to understand for urban dwellers, for Jesus is referring to a rural phenomenon – the common behavior of vultures to circle high above a carcass.

Where I live in the dry foothills of California's Sierra Nevada Mountains, the sight of circling turkey vultures is exceedingly common, as it must have been above the hills and deserts of Palestine. These vultures are majestic in their effortless soaring flight. First, one vulture will spot a dead or dying animal. Soon, from far off, others will see the lone vulture circling and join it in its vigil. When the animal is dead, the vultures descend for a meal.

Jesus' analogy refers to the gathering and circling of vultures where a carcass is found, marking its location and making it obvious from miles around. The carcass does not represent

---

[5] "Dead body" (NIV), "corpse" (ESV, NRSV), "body" (KJV) is *sōma*, "body," here, "dead body, corpse" (BDAG 983, 1a).

[6] "Carcass" (NIV, KJV), "corpse" (ESV, NRSV) is *ptōma*, "primarily, 'that which has fallen,' "a dead body: animal or human, (dead) body, corpse," especially of one killed by violence" (BDAG 895).

[7] Leviticus 11:13; Deuteronomy 14:12. Harold van Broekhoven, Jr., "Eagle," ISBE 2:1-2; R.K. Harrison, "Vulture," ISBE 4:999.

5. Parables about Readiness for Christ's Return

Jesus' body – that is pushing the parable beyond its intent. The point is that high circling of the vultures makes the location obvious from afar.

Jesus is saying that there is no need to pinpoint a location now; when Jesus comes it will not be secret, but obvious to all, in the same way that lightning and circling vultures are visible to all.[8]

> **Q19. (Luke 17:24, 37) The Analogies of the Lightning and the Vultures Gathering both teach the same simple point. What is it?**
> https://www.joyfulheart.com/forums/topic/2193-q19-lightning-and-vultures-gathering/

5.2 Watchfulness and Obedience Needed

Jesus talks about signs of the approaching End Times. Now he gives several parables on how we disciples need to behave so that we are prepared for his coming. Though the order and context vary a bit from one Gospel to another, they revolve around a common injunction:

> "You also must be ready, because the Son of Man will come at an hour when you do not expect him." (Luke 12:40; cf. Matthew 24:44; Mark 13:33)

Jesus uses the title of Son of Man during his earthly ministry, but will come as the glorious Son of Man prophesied by Daniel (Daniel 7:13-14) to set up his kingdom. His disciples must be watchful so they will be ready when he appears. These parables illustrate why watchfulness is needed and what it should look like.

---

[8] Dispensationalism (including a "secret rapture" theory) has been circulating in evangelical circles for nearly two centuries, beginning with John Nelson Darby (1800-1882) and the Plymouth Brethren in the 1830s. It was popularized in the US in the early 20th century through the Scofield Reference Bible (1909) and the Bible School Movement. Later by Hal Lindsay's book, *The Late Great Planet Earth* (1970) and the Christian apocalyptic novel Left Behind (1995) by Tim LeHaye (1926-2016) and Jerry B. Jenkins (b. 1949), ultimately resulting in a series of 16 novels (1995-2007) and a series of films in the Left Behind series (2000, 2002, 2005, 2014). The theory is that Jesus will come secretly for believers, who will be raptured suddenly without notice before the tribulation (pre-trib). Then Christ will come publicly in his glory later on after the tribulation. In other words, two comings of Christ. The problem I have with it is that the Scripture doesn't teach a secret rapture or two comings. Both the Analogies of the Lightning and the Vultures Gathering point to a sudden, visible coming of Christ. For more on this see a popular-level discussion in Marvin Rosenthal, *The Pre-Wrath Rapture of the Church* (Nelson, 1990), my study, *The Book of Revelation: Discipleship Lessons* (JesusWalk Publications, 2004, 2011), www.jesuswalk.com/revelation/ Also see my *Discipleship Training in Luke's Gospel* (JesusWalk Publications, 2010), Appendix 2G. Introduction to Eschatology. www.jesuswalk.com/luke/intro-to-eschatology.htm

Servant Parables

Jesus uses servants (usually, literal slaves) in a number of parables. In a large household with several slaves, a head servant will be in charge with others under him. (For more, see Appendix 6. Slavery in Jesus' Day.)

We're going to consider several parables that seem quite similar. But there are important differences we need to look for. Here are the servant parables we need to distinguish from one another:

Eugene Burnand, detail of 'Watchful Servants,' in *The Parables* (France, 1909), Conte crayon and charcoal.

1. Parables of the Watching Servants emphasize staying awake and alert during the master's absence (below)
2. Parable of the Wise and Faithful Steward emphasizes the leader not abusing his authority during the master's absence (below)
3. Parable of the Talents and the Parable of the Minas or Pounds both emphasize continued faithful labor about the master's business during his absence (Lesson 11.2).

Parables of the Watching Servants (Mark 13:34-37, §222; Luke 12:35-38; §158)

The Parables of the Watching Servants are found with some variations in both Mark and Luke. As I study them, I believe we are seeing two distinct versions of the same parable, a parable Jesus must have told on numerous occasions. Some might consider them different parables. Nevertheless, I'll refer to them as the Parables of the Watching Servants and we'll consider them together.

We'll start with Mark's account, and then look at a special surprise in Luke's version.

> "³² No one knows about that day or hour, not even the angels in heaven, nor the Son, but only the Father. ³³ Be on guard! Be alert! You do not know when that time will come." (Mark 13:32-33; cf. Matthew 24:36)

This is one of the main points of this series of parables. You don't know when Christ will come, so be continually alert. It is fascinating that when Jesus was in the flesh, even *he* didn't know the "day or hour." This limiting of his omniscience was part of him "emptying himself" to become a man (Philippians 2:6-7). I expect that in his present state at the right hand of the Father, he now knows the time of his coming.

Here is Mark's version of the parable.

5. Parables about Readiness for Christ's Return

> "It's like a man going away: He leaves his house and puts his servants in charge, each with his assigned task,[9] and tells the one at the door[10] to keep watch."[11] (Mark 13:34)

Notice that Mark's version talks about each servant having an assigned task – which we see spelled out in the Parables of the Pounds and Minas (Lesson 11.2).

Mark's version doesn't tell us where the master went; Luke's version tells us that he was at a wedding feast (Luke 12:36). It seems to be nearby, but the wedding party may extend into the wee hours of the morning. The servants don't know what time he'll return.[12]

Luke's version has the master commanding the servants not to go to bed and turn off the lights. He wants them ready instantly when he knocks.

> "35 "Be dressed ready for service[13] and keep your lamps burning, 36 like men waiting for their master[14] to return from a wedding banquet,[15] so that when he comes and knocks they can immediately open the door for him." (Luke 12:35-36)

The house lamps are to remain ablaze for the momentary return of the master. These could be a hanging lamp with multiple wicks, or the small clay hand lamps with a single wick. To keep them burning requires an expenditure of both effort and resources. Lamps must be refilled periodically with olive oil, the wicks must be trimmed occasionally, and they must be checked lest a breeze were to blow one out. The servants are instructed to keep tending them throughout the night so they are lit when the master returns from the party. The alternative is

---

[9] Literally, "each with his work" (ESV, NRSV). Notice that Mark's form of the parable includes the ideas of assigned tasks, perhaps a bit like the Parables of the Talents (Matthew) and Minas (Luke), Lesson 11.2.

[10] "The one at the door" (NIV), "doorkeeper" (ESV, NRSV), "porter" (KJV) is *thurōros*, "doorkeeper, gatekeeper" (BDAG 462).

[11] "Keep watch" (NIV), "stay awake" (ESV), "be on the watch" (NRSV), "watch" (KJV) is the present active subjunctive of *grēgoreō*, "to stay awake, be watchful" (BDAG 208, 1).

[12] We might be tempted here to see the wedding banquet the master is attending as an allegorical reference to the Marriage Supper of the Lamb (Revelation 19:7). I think that's the wrong direction. Our passage contains the element of the wedding banquet to indicate that the master is relatively close by and can return at any time.

[13] The phrase translated, "Be dressed and ready for service" (NIV), "stay/be dressed for action" (ESV, NRSV) is more literally rendered by the KJV: "Let your loins be girded about." Leon Morris explains, "The long, flowing robes of the Easterner were picturesque, but apt to hinder serious labor, so when work was afoot they were tucked into a belt about the waist" (*Luke*, p. 217).

[14] The word translated "master" is Greek *kyrios*, "one who is in charge by virtue of possession, owner." The word is also used as a term of respect, something like our "sir" for someone who is in a position of authority, "lord, master" (BDAG 577, 1b).

[15] "Wedding banquet" (NIV, NRSV), "wedding feast" (ESV), "wedding" (KJV) is the plural of Greek *gamos*, the "public ceremony associated with entry into a marriage relationship, wedding celebration" (BDAG 188, 1b).

a very unhappy master when he comes home to find a dismal dark house and has to bang on the barred door for a long time while his servants hurry to dress and come to the door.

In both accounts, when the master arrives, the servants are to be ready. His coming is their most important priority; their own weariness and self-indulgence must not be allowed to take over. They are servants commanded to stay awake and alert.

Mark ends the parable with the reminder that the master could come back any time of the night.

> ³⁵ Therefore **keep watch** (*grēgoreō*) because you do not know when the owner of the house will come back – whether in the evening, or at midnight, or when the rooster crows, or at dawn. ³⁶ If he comes suddenly, do not let him find you sleeping. ³⁷ What I say to you, I say to everyone: '**Watch!** (*grēgoreō*)'" (Mark 13:35-37)

Here is Luke:

> "³⁶ ... Like men **waiting** (*prosdechomai*) for their master to return ... ³⁷ It will be good for those servants whose master finds them **watching** (*grēgoreō*) when he comes." (Luke 12:36a, 37a)

Notice the key directives:

- *Prosdechomai*. "Waiting" (Luke 12:36) carries the idea of, "look forward to, wait for," with the connotation of "receive favorably."[16] This is not just a dutiful waiting, but an anticipation of one who is hoped for, expected, and looked forward to, where an extravagant welcome is prepared and ready for a moment's notice.
- *Grēgoreō*. "Watch/watching" (NIV, KJV), "(stay) awake" (ESV; NRSV, Mark), "alert" (NRSV, Luke) is "to stay awake, be watchful," then "to be in constant readiness, be on the alert."[17] It comes from a word meaning, "to wake or rouse up someone."

Our attitude is to be joyfully expectant with constant alertness and situational awareness.

The Master Serving a Meal to the Servants (Luke 12:37b)

So far, the parable has taught Jesus' disciples to be ready and vigilant for Jesus' coming. But now, in Luke only, the parable takes an unexpected twist, a role reversal.

> "I tell you the truth, he will dress himself to serve, will have them recline at the table and will come and wait on them." (Luke 12:37b)

The master they have so eagerly prepared for tells *them* to be seated at the table. He girds up his own clothing and begins to serve *them*. This isn't what you'd expect from *any* master, Jewish or Roman. Far from it! It's almost like this part of the parable becomes allegorical.

---

[16] *Prosdechomai*, BDAG 877, 2a.
[17] *Grēgoreō*, BDAG 208, 2.

5. Parables about Readiness for Christ's Return

Jesus is the Servant Leader, from whom all of us learn to serve and take on a servant mentality.

- He is the Suffering Servant of Isaiah who pours out his life unto death and is numbered with the transgressors (Isaiah 52:13 – 53:12).
- He is the Humble Servant who washes the dirty feet (and souls) of his disciples (John 13:4-17, Lesson 11.1).
- He is the Son of Man who does not come to be served, but to serve, and to give his life as a ransom for many (Mark 10:45).

Jesus upends the world system by making the last first and the first last, the poor rich and the rich poor, the servants the ones served, the meek to inherit, and the mournful to leap for joy.

And so, in Jesus' remarkable twist to the parable, the servants who wait up to all hours to welcome their master with style are rewarded to a meal he serves to them himself – a banquet! What a wonderful and unexpected blessing! I think it is intended to remind us of the feast at the End of the Age! (See Appendix 5. The Great Messianic Banquet). We also see this unexpected switch of the Lord serving the servants in Jesus' Acted Parable of Washing the Disciples' Feet (Lesson 11.1).

Even in the Wee Hours of the Morning (Luke 12:38; Mark 13:36-37)

In Luke, Jesus caps off this parable with a summary of the lessons to be learned from it. He repeats the phrase that began verse 37:

> "It will be good for those servants whose master finds them ready,[18] even if he comes in the second or third watch of the night." (Luke 12:38)

The Romans divided the night into four watches, while the Jews divided it into three.[19] Whichever system is referred to, this would represent the wee hours of the morning. Jesus says that even if the servants have to stay up into the wee hours of the morning they will be rewarded for their readiness.

The Parables of the Watchful Servants have two main themes:

1. The master's return may be delayed, and
2. The master's servants must nevertheless be ready.

Christ's return is delayed, but we must still be alert and ready for his return at any time. He doesn't give us a precise timetable. We have only the bare outlines, sign posts, event

---

[18] "Ready" (NIV), "awake" (ESV) is not in the actual text, which is literally "finds them so" (NRSV, KJV).
[19] Marshall (*Luke*, p. 537) cites Strack and Billerbeck I, 688-691 for the Jewish watches (Judges 7:19) and several verses for the Roman watch system (Matthew 14:25; Mark 6:48; 13:35; Acts 12:4).

triggers that we know will precipitate other events, but we don't have a precise timeline (contrary to what some Bible teachers might tell you).

> **Q20. (Luke 12:35-39; Mark 13:34-37) What are the main themes of the Parables of the Watching Servants? What kinds of behaviors should the parable inspire in modern-day disciples?**
> https://www.joyfulheart.com/forums/topic/2194-q20-watching-servants/

Parable of the Burglar (Luke 12:39-40; Matthew 24:43-44; §158)
(Also known as the Parable of the Thief in the Night)

In Luke's Gospel, the Parable of Watching Servants is immediately followed by the Parable of the Burglar. In Matthew, the parable follows Jesus' Parable of the Wise and Foolish Virgins (Lesson 5.2), which we'll examine after this.

One reason for the servants to be alert at night would be to welcome the late-arriving master. The other reason, this parable suggests, would be to catch a burglar who would probably choose the early hours for a break-in when everyone is asleep.

> "But understand this: If the owner of the house had known at what hour the thief was coming, he would not have let his house be broken into."[20] (Luke 12:39)

Homes in Palestine were typically barred at night. Thieves wouldn't try to storm the door – not at night when it would surely wake the inhabitants. Rather, in the dead of night, they would dig through the mud-brick wall of the house. They would ever-so-silently remove a few bricks, slide through the opening, steal valuables, and then exit without waking the family. In a larger house with rooms that weren't used for sleeping, this might be possible and hard to detect until the next morning.

Even though the Parable of the Burglar consists of just two sentences, the saying about "a thief in the night" is almost proverbial in the New Testament to describe the unannounced and unexpected coming of Jesus:

> "You know very well that the day of the Lord will come like a thief in the night." (1 Thessalonians 5:2)

> "The day of the Lord will come like a thief." (2 Peter 3:10)

---

[20] The phrase "broken into/through" is *dioryssō*. In the New Testament it is used of a thief who "digs through" the (sun-dried brick) wall of a house and gains entrance, "break through, break in" (BDAG 251).

5. Parables about Readiness for Christ's Return

> "I will come like a thief, and you will not know at what time I will come to you." (Revelation 3:3)

> "Behold, I come like a thief! Blessed is he who stays awake and keeps his clothes with him, so that he may not go naked and be shamefully exposed." (Revelation 16:15)

The only way to defeat such a robber would be to stay up all night, alert and listening for any sound or sign of entry. In the same way, Jesus will come – unanticipated, unexpected. The only way you can be ready for his Coming is to stay spiritually alert and awake. Otherwise, you will be caught unawares.

Jesus sums it up with an explicit command:

> "You also must be ready,[21] because the Son of Man will come at an hour when you do not expect him." (Luke 12:40)

The tiny Parable of the Burglar makes two points:

1. The Son of Man is coming unexpectedly, and
2. You must be alert for his coming, even if your alertness must be long-maintained.

What Constitutes Readiness?

What does readiness for the Son of Man consist of? What is this alertness? This wakefulness? And how is it degraded? Here are some of the factors.

1. **Avoiding sin.** Sin is not cost-free for the disciple, since it can dull our spiritual awareness. Yes, he will forgive, but self-indulgent moral compromise dulls us. It prevents us from walking closely with him and being spiritually alert, from being sensitive to his voice. When you sin, repent immediately!
2. **Prayer**, time communing with Jesus, is necessary so that we remain spiritually alert, spiritually awake.
3. **The Word.** Regular reading of the Scriptures keeps us alert. It is cleansing. Jesus said, "You are clean because of the word I have spoken to you" (John 15:3).
4. **Beliefs** can affect our readiness. If our theological system tells us that Jesus can't come imminently, then we tend to relax. The text tells us, "the Son of Man will come at an hour when you do not expect[22] him" (Luke 12:40b). If you don't think that it is probable that Jesus will come in your lifetime, then you are extremely vulnerable to being taken by surprise, if he were to return contrary to your doctrinal timeline.

---

[21] "Be ready" is *hetoimos*, "ready," with the verb *ginomai*, "be ready, prepare oneself" (BDAG 401, b), from the verb *hetoimazō*, "to cause to be ready, put/keep in readiness, prepare."

[22] "Expect" (NIV, ESV, NRSV), "think" (KJV) is *dokeō*, "to consider as probable, think, believe, suppose, consider" (BDAG 254, 1f).

We'll consider Jesus' related Parable of the Wise and Faithful Steward (Lesson 5.3) in a few moments, but first, the Parable of the Wise and Foolish Virgins.

Parable of the Wise and Foolish Virgins (Matthew 25:1-13; §227)
(Also known as the Parable of the Ten Maidens; Ten Virgins; Ten Bridesmaids)

In Matthew, Jesus tells a longer Parable of the Wise and Foolish Virgins about the importance of readiness for Christ's return, even though it is delayed longer than expected.

Marriage Practices in Jesus' Time

To understand this parable, we need to review marriage practices in the first century. Marriage began with a betrothal up to a year before the marriage celebration, usually arranged by parents. The man and woman would enter into a binding agreement to marry at this betrothal, more binding than our "engagement" in the West. The man would give the bride's father a bridal gift, a form of compensation to the father (some of which becomes a dowry the father gives to the daughter at the marriage to help provide economic stability to the marriage bond). The couple doesn't live together or consummate the marriage at their betrothal, though they are considered husband and wife by law and the bond cannot be broken without divorce.

William Blake, "Parable of the Wise and Foolish Virgins" (1826), watercolor, Tate Collections.

The final marriage event in this culture is a celebration. Typically, the groom and his friends go to the bride's home. Perhaps there is a brief party there. But then – usually early in the evening – they escort the bride in a festive procession to the groom's home, where a grand celebration takes place. There is probably an exchange of vows and some kind of religious ceremony, though none of these details survive from the first century AD. The groom gives his bride gifts. After the marriage feast, the bride and groom enter the nuptial chamber and the marriage is consummated.

Ten Teenage Girls

With that explanation, let's look at the parable.

> "¹ At that time the kingdom of heaven will be like ten virgins who took their lamps and went out to meet the bridegroom. ² Five of them were foolish and five were wise.

5. Parables about Readiness for Christ's Return

> ³ The foolish ones took their lamps but did not take any oil with them. ⁴ The wise, however, took oil in jars[23] along with their lamps." (Matthew 25:1-4)

The parable focuses on the period between the groom fetching the bride from her parent's home and bringing her in a grand procession to the marriage ceremony and celebration that will take place in his home.

To call them the "ten virgins" is a bit misleading, since it places the focus on their virginity. But the idea here is that these are a group of young, unmarried teenage girls. They might be junior-high or middle-school age in the American school system. In Jesus' time, girls typically married at age 14 or 15, or so.

This group of young teenage girls has decided not to go all the way to the bride's house. Rather, they have positioned themselves right on the road to the groom's house so they don't miss the procession. That is the plan.

But everything doesn't work to plan. The procession doesn't come in the early evening as expected. It is now dark outside, and the only lights they have are small hand lamps made of pottery, probably Herodian lamps, burning a flax wick that is threaded into a hole at the end of the lamp where it can draw from a small reservoir of olive oil in the base of the lamp.

Herodian Lamp, that would have been common in the time of Jesus (larger image).

Staying together as a group would provide protection. By the time they were this old, of course, they knew about how long one of these small lamps would stay lit, probably four to five hours. Some of their mothers had told them, "Be sure to take extra oil. You'll need it for the trip home." "Sure, mom." It would be like your mother telling you to take extra batteries for your flashlight on a dark night. The more mature, wiser[24] girls would take the appropriate precautions, even if only to placate their mothers. The flighty, foolish[25] girls didn't bother.

---

[23] "Jars" (NIV), "flasks of oil" (ESV, NRSV), "vessels" (KJV) is Greek *angeion*, "vessel, flask, container," e.g., for oil. It didn't refer to a specific size or special-purpose pottery, for the same name could describe a container for fish or edible snails (BDAG 7).

[24] "Wise" in verses 2, 4, 7, and 9 is *phronimos*, "pertaining to understanding associated with insight and wisdom, sensible, thoughtful, prudent, wise" (BDAG 1066).

[25] "Foolish" in verses 2, 3, and 8 is *mōros* (from which we get our word "moron"), "foolish, stupid" (BDAG 663, a).

The Bridegroom Comes (Matthew 25:5-7)

> "⁵ The bridegroom was a long time in coming, and they all became drowsy and fell asleep. ⁶ At midnight[26] the cry rang out: 'Here's the bridegroom! Come out to meet him!' ⁷ Then all the virgins woke up and trimmed their lamps." (Matthew 25:5-7)

It is midnight by the time the bridegroom's procession is spotted coming up the road. The teenage girls have fallen asleep by this time.

Suddenly they awake and look to their flickering oil hand lamps. You can turn a flashlight off to save batteries, but not an oil lamp, since you can't relight it without an ignition source. They trim the wicks, cutting off the burned end of the wick, and pulling up more wick so that it overhangs the lip of the lamp at the proper length.[27] It is only then that they would have noticed how low the oil supply in the lamp was getting. Some of their lamps were about ready to go out. Panic sets in.

Running Out of Oil (Matthew 25:8-9)

> "⁸ The foolish ones said to the wise, 'Give us some of your oil; our lamps are going out.'
>
> ⁹ 'No,' they replied, 'there may not be enough for both us and you. Instead, go to those who sell oil and buy some for yourselves.'" (Matthew 25:8-9)

At first thought, the wiser girls might seem stingy. But they are not; they are wise. They know that if they give away their supply, they won't have enough. So they tell their foolish friends to run off to the merchant who sells oil to buy some more.

No "oil vending stores" are open at this hour, but the oil merchant in their village would know them and probably sold his olive oil out of his own house anyway. So off go the foolish girls to get more oil as the wedding procession comes into view.

"I Don't Know You" (Matthew 25:10-13)

> "But while they were on their way to buy the oil, the bridegroom arrived. The virgins who were ready went in with him to the wedding banquet. And the door was shut." (Matthew 25:10)

The wise girls, lamps illuminating the way, join the procession that leads to the bridegroom's house. When everyone in the procession is inside the courtyard adjacent to the house, the door is shut. This isn't an open party where people can drift in and out. No more guests are expected.

---

[26] "Midnight" is literally, "middle of the night," *mesos*, "middle" + *nux, nukktos*, "night." By New Testament times it was more accurately determined (N. Green, "Midnight," ISBE 3:351).

[27] "Trimmed" is *kosmeō* (from which we get our "cosmetic"), to make neat or tidy" (BDAG 560, 1).

> "¹¹ Later the others also came. 'Sir! Sir!' they said. 'Open the door for us!'
>
> ¹² But he replied, 'I tell you the truth, I don't know you.'" (Matthew 25:11-12)

The foolish girls finally arrive long after the party has gotten underway and the door has been shut. They knock and call out. They bang on the door. But the doorkeeper doesn't recognize them and refuses to open the door.

It sounds reminiscent of Jesus' prediction that on the final Day of Judgment, some would be excluded from the kingdom of heaven who supposed themselves to be disciples, who may even have done some religious things, but did not really follow Jesus.

> "²² Many will say to me on that day, 'Lord, Lord, did we not prophesy in your name, and in your name drive out demons and perform many miracles?' ²³ Then I will tell them plainly, 'I never knew you. Away from me, you evildoers!'" (Matthew 7:21-23)

This sentence, "I do not know you!" is so final, so shocking. Sinners have heard for years that God will give them a second chance, but now the time for second chances is finally over. Only those who follow Jesus closely, who "keep watch" will be ready when he returns. Others will be excluded from his kingdom. The parable concludes with the words:

> "Therefore keep watch, because you do not know the day or the hour." (Matthew 25:13)

Legitimate Allegories

I believe we are intended to see:
1. Relationship between the kingdom of heaven and circumstances at a marriage feast.
2. Relationship between wise preparedness and entering the kingdom.
3. Exclusion from the kingdom for those who aren't prepared at Christ's coming.

Those vital touchpoints are clear. But what about other elements?

It is likely that the idea of the bridegroom representing the Messiah underlies the story, for Jesus refers to himself as the Bridegroom in the Parable of the Bridegroom's Guests (Lesson 7.2). And the idea of the celebration meal in the Kingdom of God is a theme throughout Jesus' teachings. (See Appendix 5. The Great Messianic Banquet.)

However, lights (in the sense of witness) that are shining rather than going out is not the point, but rather preparedness and watchfulness. The number of virgins (ten) has no significance to the parable, though among Jews it was the minimum number need to form a synagogue. Virginity or purity is not the point; virginity is mentioned only to fix the age of the participants in the story. The oil doesn't represent the Holy Spirit or good works; it just illustrates the degree of preparedness. The story includes reference to olive oil – a household staple. There is no need to make the oil into something in the story. Jesus doesn't.

Finally, falling asleep isn't the point of this parable, since both the wise and foolish girls fell asleep. The watchfulness shows itself in preparedness, not physical wakefulness at a late hour. The true intent of Jesus' parable is to be prepared even though Jesus' Coming is delayed.

> **Q21. (Matthew 25:1-13) What are the main points from the Parable of the Wise and Foolish Virgins that Jesus wants his disciples to understand and internalize? What constitutes preparedness for Christ's coming for modern-day disciples?**
> https://www.joyfulheart.com/forums/topic/2195-q21-wise-and-foolish-virgins/

5.3 Faithful Service in the Master's Absence

Jesus tells four parables about how faithful service in the master's absence is indicative of leadership potential. One is just a mention in Mark's version of the Parable of the Watching Servants that we saw above in Lesson 5.2: "It's like a man going away: He leaves his house and puts his servants in charge, each with his assigned task" (Mark 13:34a). But the other three parables are more developed, each designed to prepare disciples for a time when Jesus has returned to his Father and his return is delayed.

- Parable of the Wise and Faithful Steward
- Parable of the Talents (Lesson 11.2)
- Parable of the Minas or Pounds (Lesson 11.2)

Parable of the Wise and Faithful Steward (Matthew 24:45-51, §226; Luke 12:42-46; §§158-159)
(Also known as the Parable of the Door Keeper, and the Wise and Faithful Servant or Manager)

In Lesson 5.2 above, we've seen parables about watchfulness and readiness. Now Jesus tells a parable about the kind of faithfulness appropriate for leaders during this time of waiting for the coming of the Son of Man. The Parable of the Wise and Faithful Steward is found in both Luke and Matthew.

In Luke's version, Peter asks a question about the Parable of the Burglar (Lesson 5.2). Jesus answers Peter's question with a question:

> "Who then is the faithful and wise manager, whom the master puts in charge of his servants to give them their food allowance at the proper time?" (Luke 12:42)

The chief protagonist is "the faithful and wise manager." The noun is Greek *oikonomos*, "manager of a household or estate, (house) steward, manager."[28] This word is modified by two adjectives. The first adjective is Greek *pistos*, "pertaining to being worthy of belief or trust, trustworthy, faithful, dependable, inspiring trust/faith."[29] The second adjective is Greek *phronimos*, "pertaining to understanding associated with insight and wisdom, sensible, thoughtful, prudent, wise."[30]

The steward isn't just any servant. Perhaps not even the oldest, most experienced servant. But he is one in whom the master sees qualities of trustworthiness and prudence – wisdom. He appoints him to be in charge[31] of the other servants – especially in his absence. The main duty mentioned here is to give his fellow servants their food allowance at regular intervals.[32]

The steward is not doing something particularly flashy or creative. He is just continuing to do his duty, day after day, without fail, without forgetting, without unexplained lapses. His virtue is faithfulness. You can count on him.

Our generation shuns words like "duty" and "obligation." Jesus' message of faithfulness runs contrary to our somewhat selfish souls, but then, Jesus' teachings often grate on self-absorbed people. Jesus cares about faithfulness.

Faithful Service (Luke 12:43-44)

> "It will be good for that servant whom the master finds doing so when he returns. I tell you the truth, he will put him in charge of all his possessions." (Luke 12:43-44)

When the master returns from a journey and finds that in his absence his steward has been taking care of things without slacking off, the servant will be rewarded with a promotion. The steward's responsibility moves from just being responsible for the servants' meals. He is appointed over all the master's possessions.[33]

I think of Joseph in the Old Testament, who through faithfulness rose rapidly from being a common slave to being in charge of both Potiphar's household as well as his entire estate: "Everything he owns he has entrusted to my care" (Genesis 39:8).

---

[28] *Oikonomos*, BDAG 698, 1.
[29] *Pistos*, BDAG 820.
[30] *Phronimos*, BDAG 1066.
[31] "Put in charge of" (NIV, NRSV), "set over" (ESV), "make ruler over" (KJV) is the preposition *epi* and the verb *kathistēmi*, "to assign someone a position of authority, appoint, put in charge" (BDAG 492, 2a).
[32] "Food allowance" (NIV), "portion of food" (ESV), "allowance of food" (NRSV), "portion of meat" (KJV) is *sitometrion*, "a measured allowance of grain/food, food allowance, ration" (BDAG 925).
[33] "Possessions" (NIV, ESV, NRSV), "all he hath" (KJV) is *hyparchō*, "what belongs to someone, someone's property, possessions, means" (BDAG 1029).

Presumptive and Undisciplined Service (Luke 12:45-46)

But even wise and faithful servants can succumb to temptation. So Jesus goes on:

> "But suppose the servant says to himself, 'My master is taking a long time in coming,' and he then begins to beat the menservants and maidservants and to eat and drink and get drunk." (Luke 12:45)

Jesus has pointed to the rewards of faithfulness. Now he shifts the parable to explore the dangers fruits of unfaithfulness. The second scenario is a head servant who knows he won't be held accountable and so begins to abuse his authority and position. In Matthew, Jesus calls him "that wicked[34] servant" (Matthew 24:48). The evil servant begins to justify his actions:

> "My master is taking a long time[35] in coming." (Luke 12:45)

Note the element of delay in the master's return that was present in the Parable of the Waiting Servants (Lesson 5.2), the Wise and Foolish Virgins (Lesson 5.2), the Talents, the Minas or Pounds (Lesson 11.2), etc. Surely, Jesus is preparing his disciples for a delay in his own return.

In our parable, Jesus suggests that the head servant begins to beat[36] his fellow servants. Instead of acting as a servant, he is acting as the master and taking upon himself a master's prerogatives to discipline harshly. He indulges his whims. He abandons the self-discipline that got him appointed head servant in the first place. He gorges himself with food and wine and goes about drunk. Drunkenness is the very antithesis of the qualities of being wakeful and watching that the initial parables stressed (Luke 12:36). The unfaithful servant now lives for himself and not his master.

Unfortunately, the history of the Christian church offers abundant examples of (especially) men who started out as sincere monks and priests, but became worldly and wealthy bishops, cardinals, and popes. It took a humble St. Frances of Assisi (1181-1286 AD) to rebuke this worldliness by his vivid example of poverty filled with joy and love. I've seen humble and faithful pastors become petty tyrants, demanding personal loyalty of each member, sometimes indulging themselves with expensive cars and houses to celebrate their power. It is repugnant!

Unexpected Return and Punishment (Luke 12:46)

Now Jesus tells of the judgment falling on this corrupt head-servant.

---

[34] "Wicked" (NIV, ESV, NRSV), "evil" (KJV) is *kakos*, "pertaining to being socially or morally reprehensible, bad, evil," or even so far as, "harmful or injurious, evil, injurious, dangerous, pernicious" (BDAG 501).
[35] "Taking a long time" (NIV), "delayed" (ESV, NRSV, cf. KJV) is the verb *chronizō*, "to extend a state or an activity beyond an expected time, delay, take a long time" in doing something (BDAG 1092).
[36] "Beat" is Greek *typtō*, "to inflict a blow, strike, beat, wound" (BDAG 1020).

5. Parables about Readiness for Christ's Return

> "The master of that servant will come on a day when he does not expect him and at an hour he is not aware of. He will cut him to pieces and assign him a place with the unbelievers." (Luke 12:46)

The master's coming in Jesus' parable is sudden, but the unfaithful servant is clueless. He doesn't "expect"[37] the master or anticipate his coming. Nor does the abusive servant "know" or anticipate this hour of returning.

The punishment seems horrible, far beyond what would seem appropriate. Luke uses the verb *dikotomeō*, "cut in two," of dismemberment of a condemned person. Some suggest that Jesus may have meant this figuratively with the meaning "punish with utmost severity," but there is no support for this interpretation.[38]

In addition to dismemberment, in Luke, the unfaithful steward is assigned the portion or reward of the unbeliever, the faithless. Matthew uses the word "hypocrites." In both Matthew 18:50 and Luke 12:46, the scene moves from punishment of the servant in the parable to the End Time application of this parable, where the unfaithful and unbelieving are cast out into outer darkness, far from the joys of table fellowship in the Kingdom of God.[39] (See Appendix 5. The Great Messianic Banquet.)

Though the unfaithful steward had been a servant, since he refused to believe that his master would return to correct him, he is allotted a place with the gross unbelievers. He is stripped entirely of his relation to the master's household. How horrible!

Punishment in Proportion to Knowledge (Luke 12:47-48a, §159)

In Luke's version of the parable, Jesus adds an element of proportional punishment.

> "⁴⁷ That servant who knows his master's will and does not get ready or does not do what his master wants will be beaten with many blows. ⁴⁸ But the one who does not know and does things deserving punishment will be beaten with few blows." (Luke 12:47-48a)

A servant will be beaten in proportion to his knowledge and understanding of what his master wanted.[40] Beating slaves sounds harsh to twenty-first century ears, but in Jesus' day, beating

---

[37] "Expect" (NIV, ESV, NRSV), "aware" (KJV) is *prosdokaō*, "to give thought to something that is viewed as lying in the future, wait for, look for, expect" (BDAG 877).

[38] *Dikotomeō*, BDAG 253.

[39] In Bible days, using rods to punish was extremely common. Fathers would discipline their children with a rod; masters would discipline their servants with a rod. Punishment of criminals would sometimes be with a rod or whip (Matthew 5:29-30; 8:12; 13:50; 18:8-9; 22:13).

[40] "Beating/beaten" is *derō*, originally, "skin, flay," but in the New Testament only in imagery, "beat, whip" (BDAG 218-219). See Exodus 21:20; 2 Samuel 7:14; Job 9:34; 21:9; Psalm 89:32; Proverbs 10:13; 13:24; 14:3; 22:8, 15; 23:13-14; 26:3; 29:15; Isaiah 10:5; 30:32; Lamentations 3:1.

one's slaves was common and believed to be necessary to train them to avoid dishonesty and do right.[41] I'm sure there was often abuse, but in theory at least, discipline was not designed for cruelty, but for instruction.

Jesus tells us that the servant who knows what his master wants is held responsible to take action. If he doesn't believe his master, that doesn't alleviate his punishment. What the servant is expected to do is, in Jesus' words, to "get ready."[42]

We disciples are those servants. We are responsible for what we have been told, and we must use that knowledge to prepare ourselves for what is to come.

To Whom Much is Given, Much Is Demanded (Luke 12:48b, §159)

If verses Luke 12:47-48a explain the concept of relative responsibility for punishment, then verse 48b summarizes the concept into a principle.

> "From everyone who has been given much, much will be demanded; and from the one who has been entrusted with much, much more will be asked." (Luke 12:48b)

We see the same principle illustrated in Jesus' Parables of the Talents and Minas (Lesson 11.2).

Perhaps you are of those people who is multi-gifted. You have risen to a place of leadership. You are blessed. While those gifts God has given you certainly enable you to enrich yourself and your family – and caring for your family is important – Jesus wants you to use those gifts to help your fellow servants in the household of God and bless their lives. Remember, you are not your own; you are a servant under orders from the Master, Jesus. He has given you much; he expects much of you. Don't disappoint him!

> **Q22. (Luke 12:42-46) The Parable of the Wise and Faithful Steward is directed particularly at church leaders at various levels. Why are leaders sometimes tempted to take advantage of the perks of their position and to oppress those under their authority? What is the best antidote for these temptations? What does verse 48 teach disciples about responsibility?**
> https://www.joyfulheart.com/forums/topic/2196-q22-wise-and-faithful-steward/

---

[41] For example, see Deuteronomy 25:2-3; Psalm 89:32; Proverbs 10:13; 13:24; 14:3; 22:15; 23:13-14; 29:15; and Hebrews 12:10-11.
[42] "Get ready" (NIV, ESV), "prepare" (NRSV, KJV) is *hetoimazō*, "to cause to be ready, put/keep in readiness, prepare" (BDAG 400a).

5. Parables about Readiness for Christ's Return

For us, the struggles of this life may seem overwhelming. But there will come that day when we see his face, and the struggles of life lose their grip in the joy of his presence. In the meantime, my dear friends, remain watchful. Come soon, Lord Jesus!

Prayer

Father, it is so easy for us to fall into routines of complacency, rather than maintain a constant alertness and readiness. Jar us. Do whatever it takes to change our lazy habits into a constant seeking of your face and listening to your voice. In Jesus' name, we pray. Amen.

6. Parables about Salvation

One of Jesus' favorite themes is salvation – setting people free! He used a number of parables and analogies to teach his disciples these truths.

6.1 Analogies of Salvation

- Analogy of Spiritual Birth (John 3:3-7)
- Analogy of the Wind of the Spirit (John 3:8)
- Analogy of Lifting the Bronze Serpent (John 3:14)
- Parable of the Bread of Life (John 6:35)
- Parable of Water for Eternal Life (John 4:13-14)
- Parable of Streams of Living Water (John 7:37-39)
- Saying of the Camel and the Needle (Matthew 19:23-24; Mark 10:24-25; Luke 18:24-25)

'Eucharist,' stained glass window, St. Michael the Archangel Catholic Parish, Findlay, Ohio.

6.2 Analogies of Jesus' Death and Resurrection

- Acted Parable of the Bread and the Wine (Matthew 26:26-29; Mark 14:22-25; Luke 22:15-20)
- Acted Parable of Baptism (Mark 1:4-8; Matthew 28:19-20; Mark 16:15-16)
- Analogy of the Kernel of Wheat (John 12:24)
- Analogy of the Rooms in the Father's House (John 14:2-4)
- Parable of the Woman in Childbirth (John 16:21)

6.3 Setting People Free

- Parable of Plundering the Strongman's House (Mt 12:25-37; Mk 3:23-30; Lk 11:17-23)

6.1 Analogies of Salvation

Jesus told a number of parables to help clarify for his disciples what salvation was and what it was not. Many of these brief analogies are found in the Gospel of John.

Two caveats before we begin. First, some of these concepts like "born again" and "rivers of living water" are buzz-words or jargon, so ingrained in our Christian theology and terminology that it is difficult for us to lay that aside and look at what Jesus actually says.

Second, since some of these analogies are so central to our theology of salvation, I'm tempted to spend a lot of space putting them in context. But in a focused study of the parables, it's hard to do them justice. So, for fuller expositions, I refer you to my prior studies.

6. Parables about Salvation

John's Gospel: A Discipleship Journey with Jesus (JesusWalk Publications, 2015)
Disciple's Guide to the Holy Spirit (JesusWalk Publications, 2018)

Analogy of Spiritual Birth (John 3:3-7)
(Also known as New Birth and Second Birth)

Jesus is teaching Nicodemus, a Pharisee and member of the ruling group of Great Sanhedrin leaders in Jerusalem. Jesus insists that a person *must* be born again spiritually.

> "I tell you the truth, no one can see the kingdom of God unless he is born again." (John 3:3)

"Again" in verses 3 and 7 could be translated "from above," but Nicodemus tries to puncture Jesus' illustration of salvation as re-birth, by claiming the physical impossibility of rebirth, thus suggesting that "again" is the main idea.[1]

> "How can a man be born when he is old? Surely he cannot enter a second time into his mother's womb to be born!" (John 3:4)

But Jesus insists that a spiritual birth is necessary.

> "⁵ I tell you the truth, no one can enter the kingdom of God unless he is born of water and the Spirit. ⁶ Flesh gives birth to flesh, but the Spirit gives birth to spirit. ⁷ You should not be surprised at my saying, 'You must be born again.'" (John 3:5-7)

In verse 5, water could be interpreted as (1) amniotic fluid as symbolic of physical birth, or (2) perhaps repentance and cleansing inherent in John's water-baptism mentioned previously in John's Gospel. We can't be sure which. Verse 6 states clearly that this spiritual birth is distinct from physical birth. Thus, people are not automatically born by the Spirit – probably not Nicodemus himself at this point in his quest. Later, he comes to faith and is counted as a disciple (John 7:50; 19:39).

Jesus is talking about a new plane of life and understanding that is entirely beyond man's control. It is a birth and a new life that the Spirit gives. This "new birth," or "second birth" is as radical as our physical birth was, and is necessary to "see" (verse 3) and "enter" (verse 5) the Kingdom of God that Jesus is talking about. Of course, much more could be said about the

---

[1] "Again" (NIV, ESV, KJV, NASB), "from above" (NRSV, NJB) is *anōthen*, an adverb of place. It can mean (1) "from above," but probably is (4) at a subsequent point of time involving repetition, again, anew" (BDAG 92, meanings 1 and 4).

new birth of the Spirit that we can't get into here.[2] But second birth is a powerful image that teaches us something about spiritual life. The theological word to describe spiritual birth and life is "regeneration." As Paul puts it:

> "He saved us through the washing of rebirth[3] and renewal[4] by the Holy Spirit...." (Titus 3:5)[5]

Analogy of the Wind of the Spirit (John 3:8)

Now Jesus switches from a birth analogy to the wind. He emphasizes that the Holy Spirit cannot be manipulated. He is completely beyond man's control.

> "The wind (*pneuma*) blows wherever it pleases. You hear its sound, but you cannot tell where it comes from or where it is going. So it is with everyone born of the Spirit (*pneuma*)." (John 3:8)

"Wind" is *pneuma*, the breath of God, the same word that is translated "Spirit" at the end of verse 8. In Hebrew also, the word for spirit (*rûaḥ*) is also used for wind.

People who have been born of the Spirit, Jesus is saying, are motivated, guided, and moved by an unseen but powerful force beyond themselves. The life of the Spirit is a new level of spiritual existence, a different plane entirely. Only people who have been born of the Spirit can perceive and enter the Kingdom of God.

> **Q23. (John 3:3-8) In what way is becoming a believer in Jesus similar to a second birth? What aspects of physical birth are analogous to spiritual birth that Jesus seeks to clarify with this analogy? What about wind's characteristics are we to attribute to the**

---

[2] For a detailed study of this passage, see my *John's Gospel: A Discipleship Journey with Jesus* (JesusWalk Publications, 2015), Lesson 6. https://www.jesuswalk.com/john/06_born_again.htm In brief, the main explanations for water are: (1) Christian baptism, (2) amniotic fluid, (3) procreation (sperm), and (4) repentance and purification.

[3] "Regeneration" (ESV, KJV), "rebirth" (NIV, NRSV) in verse 5 is the Greek noun *palingenesia*, "the state of being renewed, renewal," here, "experience of a complete change of life, rebirth" of a redeemed person. (BDAG 75, 2).

[4] "Renewal" (NIV, NRSV, ESV), "renewing" (KJV) is *anakainōsis*, a Greek word not found outside of Christian literature, "renewal," of a person's spiritual birth, in Titus 3:5 and Romans 12:2 (BDAG 64), "a renewal, renovation, complete change for the better" (Thayer 342). This is a compound verb from *ana-*, "anew," repetition, renewal + *kainizō*, "to make new."

[5] See *Disciple's Guide to the Holy Spirit* (JesusWalk Publications, 2018), Lesson 4, Born of the Holy Spirit. https://www.jesuswalk.com/spirit/04_spirit_born.htm

6. Parables about Salvation

Spirit?
https://www.joyfulheart.com/forums/topic/2197-q23-spiritual-birth/

Analogy of Lifting the Bronze Serpent (John 3:14-15)

As you'll recall, Nicodemus, a highly placed inquirer, comes to Jesus at night to talk about salvation. After explaining the new birth and the wind of the Spirit, he explains faith with this analogy.

> "¹⁴ Just as Moses lifted up the snake in the desert, so the Son of Man must be lifted up,
> ¹⁵ that everyone who believes in him may have eternal life." (John 3:14-15)

For us, this seems like a rather obscure analogy, but for Jesus' Jewish listeners it taught them something. It refers to an incident when God judged the rebellion of his people in the desert with an abundance of venomous snakes whose bite was lethal. The snake danger had the intended effect. The people repented of their sin and asked Moses to take the snakes away. Yahweh tells Moses:

> "⁸ 'Make a snake and put it up on a pole; anyone who is bitten can look at it and live.
> ⁹ So Moses made a bronze snake and put it up on a pole. Then when anyone was bitten by a snake and looked at the bronze snake, he lived." (Numbers 21:8-9)

The analogy doesn't compare Jesus with a bronze snake. Rather, it involves a two-fold comparison:

1. **Lifting up**. Like the snake was lifted up, so Jesus will be lifted up both on the cross and in resurrection and ascension (see John 8:28; 12:32-34).
2. **Faith**. Just as people looked at the snake and lived, so people will look to Jesus in faith and live, that is be healed of their sin and receive eternal life.

Parable of the Bread of Life (John 6:35)

As part of a long discussion of manna, Jesus identifies himself as "the true bread from heaven" (John 6:32) The true bread doesn't give just physical life, but eternal life. Jesus spells it out using a metaphor, one of Jesus' seven "I AM" declarations in John's Gospel.

> "³⁵ᵇ I am the bread of life. ³⁶ He who comes to me will never go hungry, and he who believes in me will never be thirsty." (John 6:35-36)

Again, Jesus' words sound much like his promises of living water to the woman at the well (John 4:13-14, Lesson 6.1 below), words that bring life forever – eternal life. He says it again:

"⁴⁸ I am the bread of life. ⁴⁹ Your forefathers ate the manna in the desert, yet they died. ⁵⁰ But here is the bread that comes down from heaven, which a man may eat and not die. ⁵¹ I am the living bread that came down from heaven. If anyone eats of this bread, he will live forever." (John 6:48-51a)

Contained in Jesus' Bread of Life Discourse is the related Parable of Eating Jesus' Flesh in Lesson 9.3, where we'll dig deeper into these figures of speech.

"Bread of Life" and "Living Bread" mean bread that brings life, just as "Living Water," in the spiritual sense, means water that brings life as we see in the next analogies of salvation.

Parable of Water for Eternal Life (John 4:10, 13-14)

Life-giving Water

Now we come to a pair of parables of salvation that use the figure of "living water" – water for eternal life in John 4:13-14 and "streams of living water" in John 7:37-39. To unwrap both of these parables, we need to understand water as a symbol and the meaning of "living water."

1. Water as a symbol of life. In a largely arid land, water is a symbol of life. The patriarchs dug wells so they would have enough water for both themselves and their herds.

2. The meaning of "living water." The phrase normally referred to flowing water from a spring, stream, or river, as opposed to standing water in a pond, well, or cistern. Flowing water suggests a continuous flow. So "living water" is a symbol not just of life, but continuous, eternal, everlasting life.

Jesus' words aren't said in vacuum, but amidst a rich heritage of the Old Testament prophecies about water and salvation. For example:

> "My people ... have forsaken me,
> the spring of living water." (Jeremiah 2:13; cf. 17:13)

> You give them drink from your river of delights.
> For with you is the fountain of life." (Psalm 36:8b-9a)

'Samaritan Woman at the Well,' stained glass, Our Lady of Providence Catholic Church, St. Louis, Missouri.

> "On that day living water will flow out from Jerusalem...." (Zechariah 14:8)

Now let's examine Jesus' parables about living water, first the Parable of Water for Eternal Live (John 4:10, 13-14)

6. Parables about Salvation

The Woman at the Well

Jesus meets a Samaritan woman at Jacob's well and asks for a drink. She brings up differences between Jewish and Samaritan religious beliefs, but Jesus isn't distracted. He speaks to her deep spiritual need of salvation.

> "If you knew the gift of God and who it is that asks you for a drink, you would have asked him and he would have given you **living water**." (John 4:10)

A few minutes later he says,

> "¹³ Everyone who drinks this water will be thirsty again, ¹⁴ but whoever drinks the water I give him will never thirst. Indeed, the water I give him will become in him a **spring[6] of water** welling up[7] to eternal life." (John 4:13-14)

Jesus makes two claims for those who drink this Living Water.

1. They will never again thirst spiritually.
2. They will have eternal life.

Parable of Streams of Living Water (John 7:37-39)

A similar metaphor of spiritual life and eternal life is "rivers of living water." Jesus is in Jerusalem for the Feast of Tabernacles. This annual Jewish feast has a tradition of a daily libation, or pouring out of water that was understood by the rabbis and the people as symbolic of the outpouring of the Holy Spirit.[8] Now, at the culmination of the festival, Jesus proclaims in a loud voice:

> "³⁷ 'If anyone is **thirsty**, let him come to me and **drink**. ³⁸ Whoever believes in me, as the Scripture has said, 'Streams[9] of living water will flow[10] from within him.'[11] ³⁹ By

---

[6] "Spring" (NIV, NRSV, ESV), "well" (KJV) is *pēgē*, "a source of something that gushes out or flows, spring, fountain, flow" (distinguished from *krēnē*, "artificially constructed fountain." Ordinarily of water, "spring, fountain" (BDAG 810, 1a). "Running water," then "fount, source" (Liddell-Scott, p. 1399).

[7] "Welling up" (NIV, ESV), "gushing up" (NRSV), "springing up" (KJV) is *hallomai*, literally, "to make a quick leaping movement, leap, spring up," here used figuratively of the quick movement of inanimate things, "to spring up from a source," of water, "well up, bubble up" (BDAG 46, 2).

[8] For this Alfred Edersheim (*The Temple and Its Services as They Were at the Time of Christ* (1874), chapter 14) cites Jerusalem Talmud, *Sukkot* Vol. 1, p. 55 *a* (5.1). Also, Edersheim, *Life and Times*, book 4, chapter 7; Morris, *John*, pp. 420-21.

[9] "Streams" (NIV), "rivers" (NRSV, KJV) is *potamos*, "river, stream," from which we get our word "hippopotamus" ("horse of the river") (BDAG 856, b).

[10] "Flow" is *rheō*, "to flow with liquid," here in a transferred sense (BDAG 904, a).

[11] The river flows "from within him" (NIV), "out of his heart" (ESV, NRSV), "out of his belly" (KJV), phrases that translate the noun *koilia*. It refers to the organs of the abdomen, thought to be the "seat of inward life, of feelings and desires," what we express in English as the functional equivalent of "heart" (BDAG 550, 3).

this he meant the Spirit, whom those who believed in him were later to receive. Up to that time the Spirit had not been given, since Jesus had not yet been glorified." (John 7:37-39)

Jesus draws on Isaiah's use of water as a metaphor for salvation (Isaiah 12:3; 44:3). He speaks to the spiritual thirst of the Jewish people with both an invitation and a promise.

1. Invitation. "If anyone is thirsty, let him come to me and drink" (John 7:37). This turns my mind to several similar invitations in the Bible:

"Come, all you who are thirsty, come to the waters." (Isaiah 55:1-2)

"Come to me, all you who are weary and burdened...." (Matthew 11:28-29)

"Whoever is thirsty ... let him take the free gift of the water of life." (Revelation 22:17)

2. Universal invitation. The invitation and promise are to "whoever" (NIV, ESV) believes in Jesus – not just the Jews, but thirsty people around the world. This is his invitation to anyone even in our day who thirsts for healing, for reality, for truth, for love.

3. Promise. Jesus promises that the Holy Spirit will flow from within like an artesian well, never stopping. There is so much here to explore, but we don't have the time in this particular study.[12]

Jesus' promise here is fulfilled with the outpouring of the Holy Spirit on the Day of Pentecost and the continued presence of the Holy Spirit in each believer. This passage is the basis for a praise chorus from the Jesus Movement of the 1970s:

"There's a river of life flowing out of me,
Makes the lame to walk and the blind to see,
Opens prison doors, sets the captive free.
There's a river of life flowing out of me.
 Spring up a well within my soul,
 Spring up a well that makes me whole...."[13]

Q24. (John 4:13-14; 7:37-39) If water is symbolic of life, what is flowing or living water symbolic of in these passages? Who creates this spiritual thirst in a person? How are

---

[12] More on this in my *John's Gospel: A Discipleship Journey with Jesus* (JesusWalk Publications, 2015), Lesson 15; and my *Disciple's Guide to the Holy Spirit* (JesusWalk Publications, 2018), Lesson 4.

[13] "I've Got a River of Life," words and music by Louis Casebolt (no date).

6. Parables about Salvation 135

these promises fulfilled in believers?
https://www.joyfulheart.com/forums/topic/2198-q24-living-water/

Saying of the Camel and the Needle (Matthew 19:23-24; Mark 10:24-25; Luke 18:24-25; §189)

One of the greatest misconceptions in Judaism during Jesus' time was that a person could become righteous enough to be saved by doing good deeds. This isn't too far from American popular religion that sees people getting to heaven on good works. Of course, the cross isn't needed in a world that exalts human effort and minimizes the need for God's working. This brings us to Jesus' Saying of the Camel and the Needle.

The context is Jesus' encounter with the Rich Young Ruler. This young man was a serious, observant Jew who asks Jesus what he might do to inherit eternal life. Jesus stuns him by telling him that he needs to sell all his possessions, give the proceeds to the poor, and then follow Jesus. The man balks at this and "went away sad."

The disciples are shocked. If a wealthy man who is serious about keeping the law can't be saved, who can? In Judaism's eyes, a wealthy, young pious Jew was the very kind of person who *could* enter the Kingdom of God, that is, be saved, since he could afford to keep all the laws. That was the common wisdom. If *he* can't be saved, who can be saved?

How Hard for the Rich to Enter the Kingdom (Luke 18:24-25)

Jesus answers this question with his Saying of the Camel and the Needle.

> "²⁴ Jesus looked at [the Rich Young Ruler] and said, 'How hard it is for the rich to enter the kingdom of God! ²⁵ Indeed, it is easier for a camel to go through the eye of a needle than for a rich man to enter the kingdom of God.'" (Luke 18:24-25)

Jesus explains to his disciples about how "hard" or "difficult" it is for the rich to be saved.[14] Then Jesus declares it impossible – illustrated by a short saying or parable.

Camels were a curiosity to Israelites. Farmers didn't use them; the donkey was their animal of choice. But the camel, domesticated by 1,000 BC, was used for long-distance trade. Camels

---

[14] "Hard" (NIV, NRSV), "difficult" (ESV), "hardly" (KJV) is *dyskolos*, "pertaining to that which is difficult to fulfill or do, hard, difficult" (BDAG 265).

brought goods along the Silk Road from China though Palestine and Syria to the coast, then the goods were loaded on ships headed for Rome. Camels also carried frankincense and myrrh along the Incense Route from south Arabia.

Galilee was near a crossroads of some of these trade routes, so camels were not unfamiliar to the Galileans. Nevertheless, the camel was a wonder, the largest animal regularly seen in Palestine.

The ancients were quite familiar with sewing needles to make clothing, tents, etc. Archaeologists have found bone and ivory needles dating back tens of thousands of years. Copper and iron needles date from the fourth and third millennia BC.

At issue in Jesus' saying is the tiny opening for the thread in the eye of the needle. Some rabbinical writings have a similar expression: "Draw an elephant through the eye of a needle."[15] Both this saying and Jesus' saying share the same contrast between the huge beast and the proverbially small eye of a needle. The point of both these figures of speech is impossibility; they are proverbs of impossibility. We know this because Jesus uses the word "impossible" (*adynatos*) in Luke 18:27.

The Gate of Jerusalem Myth

For hundreds of years there have been various explanations floating around to change Jesus' teaching of "impossibility" to some kind of "you-can-do-it-if-you-really-try" approach. One of these pseudo-explanations imagines a gate through the wall of Jerusalem called "the needle's eye," so small that a laden camel couldn't get through unless it were to kneel down and be completely unloaded. Preachers and tour guides love the story. It is picturesque, but has absolutely no support in fact.[16] It also distorts what Jesus is trying to say from "impossible for man" to "possible by man."

Possible Only with God (Luke 18:26-27)

As mentioned, he disciples' were astonished at the impossibility of salvation for the rich.

"²⁶ Those who heard this asked, 'Who then can be saved?'

²⁷ Jesus replied, 'What is impossible with men is possible with God.'" (Luke 18:26-27)

---

[15] I have researched this considerably and found nothing that provides any support whatsoever for the "gate in the wall" theory. All my sources – from older commentators such as Matthew Henry (1710), to respected scholars in the *International Standard Bible Encyclopedia* (1974), to my newest scholarly commentaries on Matthew, Mark, and Luke – all of them, discredit the story as unsupported, if they mention it at all. Marshall, *Luke*, p. 687 cites *Ber.* 55b; BM 38b; Strack and Billerbeck I, 828, dating from the third century AD.

[16] See Otto Michael, TDNT 3:592-594. Marshall, *Luke*, p. 687.

6. Parables about Salvation

Even the most religious, the most pious Jews – of which the Rich Young Ruler is an example – and the most saintly Christian believer can't save themselves. Salvation is not man's work, but God's. God can do what is impossible to man. He can open the most distracted heart, cleanse the most polluted person, and flood the soul with his life-giving Holy Spirit.

> Q25. (Luke 18:24-25) Why do you think people try to distort Jesus' Saying of the Camel and the Needle from a parable of impossibility? Why is salvation impossible to humans?
> https://www.joyfulheart.com/forums/topic/2199-q25-camel-and-needle/

6.2 Parables of Jesus' Death and Resurrection

Jesus uses several analogies and parables to teach his disciples about his death and resurrection. As you may recall, three times prior to Holy Week, Jesus told his disciples about his death and resurrection, but they didn't understand it – and even refused to understand (Matthew 16:21; 17:22-23; 20:17-19).

Thus, part of Jesus' training for his disciples was to help them find ways to process his death and his resurrection. Even if they didn't understand immediately, they would be able to look back at his teachings later and realize what he was saying to them. Much of Jesus' training along this line was in the form of parables.

Acted Parable of the Bread and the Wine (Matthew 26:26-29; Mark 14:22-25; Luke 22:15-20; §236)

We are so used to the bread and the wine representing Jesus' body and blood that we hardly think of it as one of Jesus' teaching parables. But it is – perhaps the most important and enduring one, since these Words of Institution are to be spoken in every congregation every time the Lord's Supper or Eucharist, the Communion or the Mass is remembered. In Luke he says, "Do this in remembrance of me" (Luke 21:19; cf. 1 Corinthians 11:24).[17] This acted parable is designed to be remembered!

'Eucharist,' stained glass window, St. Michael the Archangel Catholic Parish, Findlay, Ohio.

---

[17] The early manuscripts of Luke 21:19 differ some. The earliest documents include a longer passage, but the Western text omits verses 19b and 20. The majority of the Editorial Committee of the United Bible Societies

Here is Matthew's version, recounting what happened on Thursday evening, just before his crucifixion the following day.

> "²⁶ While they were eating, Jesus took bread, gave thanks and broke it, and gave it to his disciples, saying, 'Take and eat; this is my body.' ²⁷ Then he took the cup, gave thanks and offered it to them, saying,
>
> 'Drink from it, all of you. ²⁸ This is my blood of the covenant, which is poured out for many for the forgiveness of sins. ²⁹ I tell you, I will not drink of this fruit of the vine from now on until that day when I drink it anew with you in my Father's kingdom.'" (Matthew 26:26-29)

By the time of the Apostle Paul, the Words of Institution had become a bit more fixed, more parallel to each other (1 Corinthians 11:23-26)

Whenever I teach about Christian Baptism and the Lord's Supper or Eucharist I risk offending people, since Christians have a wide range of beliefs about these two important sacraments (or institutions), and our respective denominational traditions have battled about doctrine for centuries. I don't write to offend. But I would be remiss, if I didn't point out that Jesus' giving the bread and cup to his followers *seems to me* to be a metaphor where the bread and wine represent Jesus' body and blood.[18]

I certainly don't want to offend my dear Roman Catholic and Orthodox brothers and sisters who believe in transubstantiation. They take Jesus' words at the Last Supper *literally*, and believe that the bread of the Eucharist *IS* the Real Body of Christ at the time it is consecrated.

On the other hand, I believe that when Jesus held out the bread before the disciples at the Last Supper and said, "This is my body given for you," he was speaking *metaphorically*. As they looked at him, they had no trouble clearly differentiating between his physical body and the loaf of bread he was holding in his physical hands. Nevertheless, though we may disagree on some understandings, we must endeavor to love one another in Christ!

Notice where Jesus says, "I will not drink of this fruit of the vine from now on until that day when I drink it anew with you in my Father's kingdom'" (Matthew 26:29). This is a

---

preferred the longer text "impressed by the overwhelming preponderance of external evidence supporting the longer form," and "explained the origin of the shorter form as due to some scribal accident or misunderstanding" (Metzger, *Textual Commentary*, pp. 149-150). Metzger gives the longer reading a {B}, "some degree of doubt" confidence rating.

[18] English words sometimes used in a discussion of the Lord's Supper include: Symbol – "something that stands for or suggests something else by reason of relationship, association, convention, or accidental resemblance." Emblem – "an object or the figure of an object symbolizing and suggesting another object or an idea." Token – an outward sign or expression." "Metaphor – "a figure of speech in which a word or phrase literally denoting one kind of object or idea is used in place of another to suggest a likeness or analogy between them" *Merriam-Webster 11th Collegiate Dictionary*.

reference to the great eschatological banquet where Abraham, Isaac, and Jacob feast with the saints of God. (See Appendix 5. The Great Messianic Banquet.)

Much more could be said about the Eucharist, of course. My main purpose here is to point to it as an acted parable, comparing the bread and the wine to his flesh and blood given for us on the cross.

> Q26. (Matthew 26:26-29; 1 Corinthians 11:23-26) How do the bread and wine remind us of Jesus' sacrifice for our sins? In what way, when we partake of the Lord's Supper, do we "proclaim the Lord's death until he comes" (1 Corinthians 11:26)? https://www.joyfulheart.com/forums/topic/2200-q26-bread-and-wine/

Acted Parable of Baptism (Mark 1:4-8; Matthew 28:19-20; Mark 16:15-16)

While we're at it, let's consider baptism as an acted parable of salvation, a symbol of cleansing from sin.

We don't have any of Jesus' own teaching about the significance of baptism, but since Jesus' ministry had a real continuity with the repentance theme of John the Baptist,[19] we can assume that his message was similar to that of his cousin.

> "⁴ And so John came, baptizing in the desert region and preaching a **baptism of repentance for the forgiveness of sins**. ⁵ The whole Judean countryside and all the people of Jerusalem went out to him. Confessing their sins, they were baptized by him in the Jordan River." (Mark 1:4-5, §1)

I'll briefly summarize what was going on here. For centuries, the Jews practiced ritual washings.[20] Jews would build a *mikvah* in their synagogues – and do so to this day – a bath for ritual purification by self-immersion. Proselytes to Judaism were baptized by immersion as an initiation.[21] John's baptism was probably understood by the Jews of his time against this background as a kind of *mikvah* of repentance in preparation for the kingdom. Jesus' disciples also conducted this kind of baptism under Jesus' direction (John 3:22, 26; 4:1-2).

When Paul describes the circumstances of his own baptism, he links baptism with cleansing. In Paul's account, Ananias says to him:

> "And now what are you waiting for? Get up, **be baptized and wash your sins away**, calling on his name." (Acts 22:16; cf. 1 Peter 3:21)

---

[19] Matthew 3:2 = Matthew 4:17; John 4:1-2.
[20] Exodus 40:30-32; Leviticus 15:18; Deuteronomy 23:11; etc.
[21] William Sanford LaSor, "Mikvah," ISBE 3:354.

Thus, baptism of believers is a metaphor of spiritual cleansing, or salvation from sin. Jesus clearly tells his followers to baptize new believers on the basis of their faith in Christ (Matthew 28:19-20; Mark 16:15-16).

In addition to cleansing, Paul also understood baptism as a symbol or metaphor of death and resurrection (Romans 6:3-4; cf. Colossians 2:12). Whenever we witness a believer being baptized, it is intended to remind us both of cleansing from sin and rising to a new life – an acted parable.

Analogy of the Kernel of Wheat (John 12:24)

When Jesus shares the Analogy of the Kernel of Wheat, the Triumphal Entry has already taken place. It is Holy Week, the last few days of Jesus' physical life on earth. He knows that the cross is coming soon, but the disciples refuse to accept it (Matthew 16:21-23). Nevertheless, Jesus patiently teaches them how to understand his death and resurrection, though on this occasion he appears to be speaking to a crowd as well as his disciples.

> "[23] The hour has come for the Son of Man to be glorified.[22] [24] I tell you the truth, unless a kernel of wheat falls to the ground and dies,[23] it remains only a single seed. But if it dies, it produces many seeds. [25] The man who loves his life will lose it, while the man who hates his life in this world will keep it for eternal life." (John 12:23-25)

Here, Jesus uses an agricultural analogy to typify both death and resurrection – a seed that is planted in the ground germinates, grows, and eventually reproduces itself many times over. Paul uses this kind of analogy too: A seed "dies" by being planted in the ground like a body in a grave (cf. 1 Corinthians 15:36). But when the seedling breaks through the earth and "rises from the dead," so to speak, it grows up to be stalk of wheat with a seed-head bearing many seeds.

The disciples didn't understand that Jesus' death on the cross enables their salvation. They didn't understand that Jesus' resurrection enables the promise of life for all. But it was so. The Analogy of the Kernel of Wheat gives Jesus' disciples another way to understand and process their Master's death and resurrection.

---

[22] When Jesus talks about the time for him to be "glorified," he seems to be referring to his death, resurrection, and ascension (John 7:39b; 12:16b, 41; Luke 4:26). This seems to be a reference to the Suffering Servant passage where the Servant will be "raised and lifted up and highly exalted" (Isaiah 52:13).

[23] Of course, from a scientific viewpoint, the seed doesn't die. But from the observation of a farmer – and this audience was made up of people who had experience with subsistence farming – it might well appear like death and burial, and resurrection glory when the seeds appear on the plant.

6. Parables about Salvation

Remember Jesus' words, "The man who hates his life in this world will keep it for eternal life" (John 12:25). We'll see that idea again when we examine Jesus' Parable of Taking Up One's Cross in the Synoptic Gospels (Lesson 8.4).

Analogy of the Rooms in the Father's House (John 14:2-4)

Another analogy Jesus uses to prepare his disciples for his death, resurrection, and ascension is his promise of preparing a place for them in his Father's House. He senses their confusion at his talk about going away (John 13:36), so he reassures them.

> "In my Father's house are many rooms; if it were not so, I would have told you. I am going there to prepare a place for you." (John 14:2)

What house is he talking about? The noun is *oikia*, "a structure used as a dwelling, house,"[24] essentially synonymous with the more common noun *oikos*, "house, household, family." Sometimes "the house of the Lord" refers to the tabernacle and later the temple in Jerusalem.[25] But here, Jesus is talking about God's heavenly dwelling.[26]

Every time I see this verse, I think of a wonderful African-American spiritual:

> "Come and go with me to my Father's house,
> To my Father's house, to my Father's house,
> Come and go with me to my Father's house,
> There is joy, joy, joy!
>
> Jesus will be there, in my Father's house....
>
> There'll be no crying there, in my Father's house...." (etc.)

In the Father's house, Jesus says, there will be many rooms. "Rooms" (NIV, ESV), "dwelling places" (NRSV), "mansions" (KJV) is *monē*, "a place in which one stays, dwelling(-place), room, abode."[27] Perhaps these might be comparable to personal apartments in the Father's heavenly palace – who knows?

Jesus says he is going there to "prepare a place"[28] for his disciples. I can remember going to my grandparents' home, with a guestroom prepared for my brother and me – clean sheets and all. Jesus is going away, not just to freshen up rooms for us in heaven, but to prepare the

---

[24] *Oikia*, BDAG 695, 1b.
[25] For example, Exodus 23:19; Judges 19:18; Psalm 27:4; John 2:16.
[26] The writer of Hebrews refers to it as the City of God (Hebrews 9:21, 24; 11:10, 16; 12:22; 13:14).
[27] *Monē*, BDAG 658, 2, from *menō*, "continue, abide, stay."
[28] "Prepare" is *hetoimazō*, "to cause to be ready, put/keep in readiness, prepare" (BDAG 440, a). "Place" is *topos*, from which we get our English words "topography, topographical, topical." *Topos* refers to "an area of any size, generally specified as a place of habitation, here, "an abode: place, room," to live, stay, sit, etc. (BDAG 1011, 1e).

"way" so we can get to heaven at all, as we'll see in verse 6: "I AM the Way." Jesus explains that he isn't just leaving, but he is coming back.

> "And if I go and prepare a place for you, I will come back and take you to be with me[29] that you also may be where I am." (John 14:3)

Where is Jesus going? He is "returning to God" (John 13:3), "going to the Father,"[30] he is going to "my Father's house" (John 14:2). The Father's house seems to be a metaphor of heaven, the very presence of God.

Parable of the Woman in Childbirth (John 16:21)

Jesus has been talking to his disciples for his death followed by resurrection, about going away and then returning. They are discouraged, confused. And so he gives them a word of comfort using the figures of a laboring mother and her newborn.

> "[20] I tell you the truth, you will weep and mourn while the world rejoices. You will grieve, but your grief will turn to joy. [21] A woman giving birth to a child has pain because her time has come; but when her baby is born she forgets the anguish because of her joy that a child is born into the world. [22] So with you: Now is your time of grief, but I will see you again and you will rejoice, and no one will take away your joy." (John 16:20-22)

My wife was a childbirth instructor for several years, so I learned that "transition" is a stage in childbirth that comes during the last part of active labor, just before birth. It can be particularly intense and painful, with contractions close together that can last as long as 60 to 90 seconds each.

Women, especially during transition, are caught in a zone of pain and sometimes panic that seems like it will never end. Their focus is so intense on the pain of bearing the child, that they can't see beyond it. But when the baby comes and the midwife puts the newborn in the mother's arms, she relaxes and breaks into a huge smile. The struggles of birth fade away in the joy of holding and nursing the new life.

Jesus is referring to the joy his disciples will experience when they see him raised from the dead in his resurrection glory. And of the lasting joy they will have in the risen Christ long after his ascension. Nearly all these disciples were martyred for their faith, but even through

---

[29] The phrase "take you to be with me" carries the idea in Greek idiom, "I will take you with me to my home" (Beasley-Murray, *John*, p. 250; Kruse, *John*, p. 297). "Take you" (NIV, NRSV, ESV), "receive you" (KJV) is *paralambanō*, "to take into close association, take (to oneself), take with/along" (BDAG 767, 1).
[30] John 14:13; 16:10, 17.

6. Parables about Salvation

the pain of that, they clung to their joy in their resurrected Lord. Because of this they were unstoppable.

I might go a step beyond that. For us, the struggles of this life may seem overwhelming. But there will come that day when we see his face, and the struggles of life lose their grip in the joy of his presence. Come soon, Lord Jesus!

6.3 Setting People Free

Jesus taught that the Kingdom of God has power to set the sinner free! Jesus told two parables about this:

1. Analogy of the Slave and the Son (John 8:34-36), where Jesus says, "If the Son sets you free, you will be free indeed." (More on this in Appendix 4.2.)
2. Plundering the Strongman's House passage (Luke 11:17-26), which we'll examine here.

The Plundering the Strongman's House passage (Luke 11:17-26) is really a cluster of three mini-parables.[31] Since they appear differently in Matthew, Mark, and Luke, we'll consider each of them separately.

- Analogy of a House Divided (in all Synoptic Gospels)
- Parable of Binding the Strong Man (in all Synoptic Gospels)
- Parable of the Empty House (in different contexts in Luke and Matthew, only)

Analogy of a House Divided (Matthew 12:25-26; Mark 3:24-26; §86; Luke 11:17-18, §149)

Jesus had become known for casting out demons. Unwilling to acknowledge God's hand in these healings and exorcisms, Jesus' enemies[32] present an alternate theory, that Jesus drives out demons because he is working for the devil himself.

> "[17] Jesus knew their thoughts and said to them: 'Any kingdom divided against itself will be ruined, and a house divided against itself will fall.[33] [18] If Satan is divided against himself, how can his kingdom stand? I say this because you claim that I drive out demons by Beelzebub.'" (Luke 11:17-18)

---

[31] In Mark's account, "Jesus called them and spoke to them in parables" (Mark 3:23), where "parables" is plural, suggesting more than one parable.

[32] Matthew identifies them as "the Pharisees" (Matthew 12:24), Mark as "the scribes" (Mark 3:22).

[33] Abraham Lincoln, 16th American president, famously used this parable in his "House Divided" speech in June 16, 1858, seeing inevitable conflict over slavery in America. "'A house divided against itself cannot stand.' I believe this government cannot endure, permanently half *slave* and half *free*. I do not expect the Union to be *dissolved* – I do not expect the house to *fall* – but I do expect it will cease to be divided. It will become *all* one thing, or *all* the other."

By Jesus' day, Beelzebul or Beelzebub had become the popular name for Satan, the prince of demons.[34] The scribes and Pharisees are attributing Jesus' success at exorcism to being empowered by Satan, the prince of demons. This is gross blasphemy and slander. It is also illogical!

Jesus uses a common-sense illustration from political life. A kingdom with a mortal conflict between leaders won't be able to continue. One party will destroy the other and the kingdom will topple.

Thus, Jesus is saying: If he is casting out Satan's demons by Beelzebub, the chief demon, then Satan's dominion cannot continue! It would by rent by internal warfare and fall. Jesus concludes his scathing criticism of his enemies' theory by noting that their own followers conduct exorcisms (Luke 11:19).

Deliverance by the Finger of God (Luke 11:20)

Now Jesus delivers a powerful challenge to his critics.

> "But if I drive out demons by the finger of God, then the kingdom of God has come to you." (Luke 11:20)

The term "finger of God" is a powerful term,[35] similar in meaning to the term "hand of God." We see it in God's powerful actions during the Exodus from Egypt and the giving of the law before Mt. Sinai (Exodus 8:19; 31:18).

Jesus is saying, If you're wrong, and God not Beelzebub, is empowering me, then the Kingdom of God has come to you and you are too blind to see it.

Parable of Binding the Strong Man (Matthew 12:29; Mark 3:27, §86; Luke 11:21-22, §149)
(Also known as the Parable of the Strong Man)

While Jesus' Analogy of the House Divided is designed to expose faulty logic, his Parable of Binding the Strong Man teaches us some amazing things about Jesus' understanding of his ministry.

---

[34] Beelzebub (sometimes spelled Beelzebul, and considered the same figure as Belial in the intertestamental literature) comes from the Hebrew *Baal*, "lord, husband," the name of an early Canaanite god. *Bul* is the Hebrew word for "house, high place, temple" (1 Kings 8:13; Isaiah 63:15). So Beelzebul means "god of the high place." However, the Jews may have purposely corrupted Beelzebul – as a sign of their disgust – into the word Beelzebub, meaning "Lord of the flies" or "god of filth" (Marshall, *Luke*, pp. 472, 473; BDAG 173).

[35] Matthew 12:28 substitutes the term, "Spirit of God."

6. Parables about Salvation

"²¹ When a strong man, fully armed,³⁶ guards his own house, his possessions are safe.³⁷ ²² But when someone stronger attacks and overpowers him, he takes away the armor in which the man trusted and divides up the spoils." (Luke 11:21-22)

Jesus is using military terms to picture an estate and outbuildings³⁸ guarded³⁹ by a fierce, well-armed warrior. He patrols the property constantly, so that no one can break in and steal the treasures within.⁴⁰

But now, an even greater warrior⁴¹ faces him in battle with a head-on attack,⁴² coming against him with greater force. This opposing warrior is stronger, bigger, more determined, and better armed. There is no comparison when it comes to strength! The stronger warrior "overcomes" or "overpowers" the weaker guard and slays him.⁴³

On the west front of Lincoln Cathedral in Lincoln, England, is an amazing frieze known as 'The Harrowing (or Plundering) of Hell,' (c. 1150 AD, restored in 2009). It shows the conflict with Satan in graphic terms. The man with the crown is, of course, Christ. The man to the right seems to be John the Baptist. Both have their feet on the devil, bound hand and foot. Christ is grasping those enslaved souls who are reaching out for his help.

As was the practice on ancient battlefields, he strips the dead warrior of his sword and shield,

---

[36] "Strong man" is the adjective *ischyros*, "strong, mighty, powerful," here, "pertaining to being strong physically, mentally, or spiritually, strong." "Fully armed" is *kathoplizō*, "arm fully, equip," here a perfect participle in the middle voice, "to arm oneself with weaponry, arm, equip oneself" (BDAG 492, a).

[37] "Safe" (NIV, ESV, NRSV), "in peace" (KJV) is two words, *en*, "in" and *eirēnē*, "peace," here, "be in peace, out of danger" (BDAG 287, 1a).

[38] "House" (NIV), "palace" (ESV, KJV), "castle" (NRSV) is the adjective *aulē*, literally, "enclosed open space, courtyard," then, "dwelling complex," either of ordinary property, "farm, house," or of royal property, the "court" of a prince, then "palace" (BDAG 150).

[39] "Guards" is *phylassō*, "to protect by taking careful measures, guard, protect" (BDAG 2b).

[40] "Possessions" (NIV), "property" (NRSV), "goods" (ESV, KJV) is the present active participle of the verb *hyparchō*, "exist, be present, be at one's disposal." As a participle it refers to "what belongs to someone, someone's property, possessions, means" (BDAG 1029, 1).

[41] "(Some) one stronger" is the comparative of *ischysros* in verse 21.

[42] "Attacks" (NIV, ESV, NRSV), "comes upon" (KJV) is *eperchomai*, "to move to or upon," here, "to come against someone with force, attack" (BDAG 361, 3).

[43] "Overpowers" (NIV, NRSV), "overcomes" (ESV, KJV) is *nikaō* (from which we get the brand "Nike"), "to win in the face of obstacles, be victor, conquer, overcome, prevail," then "to overcome someone, vanquish, overcome" (BDAG 673, 2a).

his breastplate and helmet, his belt and clothing.[44] Since the conquering warrior has no need of these himself, he "distributes" them to his fellow men in arms.[45] When he plunders the wealthy owner's treasures, those also go to his followers. To the victor goes the spoils. That is the vivid, powerful picture that Jesus paints in just two sentences.

This is a curious parable if we were to allegorize it by making the demonized man correspond to the "house" that is guarded by its owner, the prince of demons. The story applies to Jesus and Beelzebub, but not every detail. I don't think this is a simple allegory. It is rather a direct story about the superior force of Jesus the Messiah, Commander of the Armies of the Lord, overcoming the power that enslaves Satan's victims. It tells of the defeat of Satan! Satan's house contains his captives; King Jesus overcomes Satan and sets them free.

The point is that Jesus casts out demons by his superior power, not by the lesser power of Beelzebub, the prince of demons. Jesus' power is far superior to Satan's! Hallelujah.

Victorious Jesus, Mighty Warrior

Sadly, the picture of Jesus as Mighty Warrior and Savior seems to have diminished in popular preaching. But Yahweh as Mighty Warrior is a rich theme in the Old Testament. We see him as El Shaddai (Mighty God), Lord of Hosts (armies), King of Glory, Mighty Warrior, Savior, Deliverer, etc.[46] The "commander of the army of Yahweh" appears before Joshua prior to the fall of Jericho (Joshua 5:13-15). In the Garden of Gethsemane, Jesus reminds his disciples:

> "Do you think I cannot call on my Father, and he will at once put at my disposal more than twelve legions of angels?" (Matthew 26:53)

Finally, we see in the Book Revelation Jesus riding on a white horse, leading the armies of heaven to victory over Satan (Revelation 19:11-14).

Jesus is the Stronger Man who has the power to overcome the lies, enticements, and deception of the enemy that you and I face. In Him is power for our deliverance. He is our Stronger Man. He is our Savior. He is our Rescuer. He is the power of God working in us who believe (1 Thessalonians 2:13; Philippians 2:12-13). As the Apostle John put it many years later,

> "You, dear children, are from God and have overcome them, because the one who is in you is greater than the one who is in the world." (1 John 4:4)

---

[44] "Armor" is *panoplia*, "the complete equipment of a heavy-armed soldier, full armor." We see the word used in a spiritual sense in Ephesians 6:11, 13 (BDAG 754, 1). "Spoil(s)" (ESV, NIV, KJV), "plunder" (NRSV) is *skylon*, here, "armor and weapons taken ('stripped') from the body of a slain enemy," then generally, "booty, spoils" (BDAG 933), from *skyō*, "to pull off."

[45] "Distributes" is *diadidōmi*, "to apportion among various parties, distribute, give" (BDAG 227).

[46] See Ralph F. Wilson *Names and Titles of God* (JesusWalk Publications, 2010), lessons 2, 7, and 11. https://www.jesuswalk.com/names-god/2_almighty.htm

6. Parables about Salvation

Q27. (Luke 11:17-22) In the Parable of the Binding of the Strong Man, who is the strong man? Who is the stronger warrior? How does this explain Jesus' power to cast out demons? How does it explain Jesus' power to set you free? To set your friends free?
https://www.joyfulheart.com/forums/topic/2201-q27-binding-the-strong-man/

Parable of the Empty House (Matthew 12:43-45, §88; Luke 11:23-26, §150)
(Also known as the Parable of the Return of the Evil Spirit)

Finally, in this series of three mini-parables in Luke, Jesus relates the Parable of the Empty House. As we'll see Matthew includes it, but in a different setting. Mark omits it entirely. It is a difficult parable to interpret, but seems to be a story explaining the necessity for full commitment vs. neutrality.

> "23 He who is not with me is against me,[47] and he who does not gather with me, scatters. 24 When an evil ("unclean"[48]) spirit comes out of a man, it goes through arid places seeking rest and does not find it. Then it says, 'I will return to the house I left.' 25 When it arrives, it finds the house swept clean and put in order. 26 Then it goes and takes seven other spirits more wicked than itself, and they go in and live there. And the final condition of that man is worse than the first." (Luke 11:24-26)

Demons were thought to haunt desert places.[49] But the demon doesn't find a comfortable abode so it decides to return to its former "house" (*oikos*), the body of the formerly demonized

---

[47] In an unrelated incident we see what seems on the surface just the opposite of this call to decision. The disciples had reported that someone is casting out demons in Jesus' name. "Do not stop him," Jesus said. "No one who does a miracle in my name can in the next moment say anything bad about me, for whoever is not against us is for us" (Mark 9:40-41; cf. Luke 9:49-50). But this is different. It is about someone who recognizes Jesus' power and authority and is experimenting with it, not the Jewish leaders who bitterly oppose him and are trying to trap him so they can destroy him.

[48] The word translated "evil spirit" (NIV) is better translated "unclean spirit" (ESV, NRSV, KJV), since the adjective *akathartos* means "impure, unclean." It is used of "unclean" foods that could not be eaten by the Jews, as well as everything connected with idolatry. A moral sense of the word includes the ideas of "unclean, impure, vicious," and is especially used to describe demonic spirits.

[49] Isaiah 34:14 (LXX); Revelation 18:2. Morris observes, "Desert places were popularly regarded as the haunts of evil spirits and Jesus pictures this one as wandering through such waterless regions without finding rest" (Morris, *Luke*, p. 199) But Marshall notes, "The point is perhaps not the dryness but the absence of men from such desert regions, so that the demon cannot find anywhere to rest" (Marshall, *Luke*, p. 479). The Greek word *anapausis* can mean both "rest" and "a resting place" (BDAG 69, 3).

person. "When it arrives, it finds the house swept clean and put in order"[50] (Luke 11:25), so it decides to take up residence again, with lots of friends!

Context in Matthew

The parable as it appears in Matthew seems to be about Israel. In Matthew, the parable is placed following Jesus' castigation of the dullness of his generation, as "a wicked and adulterous generation" (Matthew 12:39), particularly its leaders. Jesus concludes the parable:

> "That is how it will be with this wicked generation." (Matthew 12:45)

The key idea in Matthew's version (verse 44) is that the house is "unoccupied" (NIV) or "empty" (ESV, NRSV, KJV).[51] Thus the meaning would be: In the same way as an individual is freed from a demon, so the nation of Israel was initially cleansed by the teaching of Jesus (and John the Baptist), but must continue in the teachings of Christ. Israel's leaders can't remain neutral! If they don't follow Christ's teachings, they will be overcome again by the Evil One. Thus, they will be worse off than before, since now they are guilty of rejecting the Messiah and his teaching.[52]

Context in Luke

In Luke, the parable is found right after the Parable of Plundering the Strongman's House (Luke 11:17-23, Lesson 6.3). Most commentators follow Leon Morris's interpretation of Luke's version which is more personal than national in application. Morris says,

> "When a man gets rid of an evil spirit but puts nothing in its place, he is in grave moral danger. No man can live for long with his life a moral vacuum."[53]

This is what Jesus means in Luke 11:23:

> "He who is not with me is against me, and he who does not gather with me scatters." (Luke 11:23 = Matthew 12:30)

Neither Israel nor an individual can remain neutral about the Messiah.

---

[50] The phrase "put in order" (NIV, ESV, NRSV), "garnished" (KJV) is *kosmeō* (from which we derive our word "cosmetic"), " to put in order so as to appear neat or well organized, make neat/tidy" (BDAG 560, 1).

[51] "Unoccupied" (NIV) or "empty" (ESV, NRSV, KJV) is *scholazō*, "to be without occupants, be unoccupied, stand empty" (BDAG 982, 2). Luke omits the word "empty" in the earliest texts, but seems to assume the idea anyway. Metzger (*Textual Commentary*, p. 134) sees this as a clear interpolation from Matthew, and gives the text omitting the word a {B} "some degree of doubt" confidence rating. The earliest Greek manuscripts omit "empty" (p^{75} Aleph* D Θ 700).

[52] So France, *Matthew*, p. 494; Morris, *Matthew*, p. 330; Norval Geldenhuys, *Commentary on the Gospel of Luke* (New International Commentary on the New Testament; Eerdmans, 1951), p. 351.

[53] Leon Morris, *The Gospel According to St. Luke* (Tyndale New Testament Commentaries; Eerdmans, 1974), p. 199.

6. Parables about Salvation

Just getting your life cleaned up and more orderly is a good thing – but inadequate. To be empty is to be vulnerable. Without the strong power of Jesus in our lives, we set ourselves up to be oppressed by evil in some other form. Emptiness represents a lack of commitment, lack of purpose, lack of focus. There can be no spiritual neutrality!

Jesus' parables of salvation are so rich, so deep, so powerful! Meditate on them so you will grow as a disciple!

Prayer

Father, thank you for your Son's death on the cross on our behalf, and for his resurrection. Thank you for a second birth. Teach us disciples how to pass on these truths to others, to those who have never heard the good news of abundant life and deliverance from sin. In Jesus' name, we pray. Amen.

7. Parables about the Nature of Christ's Kingdom

Jesus' kingdom is different from others. It is different from political empires and from church institutions. As Jesus explained to Pilate:

"My kingdom is not of this world."

Jesus' Kingdom operates on a different plane altogether.

We have the luxury of hindsight, but the disciples are having trouble understanding the nature of the Kingdom of God that Jesus is proclaiming. They have their expectations of a messianic overthrow of the Roman oppressors and a restoration of David's throne. But they have little understanding of the true nature of the Kingdom of God of which they are ambassadors-in-training. So Jesus tells parables to explain what this Kingdom is like by comparing it to things they already understand,

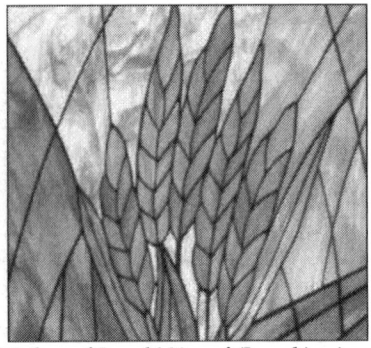

'Tribes of Israel,' Yossef (Joseph) window, stained glass, modern Synagogue of Shilo, Israel.

"What is the kingdom of God like? What shall I compare it to?" (Luke 13:18)

In this lesson I have grouped parables that focus on the *nature* of Jesus' Kingdom. Many parables could be included here that are treated in other lessons, so my selection is somewhat arbitrary.

7.1. Small but Expanding
- Parable of the Mustard Seed (Matthew 13:31-32; Mark 4:30-32; Luke 13:18-19)
- Parable of the Yeast or Leaven (Matthew 13:33; Luke 13:21)
- Parable of the Seed Growing by Itself (Mark 4:26-29)

7.2 John the Baptist and Jesus the Messiah
- Parable of the Bridegroom's Guests (Matthew 9:14-15; Mark 2:18-20; Luke 5:33-35)

7.3 The Old and the New
- Parable of the Unshrunk Cloth (Matthew 9:16; Mark 2:21; Luke 5:36)
- Parable of the Wineskins (Matthew 9:17; Mark 2:22; Luke 5:37-39)

7.4 The Flock of the Kingdom
- Parables of the Good Shepherd and the Sheep Gate (John 10:1-10)

7. Parables about the Nature of Christ's Kingdom

The Kingdom of God is Like....

Jesus begins eleven parables with the words, "The kingdom of heaven/God is like...." "Kingdom of heaven" is Matthew's way of saying "Kingdom of God" (Mark and Luke), in a way that didn't offend his Jewish readers who avoid uttering the name of God. Most of these parables we consider elsewhere.[1] But here we'll examine three parables that begin with the words, "The kingdom of heaven/God is like...."

1. Parable of the Mustard Seed,
2. Parable of the Yeast or Leaven, and
3. Parable of the Seed Growing by Itself.

7.1. Small but Expanding

We begin our study of the nature of Jesus' Kingdom with a pair of parables that make the point that the Kingdom is small but expanding rapidly to become quite large. In Matthew both occur as part of the "parables chapter," Matthew 13. In a similar setting, Mark only includes the Parable of the Mustard Seed. In Luke, the parables occur amidst other parables and the healing of the bent-over woman.

Parable of the Mustard Seed (Matthew 13:31-32; Mark 4:30-32; Luke 13:18-19; §97)

Jesus uses the contrast between the proverbial "smallest seed" in the Parable of the Mustard Seed.

> "Then Jesus asked, 'What is the kingdom of God like? What shall I compare it to? It is like a mustard seed, which a man took and planted in his garden. It grew and became a tree, and the birds of the air perched in its branches.'" (Luke 13:18-19)

Matthew and Mark note that the mustard seed was considered by the Jews as the smallest of seeds. This isn't a scientific statement, only a commonly accepted generalization. Elsewhere, Jesus uses the mustard seed to describe the tiniest amount of faith.[2]

"Mustard" is usually identified as *Sinapis nigra*, "black mustard," which grows to a shrub about 4 feet high, but occasionally can grow to 15 feet high and would qualify as a "tree." Three varieties of mustard were grown in gardens because of their aromatic seeds.[3] Jesus

---

[1] Parable of the Unmerciful Servant (Lesson 1.2); Parable of the Marriage Feast (Lesson 2.2); Weeds or Tares (Lesson 4.2); the Net (Lesson 4.2); the Laborers in the Vineyard (Lesson 4.3); the Hidden Treasure (Lesson 8.5); Pearl of Great Price (Lesson 8.5); and Scribes of the Kingdom (Lesson 12.4).
[2] Analogy of the Faith of a Mustard Seed, Lesson 10.4.
[3] R.K. Harrison, "Mustard," ISBE 3:449.

mentions the growth, but the main emphasis seems to be on the beginning (very small) and the end (very large). Small beginnings, large endings.

Birds Perching in Its Branches (Luke 13:19b)

There's one more detail to consider:

"The birds of the air perched in its branches." (Luke 13:19b)

Probably all that means is that the tree was large enough to sustain life around it as a mini-ecosystem. This isn't just a marginal tree, but one that provides support for wildlife. Some think that the birds of the air represent the Gentile nations seeking refuge with Israel.[4] That may be so (as a secondary allegory), but I think "the birds of the air perched in its branches" is the way Jesus rounded out his story, in words echoing Daniel 4:12, 21 and Ezekiel 17:23; 31:6.[5]

Here the birds don't represent enemies, but rather welcome guests (contrary to birds in the Parable of the Sower, Lesson 8.1). Jesus' use of examples is flexible. Just because an item was used for evil in one parable doesn't mean it has to have the same significance in another.

The point is that the proverbial tiniest seed can produce a tree. So the Kingdom, though small now, will grow exponentially into a large kingdom with major significance of its own.

Parable of the Yeast or Leaven (Matthew 13:33, §98; Luke 13:20-21, §164)

The Parable of the Leaven makes a similar point.

"Again he asked, 'What shall I compare the kingdom of God to? It is like yeast[6] that a woman took and mixed into a large amount of flour until it worked all through the dough.'" (Luke 13:20-21)

In the West we commonly purchase baker's yeast compressed in small blocks (from the late 18th century) or in dry granulated form in small packets (from World War II). But in Jesus' day, a portion of leavened fermented dough from the previous day's baking was set aside and, after softening with water, was mixed with the dough for the next day's baking, passing on the live yeast from one batch to the next.[7] Leaven was commonly used in baking the round, relatively flat barley or wheat loaves that were the common fare of the Israelites.

---

[4] They cite Daniel 4:12, 21; Psalm 104:13; Ezekiel 17:23; 31:6; and 1 Enoch 90:30.
[5] Jeremias, *Parables*, p. 147. Dodd, *Parables*, p. 153. T.W. Manson, *The Sayings of Jesus* (Eerdmans/SCM Press, 1957).
[6] *Zumē*, "fermented dough, leaven." The rendering "yeast" popularly suggests a product foreign to ancient baking practice (BGAD 429, 1).
[7] Adrianus Van Selms, "Bread," ISBE 1:540-544.

7. Parables about the Nature of Christ's Kingdom

Jesus compares the Kingdom of God to a small lump of yeasty dough that is kneaded into a large amount of flour until it is homogenized.

If you've never baked a loaf of bread, you may not understand the radical difference that yeast makes. You take flour, water, a bit of oil, and salt and knead them together with some softened yeast. It is pretty compact at this point, and, if you were to bake now, the bread would come out heavy and hard.

As the yeast begins to metabolize the sugars in the dough, it forms carbon dioxide that puffs into tiny gas pockets all throughout the dough. The gas can't escape because of the elastic gluten in the flour, so these pockets of gas stay in the loaf making the lump of dough larger – rising. When the loaf finally goes into the oven, the gas expands even more as the temperature rises, until the dough finally bakes, holding the shape of those tiny gas pockets, now filled with air, making a light, tasty loaf.

John Everett Millais, 'Parable – The Leaven' (c. 1860), watercolor on paper, 5.3 x 4.2 inches, Aberdeen Art Gallery, Aberdeen, Scotland.

And as the bread rises, the size increases many-fold. When I bake bread, I use a large pottery bowl and place the kneaded lump dough in the bottom of the bowl. By the time it has risen, the dough is nearly overflowing the bowl.

What's the point of the parable? A small amount of yeast will leaven a large amount of dough. Small beginnings, large endings.

Occasionally people get confused about this parable. They reason that since leaven is sometimes used negatively elsewhere in the Bible,[8] that it must be negative in the Parable of the Leaven. Not so. Jesus shows quite a bit of flexibility in using comparisons. In Jesus Analogy of the Yeast of the Pharisees (Lesson 9.2), for example, Jesus makes the same point about yeast as in this parable, warning his disciples against the hypocrisy of the Pharisees that can start small and grow to become large and pervasive.

Small Beginnings, Much Discouragement

Sometimes we get discouraged. What we've worked so hard to do seems so small and insignificant, like a mustard seed or a bit of yeast – so small, so hopeless, so tiny. The disciples may have felt that way about the Kingdom of God. Here is an itinerant carpenter-preacher speaking in villages in a minor Roman province. Not very impressive when you look at the big picture. But within a single generation after Christ's death, Christianity had spread all over

---

[8] Luke 12:1; 1 Corinthians 5:6-8; Galatians 5:9.

the Roman empire and beyond – India to the East, Ethiopia to the South, and Britannia to the West.

Just because the Kingdom doesn't seem very great as yet, Jesus is saying that it will grow. The Kingdom of God begins as small and insignificant, but grows to become large and powerful. Mustard seeds versus trees, tiny leaven-lumps versus large bread loaves, fresh and fragrant from rising, and ready for the oven.

There's an old hymn with a chorus that begins, "Little is much when God is in it."[9] The Prophet Zechariah warns fragile Israel after the Exile:

> "Don't despise the day of small things." (Zechariah 4:10)[10]

Too often we, like Jesus' first disciples, are tempted to give up when we see the tiny, struggling beginnings and think that's all there will be. But the seeds we sow today will grow great crops in season, even if we never live to see them. "We walk by faith, not by sight" (2 Corinthians 5:7, KJV).

> **Q28. (Luke 13:18-21) What lesson did Jesus intend his disciples to learn from the Parables of the Mustard Seed and the Yeast or Leaven? Why might the disciples be discouraged by the "size" of the Kingdom? Why are we sometimes discouraged in Christian work? Why are patience and faith so important for disciples?**
> https://www.joyfulheart.com/forums/topic/2202-q28-mustard-seed-and-leaven/

Parable of the Seed Growing by Itself (Mark 4:26-29, §95)
(Also known as the Parable of the Seed Growing Secretly)

There is a third parable that illustrates the growth of the Kingdom, found only in Mark, right before the Parable of the Mustard Seed in Mark's chapter of parables.

> "²⁶ This is what the kingdom of God is like. A man scatters seed on the ground.
> ²⁷ Night and day, whether he sleeps or gets up, the seed sprouts and grows,[11] though

---

[9] "Little is Much When God Is in It" is the title of a 1924 gospel hymn by Kittie L. Suffield.
[10] See my article "Don't Despise the Day of Small Things" www.joyfulheart.com/encourag/small-tg.htm
[11] "Sprout/s" (NIV, ESV, RSV), "spring" (KJV) is *blastanō*, "to emerge as new growth, bud, sprout" (BDAG 177, 2). "Grows" (NIV) is *mēkunō*, "make long," middle, become long, grow (long)" (BDAG 648).

he does not know how.[12] 28 All by itself[13] the soil produces grain – first the stalk, then the head, then the full kernel in the head. 29 As soon as the grain is ripe,[14] he puts the sickle[15] to it, because the harvest has come." (Mark 4:26-29)

Jesus' society is primarily agricultural. Everyone outside of a large city – even craftsmen – would have a garden plot and perhaps a sheep, cow, or goat. Planting was familiar. This parable, however, assumes large scale planting, such as a field of barley or wheat.

Jesus describes the course of growth:

"First the stalk, then the head, then the full kernel in the head." (Mark 4:28b)

Of course, the farmer is active in weeding and protecting the growing crop, and perhaps watering, but he doesn't have any part in its actual growth. He starts the process by sowing and completes it by harvesting.

What does it mean? Some have focused on the inactivity of the farmer, though the text doesn't actually mention it. Others have allegorized the parable – the sower is Jesus, they say, and the harvest is the End Time. Probably the eschatological harvest is in mind in this parable, but that isn't the point of the parable. The key phrase is "by itself" or "of itself."

"**All by itself** the soil produces grain[16] – first the stalk, then the head, then the full kernel in the head." (Mark 4:28)

The Greek word is *automatos* (from which we get our word "automatic"). It means, "pertaining to something that happens without visible cause, by itself."[17] It is used elsewhere of doors opening themselves, of plants growing without help, etc.[18]

This is a parable of inevitability and thus an encouragement to patience. The seed has been planted already by God and its growth is evident in the ministry of Jesus. And just as surely

---

[12] "How" is the particle *hōs*, here, "a comparative particle, marking the manner in which something proceeds, "as, like," corresponding to *outōs* – "so, in such a way." In our passage, "(in such a way) as he himself does not know = he himself does not know how, without his knowing (just) how" (BDAG 1103, 1a).

[13] "All by itself" (NIV), "by/of itself/herself" (ESV, NRSV, KJV) is *automatos* (from which we get "automatic"), "pertaining to something that happens without visible cause, by itself" (BDAG 152).

[14] "Is ripe" (NIV, ESV, NRSV), "is brought forth" (KJV) is *paradidōmi*, "to make it possible for something to happen, allow, permit," here, "when the (condition of the) crop permits" (BDAG 763, 4).

[15] "Sickle" is *drepanon*, "an agricultural implement consisting of a curved blade and a handle, used for a variety of purposes, sickle" (BDAG 261).

[16] Of course, we know (and Jesus' hearers knew) that the seed produces the growth of the plant, but only after the seed has been planted in the soil and flourishes with the moisture the soil provides (John 12:24).

[17] *Automatos*, BDAG 152.

[18] Acts 12:10; Leviticus 25:5, 11 (LXX); Josephus, *Antiquities*, 1:54; 12:317; *Life* 11), etc.

as planting the seed will lead to an inevitable harvest, so the Kingdom of God is growing and maturing, and the harvest will come in due time at the End of the Age.[19] As James tells us:

> "Be patient, then, brothers, until the Lord's coming. See how the farmer waits for the land to yield its valuable crop and how patient he is for the autumn and spring rains. You too, be patient and stand firm, because the Lord's coming is near." (James 5:7-8)

We too must be patient, because though delayed, the Harvest of the Kingdom will surely come!

7.2 John the Baptist and Jesus the Messiah

Parable of the Bridegroom's Guests (Matthew 9:14-15; Mark 2:18-20; Luke 5:33-35; §54)

Jesus has been criticized by the Pharisees and teachers of the law that his disciples didn't fast like "serious" followers of God, such the Pharisees and the disciples of John the Baptist.

> "They said to him, 'John's disciples often fast and pray, and so do the disciples of the Pharisees, but yours go on eating and drinking.'" (Luke 5:33)

What's wrong your disciples – and by clear implication – what's wrong with you?

The Bridegroom's Celebration

> [34] Jesus answered, 'Can you make the guests of the bridegroom fast while he is with them? [35] But the time will come when the bridegroom will be taken from them; in those days they will fast.'" (Luke 5:33-35)

Jesus answers by referring to his disciples as "guests of the bridegroom." You don't fast at a wedding celebration.

Weddings in Jesus' day, as in ours, are joyous affairs. The custom in those days was that the bridegroom and his family were to put on the celebration (John 2:9-10), not the bride's family as in American custom. As we saw in the Parable of the Wise and Foolish Virgins

---

[19] Hunter sees this parable as "a call to patience.... Stage by stage, quietly but irresistibly, it grows to harvest, whether men will or no" (Hunter, *Parables*, p. 45). Jeremias says, "With the same certainty as the harvest comes for the husbandman after his long waiting, does God when his hour has come, when the eschatological term is complete, bring in the Last Judgment and the Kingdom" (Jeremias, *Parables*, pp. 151-152). France sees this as a parable "about rightly interpreting and responding to the period of apparent inaction of the kingdom of God. Despite appearances to the contrary, it is growing, and the harvest will come. But it will come in God's time and in God's way, not by human effort or in accordance with human logic" (France, *Mark*, p. 215). Snodgrass puts it this way: "Jesus' ministry has inaugurated a sequence of action leading to the fullness of God's kingdom, just as surely as sowing sets in play a spontaneous process leading to harvest" (Snodgrass, *Stories*, p. 189).

(Lesson 5.2), the groom would go to the bride's home to fetch her and her attendants, and the couple would lead them in a procession to the groom's house where the celebration would take place. Though the consummation would take place that night, the party might go on for as long as a week with friends and family who had traveled some distance to attend.

Jesus is saying in this parable that, just as you don't fast while the bridegroom hosts the wedding celebration, neither should my disciples fast while I am ushering in the Kingdom of God. It is a time for celebration, not for mourning. Then he adds, darkly,

> "But the time will come when the bridegroom will be taken from them; in those days they will fast." (Luke 5:35)

Jesus knew that his crucifixion and death lay ahead and refers to it here. Interestingly, John the Baptist told the Parable of the Bridegroom's Friend, with Jesus as the Bridegroom and himself as the best man (see Appendix 4.2). "He must increase, but I must decrease."

The Biblical Imagery of Wife and Bride

Jesus clearly identifies himself with the bridegroom in this parable. It is a powerful image! This wedding analogy carries with it the overtones from the Old Testament of Israel as the bride of God,[20] which the New Testament carries forward to the Church as the bride of Christ,[21] culminating in the great Marriage Supper of the Lamb (Revelation 19:6-9).

Having said that, I doubt that Jesus is referring *directly* to this theme of the Bridegroom and the Bride, or he would have spelled it out more explicitly.[22] Rather he is probably using this simple analogy of rejoicing with a bridegroom to explain why this wasn't to be a time of fasting, but a time of rejoicing in the Messiah and the Kingdom he is bringing.

7.3 The Old and the New

Immediately, following Jesus' Parable of the Bridegroom's Guests, Jesus gives a pair of parables to explain that his coming Kingdom is different than what people expect. It doesn't follow the old tried-and-true traditions. It is new and exclusive and must not be considered the same as the past. These are the Parable of the Unshrunk Cloth and the Parable of the Wineskins.

---

[20] Isaiah 62:4-5; Jeremiah 2:2; 3:20; Ezekiel 16:8; 23:4; Hosea 2:19-20.

[21] 2 Corinthians 11:2; Ephesians 5:25-32; Revelation 19:7-8; 21:2; 22:17.

[22] In Jesus' day, the term "bridegroom" didn't seem to be laden with Messianic connotations, though France concludes, "This verse ... may be properly read as a veiled messianic claim" (France, *Mark*, p. 139). Reference to the Messiah as bridegroom in the Old Testament and later Jewish writings wasn't pronounced, though a couple of Qumran references could be interpreted as possibly messianic (D.J. Williams, "Bride, Bridegroom," DJG 87, citing Jeremias *nymphē, nymphios*, TDNT 4:1099-1106). Snodgrass, *Stories*, p. 514; Jocelyn McWhirter, "Bride, Bridegroom," DJG2, p. 97.

Parable of the Unshrunk Cloth (Matthew 9:16; Mark 2:21; Luke 5:36; §54)

As you recall, the Pharisees and scribes are insisting that Jesus and his disciples should fast. In response, Jesus explains in these parables why it is important that he doesn't fit his new teaching into their mold. First, he uses the metaphor of patched garments:

> "No one sews a patch of unshrunk[23] cloth on an old garment, for the patch will pull away from the garment, making the tear worse." (Matthew 9:16)

As I write this it is a popular fashion for young women (and some men) to wear jeans that are frayed and torn at the knees. They are marketed as "ripped," "torn," or "distressed." No patches. But in Jesus' day clothing was expensive. Keeping clothing in repair was a point of pride. Thus, patching one's clothing was a common task and Jesus' hearers would know the problems inherent in patching. Patching with unshrunk cloth would cause the patch to tear from its stitches when it was washed and shrunk the first time.

Jesus is saying that to try to attach the new to the old won't look right and will eventually tear again.

Parable of the Wineskins (Matthew 9:17; Mark 2:22; Luke 5:37-39; §54)

Jesus makes the same point with a parable about new wine and old.

> "37 And no one pours new wine into old wineskins.[24] If he does, the new wine will burst the skins, the wine will run out and the wineskins will be ruined. 38 No, new wine must be poured into new wineskins." (Luke 5:37-38)

Jesus is referring to fairly large wine containers made of the skins of goats used to store the wine while it fermented.[25]

---

[23] "Unshrunk" (NIV, ESV, NRSV), "new" (KJV) is *agnaphos*, "pertaining to cloth fresh from the weaver's loom, not fulled, unshrunken, unsized, new" (BDAG 12). Matthew and Mark make explicit the "unshrunk (*agnaphos*) cloth" that is implied by Luke's "new (*kainos*) garment" (Matthew 9:16; Mark 2:21).

[24] "Wineskins" (NIV, ESV, NRSV), "bottles" (KJV) is *askos*, "a leather bag," especially, "wine-skin" (BDAG 143).

[25] The KJV translation "bottles" may confuse us, but "bottle" was used in Elizabethan English of a container made of skin to store liquids, common from medieval times through the eighteenth century.

Winemaking

In Jesus' day, wine was made by treading on the grapes barefoot in a wine press, a square or circular pit hewn out of the rock, or dug out and lined with rocks and sealed with plaster.[26] The juice from the pit then flowed through a channel into a lower vessel, a wine vat which functioned as a collecting and fermenting container for the grape juice or "must."

In the warm climate of Palestine, grape juice began to ferment very quickly and there was no easy way to prevent fermentation. After the first state of fermentation had taken place in the wine vat, the wine was separated from the lees (that is, sediment of dead yeast, tartar crystals, small fragments of grape skins, etc.) and strained through a sieve or piece of cloth (cf. Matthew 23:24). After four to six days, it was poured into clay jars (Jeremiah 48:11) or animal skins for storage and further fermentation.[27]

Wineskins were made of whole tanned goatskins or sheepskins where the legs and tail were cut off and sewn shut.[28] A skin might hold about 8 to 10 gallons (30 to 40 liters), depending upon the size of the animal.

Niko Pirosmani, 'Porter with a Wineskin' (before 1919), oil on oilcloth, 15 x 34 cm. State Museum of Fine Arts, Tbilisi, Republic of Georgia.

Imagine a large leather bag with nubbins bulging out where the legs and tail once were, the neck tied off where the wine has been poured in. The whole large skin would be bulging almost to bursting as the carbon dioxide gas generated by the fermentation process stretched it to its limit. This image is well described by Job:

> "For I am full of words,
> and the spirit within me compels me;
> inside I am like bottled-up wine,
> like new wineskins ready to burst." (Job 32:18-19)

Fermentation in the wineskin might continue for another two to four months until the process slows down and stops.[29] By that time the skin has been stretched to its limit and the alcohol level is about 12%. The collagen protein that gives the leather its elasticity has been

---

[26] See Isaiah 63:2-3; Job 24:11b; Lamentations 1:15; Joel 3:13; Matthew 21:33; Revelation 14:19-20; 19:15, where treading the winepress was a symbol of judgment.
[27] Barry L. Bandstra, "Wine Press, Winevat," ISBE 4:1072; and Duane F. Watson, "Wine," DJG 870-873.
[28] 1 Samuel 1:24; 10:3; 16:20; 25:18; 2 Samuel 16:1.
[29] Watson, DJG 871.

stretched out by the pressure and denatured by the alcohol, destroying its natural resiliency. The skin's ability to contract and stretch again has been lost.

New Wine in Old Wineskins (Luke 5:37-38)

Jesus' hearers knew all about wineskins and the aging of leather.

> "No one pours new wine into old wineskins. If he does, the new wine will burst the skins, the wine will run out and the wineskins will be ruined. No, new wine must be poured into new wineskins." (Luke 5:37-38)

Here is the same contrast of old and new that we saw in the Parable of the Unshrunk Cloth. His point is the same: you can't join the new to the old or you'll ruin both the new wine and the old skin. The gas pressure from the fermentation would eventually be so great that the inflexible old skin would rupture and the new wine would gush out onto the ground and be wasted.

The Old Is Better (Luke 5:39)

What is Jesus getting at? Jesus has come with a radical gospel of Good News to the poor, the disenfranchised, the oppressed, the sick, the brokenhearted (Luke 4:18-19). He speaks with authority, rather than the casuistry, the tortured interpretations of religious texts, used by the scribes of his day. Their man-made rules of who a person can eat with and how he should fast would just get in the way. They are externals. Jesus, on the other hand, is aiming to expose afresh the heart of the ancient faith. He helps them to return anew to love for God and for one's neighbor, to do mercy and love justice and walk humbly with their God (Micah 6:8). These are the core of the Hebrew faith – its true life, not the dead Pharisaical external traditions that offer an appearance of piety but don't change the heart (see Colossians 2:23).

You may think that this is a dead issue, but it has a way of raising its head again and again. Paul, trained as a strict Pharisee, grasps the radical nature of salvation by grace through faith, and goes preaching it boldly throughout the Mediterranean. Soon he is called on the carpet to explain why he isn't imposing the familiar Jewish regulations on his Gentile converts (Acts 15). Again and again, he has to insist that we are free in Christ, so we must not become entangled again in a legalistic religion trying to pass itself off as Christianity (Galatians 5). The Judaizers tried to infect church after church with their legalism; the recipients of the Letter to the Hebrews are tempted to turn again to the regulations of Judaism. Yes, legalism and an external faith are problems of every generation.

Comparing the Old and New Wine (Luke 5:39)

At the close of Luke's parable of the wineskins, Jesus adds a sentence not found in Matthew and Mark.

7. Parables about the Nature of Christ's Kingdom

> "And no one after drinking old wine wants the new, for he says, 'The old is better.'"
> (Luke 5:39)

Old wine has had a chance to mellow; new wine is more raw and biting, less pleasing to the taste, having not yet finished the process of fermentation.

Jesus is saying that it is easier to fall back to what is familiar and comfortable, rather than launch out into a life guided not by laws and regulations, but led by the Voice of the Spirit of God. The two are opposites, the old and the new. You cannot combine them without destroying both.

Pastors and church planters face this. Pastoring a long-established congregation generally offers greater security and predictability than starting a new congregation from scratch. But for all the difficulties and hardships of church planting, change is much easier in a new church than with the traditionalists, and you're able to reach many more non-Christians with the gospel in a new church designed to minister to a particular unreached slice of the culture. In an established church, it is extremely difficult to shift focus to the lost and needy of the community without major resistance.

The New Wine may not be as smooth to the tongue and finely aged. It may be a bit sharp and unrefined. But it is alive. You can't contain it in old structures. You must find new wineskins for it or none at all.

Integrating the New with the Old

That is not to say that Jesus' threw out the Old Covenant. He makes it very clear in the Sermon on the Mount that he comes to fulfill the law, not to abrogate it (Matthew 5:17-20). Jesus didn't come to set aside the law, but to strip away the Pharisees' precious oral tradition so people can see the true power and spirit of the law, and repent, preparing for the coming of the Kingdom. The Spirit Jesus sends now fulfills the law within us (Romans 8:1-4; Galatians 5:16-23).

> **Q29. (Luke 5:36-39) What did Jesus intend his disciples to learn from the Parables of the Unshrunk Cloth and the Wineskins? Why are we tempted to say, "The old wine is better?" How might our church traditions limit the Holy Spirit's work in our day? How do these parables illustrate the need for newly planted churches?**
> **https://www.joyfulheart.com/forums/topic/2203-q29-unshrunk-cloth-and-wineskins/**

Another parable that contrasts the old and the new is the Parable of the Scribes of the Kingdom (Matthew 13:51-52). It compares a Jesus-follower to a person who finds both old and new treasures in his treasure box. We'll examine it in Lesson 12.4.

7.4 The Flock of the Kingdom

As Jesus explains what the Kingdom of God is like, he uses analogies of a shepherd with the sheep. The analogy of the shepherd and sheep is a common one in the Bible and rich in meaning. Jesus uses the shepherd/sheep analogy quite often.

- Parable of the Lost Sheep (Luke 15:1-6, Lesson 1.1).
- Parable of the Sheep and the Goats (Matthew 25:31-46, Lesson 4.2)
- Analogies of Lost Sheep (Matthew 9:36; 10:5-6; 15:24; Lesson 12.1).
- Parables of the Good Shepherd and the Sheep Gate (John 10:1-18; Lesson 7.4)

But here, especially, in the Parables of the Good Shepherd and the Sheep Gate we see several sheep/shepherd analogies used together as Jesus explains his role in caring for his "sheep."

Parables of the Good Shepherd and the Sheep Gate (John 10:1-18)

Rather than seeing this discourse as a narrative, it is best understood as a series of teachings, spiritual lessons drawn from sheep-herding. We can see four primary analogies drawn from the pastoral images that weave through this discourse:

Statue of the Good Shepherd (c. 300-350), marble, 39 inches high. Rome, from Catacomb of Domitilla, Vatican, Museo Pio Cristiano.

1. The Sheep-pen (verses 1-2).
2. The Shepherd's voice (verses 3-5).
3. The Gate or Door of the sheep-pen (verses 6-9).
4. The Good Shepherd who lays down his life for the sheep (verses 10-18).

Rather than treat them as separate parables, however, I think it is more useful to refer to them together as Parables of the Good Shepherd and the Sheep Gate.

7. Parables about the Nature of Christ's Kingdom

Shepherds as Leaders

Throughout the ancient Near East, rulers and leaders were often spoken of as "shepherds" of their people. Ezekiel indicts Israel's shepherds – both kings and spiritual leaders – for caring only for themselves, not feeding the sheep, not healing the wounded sheep, not searching for the strays, and allowing the flock to be scattered (Ezekiel 34:2-5, 10-12). In John 9, Jesus has just dealt with the spiritual blindness of Jerusalem's shepherds, the scribes and Pharisees and members of the Sanhedrin. They weren't really interested in the sheep, only in finding cause to destroy the true Shepherd who *did* care about the flock.

The Kingdom of God is different from earthly kingdoms where the kingdom exists for the whims of the king. In God's Kingdom, the Shepherd King actually cares about his subjects and lays down his life to save them. Hallelujah.

Analogy of the Sheepfold and the Shepherd (John 10:1-2)

The first analogy Jesus draws from shepherding relates to the sheep-pen where the sheep are kept at night.

> "[1] I tell you the truth, the man who does not enter the sheep pen by the gate, but climbs in by some other way, is a thief and a robber. [2] The man who enters by the gate is the shepherd of his sheep." (John 10:1-2)

Jesus has in mind an enclosed pen, open to the sky, with a doorway[30] through which the sheep might enter.[31] Such an enclosure would protect the sheep from straying at night and from attack by wild animals, such as lions, wolves, and bears.

A pen might have been constructed next to the family's house. But I think Jesus has in mind a sheep-pen out on the grazing fields some distance from town. Such a pen would likely be made of rocks piled up to make an enclosure, since wood is scarce in this hilly, rocky terrain. A gate might have been constructed from wood or scrub brush on a crude hinge. Or perhaps the shepherd himself might sleep in the doorway

Stone sheepfold, Ameixiel Photo by Muffinn. Wikipedia, under Creative Commons Attribution 2.0 license.

---

[30] "Gate" (NIV), "door" (KJV) is *thyra*, "door," here, "a passage for entering a structure, entrance, doorway, gate" (BDAG 462, 2b).

[31] "Pen" or "fold" is *aulē*, "an area open to the sky (frequently surrounded by buildings, and in some cases partially by walls), enclosed open space, courtyard," here fold for sheep (BDAG 150, 1), in verses 1 and 16.

so that no one could get to the sheep except by climbing over his body. More on that in a moment.

In this first analogy, Jesus speaks of thieves who would try to climb over the fence or wall to steal a sheep. A shepherd or the owner of the sheep would use the gate, which would be closed and guarded at night. Only thieves[32] or bandits[33] would try to get in undetected some other way.[34]

The "thieves and robbers" in this analogy are, of course, the religious leaders who take advantage of their positions of trust to ravage God's flock. Among Jesus "woe to the Pharisees" discourse, he says.

> "You travel over land and sea to win a single convert, and when you have succeeded, you make them twice as much a child of hell as you are." (Matthew 23:15)

The identity of the "sheep-pen" isn't as clear. Israel? The church? We're not sure. Making a point with such an analogy doesn't require every element to be identified.

Analogy of the Shepherd's Voice (John 10:3-5)

Jesus' point, however, is that the legitimate shepherd comes in through the gate and his sheep know him.

> "³ The watchman opens the gate for him, and the sheep listen[35] to his voice. He calls[36] his own sheep by name[37] and leads them out. ⁴ When he has brought out all his own, he goes on ahead of them, and his sheep follow him because they know his voice. ⁵ But they will never follow a stranger; in fact, they will run away from him because they do not recognize a stranger's voice." (John 10:3-5)

Verse 3 mentions a gatekeeper.[38] When several flocks would be put in the same pen on a remote sheep-field, each of the shepherds in turn would agree to act as the gatekeeper for one of the watches of the night. Of course, the gatekeeper on duty would open up for a shepherd whose flock was contained within.

---

[32] "Thief" is *kleptēs* (from which we get our word, "kleptomaniac"), "thief" (BDAG 574).
[33] "Robber" (NIV, KJV), "bandit" (NRSV) is *lēstēs*, "robber, highwayman, bandit" (BDAG 594, 1).
[34] "Some other way" is *allachothen*, "from another place" (BDAG 46).
[35] "Listen" (NIV), "hear" (NRSV, KJV) is *akouō*, "hear," but here with the idea of "to give careful attention to, listen to, heed someone" (BDAG 38, 4).
[36] "Calls" is *phōneō*, "to produce a voiced sound/tone, frequently with reference to intensity of tone," here, "to call to oneself, summon" (BDAG 107, 3).
[37] "By name" (*kat' onoma*).
[38] "Watchman" (NIV), "gatekeeper" (NRSV, ESV), "porter" (KJV) is *thyrōros*, "doorkeeper, gatekeeper" (BDAG 462).

When you have several flocks penned together for the night, the way they get sorted out in the morning is by each sheep recognizing its own shepherd's voice and coming when he calls them out of the pen for another day of grazing. The shepherd might even have a name for every sheep that he might call out if the sheep didn't come when he called the flock. Jesus is referring to the intimate relationship between the shepherd and his own sheep – mutual knowledge.

George Adam Smith, who traveled in the Holy Land at the end of the nineteenth century before its modern development and westernization, relates an incident that illustrates this passage:

> "Sometimes we enjoyed our noonday rest beside one of those Judean wells, to which three or four shepherds come down with their flocks. The flocks mixed with each other and we wondered how each shepherd would get his own again. But after the watering and the playing were over, the shepherds one by one went up different sides of the valley, and each called out his peculiar call; and the sheep of each drew out of the crowd to their own shepherd, and the flocks passed away as orderly as they came."[39]

The sheep knows its shepherd's voice.

I believe that one of the neglected, seldom-taught skills necessary to being a disciple, is to learn to discern Jesus' voice. We hear many voices – the pressures of our society's expectations, our family's desires, our own selfish desires, our own inner voices. It is possible to hear Jesus' voice and distinguish it from the others, but we must make a practice of learning which is which. It is good to learn this with the help of a more mature Christian brother or sister.

Once we learn to discern Jesus' voice – the leading of the Spirit, same thing – then he can guide us, teach us, and use us much more effectively than before. For more on this see my study, *Listening for God's Voice: A Discipleship Guide to a Closer Walk* (JesusWalk Publications, 2018). www.jesuswalk.com/voice/

Q30. (John 10:1-5) Why is knowing the Shepherd's voice and obeying it so very important for disciples? What happens when we act independently of the Shepherd? What causes sheep to stray?
https://www.joyfulheart.com/forums/topic/2204-q30-shepherds-voice/

---

[39] George Adam Smith, *The Historical Geography of the Holy Land* (New York: A.C. Armstrong and Son, 1900), p. 312.

Analogy of the Gate for the Sheep (John 10:6-9)

The analogy is confusing to some of Jesus' hearers, so he explains it a bit more, at the same time adding new elements and shifting the analogy some.

> "⁶ Jesus used this figure of speech[40], but they did not understand what he was telling them. ⁷ Therefore Jesus said again, 'I tell you the truth, I am the gate for the sheep. ⁸ All who ever came before me were thieves and robbers, but the sheep did not listen to them. ⁹ I am the gate; whoever enters through me will be saved. He will come in and go out, and find pasture[41].'" (John 10:6-9)

Jesus shifts his analogy from the multiple-flock sheep pen with an assigned gatekeeper to one in which all the sheep in the pen belong to the same shepherd on a particular night.

In this third of his "I AM" declarations, Jesus says in verse 7b, "I am the gate/door for the sheep.[42] Perhaps he is comparing himself to a gate to protect the sheep, swinging open on hinges to let the sheep through. But there is another possibility, illustrated by a story told by George Adam Smith to Bible commentator G. Campbell Morgan.

> "[Smith] was one day travelling with a guide and came across a shepherd and his sheep. The man showed him the fold into which the sheep were led at night. It consisted of four walls, with a way in. [Smith] said to him, 'That is where they go at night?' 'Yes,' said the shepherd, 'and when they are there, they are perfectly safe.' 'But there is no door,' said [Smith]. 'I am the door,' said the shepherd. '... When the light has gone and all the sheep are inside, I lie in that open space, and no sheep ever goes out but across my body, and no wolf comes in unless he crosses my body; I am the door.'"[43]

However, we understand Jesus' words, whether as a swinging gate or the shepherd's own body serving as a gate, Jesus teaches that he is both the Protector (Savior) of the sheep, and their Point of Access to life beyond the fold – pasture, water, life, and ultimately, the Kingdom of God in the presence of the Father.

Abundant Life (John 10:10)

Now Jesus repeats and amplifies this idea further.

---

[40] *Paroimia*, "pithy saying" (BDAG 779, 2). For more on this see Appendix 3. A Vocabulary for Parables and Analogies.

[41] "Pasture" is *nomē*, generally, "pasturing-place, grazing land, pasturage" (BDAG 675, 1).

[42] See my study, *John's Gospel: A Discipleship Journey with Jesus* (JesusWalk Publications, 2015, Appendix 4. The "I Am" Passages in John's Gospel (www.jesuswalk.com/john/appendix_4.htm).

[43] Morris, *John*, p. 507, n. 30, citing G. Campbell Morgan, *The Gospel According to John* (London and Edinburgh, 1951). In the fuller quote, Smith explains that the shepherd "was not a Christian man, he was not speaking in the language of the New Testament. He was speaking from the Arab shepherd's standpoint."

7. Parables about the Nature of Christ's Kingdom

"The thief comes only to steal and kill and destroy;[44] I have come that they may have life, and have it to the full." (John 10:10)

Jesus is the herd's protection against thieves, who are the false Jewish religious leaders. Jesus' motive is for the sheep to have a full life – protection from wolves and thieves, as well as pasture, water to drink, and the shepherd's experienced hands to rescue them and bind up their wounds. The words of the Twenty-Third Psalm come to mind:

> "[1] The LORD is my shepherd;
> I shall not want.
> [2] He makes me lie down in green pastures.
> He leads me beside still waters.
> [3] He restores my soul.
> He leads me in paths of righteousness for his name's sake.
> [4] Even though I walk through the valley of the shadow of death,
> I will fear no evil,
> for you are with me; your rod and your staff,
> they comfort me...." (Psalm 23:1-4, ESV)

Some see the Christian life as no fun, somehow constrained and diminished by the restrictions of Jesus' commands. But true disciples realize that only in Jesus' care can they truly flourish. They are healed within and protected without. They can live life to the full[45] as it was intended to be lived.

Analogy of the Shepherd Laying Down His Life for the Sheep (John 10:11-13)

Now Jesus changes the analogy once again. In verse 10a, the threat was thieves who would try to break into the fold. In verse 11, the figure turns to threat from predators – a wolf, bear, or lion. The predator's strategy would be to suddenly attack the flock, which will scatter. The predator then would go after the slowest sheep to react – usually the youngest or weakest of the flock.

> "[11] I am the good shepherd. The good shepherd lays down[46] his life for the sheep. [12] The hired hand is not the shepherd who owns the sheep. So when he sees the wolf

---

[44] "Destroy" is *apollymi*, "ruin, destroy," especially, "put to death" (BDAG 116, 1aα).

[45] In verse 10b, "to the full" (NIV), "abundantly" (NRSV, KJV) is *perissos*, "exceeding the usual number or size ... pertaining to being extraordinary in amount, abundant, profuse," here, "going beyond what is necessary" (BDAG 805, 2a).

[46] "Lays down" (NIV, NRSV) is *tithēmi*, "put, place," here, in the sense, "lay down or give (up) one's life" (verses 11, 15, 17, and 18; also in John 13:37-38; 15:13; and 1 John 3:16) (BDAG 1003, 1bβ). In verses 11 and 15 (but not verse 17 and 18), KJV text is "giveth," *didōmi*, "give," supported by p⁴⁵ Aleph* D. The Editorial Committee prefers *tithēmi*, which they say is characteristically Johannine, while *didōmi* is found in the

coming, he abandons[47] the sheep and runs away.[48] Then the wolf attacks[49] the flock and scatters[50] it. [13] The man runs away because he is a hired hand and cares[51] nothing for the sheep." (John 10:11-13)

A hired hand – here again probably representing the Jewish leaders – isn't willing to risk his life fighting off a dangerous animal like a wolf. But the owner of the sheep doesn't run. Rather he stands up to the predator, ready to "lay down his life for the sheep." We think of David as a young shepherd, who explained to Saul, just before going out to defeat Goliath:

> "Your servant has been keeping his father's sheep. When a lion or a bear came and carried off a sheep from the flock, I went after it, struck it and rescued the sheep from its mouth. When it turned on me, I seized it by its hair, struck it and killed it." (1 Samuel 17:34-35)

Of course, when Jesus talks about laying down his life for the sheep, he is not talking merely about taking risks to protect the sheep from predators. This is a thinly veiled reference to his death on the cross, to bear our sins to deliver us from sin and its consequences.

This theme of the shepherd laying down his life for the sheep is repeated five times in this discourse. It is therefore vital for us to grasp its importance.

> "The good shepherd **lays down** his life for the sheep." (verse 11)
>
> "I **lay down** my life for the sheep." (verse 15)
>
> "I **lay down** my life – only to take it up again. (verse 17)
>
> "No one takes it from me, but I **lay it down** of my own accord." (verse 18a)
>
> "I have authority to **lay it down** and authority to take it up again." (verse 18b)

Verses 17 and 18 talk about laying down his life, but verses 11 and 15 give the *reason*: "for the sheep," indicating a sacrifice made on behalf of another.[52]

Synoptic Gospels (Matthew 20:28; Mark 10:45). They give *tithēmi* a {B} "some degree of doubt" confidence rating (Metzger, *Textual Commentary*, p. 230).

[47] "Abandons" (NIV), "leaves" (NRSV, KJV) is *aphiēmi*, here, "to move away, with implication of causing a separation, leave, depart from ... abandon" (BDAG 156, 3a).

[48] "Runs away" (NIV, NRSV), "flees" (ESV, KJV) is *pheugō*, "to seek safety in flight, flee" (BDAG 1052, 1).

[49] "Attacks" (NIV), "snatches" (NRSV), "catcheth" (KJV) is *harpazō*, "snatch, seize," that is, take suddenly and vehemently, "to make off with someone's property by attacking or seizing, steal, carry off, drag away something" (BDAG 134, 1).

[50] "Scatters" is *skorpizō*, "to cause a group or gathering to go in various directions, scatter, disperse" (BDAG 931, 1).

[51] "Care" is *melomai*, "be an object of care, be a cause of concern" (BDAG 628).

[52] The preposition *hyper* is used with the genitive case: "a marker indicating that an activity or event is in some entity's interest, for, in behalf of, for the sake of someone/something" (BDAG 1030, 1aε). We also see this expression of "laying down one's life" at John 13:37-38; 15:13; and 1 John 3:16. The Greek parallels that use the verb *tithēmi*, "to put, lay," all denote taking a risk rather than full sacrifice of life as in John. This is John's

I Am the Good Shepherd (John 10:11, 14)

In verses 11 and 14, "I am the Good Shepherd," is the fourth of John's seven "I AM" declarations.[53] The "Good Shepherd" is prepared to lay down his life for his sheep. The Greek word for "good" is *kalos*, which may also carry the idea of "beautiful" – the "Beautiful Shepherd" (though that is probably an over-translation).[54] It also carries the ideas of the "Noble Shepherd"[55] – one who stands up for his sheep and does not run away when his life is threatened.

Mutual Knowledge (John 10:14-15)

> "[14] I am the good shepherd; I know[56] my sheep and my sheep know me – [15] just as the Father knows me and I know the Father – and I lay down my life for the sheep." (John 10:14-15)

Jesus is referring to the mutual, intimate knowledge of the shepherd for the sheep, the shepherd who can call each of them by his or her special name (verse 3). He knows their peculiarities and weaknesses, and accommodates for these as he shepherds them. And in turn, they trust their shepherd because he always looks out for them. He rescues them when they get lost or caught in something. Heals them when they are sick or injured. Brings them to the best places to graze and water. They can trust him, so when he speaks, they listen and follow.

Verse 15a suggests that this intimate knowledge and love between the shepherd and his sheep is a picture of the intimate knowledge, love, and trust between the Son and the Father.

My dear friend, how intimate is your knowledge of your Shepherd? How much do you trust him to lead you better than you can lead yourself? How much do you love him? How much do you listen for his voice, or do you let it be drowned out by the noise of the world? He longs for you to know him and love him as he knows you.

Q31. (John 10:6-15) Why does a true shepherd "lay down his life for the sheep"? How did Jesus' do this for his disciples? For us? In what way did Jesus intend his disciples to learn that they, too, must be willing to lay down their lives for the sheep? Can you

---

way of reproducing Jesus' saying in Mark 10:45, to "give his life as a ransom for many" (Christian Maurer, *tithēmi*, TDNT 8:156-157).

[53] See my study, *John's Gospel: A Discipleship Journey with Jesus* (JesusWalk Publications, 2015, Appendix 4. The "I Am" Passages in John's Gospel (www.jesuswalk.com/john/appendix_4.htm).

[54] Morris, *John*, p. 509, n. 34, citing Rieu.

[55] Beasley-Murray, *John*, p. 170.

[56] "Know" four times in verses 14 and 15 is the generic word *ginōskō*, "to know," here of persons, "know someone" (BDAG 200, 6aβ).

think of any examples where Christ's servants have done this?
https://www.joyfulheart.com/forums/topic/2205-q31-laying-down-his-life/

Prayer

Father, mature us as disciples. Help us to see not our own smallness, but your greatness, not our own importance, but your preeminence. And help us to let go of the traditions and self-imposed restraints that prevent your power from breaking forth into the world. Forgive us, and lead us to better things. We pray in Jesus' name, Amen.

8. Parables about Responding to the Kingdom

Jesus tells parables to train his disciples, to help them understand, to help them grasp what is very, very new to them. One area they need to understand is receptivity. Who will have ears to hear? What does real faith look like in contrast to pseudo-faith? Jesus Messiah was rejected by his own people.

"He came to that which was his own, but his own did not **receive** him." (John 1:11)

These parables we'll look at here examine various degrees of receptivity, as well what pushing into the Kingdom and knowing the Lord look like when they are authentic.

8.1 Receptivity to the Kingdom

- Parable of the Sower (Matthew 13:1-9, 18-23; Mark 4:3-9, 13-20; Luke 8:4-8, 11-15)
- Saying: Pearls before Swine (Matthew 7:6)

James J. Tissot, "The Sower" (1886-96), gouache over graphite on gray wove paper, 9.75 x 5.4 inches, Brooklyn Museum, New York.

8.2 Forcible Nature of Discipleship

- Parable of the Narrow Door (Luke 13:23-27)

8.3 The Priority of Discipleship

- Analogy of Foxholes and Nests (Matthew 18:19-20; Luke 5:57-58)
- Analogy of Dead Burying the Dead (Matthew 18:21-22; Luke 9:59-60)
- Analogy of Looking Back from the Plow (Luke 9:61-62)

8.4 Counting the Cost of Discipleship

- Parable of the Tower-Builder (Luke 14:28-30)
- Parable of the Warring King (Luke 14:31-32)
- Parable of Taking Up One's Cross (Matthew 16:24-25; Mark 8:34-35; Luke 9:23-24; Matthew 10:37-39; Luke 14:25-27)

8.5 Ultimate Prize of the Kingdom

- Parable of the Hidden Treasure (Matthew 13:44)
- Parable of the Pearl of Great Price (Matthew 13:45-46)

8.1 Receptivity to the Kingdom

Parable of the Sower (Matthew 13:1-9, 18-23; Mark 4:3-9, 13-20; Luke 8:4-8, 11-15; §§90, 93)
(Also known as the Parable of the Soils)

One of the most difficult experiences for disciples in any age is to see people begin the journey of following Jesus, only to fall back, and ultimately fall away. It can be deeply discouraging and make you doubt yourself and your ministry!

To teach his disciples about this, Jesus tells the Parable of the Sower. It could well be called the Parable of the Soils, since the quality of the soils is the distinguishing factor in the parable, not the sower or the seed sown. The parable is found in all three Synoptic Gospels; we'll follow Matthew's account, found in Matthew's "parables chapter." As we begin to examine it, we'll observe that this parable is a fairly involved allegory.

The setting is outdoors with a huge crowd of people.

> "[1b] Jesus went out of the house and sat by the lake. [2] Such large crowds gathered around him that he got into a boat and sat in it, while all the people stood on the shore." (Matthew 13:1-2)

In each Gospel, the size of the crowd is mentioned. As Jesus tells the parable, he knows that many of his hundreds of hearers this day will not be open or receptive, or will begin with enthusiasm only to fall away.

Carl Reuben Schmidt (California artist, 1885-1969), 'Jesus Teaching from a Boat,' oil on canvas, 38 x 48 inches, in a private collection.

Seeds on the Path, Rocky Soil, Thorns, and Good Soil (Matthew 13:3-8)

The kind of sowing Jesus describes involves taking a handful of seed and scattering it evenly onto the field. Israelites were familiar with two grain crops – barley in the areas with poorer soil and wheat in the better land.

> "[3] Then he told them many things in parables, saying: 'A farmer went out to sow his seed. [4] As he was scattering the seed, some fell along the path, and the birds came and ate it up.'" (Matthew 13:3-4)

The path is the narrow strip of hard-trampled dirt along which the farmer and his family walk through the field. Of course, the farmer doesn't *deliberately* sow seed on the hard-packed soil, but some of the seed falls there anyway. Because the soil of the path isn't broken up, the seed remains on the surface of the ground, "and the birds came and ate it up." Birds are opportunists.

> "⁵ Some fell on rocky places, where it did not have much soil. It sprang up quickly, because the soil was shallow. ⁶ But when the sun came up, the plants were scorched, and they withered because they had no root." (Matthew 13:5-6)

Some seed falls on rocky places.[1] These aren't surface rocks, but slabs of limestone just under the surface in certain parts of the field with an inch or two of soil over them. The limestone would hold the warmth of the sun throughout the night, and for a while, the new plants will spring up and grow vigorously – until they run out of moisture. Then, when the heat comes, since the plants can't get a root down into deep soil, they quickly wither and die.

> "Other seed fell among thorns, which grew up and choked the plants." (Matthew 13:7)

No farmer purposely scatters seed into thorns. But there may be thorn seed in the soil in certain spots. Thorns suck up the water, leaving little for the grain. They shade out the grain and the thorns make it impossible to harvest whatever seed heads may ripen.

> "Still other seed fell on good soil, where it produced a crop – a hundred, sixty or thirty times what was sown." (Matthew 13:8)

A ripening field of wheat is a wonder to behold – "amber waves of grain." In a good year, a field might yield 100 grains of wheat for every grain that was sown – a hundred-fold. That is the goal. That is the dream in the farmer's hopeful eyes as he sows the wheat. Sure, a few grains may fall on the path, some on the thin soil over a limestone shelf, and some in a thorny area. But most, he hopes, will grow up strong and flourish in the sun, producing an abundant harvest.

Why Jesus Taught in Parables (Matthew 13:9-17)

What is Jesus getting at? Good parables can both clarify and confuse. Jesus concludes the parable in a strong voice that carries to the hundreds listening from the shore:

> "He who has ears, let him hear." (Matthew 13:9)

Jesus is challenging the hearers to *understand* what they are hearing, to be discontent until they probe and learn, until they apply and obey what they have heard. But he realizes that they do *not* all care to know and understand. Many are spiritually dull.

The scene changes as Jesus speaks to his own disciples later. What he says is hard to understand, especially for us today.

> "¹⁰ The disciples came to him and asked, 'Why do you speak to the people in parables?'

---

[1] "Rocky places" is *petrōdēs*, "pertaining to rocky area with little topsoil, rocky, stony" (BDAG 810).

> ¹¹ He replied, 'The knowledge of the secrets of the kingdom of heaven has been given to you, but not to them. ¹² Whoever has will be given more, and he will have an abundance. Whoever does not have, even what he has will be taken from him.'" (Matthew 13:10-13)

In other words, not everyone is able to understand and grasp spiritual truth. They don't have "ears to hear." Some people are unreceptive.

Jesus explains that God had revealed this same truth to Isaiah. God had called Isaiah in an amazing vision of the heavenly throne room and had cleansed his lips with a coal from the holy altar. "Who will go?" God asks. Isaiah responds, "Here am I. Send me" (Isaiah 6:8).

Then God instructs Isaiah to preach to a people who have closed ears and calloused hearts, who ultimately will not heed Isaiah's message, but rather reject it. Yet, he is to speak to them anyway. Jesus quotes Isaiah 6:9-10 as the reason he speaks in parables.

> "¹³ This is why I speak to them in parables:
>
> 'Though seeing, they do not see;
> though hearing, they do not hear or understand.'
>
> ¹⁴ In them is fulfilled the prophecy of Isaiah:
>
> 'You will be ever hearing but never understanding;
> you will be ever seeing but never perceiving.
> ¹⁵ For this people's heart has become calloused;
> they hardly hear with their ears,
> and they have closed their eyes.
> Otherwise[2] they might see with their eyes,
> hear with their ears,
> understand with their hearts
> and turn, and I would heal them.'" (Matthew 13:13-15)

It isn't that God doesn't want to heal them, he does. But because they have shut themselves off from God's message, they *won't* see, they *won't* hear, they *won't* understand, nor will they repent so they can be healed. Other translations help us catch the sense of verse 15:

> "This people's heart has grown coarse, their ears dulled, they have shut their eyes tight to avoid using their eyes to see, their ears to hear, their heart to understand, changing their ways and being healed by me." (New Jerusalem Bible)

---

[2] In Matthew the word translated "otherwise" (NIV, NASB), "lest" (ESV, KJV), "so that" (NRSV) is not in the Greek text. Verse 15b reads literally, "not to see with their eyes and hear with their ears...."

8. Parables about Responding to the Kingdom

"They have stopped their ears and have closed their eyes. Otherwise, their eyes would see, their ears would hear, their minds would understand, and they would turn to me, says God, and I would heal them.'" (Good News Translation)

It is the old, old story of the Jews rejecting the prophets God sends to them.[3] Even when the Messiah himself comes in the flesh, they will not, they *refuse* to hear. Note that Isaiah's prophecy here is quoted on three different occasions in the New Testament to explain why the Jews reject the message of Jesus![4]

Please understand this! Jesus is saying to his disciples: Not everyone will hear. Not everyone will be receptive. Shortly, he will help them understand the Parable of the Soils that explains receptivity, but first he blesses them:

"[16] But blessed are your eyes because they see, and your ears because they hear. [17] For I tell you the truth, many prophets and righteous men longed to see what you see but did not see it, and to hear what you hear but did not hear it." (Matthew 13:16-17)

The Seed is the Word, the Message about the Kingdom (Matthew 13:18-19a)

Now Jesus begins the interpretation. This parable is about how people listen, how they hear "the message of the kingdom."[5]

"[18] Listen then to what the parable of the sower means: [19] When anyone hears the message about the kingdom...." (Matthew 13:18-19a)

"Word" (ESV, NRS, KJV), "message" (NIV) is *logos*, "a communication whereby the mind finds expression, word, chiefly oral."[6] What is the message or word of the Kingdom? It is that

- The Messiah has come and he is Jesus Christ the Lord.
- That before him every knee will bow.
- That Jesus reigns! He delivers! He rescues! He sets free!
- That to welcome him you must humble yourself and repent of your sins.

The messenger may be Jesus, or the apostles, or modern-day disciples. But the power is in the message, the Word. The writer of Hebrews says,

"For the word of God is living and active. Sharper than any double-edged sword, it penetrates even to dividing soul and spirit, joints and marrow; it judges the thoughts and attitudes of the heart." (Hebrews 4:12)

---

[3] Zechariah 7:11; Jeremiah 5:21, 23; Ezekiel 12:2.
[4] Matthew 13:13-15 = Mark 4:12 = Luke 8:10; John 12:40; Acts 29:27.
[5] Luke explains, "The seed is the word of God" (Luke 8:11). Mark tells us, "The farmer sows the word" (Mark 4:14).
[6] *Logos*, BDAG 599, 1a.

The Apostle Paul, who sowed the Word for most of his adult life, testifies about it:

> "I am not ashamed of the gospel, because **it is the power of God for the salvation** of everyone who believes: first for the Jew, then for the Gentile." (Romans 1:16)

It is immaterial who sows the seed – a bird, Johnny Appleseed, Jesus, Billy Graham, a Sunday school teacher, a parent, a friend. The power is in the seed itself. The seed alone has the power to grow, the power of life. Sowers are to sow – regularly, faithfully, whether it is inconvenient or not (2 Timothy 4:2; 2:15).

Hard-Packed Hearts (Matthew 13:19)

> "When anyone hears the message about the kingdom and does not understand[7] it, the evil one comes and snatches away[8] what was sown in his heart. This is the seed sown along the path." (Matthew 13:19)

On the hard-packed path between fields the seed never sinks into the soil. The devil, represented here by birds, gobbles up the seed before it can have any effect. These are the unreceptive unbelievers who hear, but have closed minds. The words just bounce off them.

I'm going to step outside the parable for a moment to say that soil quality can change – and sometimes change very rapidly. This isn't Jesus' point, and he doesn't even mention it in this connection. But think of what one plow furrow would do to the receptivity of the hard-packed "path." Life's troubles and problems often have the effect of running a plow through our carefully constructed lives and demolishing the values we once held to be true. Your friends may be utterly closed now. Accept that. But be alert to the circumstances that God may bring into their lives that will make them receptive to the Word.

Rocky Hearts (Matthew 13:20-21)

> "The one who received the seed that fell on rocky places is the man who hears the word and at once receives it with joy. But since he has no root, he lasts only a short time. When trouble or persecution comes because of the word, he quickly falls away." (Matthew 13:20-21)

Though Jesus doesn't say so directly, I think the rock represents people who have surface enthusiasm, but a hard heart. These people can be sorry for their sins and pray the "sinner's prayer." But, in fact, they haven't really internalized King Jesus' teachings and restructured their lives around him.

---

[7] "Understand" is *suniēmi*, "to have an intelligent grasp of something that challenges one's thinking or practice, understand, comprehend" (BDAG 972.) Originally, to set or bring together,' here "to set or join in the mind." "To understand" (Thayer 605).

[8] "Snatch away" (NIV, ESV, NRSV), "catch away" (KJV) is *arpazō*, "to grab or seize suddenly so as to remove or gain control, snatch/take away forcefully" (BDAG 134, 2a).

You could say that they have sorrow over their sins, but lack real repentance (*metanoia*, "a change of mind"). Deep wrenching sobs may be embarrassing, but tears often represent the destruction of an old value system and the foundations of a new one being laid in the heart. The heart is rent. (The English word "rend" means "to remove from place by violence, to wrest, to tear.") I'm not saying that weeping is necessary to salvation, only that true repentance *is* necessary to the process. Where this doesn't happen, we have the kind of people whom Jesus describes here, with surface growth, but who fall away in time of testing.

"Trouble"[9] or "persecution"[10] for the faith show their faith to be what it is – surface only. When the "heat" is on, these surface believers wither.

> **Q32. (Matthew 13:20-21) Why, according to the Parable of the Sower, why do some people fall away so quickly? What is their problem?**
> **https://www.joyfulheart.com/forums/topic/2206-q32-sower/**

Thorn-choked Hearts (Matthew 13:22)

> "The one who received the seed that fell among the thorns is the man who hears the word, but the **worries of this life** and the **deceitfulness of wealth** choke it, making it unfruitful." (Matthew 13:22)

Each of the Synoptic Gospels gives slightly different causes for unfruitfulness here. When you compare the various accounts you see the following four causes of unfruitfulness:

1. **Worries of this life** (Matthew, Mark, Luke)
2. **Deceitfulness of wealth** (Matthew, Mark), **riches** (Luke)
3. **Desires for other things** (Mark)
4. **Pleasures** (Luke)

---

[9] "Trouble" (NIV, NRSV), "tribulation" (ESV, KJV) is *thlipsis*, literally, "pressing, pressure," here used in the metaphorical sense, "trouble that inflicts distress, oppression, affliction, tribulation" (BGAD 457, 1).

[10] "Persecution" is *diōgmos*, "a program or process designed to harass and oppress someone, persecution" (BDAG 253).

Each of these can "choke" the growing plant of faith. The word is *sympnigō* "to check the growth or well-being of something by pressure, choke"[11] from *pnigō*, "to stifle, choke, strangle, suffocate."[12]

1. Worries, Cares (Matthew, Mark, Luke). At the top of the list are "worries" (NIV), "cares" (ESV, NRSV, KJV), *merimna*, "anxiety, worry, care."[13] Worry is the opposite of trust – and trust is the root idea of faith. All of us have anxieties; Jesus certainly did. But it is how we handle them that decides whether they choke out spiritual life or cause it to flourish. Being consumed with life's worries may be choking *your* spiritual life. Worry competes with faith for your time and your very life-force. It strangles your relationship with God and the growth of the Word in your life. Determine now to call on him continually to help you, and then trust that he will keep his promises. Cultivate an attitude of trust.

2. Deceitfulness of wealth (Matthew, Mark), riches (Luke). Second on the list is "riches" or "wealth," that is, "the abundance of many earthly goods, wealth."[14] Especially dangerous is the "deceitfulness" or "lure"[15] of wealth (Matthew, Mark).

Riches aren't evil in themselves. It is the "*love* of money"[16] that is a root of all kinds of evil (1 Timothy 6:10a). Riches aren't evil in themselves, but "eagerness[17] to be rich" can cause people to wander from the faith (1 Timothy 6:10b). Riches aren't evil, but Mammon[18] can become a very real competitor to serving God himself (Matthew 6:24). The problem is that riches touch the covetousness or greed deep within fallen man and often take a powerful hold. Money can deceive us, and when it does it can keep fruit from ripening on your seedheads so there is no crop for the harvest. (For parables on this see Lesson 10.2).

---

[11] *Sympnigo,* BGAD 959, 1. This is a compound word, with the Greek preposition *syn-*, "together, i.e., several ... things united or all in one" (Thayer 599, II, 2). *Pnigō* is a very strong, evocative word, and seems to be heightened by the preposition in its compound form in our passage. Whereas one thorn weed might choke the wheat or barley, all the thorn plants together (Greek *syn-*) "choke utterly" (Thayer 597). In Classical Greek, the word is used to describe a number of rather gruesome and violent incidents, as you might imagine.

[12] Hans Bietenhard, "*pnigō ktl.*," TDNT 6:455-458.

[13] *Merimna*, BDAG 632.

[14] *Ploutos*, BDAG 832.

[15] "Deceitfulness" (NIV, ESV, KJV), "lure" (NRSV) is the noun *apatē*, "deception, deceitfulness," then "pleasure, pleasantness" that involves one in sin (BDAG 59, meanings 1 and 2).

[16] *Philarguria*, "love of money, avarice, miserliness" (BDAG 1056).

[17] *Oregō*, literally, 'stretch oneself, reach out one's hand,' here figuratively, "to seek to accomplish a specific goal, aspire to, strive for, desire" (BDAG 721).

[18] *Mamōnas*, "property, wealth" (BDAG 614).

8. Parables about Responding to the Kingdom

3. Desire for Other Things (Mark). Desire[19] for things not ours is the root of the Tenth Commandment, "You shall not covet" (Exodus 20:17). We see and hear advertisements day by day that make us desire things we don't need. Add to that a corrupt heart, and it is easy to choke off the growth of the Word in us.

4. Pleasures (Luke). Finally, we come to "pleasures" (Luke 8:14), Greek *hēdonē*,[20] from which we get our word "hedonism." Everybody wants to be happy. But sometimes our pursuit of happiness can be twisted into an all-out pursuit of pleasure. Our society has turned "duty" into a negative, and "self-indulgence" into a positive. Our songs croon, "How can it be so wrong, when it feels so right?"[21] Too often we have replaced righteousness and honor and self-sacrifice with a pursuit of pleasure, of recreation, that can choke the growth of Jesus' Word in us and keep us from maturing and producing usable fruit. Weekend sports and recreation has displaced church-going in many a family.

Were They Really Christians?

I am often asked the question concerning the rocky soil and thorny believers: "Were they really Christians?" That's hard to answer – and Jesus doesn't answer it here. He only describes people who seem believe for a while and receive the word with joy when they hear it. To first appearances, these people seem to be Christians, but they don't persevere in faith, they "fall away." They could be (1) counterfeit, (2) weak, or (3) apostate Christians – and we may never know which.[22]

Is your life choked by worry, love of money, or hedonism? You must seek Jesus with all your heart, or you may end up self-deceived.

> "Not everyone who says to me, 'Lord, Lord,' will enter the kingdom of heaven, but only he who does the will of my Father who is in heaven." (Matthew 7:21)

My wife and I have a few pear trees in what was once a commercial fruit orchard. Most years, these trees will still bear a few pears, but they have to compete with other things that have grown up around it and the fruit never ripens properly. The fruit is hard and bitter, not soft, succulent, and sweet like a ripe pear. No farmer in his right mind would try to sell that kind of fruit or feed it to his family. It is worthless.

---

[19] "Desire" (NIV, ESV, NRSV), "lust" (KJV) is *epithumia*, "a great desire for something, desire, longing, craving." The word can also include "a desire for something forbidden or simply inordinate, craving, lust," which could encompass a wide range of vices, including sexual desires (BDAG 372, 1a).

[20] *Hēdonē*, "state or condition of experiencing pleasure for any reason, pleasure, delight, enjoyment, pleasantness" (BDAG 434, 1).

[21] "How Can It Be Wrong (When It Feels So Right)," words by Norro Wilson, sung by Barbara Mandrell and David Houston (1972, Sony Music Entertainment).

[22] For more on this, see my "Brief Look at TULIP Calvinism," an appendix to my *Grace: Favor for the Undeserving* (JesusWalk Publications, 2022), www.jesuswalk.com/grace/tulip-calvinism.htm

Q33. (Matthew 13:22) How do "thorns" prevent the Word of God from maturing in our lives? What is the difference between a genuine "disciple," follower or learner of Rabbi Jesus, and a person who holds a Christian belief system? What can you do to clear your life of the thorns that prevent Christ's work from maturing in you?
https://www.joyfulheart.com/forums/topic/2207-q33-thorns/

Receptive Hearts (Matthew 13:23)

But now we come to the fourth type of soil – "good soil.

> "But the one who received the seed that fell on good soil is the man who hears the word and understands it. He produces a crop, yielding a hundred, sixty or thirty times what was sown." (Matthew 13:23)

"Good soil," represents hearers who possess "a noble and good heart" (Luke 8:15) and understand the word.

The final characteristic of good soil and a good heart is a harvestable crop. I say harvestable, because sometimes a crop is so sparse it isn't worth the time to harvest and process. The farmer just turns it under to fertilize the next year's crop. But a good heart produces fruit – lots of fruit.

What does fruit indicate? (1) The development of a godly character, the fruit of the Spirit (Galatians 5:22-23). (2) The result or fruitfulness of our spiritual gifts, the tools that God gives Christians to help build up the Church, the body of Christ. If God has given you the gift of teaching, then what is the fruit of teaching? People who learn under your ministry. A teacher who has class after class of knowledgeable pupils is considered successful, fruitful. If your gift is pastoring or shepherding, then the fruit will be a well-cared-for flock. If it is administration, the fruit is a well-set-up, well-run organization of people all working toward the same goal. You get the idea.

Sometimes people think that fruit means "souls" we have won to Christ. Certainly, new believers are the natural result of witnessing and sharing the Good News. All Christians are called to do that. But some, those with a special gift of evangelism, will have many "souls" as a result of their ministry, because that is their particular spiritual gift. We don't have to be someone we are not, but we are to seek God for what he calls *us* to do, and then seek to be fruitful and effective in that to which he calls us.

Not all who begin in Jesus' Kingdom are good soil for sustained growth. Until we understand this, we are ripe for disillusionment. And when we are disillusioned, we quit sowing the seed. We become worthless as laborers in the fields. When we do understand it, we concentrate our efforts on the good soil.

Jesus' point here was not to root out the thorns and weeds in your life (though that is a good thing), but rather to be aware that rocky soil and weeds in your hearers will prevent fruitfulness. Don't be surprised or taken aback at this. Jesus is preparing his disciples for the unfruitful, as well as the somewhat fruitful and very fruitful.

Saying: Pearls before Swine (Matthew 7:6, §37)

The Parable of the Sower (Lesson 8.1) is about the receptivity. In the Sermon on the Mount we find a short saying or proverb that may be relevant here:

> "Do not give dogs what is sacred;[23] do not throw your pearls to pigs. If you do, they may trample them under their feet, and then turn and tear you to pieces." (Matthew 7:6)

Dogs in Jesus' day weren't thought of as pets, but unclean scavengers. Of course, pigs were considered unclean animals and forbidden for Jews to eat. Both wild dogs and hungry pigs can be dangerous. Pearls (as we'll see in the Parable of the Pearl of Great Price, Lesson 8.5), were highly valued in ancient times, used by the wealthy for necklaces and other ornaments. Thus, the word "pearl" came to be a figure of speech for something of supreme worth.[24]

So, in this short proverb, Jesus is saying, don't entrust something precious to people who cannot or will not appreciate it – who, in another figure, don't have "ears to hear." To do so can be dangerous.

---

[23] *Hagios*, "pertaining to being dedicated or consecrated to the service of God" (BDAG 10, 2aα).
[24] Frederick Hauck, *margaritēs*, TDNT 472-473; BDAG 626.

8.2 Forcible Nature of Discipleship

We've looked at those who are spiritually dull. Now we see what spiritual openness looks like in contrast by means of Jesus' Parable of the Narrow Door.

Parable of the Narrow Door (Luke 13:23-27, §165)

Jesus tells two parables that seem on the surface to be similar – the Parable of the Narrow and Wide Gates (Lesson 3.2) and the Parable of the Narrow Door. They both teach that only a few will be saved and that the entrance is narrow. But they are different parables, and you'll see in a moment why I've separated them.

	Parable of Narrow and Wide Gates Matthew 7:13-14 (Lesson 3.2)	**Parable of Narrow Door** Luke 13:23-27 (Lesson 8.2)
Portal	"**Gate**" (*pulē*) literally of gates of cities[25]	"**Door**" (*thura*), door to a house[26]
Destination	Roads, Ways	House

Let's see the unique message that Jesus' Parable of the Narrow Door has for disciples. The context is Jesus teaching in the towns and villages along his way to Jerusalem. In one town someone asks him a question:

Question: "Lord, are only a few people going to be saved?" (Luke 13:23)

The question is about the *number of people* who will be saved; Jesus' response acknowledges that, indeed, many people won't make it, but his answer is more about the *type of people* who will be saved.

Answer: "'Make every effort to enter[27] through the narrow door, because many, I tell you, will try to enter and will not be able to." (Luke 13:24)

Jesus' answer to the question introduces the image of a narrow door to the Kingdom that many people are urgently trying to get in at once. The door seems jammed with people, so not everyone that wants to can get in.

---

[25] "Gate" is *pylē*, "gate, door," literally of gates of cities (BDAG 897, b).

[26] "Narrow gate" (NIV, ESV, KJV), "strait gate" (KJV) Narrow door" (NIV, ESV, NRSV), "strait gate" (KJV) is two words: *thyra*, "door, a passage for entering a structure, entrance, doorway, gate" (BDAG 462), probably the door to a house or courtyard. "Narrow" or "strait" is *stenos*, in reference to dimension, "narrow." In Greek literature it is used of gates, doors, prison cells, and pathways (BDAG 942-943). The related verb *stenochōreō* means "to crowd, cramp, confine, restrict" (BDAG 942).

[27] "To enter" is *eiserchomai*, twice in verse 24, "to move into a space, enter" (BDAG 293, 1aγ).

8. Parables about Responding to the Kingdom

Push, Shove, and Elbow Your Way Inside (Luke 13:24a)

The parable includes a command to the listeners:

> "**Make every effort** to enter through the narrow door...." (Luke 13:24a)

"Entering" the Kingdom is a frequent concept in Jesus' teaching,[28] and seems the goal here. Jesus uses this parable to exhort his disciples. "Make every effort" (NIV), "strive" (ESV, NRSV, KJV) is the verb *agōnizomai* (from the same root as our word "agony"), a word from the realm of athletics, "engage in a contest" at the games, then more generally, "to fight, struggle." The word is used of wrestling in prayer (Colossians 4:12) and "fighting the good fight" (1 Timothy 6:12; 2 Timothy 4:7). Danker translates the phrase in our verse, "strain every nerve to enter."[29]

This parable teaches us not to be passive about the Kingdom. Nor are we to be gentlemanly or ladylike and let others go in ahead of us. Rather, we are to struggle, maybe even push and shove to get in while we can. Elsewhere, Jesus talks about the urgency needed:

> "The Law and the Prophets were proclaimed until John. Since that time, the good news of the kingdom of God is being preached, and everyone is *forcing*[30] *his way into it.*" (Luke 16:16; cf. Matthew 11:12)

Why can't they get in? Is the way barred? No. We know from Jesus' other teachings that entry into the Kingdom of God requires repentance and change. Many, many want the goal – the inheritance of the Kingdom, a place in heaven – so long as it costs them nothing, especially their allegiance and obedience. And so they try to enter, but do not succeed when they learn the cost. Prime example: the Rich Young Ruler.

Closing the Door (Luke 13:25-27)

Now Jesus seems to take the simple parable and extends it to teach an additional truth. The main parable is struggling to get in a narrow door, the number will be few. The extension to the parable is about the master of the house closing the door and shutting some people out.

Finally the host "gets up and closes the door..." (Luke 13:24). Apparently, the host is seated or reclining at the banquet table, but it is time to begin and he deliberately gets up and shuts the door. No more guests can enter. Now is time for the banquet to begin.

> "25 Once the owner of the house gets up and closes the door, you will stand outside knocking and pleading, 'Sir, open the door for us.'
>
> But he will answer, 'I don't know you or where you come from.'
>
> 26 Then you will say, 'We ate and drank with you, and you taught in our streets.'

---

[28] Matthew 5:20; 7:21; 11:12; 18:8-9; 19:17, 24; Mark 9:43, 45, 47; 10:15, 23ff; Luke 16:16; 18:17, 25; John 3:5.
[29] *Agōnizomai*, BDAG 17, 2b.
[30] "Forces/is forcing/by force" (ESV, NIV, NRSV), "presseth" (KJV) is the present middle indicative of, "to inflict violence on, dominate, constrain," then "to gain an objective by force, use force" (BDAG 175, 2).

²⁷ But he will reply, 'I don't know you or where you come from. Away from me, all you evildoers!'" (Luke 13:25-27)

Members of the crowd are claiming a relationship. Notice that we've moved beyond the "owner of the house" to Jesus himself teaching in the streets and anonymous crowds changing to "you" (verse 26), his immediate hearers. The parable is getting personal!

We see the same idea in the Sermon on the Mount, though not in a parable there.

"²¹ Not everyone who says to me, 'Lord, Lord,' will enter the kingdom of heaven, but only he who does the will of my Father who is in heaven. ²² Many will say to me on that day, 'Lord, Lord, did we not prophesy in your name, and in your name drive out demons and perform many miracles?' ²³ Then I will tell them plainly, 'I never knew you. Away from me, you evildoers!'" (Matthew 7:21-23)

Notice that in the Matthew passage, the outsiders claim to have given prophecies and performed miracles and exorcisms in Jesus' name, but they are still outside. Since they don't do the will of the Father, they aren't true disciples. They go through the motions of what disciples do, but they aren't surrendered to God in their hearts.

You see the same kind of dismissal in the Parable of the Wise and Foolish Virgins (Lesson 5.2). There, the girls who didn't bring enough oil arrive at the wedding celebration too late.

"¹⁰ᵇ And the door was shut. ¹¹ Later the others also came. 'Sir! Sir!' they said. 'Open the door for us!' ¹² But he replied, 'I tell you the truth, I don't know you.'" (Matthew 25:10b-12)

Scary words: "I don't know you!" We must strive to enter the door of salvation, to follow Jesus closely, and to be prepared to follow him even though his coming might be delayed. Profession of faith is one thing. As James says, "Even the demons believe – and shudder" (James 2:19). But the actions that follow faith indicate true faith.

Back to our Parable of the Narrow Door. The householder dismisses the crowd outside as "evildoers."³¹ It isn't just they haven't been able to crowd into the house, but there is some moral lack in their lives that has prevented them from entering a house that represents the Kingdom of God.

The parable morphs again in verses 28-30, where inside the house with the closed door there is a feast going on that appears to be the long-awaited eschatological banquet. (For more on this see Appendix 5. The Great Messianic Banquet.)

---

[31] "Evildoers" (NIV, NRSV), "workers of evil" (ESV), "workers of iniquity" (KJV) is two words: *ergatēs*, "worker, laborer, doer" BDAG 390, 2); and *adikia*, "the quality of injustice, unrighteousness, wickedness, injustice" (BDAG 20, 2).

> Q34. (Luke 13:23-27) Beyond the message that few will be saved, what is the unique message of the Parable of the Narrow Door? Why must would-be disciples be aggressive in order to enter the Kingdom? What happens if we don't aggressively seek God? Why do you think Jesus told this parable to his disciples?
> https://www.joyfulheart.com/forums/topic/2208-q34-narrow-door/

8.3 The Priority of Discipleship

The Parable of the Narrow Door (Lesson 8.2) suggests that becoming a disciple isn't something that happens easily, that you just ease into the Kingdom. No, there is a kind of forceful entry. You need to really want it! Jesus teaches asking, seeking, knocking. It is active, not passive.

Now in three analogies we see how Jesus seems off-putting to people who too casually ask to be his followers. These analogies occur in Matthew when "Jesus saw a crowd around him." Popularity and crowds don't necessarily indicate sincere discipleship. Jesus needs to do some sorting of applicants.

I once asked Waldron Scott, a popular leader in the Navigators, how he determined with whom to invest his life with one-on-one discipleship? In predictable Navigators' style, he said he gave young men several verses to memorize and asked them to come back to see him when they had memorized them all. The few that did, he said, might be good candidates to spend time with. In these three analogies that appear one after another in Luke, Jesus seems to be setting up barriers to discourage those who aren't serious.

Analogy of Foxholes and Nests (Matthew 18:19-20, §49; Luke 9:57-58, §138)

The first parable in Matthew begins with a person identified as a scribe or teacher of the law – a Bible expert from Jerusalem who has been impressed with his teaching. Luke just refers to him as "a man."

> "[57] As they were walking along the road, a man said to him, I will follow you wherever you go.' [58] Jesus replied, 'Foxes have holes and birds of the air have nests, but the Son of Man has no place to lay his head.'" (Luke 9:57-58)

Even birds and animals have homes, Jesus is saying. If you follow me on my itinerant mission, you will have no home. I call you to be a sojourner. The reality of significant hardship might discourage some "fair-weather Christians."

Analogy of the Dead Burying the Dead (Matthew 18:21-22, §49; Luke 9:59-60, §138)

Matthew identifies the next seeker as already being a "disciple" or follower. In Luke he is "another man."

> "⁵⁹ He said to another man, 'Follow me.' But the man replied, 'Lord, first let me go and bury my father.' ⁶⁰ Jesus said to him, 'Let the dead bury their own dead, but you go and proclaim the kingdom of God.'" (Luke 9:59-60)

If the man's father has actually just died, the man would be home making arrangements for the burial. Rather, the man is saying. I have responsibilities to my father as long as he lives. I'm not free to follow you right now, but after my father dies, then I'll follow you right away.

Jesus' answer seems harsh:

> "Let the dead bury their own dead, but you go and proclaim the kingdom of God." (Luke 9:60)

He's saying, let the spiritually dead bury the physically dead. But you, since you are spiritually alive, you should be preaching the gospel while there is still time to do so. There is an urgency! This parable immediately precedes the sending out of the Seventy to preach two by two.

Later, Jesus tells his disciples,

> "If anyone comes to me and does not hate his father and mother, his wife and children, his brothers and sisters – yes, even his own life – he cannot be my disciple." (Luke 14:26)

Following Jesus comes even before family responsibilities. Jesus must be number one, not number two after family.

Analogy of Looking Back from the Plow (Luke 9:61-62, §138)

This incident is found only in Luke, the third of three such analogies given one after another in Luke's Gospel.

> "⁶¹ Still another said, 'I will follow you, Lord; but first let me go back and say good-by to my family.' ⁶² Jesus replied, 'No one who puts his hand to the plow and looks back is fit for service in the kingdom of God.'" (Luke 9:61-62)

Jesus responds to the excuse of family again with a sense of priority and urgency. In light of the immediate mission ahead in the very next chapter – the sending out of the Seventy to the villages (Luke 10) – for this man to go home will mean that he will miss out, though his request seems reasonable enough.

8. Parables about Responding to the Kingdom

I sometimes hear people in their twenties say something like, "When I'm young I want to be free to enjoy myself. Later on, then maybe I'll settle down." I believe in Jesus, but I'm not ready to get too serious about it right now. When I get older, I will. What an insult to Jesus!

> "No one who puts his hand to the plow and looks back is fit for service in the kingdom of God." (Luke 9:62)

When you plow – with a mule or a diesel tractor – never ever try to plow while looking over your shoulder. If you do, your rows are crooked and your field is difficult to plant and harvest. Rather, plowmen fix their eyes on a point at the far end of the field and move steadily toward it, not veering to the right side or to the left.

To "put your hand to the plow," means to begin the task of plowing. Jesus isn't saying you can't glance back momentarily. But he is saying you can't continue to look back once you've begun to plow. If you do, you're not "fit for service" (NIV), "fit" (ESV, NRSV, KJV)[32] for Jesus' Kingdom.

> Q35. (Luke 9:57-62) What do these three analogies tell us about Jesus' requirements for his disciples? Why is Jesus so urgent? What was he seeking to teach would-be disciples about their priorities?
> https://www.joyfulheart.com/forums/topic/2209-q35-urgency/

8.4 Counting the Cost of Discipleship

Next, we examine several analogies and parables that teach us to calculate whether we really have enough desire to become a disciple. Luke tells us, "Large crowds were traveling with Jesus, and turning to them he said...." (Luke 14:25). It is time for Jesus to ask his multitude of "fans" for real commitment. The Parables of the Tower-Builder and the Warring King are found only in Luke in the context of "hating" his family, that is, putting allegiance to Jesus as their number one priority (Luke 14:26-27). The Parable of the Tower-Builder immediately follows the Parable of Taking Up One's Cross (Luke 14:25-27), which we'll consider shortly.

Parable of the Tower-Builder (Luke 14:28-30, §171)
(Also known as the Parable of the Tower)

> "²⁸ Suppose one of you wants to build a tower. Will he not first sit down and estimate the cost to see if he has enough money to complete it? ²⁹ For if he lays the foundation

---

[32] *Euthetos*, originally, "well-placed," then in reference to that which is well suited for something, "fit, suitable, usable, convenient" (BDAG 405)

and is not able to finish it, everyone who sees it will ridicule him, ³⁰ saying, 'This fellow began to build and was not able to finish.'" (Luke 14:28-30)

Jesus' example is from the realm of construction. He describes a tower, *pyrgos*, "a tall structure used as a lookout" (or possibly a tower-shaped building, farm building)."[33] Before beginning something of this magnitude, he says, you must first carefully calculate the cost.[34]

Down the street from the house where I lived as a boy, a lot was cleared, the foundation poured, and the rough framing for a home partly completed. Then one day, the workmen abruptly left. The unfinished house stood like this for many years, a monument to poor planning, to running out of money, to not counting the cost ahead of time.

Jesus is saying: If you don't have the wherewithal or willingness to see it through, don't even attempt the journey. Discipleship is a decision that demands the utmost seriousness and commitment. Be very, very sure you want to follow Jesus as his disciple.

Parable of the Warring King (Luke 14:31-32, §171)
(Also known as the Parable of the King Going to War)

Jesus' second parable in this context is from the field of military endeavor.

"³¹ Or suppose a king is about to go to war against another king. Will he not first sit down and consider whether he is able with ten thousand men to oppose the one coming against him with twenty thousand? ³² If he is not able, he will send a delegation while the other is still a long way off and will ask for terms of peace." (Luke 14:31-32)

Israel has always been located on a highway between major powers. Egypt is to the south. To the north are Syria, Assyria, Babylon, Greece, and Rome. Palestine has seen the marching of great armies and has its share of bloody battlefields. Many times, Israel's kings were required to decide if they could win a battle, and, if they determined that they were outnumbered, surrender to the stronger commander, rather than face slaughter in war. Bravado doesn't count. Careful consideration of our ability to follow through does.

Oh, there were exceptions, such as Gideon and his band of 300. But Jesus is talking about the normal situations that face kings and nations, businesses and families. Can we afford this? Can we pay this bill on time? If not, what can we do to stave off bankruptcy?

Everything (Luke 14:33)

Jesus ends this pair of parables with the conclusion:

---

[33] *Pyrgos*, BDAG 899, meanings 1 and 2.
[34] "Estimate the cost" (NIV, NRSV), "count the cost" (ESV, KJV) is two words: *psēphizō*, "calculate a total, count (up), calculate, reckon" (BDAG 1098, 1); and *dapanē*, "cost, expense" (BDAG 212).

"In the same way, any of you who does not **give up everything he has** cannot be my disciple." (Luke 14:33)

"Give up" (NIV, NRSV), "renounce" (ESV), "forsake" (KJV) is *apotassō*, literally, "separate yourself from, "here, "to renounce interest in something, renounce, give up."[35] Green sees this attitude as basic.

> "The distinctive property of disciples is the abandonment with which they put aside all competing securities in order that they might refashion their lives and identity according to the norms of the kingdom of God."[36]

We see this attitude personified in some famous disciples: fishermen leaving their nets (Luke 5:11), a tax collector walking away from a lucrative business (Luke 5:27-28), Zacchaeus giving half his fortune to the poor (Luke 19:8). And, famously, the Rich Young Ruler refusing to renounce all he had and walking away from Jesus (Luke 18:22).

Discipleship will take everything you have and more. Discipleship will figure in every future decision of your life. The will of God will be first in your priority from now on. If you don't have the ability or willingness to give following Jesus your all, then don't begin.

What is there that keeps you from following fully? What must you commit to Christ's cause so that you don't come up short and are recaptured by it? Money kept the Rich Young Ruler's from following. What has a hold on your heart?

Q36. (Luke 14:25-32) Are Jesus' demands of his disciples too uncompromising? Are we too compromising with the world's demands? What do you need to completely surrender so Jesus has all of you?
https://www.joyfulheart.com/forums/topic/2210-q36-cost-of-discipleship/

Parable of Taking Up One's Cross (Matthew 16:24-25; Mark 8:34-35; Luke 9:23-24; §123; and Matthew 10:37-39, §62; Luke 14:25-27, §171)

Now we turn to a cryptic, and often misunderstood, parable that is central to true discipleship, Jesus' Parable of Taking Up One's Cross. We know it is central because Jesus shares it in at least two different contexts in the Synoptic Gospels.

1. Jesus' revelation of his crucifixion at Caesarea Philippi, and
2. Two parables on counting the cost of discipleship (that we just looked at above)

---

[35] "Give up" (NIV, NRSV), "renounce" (ESV), "forsaketh" (KJV) is *apotassō* (Thayer 69, 1; BDAG 123, 2).
[36] Green, *Luke*, p. 567. I.G. Herr, "Salt," ISBE 4:286-287.

Jesus also alludes to it in John's Gospel.[37] Let's dig deeper.

Context 1. Jesus' Revelation of His Crucifixion at Caesarea Philippi

We see this saying immediately after Jesus' first declaration to his disciples at Caesarea Philippi that he would be killed and raised from the dead, Peter responds by saying, "That will never happen to you." Jesus corrects him very sharply (Matthew 16:22-23). Then Jesus gives a vitally important saying that is almost a riddle, found in all three Synoptic Gospels. We'll follow Luke's version. The parable of bearing one's cross is in verse 23; the explanation of the parable is in verse 24.

> "[23] If anyone would come after me, he must deny himself and take up his cross daily and follow me. [24] For whoever wants to save his life will lose it, but whoever loses his life for me will save it." (Luke 9:23-24)

The context is clearly the danger of losing one's life, for Jesus has just told the disciples he would be killed. We know this saying is vital, because it applies to *anyone* who "would come after me," that is, anyone who would follow him as an adherent or disciple.[38]

Taking Up One's Cross

The key to understanding this passage is to discern the meaning of the metaphor, "to take up one's cross." Our culture uses the idea of "my cross to bear" in the sense of one's burden[39] or destiny. One of the dictionary definitions of the English noun "cross" is "an affliction that tries one's virtue, steadfastness, or patience."[40] But that is *not* what Jesus is teaching here!

Jesus is speaking literally, of a wooden cross, a common instrument of torture and execution in his culture. Jesus isn't talking about a mere burden or trial or difficulty. He is talking about death.

Here is the crux of the parable: Just as a condemned man would carry the cross-beam of his cross to the place of crucifixion according to Roman custom, so each of Jesus' disciples must *daily* be willing to die. Prepared to die, if necessary. The reason is this: when a disciple has accepted death, then no man can control him with fear; he belongs fully to Jesus, come what may.

What does all this mean? Let's look at it piece by piece in Luke's version

---

[37] John 12:25 (Lesson 6.2).
[38] "Come after," the common verb *erchomai*, "come." Used with an improper preposition *opisō*, "after." With the verb *erchomai*, it means, "come after someone, follow someone" (at the same time in the transferred sense, "be an adherent/follower") (*opisō*, BGAD 716, 2a).
[39] For example, "It's Not My Cross to Bear," by Gregg Allman, copyright ©1969, 1974.
[40] *Merriam Webster*, p. 276.

"If anyone would come after me, he must deny himself and take up his cross daily and follow me." (Luke 9:23)

1. Denying oneself. The Greek word is *arneomai*, originally, "refuse, disdain," here "to refuse to pay any attention to, disregard, renounce," here, "act in a wholly selfless way."[41] Discipleship means deliberately choosing to follow another person's way rather than choosing your own way.

2. Picking up the cross. The verb *airō* means basically, "to lift up, take up, pick up." Here, it means, "to lift up and move from one place to another, take/carry (along)."[42] Picking up one's cross here suggests a voluntary action of accepting the sentence of death and all that means, and carrying it with one.

3. Picking it up daily. Luke's version of the saying adds the word daily, every day,[43] implied in Matthew and Mark. Like putting on our clothes for the day, we pick up our willingness to go to death for Jesus.

4. Following Jesus. The verb is the characteristic word for following someone as a disciple.[44]

Context 2. Allegiance to Jesus Must Come before Family Obligations

The saying is found in a second context, where Jesus demands that his disciples place allegiance to himself over family obligations. It is a hard saying.

Matthew gives it among Jesus' instructions prior to the sending out of the Twelve.

"[37] Anyone who loves his father or mother more than me is not worthy of me; anyone who loves his son or daughter more than me is not worthy of me; [38] and anyone who does not **take his cross and follow me** is not worthy of me. [39] Whoever finds his life will lose it, and whoever loses his life for my sake will find it." (Matthew 10:37-39)

Luke includes this saying at a time when large crowds are following Jesus, just prior to his Parables of the Tower-Builder and the Warring King that we just considered above. Luke's version is striking because he speaks in hyperbole and uses the word "hate"[45] in place of "love more than."

---

[41] *Arneomai*, BDAG 132, 4.
[42] *Airō*, BDAG 28, 2a.
[43] *kath hēmeran*, literally "daily, every day." The preposition *kata* is used distributively of time, "every" (BDAG 512, 2c).
[44] *Akoloutheō*, BDAG 36, 3.
[45] "Hate" is *miseō*, "hate". Danker notes, depending on the context, this verb ranges in meaning from 'disfavor' to 'detest.' The English term 'hate' generally suggests affective connotations that do not always do justice especially to some Semitic shame-honor oriented use of μισέω = śānē' (e.g., Deuteronomy 21:15, 16) in the sense, 'hold in disfavor, be disinclined to, have relatively little regard for,' here 'to be disinclined to, disfavor, disregard' in contrast to preferential treatment (BDAG 652, 2).

> ²⁶'If anyone comes to me and does not hate his father and mother, his wife and children, his brothers and sisters — yes, even his own life — he cannot be my disciple. ²⁷ And anyone who does not **carry his cross and follow me** cannot be my disciple.'" (Luke 14:26-27)

You must "hate" your family, he says, even your own life, if you want to be my disciple. The commitment is so great that it even overrides the ties of family, which in Middle Eastern culture were predominant.

The Apostle Paul understood well what this meant and lived it out day by day until the final day he was beheaded by the Roman emperor. In three classic passages he expresses this concept in different ways:

> "I have been crucified with Christ and I no longer live, but Christ lives in me." (Galatians 2:20a)

> "For you died, and your life is now hidden with Christ in God." (Colossians 3:3)

> "I die every day." (1 Corinthians 15:31)

It is said of missionaries of the nineteenth century, embarking on missions overseas, that they often packed their belongings in a coffin instead of a trunk so they would have something to be buried in. They never expected to return.

The Paradox of Saving and Losing One's Life

Jesus concludes this saying with a paradox. We find this saying in four different contexts – so it must have been something Jesus said to his disciples again and again. "Survive at all costs," is the flawed philosophy of our world. Losing your life for Christ is the philosophy of a disciple.

1. Caesarea Philippi

> "For whoever wants to save his life will lose it, but whoever loses his life for me will find it." (Matthew 16:25 = Mark 8:35 = Luke 9:24)

2. Instructions for Sending Out the Twelve

> "For whoever wants to save his life will lose it, but whoever loses his life for me will save it." (Matthew 10:39)

3. End Time Teaching

> "For whoever wants to save his life will lose it, but whoever loses his life for me and for the gospel will save it." (Luke 17:33)

4. Jesus' Teaching about His Time to Be Crucified

> "The man who loves his life will lose it, while the man who hates his life in this world will keep it for eternal life." (John 12:25)

8. Parables about Responding to the Kingdom

Martyrdom of St. Polycarp

I can picture in my mind the frail Polycarp (69-155 AD), white-haired Bishop of Smyrna, as he stands before the Roman proconsul about 155 AD in a stadium full of Romans chanting, "Away with the atheists!" (Christians were called "atheists" because they did not believe in the traditional Roman gods.) Polycarp is so old that that in his youth Polycarp had been a disciple of the Apostle John himself.[46] But soldiers haul him roughly into the arena full of the shouting populace.

Raymond Charles Péré (1854-1929), 'Martyrdom of St. Polycarp,' Fresco, Church of St. Polycarp, Smyrna (modern day Izmir, Turkey)

> "When the magistrate pressed him, and said, 'Swear, and I will release you; revile Christ,'
> Polycarp said, 'Eighty-six years have I been serving him, and he has done me no wrong; how then can I blaspheme my king who saved me?'"[47]

Refusing to recant, he is bound to a stake and burned before the eyes of the multitude, after uttering a final prayer:

> "...Wherefore I praise you also for everything; I bless you, I glorify you, through the eternal high priest, Jesus Christ, your beloved Son, through whom, with him, in the Holy Spirit, be glory unto you, both now and for the ages to come, Amen."

"Carrying one's cross" doesn't mean carrying one's own burdens. Rather it is an image of Roman execution by crucifixion, where the condemned man carried his cross to the place of execution. Unless you stand willing to die for me every day, Jesus is saying, you can't be my disciple.

> **Q37. (Luke 9:23-24, etc.) What does it mean to take up your cross daily? What does this have to do with "losing your life for me." What are the consequences in one's Christian walk if a disciple wants to take this step of commitment? How does this contrast with trying to save one's life?**
> https://www.joyfulheart.com/forums/topic/2211-q37-take-up-your-cross/

---

[46] *Ante-Nicene Fathers*, Vol. 1, Fragments of the Lost Writings of Irenaeus, II.
[47] Eusebius, *Church History* 4, 15, 20.

8.5 Ultimate Prize of the Kingdom

Half-way through Matthew 13 you find a pair of parables that underscore the great value of obtaining the Kingdom. Each begins with the phrase, "The kingdom of heaven is like...." This is how it is in the Kingdom!

Parable of the Hidden Treasure (Matthew 13:44, §101)

> "The kingdom of heaven is like treasure[48] hidden[49] in a field. When a man found it, he hid it again, and then in his joy went and sold all he had and bought that field." (Matthew 13:44)

In our day, we can store treasure in the bank or in a safe deposit box. But in Jesus' day, burying treasure was an extremely common way of safeguarding it. In fact, according to rabbinical law, burying a treasure was the most secure way of protecting it.[50] One's treasure might be stolen by thieves or plundered by foreign invading armies. But if it were hidden skillfully, rarely would it be detected.

But people often died in such invasions or passed on without disclosing the location of their treasure-trove to a relative. In that case, a hoard of coins or jewels buried in a pottery jar might be discovered that would make its finder rich. Today, people dream of getting rich by winning the lottery, but ancient literature is full of stories of people finding buried treasure and becoming fabulously wealthy.

Sir John Everett Millais, "The Hidden Treasure" (1860, watercolor on paper, 5.3x4.2 inches, Aberdeen Art Gallery, Aberdeen, Scotland

In Jesus' story, a man found the treasure in a rural field.[51] Perhaps he was employed as a laborer and his plow hit the container. Or perhaps erosion had uncovered a portion of the treasure. We don't know.

When the man finds the treasure, he is overcome with joy. He doesn't take the treasure immediately, but reburies it to hide and protect it, and then sells everything he has to purchase the land[52] to make his discovery of the fortune both reasonable and legal. It is quite possible

---

[48] "Treasure" is *thēsauros* (from which we get our English word "thesaurus"). It means, "that which is stored up, treasure" (BDAG 456, 2).

[49] "Hidden" is *kryptō* (from which we get our word, "cryptography"), which means, "to keep something from being divulged or discovered, conceal, hide," of something put in a specific place (BDAG 573, 2).

[50] Jeremias (*Parables*, p. 61, fn. 51) notes that according to rabbinical law, anyone who buried a pledge or deposit immediately upon receipt of it, was free from liability if it went missing (*b.B.M.* 42a).

[51] *Agros*, "field, land, countryside," here, "land put under cultivation, arable land, field" (BDAG 15, 3).

[52] *Agorazō*, "to acquire things or services in exchange for money, buy, purchase," both in verse 44 and verse 46 (BDAG 14).

8. Parables about Responding to the Kingdom

that the original owner of the treasure had died decades or centuries before. Then he sells everything he has and buys the field.

Some have questioned the ethics of the man's purchase without disclosing the treasure, but ethics wasn't Jesus' point.[53] There are two keys to understanding this parable:
1. "In his joy" and
2. "Sold all he had."

In the parable, the man is overcome with joy is in his good fortune of finding a huge treasure hoard that will make him rich for life. Anything he spends to gain legal right to that treasure is worth it, since its value is so exceedingly greater. The emphasis here is on the importance of parting with everything we have and own in order to obtain something inestimably greater. This is not a parable about buying salvation, but of the incredible value of salvation that far surpasses any amount a poor man might be able to scrape together to try to acquire it.

Parable of the Pearl of Great Price (Matthew 13:45-46, §101)

While the subject of the Parable of the Hidden Treasure is a poor man, the subject of the next parable is a wealthy man.

> "⁴⁵ Again, the kingdom of heaven is like a merchant looking for fine pearls. ⁴⁶ When he found one of great value, he went away and sold everything he had and bought it." (Matthew 13:45-46)

He is called a "merchant," a wholesale dealer in contrast to a retailer.[54] He specializes in searching for[55] and acquiring fine[56] pearls to sell to retailers. He is doubtless wealthy, used to spending and receiving large sums of money.

---

[53] According to rabbinical law, it might have been possible to claim legal ownership of personal property that had been found on another's land, but if he had been on the land as an agent or employee of another (say a farm hand), his legal right might have been clouded. Morris (*Matthew*, p. 359, fn. 105) cites *B. Bat* 86a. France (*Matthew*, p. 540-541, fn. 11) cites J.D.M. Derrett, *Law*, 1-16, for an explanation and defense of the finder's action according to both Roman and Jewish law. Edersheim (*Life and Times*, 2:595) asserts that the finder's action "was, at least, in entire accordance with Jewish law," citing *B. Meta* 25 a, b. Jeremias (*Parables*, p. 99, fn. 33) notes that his action was "formally legitimate, as he first bought the field," and cites *Midr. Cant.* 4:12; *Mek. Ex* on 14:5; and *Kidd* 1.5, that movable effects are included in the purchase of property.

[54] "Merchant" is the noun *emporos*, "'one who boards a ship as passenger', then, especially one who travels by ship for business reasons, merchant." Here it "denotes a wholesale dealer in contrast to *kapēlos*, retailer" (BDAG 325).

[55] "Looking for" (NIV), "in search of" (NRSV), "seeking" (KJV) is *zēteō*, "try to find something, seek, look for" in order to find, here in the special sense, "seek to buy" (BDAG 428, 1b). In "seek first his kingdom and his righteousness..." (Matthew 6:33), it has the meaning, "desire to possess something" (BDAG 428, 3a).

[56] "Fine" (NIV, ESV, NRSV), "goodly" (KJV) is *kalos*, "pertaining to meeting the high standards or expectations of appearance, kind or quality." Here, "good, useful" ... "fine pearls" (BDAG 504, 2a).

Pearls were highly valued in ancient times. This was before the time of cultured pearls, so pearls were not plentiful. They were regarded as precious stones in antiquity, taken by divers from the Red Sea, the Persian Gulf, and the Indian Ocean. Pearls were used for necklaces and other ornaments, and could be extremely costly, so the word "pearl" came to be a figure of speech for something of supreme worth.[57] Ancient literature tells of pearls worth millions of dollars. Caesar presented Brutus' mother with a pearl worth 6 million sesterces (hundreds of thousands of dollars). Cleopatra is said to have possessed a pearl worth 100 million sesterces.[58]

Thus, when the pearl merchant in Jesus' parable finds one "pearl of great price" (KJV), "great value" (NIV, NRSV, ESV),[59] he liquidates all his assets down to the last penny – "sold everything he had" – and then rushes back to buy the wonderful pearl that has enchanted him.

Harold Copping (British illustrator, 1863-1932), "The Merchant Finds the Pearl of Great Price."

Jesus' point in the Parable of the Pearl of Great Price is similar to the Parable of the Hidden Treasure. When you find such a valuable pearl, it is worth selling everything you own to obtain it, whether to admire, as some contend,[60] or to sell for a much greater profit. When you find the ultimate pearl, you spare nothing to make it your own.

The Kingdom of God is like this. Those who understand its value give everything they have to obtain it. There is a wonder, a desire, an urgency. This isn't passive, but an active entering in. The cost of discipleship is high, but the rewards are unimaginably great!

> **Q38. (Matthew 13:44-46). If you were to objectively assess your life, career, family, values, and possessions, is there anything more important, anything of greater value to you than your relationship with Jesus? How would you *objectively* prove to a friend**

---

[57] Frederick Hauck, *margaritēs*, TDNT 472-473.
[58] Jeremias (*Parables*, p. 199, fn. 36 and 37) cites Suetonius, *De vita Caesarum*, 50, and Plinius, *Nist. nat.*, IX, 119ff.
[59] *Polytimos*, "pertaining to being very high on a monetary scale, very precious, valuable" (BDAG 850). Used regarding precious ointment (Matthew 26:27) and of "faith which is more precious than gold" (1 Peter 1:7).
[60] Morris (*Matthew*, p. 360) and France (*Matthew*, p. 541) suggest that he didn't purchase the pearl to resell, but only to gaze at and admire, thus impoverishing himself. But that interpretation seems to exaggerate the reason why a pearl wholesaler would give anything to purchase this pearl.

that Jesus is first in your life?
https://www.joyfulheart.com/forums/topic/2212-q38-ultimate-prize/

Jesus told many parables to help his disciples understand that following him was to be their highest priority. He compares entering the Kingdom to squeezing through a narrow door, not looking back from the plow, making sure you have what it takes to see it through, taking up your cross, and obtaining the greatest treasure of all. Follow him with all your heart, my friend.

Prayer

Father, as I consider Jesus' demands on me as a disciple, I am shocked and humbled. He wants my all. He demands to be first. He calls me to push everything aside to be part of his Kingdom. Forgive me for my passivity and self-satisfaction. Resharpen the blade of my discipleship, I pray, in Jesus' name. Amen.

9. Parables about Disciple Character

Jesus' mission is to build disciples who will carry on his work and build his Church after his resurrection. So it is not surprising that a number of parables are designed to teach what a disciple should look like. In this lesson we'll look at the character qualities of disciples.[1] Then in succeeding lessons we'll examine the values and practices of disciples.

9.1 Humility

- Parable of the Pharisee and Tax Collector (Luke 18:9-14)
- Parable of Becoming Like Little Children (Matthew 18:3-4)
- Parable of Welcoming Little Children (Matthew 19:13-15; Mark 10:13-16; Luke 18:15-17)
- Parable of Places at the Table (Luke 14:7-11)

9.2 Avoiding Hypocrisy

- Analogy of the Yeast of the Pharisees (Matthew 16:5-12; Mark 8:15; Luke 12:1)

9.3 Abiding

- Parable of the Vine and the Branches (John 15:1-9)
- Parable of the Bread of Life (John 6:35)
- Parable of Eating Jesus' Flesh (John 6:53-58)
- The Analogy of the Yoke (Matthew 11:28-30)

9.1 Humility

To begin, we'll examine two parables in Luke's Gospel, one following the other, that teach humility: the Parable of the Pharisee and Tax Collector and the Parable of the Little Children (Luke 18:15-17).

Stained glass window by Sylvia Nicolas in the St Dominic Chapel of Providence College, Providence, Rhode Island. Photo: Fr. Lawrence, OP. Attribution-NonCommercial-NoDerivs 2.0 Generic Creative Commons license.

---

[1] Related to the character of disciples are a pair of analogies: the Analogy of the Light of the World and Analogies of Walking in Light and Darkness. It is important that disciples walk in righteousness and in the presence of the Lord. These are reviewed in Appendix 4.1.

9. Parables about Disciple Character

Parable of the Pharisee and Tax Collector (Luke 18:9-14, §186)
(Also called the Parable of the Pharisee and the Publican)

The Parable of the Pharisee and the Tax Collector, found only in Luke, is about humility – and a judgment on the pride of the Pharisees and Scribes. Jesus is speaking to a mixed crowd of both disciples and others.

> "To some who were confident[2] of their own righteousness and looked down[3] on everybody else, Jesus told this parable." (Luke 18:9)

When we move from righteous living – which is good and right – to a place of trusting in that righteous living to impress God, then we commit a fatal error, for righteousness turns to pride, and pride leads us to look down on those whom we consider morally inferior to us.

Pharisees and Tax Collectors (Luke 18:9-10)

Jesus sets the scene.

> "Two men went up to the temple to pray, one a Pharisee and the other a tax collector." (Luke 18:10)

James J. Tissot, 'The Pharisee and the Publican' (1886-96), gouache on board. Brooklyn Museum, NY.

As we discussed in Lesson 2, the Pharisees were members of an exacting party of the Jews who believed in strictly observing God's law, as well as the oral law.

Tax collectors, on the other hand, were universally despised. They collected taxes for the hated Romans and had a reputation for overcharging. They worked on a tax farming system. A chief tax collector would bid on the contract for collecting taxes in a certain district. If he won the contract, he would be responsible for delivering to the Romans the amount of money agreed upon. Whatever he could collect above that, he could keep. Chief tax collectors would employ others who resided in the various villages and sections of town to actually collect the tolls, taxes, and tariffs.

Tax collectors were considered by the populace as turncoats and traitors. And crooks – since they commonly assessed taxes beyond what was legal. If a farmer, businessman, or

---

[2] "Confident" (NIV) or "trusting in" (ESV, NRSV, KJV) is *peithō*, which can mean variously, "convince, persuade," here, "to be so convinced that one puts confidence in something ... depend on, trust in" (BDAG 792, 2a). "Righteousness" is *dikaios*, "pertaining to being in accordance with high standards of rectitude, upright, just, fair" (BDAG 246-247).
[3] "Looked down on" (NIV), "treated/regarded with contempt" (ESV, NRSV), "despised" (KJV) is *exoutheneō*, "to show by one's attitude or manner of treatment that an entity has no merit or worth, disdain."[3]

caravanner couldn't or wouldn't pay, they would turn him over to the soldiers. Extortion and threats were part of the system.

There couldn't be a greater contrast between them – the righteous Pharisee and the morally bankrupt, turncoat tax collector.

Priding Oneself (Luke 18:12)

Now Jesus, the master storyteller, sets the figures into action.

> "The Pharisee stood up and prayed about himself[4]: 'God, I thank you that I am not like other men – robbers, evildoers, adulterers – or even like this tax collector. I fast twice a week and give a tenth of all I get.'" (Luke 18:11-12)

Jews usually prayed standing, looking up to heaven with hands raised. The Pharisee's entire prayer is about himself. He thanks God – not for blessings – but that he isn't a sinner like others. The Pharisee also reminds God of how pious he is – fasting twice a week and scrupulously tithing.

Humbling Oneself (Luke 18:13)

Now Jesus presents his opposite.

> "But the tax collector stood at a distance. He would not even look up to heaven, but beat his breast and said, 'God, have mercy on me, a sinner.'" (Luke 18:13)

Jesus describes the man's body language.

- **Standing at a distance**. He doesn't feel worthy to draw close to God or the temple.
- **Not raising his eyes to heaven**, but standing with head level or bowed, an acknowledgement of guilt.
- **Beating his breast,** a sign of mourning.[5]

The tax collector's prayer is remarkable and short. Instead of telling God all the good things about himself, he describes himself as a sinner.[6] He makes no excuses for his behavior, offers

---

[4] The Greek words are variously translated "about himself" (NIV), "standing by himself" (ESV, NRSV), "with himself" (KJV). The phrase is difficult, spawning some textual variants. Marshall (*Luke*, p. 679) says that this "should be understood as representing an Aramaic ethic dative, which emphasizes the verb: 'The Pharisee, taking his stand, prayed'" (citing Black, Jeremias, and Manson).

[5] Gustav Stählin, *pypto*, TDNT 8:260-269, especially p. 262, fn 18, and p. 264. Josephus, a Pharisee who lived a few decades after Jesus, described David's mourning for his son Absalom in this way: "David ... wept for his son, and beat his breast, tearing [the hair of] his head, tormenting himself all manner of ways..." (*Antiquities* 7,10,5).

[6] *Hamartōlos*, "pertaining to behavior or activity that does not measure up to standard moral or cultic expectations, sinner" (BDAG 51-52). *Hilaskomai* calls for forgiveness from one who has been wronged, while *eleeō* asks for compassion and pity for one in tragic circumstances.

9. Parables about Disciple Character

no mitigating circumstances. He confesses his sinfulness before God and takes full responsibility for it.

Then he asks for mercy.[7] For the tax collector to ask for forgiveness and restoration of his relationship with God is a bold and faith-filled act for a man so utterly despised by society. He is obviously humble and repentant of his sins, but his faith has made him bold to ask for something that he has no right to expect – forgiveness and restoration to God.

Justification before God (Luke 18:14a)

Having contrasted the Pharisee's self-righteous and disdainful piety with the tax collector's sincere and faith-filled penitence, Jesus pronounces judgment:

> "I tell you that this man, rather than the other, went home justified before God." (Luke 18:14a)

"Justified" means freed of all charges against him.[8]

The Pharisees present must have been livid with anger. The crowd was amazed, wondering, pondering, perplexed. But the prostitutes and tax collectors, the thieves and adulterers in the audience may have been weeping, for Jesus had declared that it was possible for them to be saved, to be forgiven, to be cleansed, to be justified before God. Jesus had given them hope.[9]

Exalting or Humbling Oneself (Luke 18:14b)

Finally, Jesus brings home the application of the parable:

> "For everyone who exalts himself will be humbled, and he who humbles himself will be exalted."[10] (Luke 18:14b)

Jesus turns the normal way of things upside down[11] as he highlights a paradox of the spiritual life – exalting oneself leads to humbling, while humbling leads to exaltation. Jesus' brother James carries on this theme, when he says:

---

[7] *Hilaskomai*, "to cause to be favorably inclined or disposed, propitiate, conciliate." When used in the passive, of one addressed in prayer, "to act as one who has been conciliated, be propitiated, be merciful or gracious" (BDAG 473-474).

[8] "Justified" is *dikaioō*, "to render a favorable verdict, justify, vindicate, treat as just ... to be found in the right, be free of charges" (BDAG 249).

[9] Jesus did not absolve them of their responsibility to repay those they had cheated. Zacchaeus did so willingly (Luke 19:8), but Jesus' point here wasn't repayment but a humble heart.

[10] The word "exalt" is Greek *hypsoō*, "to cause enhancement in honor, fame, position, power, or fortune, exalt" (BDAG 1045-1046). "Humble" is Greek *tapeinoō*, "to cause to be or become humble in attitude, humble, make humble" (BDAG 990).

[11] This is similar to the saying that the first will be last and the last first that we examined in the Parable of Taking Up One's Cross (Lesson 8.4).

"... But he gives us more grace. That is why Scripture says: 'God *opposes* the proud but gives grace to the humble.'" (James 4:6)

When we are proud, we make ourselves into God's opponent, his enemy.

The lessons for would-be disciples are obvious.

1. Grace. We are saved by God's atonement and mercy, not by our righteous deeds.

2. Pride. God abhors the haughty, but welcomes the humble. We must guard against the sin of pride that is so repugnant to God. Instead, we must humble ourselves and be thankful for the grace of God.

3. Superiority. We cannot, we must not look down on others. While they may be gross sinners, they are certainly not beyond God's forgiveness. In the final analysis, the only thing that saves either of us will be God's forgiveness, and not our purity.

Is Jesus trying to undermine piety and obedience? By no means! But this parable attacks any pride and sense of superiority that our piety and obedience may foster. Faith and humility are marks of the men and women who follow Jesus.

> **Q39. (Luke 18:9-14) Why do you think the Pharisee is so convinced of his righteousness? What do you think are his actual sins? What is so remarkable about the tax collector's prayer? Why is it easier to promote ourselves in front of others rather than humble ourselves? Why did Jesus tell this parable for his disciples?**
> https://www.joyfulheart.com/forums/topic/2213-q39-pharisee-and-tax-collector/

Parables of the Little Children

As mentioned, the Parable of the Pharisee and the Tax Collector is followed immediately by the Parable of Welcoming Little Children.

Jesus repeated the parable in different ways so his disciples would get the point. In Matthew we see two instances:

- Matthew 18:3-4. Parable of Becoming Like Little Children
- Matthew 19:13-15. Parable of Welcoming Little Children

I think we are seeing two distinct parables here.

9. Parables about Disciple Character

Parable of Becoming Like Little Children (Matthew 18:3-4, §129)

In Matthew 18, the disciples have been arguing about who is the greatest. So Jesus calls a child to stand in their midst as he teaches them. Then he says:

> "³ I tell you the truth, unless you **change** and **become like little children**, you will never enter the kingdom of heaven. ⁴ Therefore, whoever **humbles himself like this child** is the greatest in the kingdom of heaven." (Matthew 18:3-4)

Pride can prevent a person from entering the Kingdom, Jesus is saying. The disciples need to change![12] And then he uses as pair of similes (with "like" or "as,"[13] a very basic kind of comparison) to explain what he means by two actions:

James J. Tissot, detail of 'Jesus and the Little Child' (1886-94), gouache on gray wove paper, 5.7 x 9.3 in., Brooklyn Museum, New York.

1. "**Become**[14] **like** little children" (verse 3)
2. "**Humbles**[15] **himself like** this child" (verse 4)

Sometimes people wonder what Jesus means when he tells his disciples to become like children. Is it childlike simplicity? Is it innocence?[16] Is it faith? As we see in Matthew 18:4, Jesus makes it explicit: it is childlike humility.

---

[12] "Change" (NIV, NRSV), "turn" (ESV), "be converted" (KJV) is *strephō*, "turn," here, "to experience an inward change, turn, change," "make a turn-about, turn around" (BDAG 948-949, 5).

[13] "Like" (NIV, ESV, NRSV), "as" (KJV) in verses 3 and 4 is *hōs*, used as a conjunction marking a point of comparison, "as," "if you do not become child-like..." (BDAG 1104, 2cβ).

[14] "Become" is *ginomai*, "be, become," here, "to experience a change in nature and so indicate entry into a new condition, become something" (BDAG 198, 5b).

[15] "Humbles himself" is *tapeinoō*, "to cause to be or become humble in attitude, humble, make humble" in a favorable sense (BDAG 990, 3).

[16] A careful study by Albrecht Oepke demonstrates that the principle of the innocence of children is alien to the Old Testament. True, children were not held responsible for sin even up to nine years of age, but the concept of the evil impulse is there from conception or birth. In Scripture, not until the Apostle Paul (1 Corinthians 14:20) does the idea of children's innocence even appear. And in Paul and other epistles, a much more common theme is that of the immaturity and inferiority of the child (1 Corinthians 3:1; 13:11; 14:20; Galatians 4:1, 3; Ephesians 4:14; Hebrews 5:13; 1 Peter 2:1-2), following the view of "foolishness" bound up in the heart of a child (Proverbs 22:15; 29:15) (Albrecht Oepke, *paidon*, TDNT 5:636-654).

Parable of Welcoming Little Children (Matthew 19:13-15; Mark 10:13-16, Luke 18:15-17; §188)

There is a second parable about little children found in all three Synoptic Gospels.[17]

> "People were bringing little children to Jesus to have him touch them, but the disciples rebuked them." (Mark 10:13)

Presumably, parents wanted Jesus to touch[18] the babies and young children[19] in an act of blessing, like elders or scribes did in the temple on the evening of the Day of Atonement.[20]

But the disciples would have none of it. Jesus was about important business – teaching and healing. They couldn't allow this work to be interrupted by mere children constantly running up.

They began to stop the little children, and rebuke[21] the parents in no uncertain terms. While children were prized by parents – male children especially – in society as a whole, they were largely ignored as unimportant. They weren't considered worthy of much adult attention outside their families.

James J. Tissot, 'Suffer the Little Children to Come unto Me' (1886-94), gouache on gray wove paper, Brooklyn Museum, New York.

Mark tells us that Jesus was "indignant,"[22] angry with his disciples' arrogance.

---

[17] In Matthew and Mark, this parable follows Jesus' teaching on divorce. In Luke it follows the Parable of the Pharisee and Tax Collector, which carries a similar theme of humility.

[18] "Touch" is Greek *haptō*, "to make close contact, 'touch,' frequently of touching as a means of conveying a blessing," though in our passage the word may also convey the idea of "to hold" (BDAG 126, 2c).

[19] In this incident they were *little* children. The word translated "babies" is *brephos*, "a very small child, baby, infant" (BDAG 183, 2). In the parallel passages (Matthew 19:13; Mark 10:13) and verse 16 of our passage, another word for "child" is used: Greek *paidion*, "very young child, infant," used of boys and girls (BDAG 749, 1a). *Paidion* is a diminutive of *pais*, the general word for child. In Classical Greek, Hippocrates used *paidion* of a child up to 7 years old, while *pais* described a child from 7 to 14 years of age (Hippocrates, *De Hebdomadibus*, 5; cited in Albrecht Oepke, *pais, ktl.*, TDNT 5:636-654).

[20] Marshall, *Luke*, p. 682, cites Soph. 18:5; Strack and Billerbeck 2:138; Joachim Jeremias, *Infant Baptism in the First Four Centuries* (London, 1960), p. 49.

[21] "Rebuked" (NIV, ESV, KJV), "sternly ordered" (NRSV) is the imperfect active indicative of *epitimaō*, "to express strong disapproval of someone, rebuke, reprove, censure," also "speak seriously, warn" in order to prevent an action or bring one to an end (BDAG 384, 1).

[22] "Indignant" (NIV, ESV, NRSV), "displeased" (KJV) is *aganakteō*, "be indignant against what is assumed to be wrong, be aroused, indignant, angry" (BDAG 5).

9. Parables about Disciple Character

> [14] When Jesus saw this, he was indignant. He said to them, 'Let[23] the little children come to me, and do not hinder[24] them, for the kingdom of God belongs[25] to such as these. [15] I tell you the truth, anyone who will not receive[26] the kingdom of God like a little child will never enter it.' [16] And he took the children in his arms, put his hands on them and blessed them." (Mark 10:14-15)

Thus, there are two similes or comparisons here.

1. Possession of the Kingdom "to **such as**[27] these [children]," and
2. Receiving or welcoming the Kingdom "**like**[28] a little child."

Notice, Jesus doesn't say that the Kingdom belongs to little children or that they are already in the Kingdom. He says that those who inherit or possess the kingdom will be "like" these children.

What characteristic of children is Jesus pointing to as an essential characteristic of disciples? Several possibilities have been mentioned:

1. Innocence. Judaism, however, didn't emphasize a child's innocence. Rather, it observed a child's immaturity and foolishness, as mentioned in the Parable of Becoming Like Little Children above.

2. Openness, trust, and receptivity. Surely the children come running to Jesus with complete openness and trust, and this is an essential characteristic of disciples. But nothing in the context of the passage seems to point to this interpretation.

3. Humility. Humility is the point, I believe, based on Jesus' explicit statement in Matthew 18:3-4. To Jesus, the children's humble station is itself symbolic of the humility required to approach God.

How do the little children come to Jesus? Freely, openly, humbly. They come to God with no posturing of worthiness, like the Pharisee in the preceding Parable of the Pharisee and Tax

---

[23] "Let" (NIV, ESV, NRSV), "suffer" (KJV) is *aphiēmi*, here, to convey a sense of distancing through an allowable margin of freedom, "leave it to someone to do something, let, let go, allow, tolerate" (BDAG 157, 5a).

[24] "Hinder" (NIV, ESV), "stop" (NRSV), "forbid" (KJV) is *kōluō*, "to keep something from happening, hinder, prevent, forbid" (BDAG 579, 1a).

[25] "Belongs" (NIV, ESV, NRSV), "is" (KJV) is the extremely common verb *eimi*, "to be," here in the sense of "to belong to someone or something through association or genetic affiliation, be, belong" with the simple genitive (BDAG 285, 9).

[26] "Receive" is *dechomai*, "take, receive," here, "to be receptive of someone, receive, welcome" (BDAG 221, 3).

[27] "To such as these" (NIV, NRSV), "to such" (ESV), "of such" (KJV) is a definite article and the pronoun *toioutos*, in the genitive, "pertaining to being like some person or thing mentioned in a context, "of such a kind, such as this, like such," here as a substantive, "such a person, either in such a way that a definite individual with special characteristics is thought of, or that any bearer of certain definite qualities is meant" (BDAG 1009, caא).

[28] "As" is *hōs*, here, a conjunction marking a point of comparison, "as" (BDAG 1004, 2cβ).

Collector (Luke 18:11-12). Rather, they come because Jesus calls them to him. They come in simple faith, like the tax collector (Luke 18:13).

These parables of becoming like children teach us that we must come to Jesus with lack of pretension. Humility is appropriate, with a recognition of God's grace and mercy allowing us to approach at all. We can only enter the kingdom when we come depending upon Jesus and not ourselves.

This is good news! Coming to Jesus has nothing to do with your worthiness and everything to do with his willingness to forgive, cleanse, and transform you.

Q40. (Mark 10:13-16; Luke 18:15-17). According to Mark 10:13-16, what characteristic of children is necessary for salvation? What characteristic were the disciples showing in rebuking the parents? When arguing about who was greatest? Why is humility essential to repentance? To learning? To obedience? Why did Jesus give his disciples the saying of becoming like little children?
https://www.joyfulheart.com/forums/topic/2214-q40-little-children/

Parable of Places at the Table (Luke 14:7-11, §169)

Jesus offers another parable on humility only in Luke, given on the occasion of him being invited to a Sabbath meal at the home of a prominent Pharisee who is trying to catch him in some error (Luke 14:1). Jesus heals a guest with dropsy, even though the Pharisees are shocked that he heals on the Sabbath. Jesus explains with an analogy of how people would rescue an ox or son in danger, even if it were the Sabbath.[29] Then he begins a teaching that culminates in his Parable of the Great Banquet that we examined in Lesson 2.2. The teaching begins simply:

> "When he noticed how the guests picked the places of honor at the table, he told them this parable...."[30] (Luke 14:7)

James J. Tissot, 'The Meal in the House of the Pharisee' (1886-94), gouache on gray wove paper, Brooklyn Museum, New York.

---

[29] See the Analogy of Rescuing from a Well, Appendix 4.3.

[30] Though Luke calls it a "parable" (*parabolē*), some suggest translating the word as "rule" (Jeremias, *Parables*, p. 20) or "counsel" (Green, *Luke*, p. 551). Some dispute that our next parable is a an "real" parable because it isn't a story that makes a point so much as an instruction on how people should act when invited to a banquet, an instruction that had a background in Jewish writings (Proverbs 25:6-7; Sirach 3:17-20). But, as we'll see, this is a parable because Jesus is giving a scenario of how to act at a contemporary banquet, and

9. Parables about Disciple Character

Picking the Best Places for Yourself (Luke 14:8-9)

Upon observing guests scrambling for the best places at the meal to which he was invited, Jesus says:

> [8] "When someone invites you to a wedding feast, do not take the place of honor, for a person more distinguished than you may have been invited. [9] If so, the host who invited both of you will come and say to you, 'Give this man your seat.' Then, humiliated, you will have to take the least important place." (Luke 14:8-11)

Where one sits vis-à-vis the host is a public advertisement of one's status.[31] Even Jesus' own disciples, James and John, had their mother try to intervene for them so they would have the preferred places in seating order next to his throne – one on his right and the other on his left (Matthew 10:21-23). At a Jewish meal, the most coveted place seems to be at the head end of the table or the middle of the middle couch.[32]

Taking the Lowest Place (Luke 14:10-11)

Jesus has painted the picture. Now he draws conclusions from it.

> "When you are invited, take the lowest place, so that when your host comes, he will say to you, 'Friend, move up to a better place.' Then you will be honored in the presence of all your fellow guests. For everyone who exalts himself will be humbled, and he who humbles himself will be exalted." (Luke 14:10-11)

Jesus recommends to the group that they should deliberately take a more humble spot. Then they might be happily surprised when the host asks them to move closer to him. The "moral" of the story given here repeats the moral of other parables we've seen.

Places at the Table: "For everyone who exalts himself will be humbled, and he who humbles himself will be exalted" (Luke 14:11).

Pharisee and Tax Collector: "For everyone who exalts himself will be humbled, and he who humbles himself will be exalted." (Luke 18:14b)

Becoming Like Little Children: "Therefore, whoever humbles himself like this child is the greatest in the kingdom of heaven." (Matthew 18:3-4)

---

then comparing it to how we are to humble ourselves prior to the Great Messianic Banquet (see Appendix 5), and how God will exalt us or humble us in his Kingdom (verse 11). Marshall (*Luke*, p. 581) comments: "This could be simple worldly advice to guests, and it is amply paralleled in Jewish writings. But it is presented here as a parable.... This is confirmed by the conclusion in verse 11 which speaks of the humiliation and exaltation of men by God. Hence the advice given (while good and valid on a worldly level) is a parable of how men should behave over against God." So also, Hunter, *Parables*, p. 58.

[31] Green, *Luke*, p. 550.
[32] Marshall, *Luke*, p. 581 cites Strack and Billerbeck, IV:2, 618.

It is not just a dinner host who might humble you, Jesus is saying, but God himself. Therefore, don't presume on your position, but be humble before God; let God exalt you, not yourself. Jesus continues by teaching these guests the Parable of the Great Banquet (Lesson 2.2). Humility is an important key to the Kingdom of God.

Both Peter and James make this point powerfully in their epistles while quoting Proverbs 3:34.

> "Clothe yourselves with **humility** toward one another, because, 'God opposes the proud but gives grace to the **humble**.' **Humble yourselves**, therefore, under God's mighty hand, that he may lift you up in due time." (1 Peter 5:5b-6)

> "He gives us more grace. That is why Scripture says: 'God opposes the proud but gives grace to the **humble**.' **Submit yourselves**, then, to God...." (James 4:6-7a)

Q41. (Luke 14:7-11) Why do people push themselves forward? According to verse 11, what will happen to them? Why is humility so important a lesson for Jesus' disciples? What is the danger to us, if we don't learn and internalize this lesson?
https://www.joyfulheart.com/forums/topic/2215-q41-self-advancement/

9.2 Avoiding Hypocrisy

Of course, where pride is unchecked by humility, hypocrisy is close at hand. Jesus makes a special point to warn his disciples about it.

Analogy of the Yeast of the Pharisees (Matthew 16:5-6, 11-12; Mark 8:14-15, §120; Luke 12:1, §154)

The Pharisees put on a veneer of holiness. They flaunted their piety by praying loud, long, pious prayers in the synagogues and street corners (Matthew 6:5-8). They loved to be publicly honored (Matthew 23:5-12). They had a reputation of keeping every tiny commandment of both the written law, the Torah, and the oral law, known as "the tradition of the elders" (Matthew 15:12). But, as we saw in the Analogy of Cleansing the Cup (Lesson 3.1), the Pharisees were guilty of gross hypocrisy – pretending strict holiness, at the same time as they are filled with judgmentalism, pride, and plots to kill the Son of God.[33]

Jesus gave his disciples a brief saying about this – twice. The first occasion is a discussion about forgetting to bring bread on a trip. Jesus picks up on this to talk about the formation of bread with yeast (Matthew 16:5-12; Mark 8:14-15).

---

[33] Matthew 6:1-8; Mark 7:6; 12:13-17; Luke 6:41-42; 13:10-17. Many of the "woes" against the scribes and Pharisees are prefaced in Matthew 23 with the phrase "you hypocrites."

9. Parables about Disciple Character

"'Be on your guard against **the yeast of the Pharisees and Sadducees.**' [12] Then they understood that he was not telling them to guard against the yeast used in bread, but against the teaching of the Pharisees and Sadducees." (Matthew 16:11-12)

The Pharisees' teaching was faulty, but especially their hypocrisy – teaching one thing and doing another.[34]

The second time Jesus gives this analogy is to his disciples in the midst of a huge crowd that are milling around. This is the one found in Luke's Gospel.

"Be on your guard against **the yeast of the Pharisees**, which is hypocrisy." (Luke 12:1)

Jesus is telling his disciples to be on guard against[35] – fully aware of, constantly on the lookout for in themselves[36] – the Pharisees' characteristic sin of hypocrisy.

This saying, this brief parable, compares the sin of hypocrisy to yeast or leaven.[37] Leaven is used in New Testament teaching in both positive and negative ways:

- **Positively**. The kingdom of heaven is compared to leaven. (Matthew 13:33; Luke 13:21; Lesson 7.1).
- **Negatively**. The hypocritical teaching of the Pharisees, Sadducees, and Herod is compared to leaven. (Matthew 16:6, 11-12; Mark 8:15; Luke 12:1; Lesson 9.2).
- **Negatively**. Boasting over tolerance of sin in their midst is compared to yeast that can affect the whole congregation, with clear references to Passover (1 Corinthians 5:6-8)
- **Negatively**. Belief in salvation by works is compared to yeast that will affect the entire batch of dough. (Galatians 5:9)

I believe that the point of yeast in Jesus' words here is yeast's ability to influence other dough by contact with it and to become pervasive throughout the whole lump of dough.[38] When Jesus says, watch out for the yeast of the Pharisees, he is saying, be careful that the mindset of the Pharisees doesn't influence you, too, starting small and growing to become large.

---

[34] "Do everything they tell you. But do not do what they do, for they do not practice what they preach." (Matthew 23:3)

[35] "Be on your guard" (NIV), "beware" (ESV, NRSV, KJV) is *proseuchō*, "to be in a state of alert, be concerned about, care for, take care" (BDAG 879, 1).

[36] The object of the verb *prosechō* ("beware") is *heautou*, "self," that is, "Beware of hypocrisy in yourself."

[37] *Zumē*, "fermented dough, leaven" (BDAG 429).

[38] See R.K. Harrison, "Leaven," ISBE 3:97-98. Marshall (*Luke*, p. 511) sees leaven here "used metaphorically of the pervasive influence of the thing signified." Hans Windisch (*zumē, ktl.*, TDNT 2:902-906, especially p. 906), observes, "The concept of *zumē* may be neutral. For the idea is that every man has a leaven. That is to say, every man or teacher exerts an influence, whether for good or for bad. The emphasis, then, is not on the [leaven] but on the genitive: [the Pharisees]."

Danger of Hypocrisy for Christians

Hypocrisy (*hypokrisis*) is so easy to fall into. The word was used in classical Greek in the sense of "act a part in a drama." Greek-speaking Jews frequently use the word group in the sense of "pretending" or "playing a part with intent to deceive."[39] In the New Testament the word is used in the sense of "to create a public impression that is at odds with one's real purposes or motivations, play-acting, pretense, outward show, dissembling."[40]

I've been around churches long enough – and am introspective enough – to know that we can easily deceive ourselves and others. We put on a good front of being good Christians, but struggle with sin and pain and brokenness. Be careful, Jesus is saying, look out for, be on guard against hypocrisy growing in you, my disciples, starting small, perhaps, but growing and taking you over. The embarrassment of transparency is to be preferred over the duplicity of hypocrisy.

The Only Antidote to Hypocrisy

The only antidote I know to hypocrisy is the willingness to contritely confess our sins quickly and openly to those before whom we have sinned. This kind of humble piety is fertile soil for spiritual growth.

Let's say that you use profane vocabulary at work, but never at home or at church. You feel like a hypocrite, and this keeps you from even mentioning at work that you are a Christian or that you go to church. You don't want to bring discredit upon Christ and his church, so you do not identify yourself with him for fear of being branded a hypocrite. But you *are* a hypocrite. You put on a show for each group. Instead of being a single, integrated person you are two-faced.

This is how I believe you can get this two-facedness straightened out. Say something like this individually to your friends at work.

> "I owe you an apology. I am a Christian, but I really haven't been acting like it here at work. My language has been pretty profane and my jokes sometimes pretty obscene. Some of my business practices have been questionable, too. I haven't been a very good example of a Christian at all.

> "But I want to try to change that. Though I'm never going to be a perfect Christian, I'm afraid, I really want to be consistent with what I believe. So please forgive me for my hypocrisy and inconsistency and bear with me while I try to get my act together. Thanks for taking the time to understand."[41]

---

[39] Robert H. Smith, "Hypocrite," DJG 351-353.
[40] *Hypokrisis*, BDAG 1038.
[41] Years ago, I wrote a short story, "God's Man at Bearcat Tool and Die," to illustrate this. www.joyfulheart.com/maturity/bearcat.htm

None of this is easy. When we say something like this our friends may or may not accept it at face value. The word will get around and people will test us to see if we mean what we say. We'll blow it inevitably, and have to confess and apologize again. And that's hard on the ego.

But I see this as the humble life of a sincere follower of Jesus who takes pains not to come across as "holier than thou," even though this *will* be mistaken for being "holier than thou" by those who feel conviction as a result.

The antidote to hypocrisy is transparency, integrity between our beliefs and our actions, with confession and apology when we are inconsistent.

We Christians have a serious public relations problem. Our Savior preached love and forgiveness, but we Christians have a reputation in the world of being judgmental hypocrites. This is the characteristic sin attributed to Christians. How did the world form this opinion? By watching Christians.

Because hypocrisy is so pervasive among Christians, we must be very, very zealous to be cognizant of and wary of the "yeast" of the Pharisees – hypocrisy. If we disciples fail to take heed, our hypocrisy is capable of so clouding the gospel of God's love, that it will prevent millions from being saved.

> Q42. (Luke 12:1; Matthew 16:11-12) Why is hypocrisy easy to detect in others, but difficult to detect in ourselves? Why is hypocrisy so deadly to spiritual growth? To witness? To obedience? To being a disciple? What is the antidote for hypocrisy?
> https://www.joyfulheart.com/forums/topic/2216-q42-hypocrisy/

9.3 Abiding

We've looked at parables about humility and hypocrisy. Now let's examine several parables that relate to abiding, remaining, staying very close to Jesus.

Parable of the Vine and the Branches (John 15:1-8)

One of the most beautiful and powerful parables along this line is found in his Parable of the Vine and the Branches. John 15 begins with one of Jesus' seven "I AM" declarations.

> "¹ I am the true vine, and my Father is the gardener.
> ² He cuts off every branch in me that bears no fruit, while

Icon of Christ the True Vine (late 20th century), Dormition Convent, Parnes, Greece, based on an early 15th century by Angelos Akotantos at Malles, Hierapetra.

every branch that does bear fruit he prunes so that it will be even more fruitful." (John 15:1-2)

As you examine this parable, you see that it isn't a story with a plot that unfolds like some of Jesus' famous parables, but rather extended observations on a metaphor of a vine and branches – and a vintner's decisions on how to prune his vineyard for maximum harvest.

This parable contains some of the most important and beloved passages in the Bible about the disciple's love relationship with Jesus – the characteristic of abiding with Christ.

Israel, God's Vineyard

The vine[42] was one of the quintessential plants of Israel representing national peace and prosperity – "every man under his vine and fig tree."[43] Moreover, the vineyard is often used to identify Israel itself, referred to by the prophets as "my vineyard" (Isaiah 3:14).

In Isaiah's Song of the Vineyard (Isaiah 5:1-7), the vineyard is the "house of Israel" that yields only the bad fruits of injustice and oppression. But in the Day of the Messiah, Isaiah prophesies, this vineyard will flourish (Isaiah 27:2-3). Psalms, Ezekiel, Jeremiah, Hosea, and Micah all use the figure of Israel as the Lord's vineyard.[44] Jesus himself carried on this identification of Israel as God's vineyard in his Parable of the Tenants (Lesson 2:3) and Parable of the Laborers in the Vineyard (Lesson 4:3).

So for Jesus to say, "I am the true vine," is an announcement that, as the Messiah, he now becomes the true Israel, the true locus for God's people. When you think about it, it is an astounding revelation!

"I am the true vine, and my Father is the gardener." (John 15:1)

In this metaphor, Jesus is the "true vine," we are the branches, and the Father is the gardener, vinedresser[45], the one who tenderly cares for the vine, cutting and pruning so that it produces the maximum amount of fruit possible.

Pruning for Increased Harvest (John 15:2-3)

Pruning a vineyard is both an art and a science.

---

[42] "Vine" is *ampelos*, "vine, grapevine" (BDAG 54, a).

[43] 1 Kings 4:25; 2 Kings 18:31; Zechariah 3:10; Micah 4:4.

[44] Psalm 80:8-16; Ezekiel 15:1-8; 17:1-21; 19:10-14; Jeremiah 2:21; 12:10; Hosea 10:1-2; Micah 7:1.

[45] "Gardener" (NIV), "vinegrower" (NRSV), "vinedresser" (ESV, RSV), "husbandman" (KJV) is *geōrgos*, generally, one who is occupied in agriculture or gardening, "farmer," then, "one who does agricultural work on a contractual basis, vine-dresser, tenant farmer" (BDAG 196, 2). This is a compound noun, from *ge*, "land" + *ergon*, "worker."

9. Parables about Disciple Character

> "² He cuts off every branch in me that bears no fruit, while every branch that does bear fruit he prunes so that it will be even more fruitful ³ You are already clean because of the word I have spoken to you." (John 15:2-3)

Since there are several vineyards within one quarter mile of my house – and the owner a personal friend – I've had considerable opportunity over the years to observe the cycles of pruning, growth, and harvest.

A grapevine consists of the woody trunk with one or more cordons, woody extensions of the trunk that remain from year to year. Together, the trunk and cordons are what Jesus refers to as the "vine." The fruitfulness comes from the canes, shoots, or spurs that grow from these woody cordons. These canes, shoots, or spurs Jesus is calling the "branches."[46] The fruit forms from buds on the new canes. The old canes do not produce again.

Pruning takes experience and skill. After the harvest, winter comes when the leaves fall off and the vine goes dormant. During this time, before the new buds of spring, the pruning takes place. Our text discusses two operations – (1) removing unfruitful branches, and (2) pruning the fruitful ones.

The vinedresser looks for any shoots that didn't bear fruit the previous season, due to disease or damage of one kind or another.

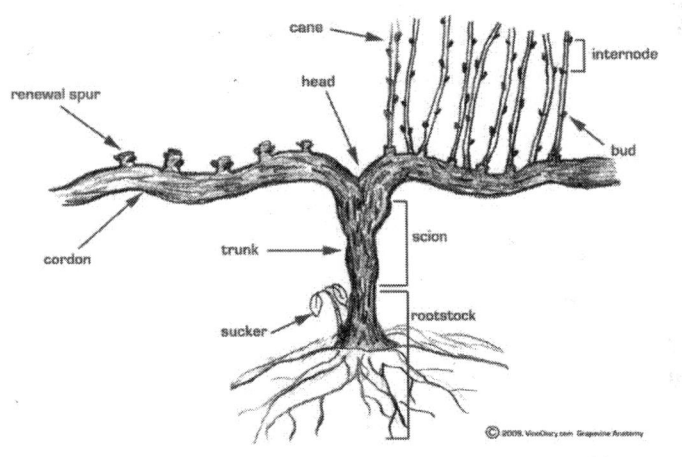

Grapevine Terminology. Diagram © 2009, VinoDiary.com. Used by permission. Larger image.

These he cuts off[47] entirely so that the energy of the plant is not wasted on unfruitful or diseased branches, but can go into branches that do bear fruit.

Common practice in our day is for the fruitful branches to be pruned back to the first two nodes on the old shoot to form new canes for next year's growth. Without pruning, the fruit

---

[46] "Branch" is *klēma*, "branch," especially of a vine (BDAG 547).

[47] "Cuts off" (NIV), "removes" (NRSV), "takes away" (ESV, KJV) is *airō*, "lift up," here, "to take away, remove, or seize control" without suggestion of lifting up, "take away, remove" (BDAG 29, 3). Some writers have suggested that *airō* should be rendered "lifted up" rather than "take away." That fruitless branches are lifted up from the ground so they can be exposed to the sun and will begin to bear fruit. However, there is no evidence that this was the practice of viticulture, ancient or modern (D. A. Carson, *The Gospel According to John* (Pillar New Testament Commentary; Eerdmans, 1991), p. 518). It is an attempt to avoid the concept that unfruitful Christians are "cut off." But, as I explain in the text, Jesus has in mind the nation of Israel being cut off for unfruitfulness.

season will be dramatically diminished. The vine will begin to grow wild, producing some grapes, but making it hard for the plant to get enough light and making it difficult to harvest the grapes that are produced. Pruning shocks the plant, to be sure, but in the hands of a skillful vinedresser, the vine remains healthy and produces maximum fruit year after year.

Purposes of Pruning

After getting rid of the dead wood, the vinedresser gets down to the exacting work of pruning each shoot or branch. The purposes of pruning are to:

- Stimulate growth,
- Allow the vinedresser to shape the vine,
- Produce maximum yield without breaking the branches with too many clusters for them to bear,
- Protect against mildew,
- Produce better quality wine, with more highly concentrated and flavorful grapes.

Of course, the Father does pruning in our lives, too, so that you and I will become healthy and bear much spiritual fruit. When I had an Internet marketing business, I tried to practice the principle in January of each year to deliberately cut off the least effective parts of my business – the bottom 10% – so I could free up time and resources for new opportunities.

You may be spending lots of time in activities that are fruitless. I can remember God telling me when I was in college to throw away my cherished notebook of folk music so I could concentrate on music that honored him. Sometimes we suffer losses and grieve about them, but find that God is redirecting and healing us. If we want the Vinedresser's skill to make us whole and fruitful, we must trust him and must be obedient,

Cleansed by the Word (John 15:3)

Now we come to a curious verse.

> "² He cuts off[48] every branch in me that bears no fruit, while every branch that does bear fruit he prunes (*katharizō*) so that it will be even more fruitful. ³ You are already clean (*katharizō*) because of[49] the word I have spoken to you." (John 15:2-3)

"Prune" (NIV, NRSV, ESV), "purge" (KJV) in verse 2 translate the verb *katharizō*, "to clean, cleanse." "Clean" in verse 3 is a participle of the same word. Jesus' word is a cause of that moral and spiritual cleansing in us.[50]

---

[48] "Cuts off" (NIV), "takes away" (ESV, KJV), "removes" (NRSV) is *airō*, "to take away, remove, or seize control without suggestion of lifting up, take away, remove." (BDAG 28, 3).

[49] In the clause, "because of (*dia*) the word I have spoken to you" (NIV, ESV), the preposition *dia* with the accusative is a "marker of something constituting cause" (BDAG 225, B2a).

[50] *Katharizo*, "to cause something to become clean, make clean," here, "to remove superfluous growth from a plant, clear, prune" (BDAG 488, 1b).

Jesus is speaking to his disciples. The effect of obedience and "holding to" or abiding in Jesus' teaching is freedom from slavery to sin and separation from evil. As Jesus told his disciples on another occasion.

> "If you hold (*menō*) to my teaching, you are really my disciples. Then you will know the truth, and the truth will set you free." (John 8:31-32)

God's Word, when received, has a washing, cleansing, pruning, faith-producing effect on us.[51]

Cutting Withered Branches (John 15:2a, 6)

Two verses in Jesus' teaching talk about cutting off branches that sometimes raise questions. Believers sometimes fear that they'll be cut off for their sins.

> "He cuts off every branch in me that bears no fruit...." (John 15:2a)

> "If anyone does not remain in me, he is like a branch that is thrown away and withers[52]; such branches are picked up, thrown into the fire and burned." (John 15:6)

Since Jesus the True Vine represents true Israel, the Father is pruning off those who rebel against the Messiah, those who bear no fruit, those who are already dead.

I live on a property with hundreds of native oak trees. Not infrequently, as I walk around the property, I'll see a tree with a branch that is dry and brown. It may be diseased. It may have broken from high wind. Its vital connection with the trunk, however, has been severed and the sap no longer flows into the branch, bringing life. Soon the leaves turn brown and fall off. The wood becomes brittle. It is dead. When I get around to it, I cut the larger pieces for firewood and put the smaller branches into a burn pile – or grind it into wood chips with a chipper.

When Jesus speaks here about withered branches being burned, is he talking about backslidden Christians or apostate Christians? I don't think so, at least not directly. Rather, he is talking about the Jewish nation, God's vineyard, whose leaders had rejected their Messiah, the True Vine. We shouldn't be afraid that God is going to cut us off for our sins. No. Jesus died for our sins. If you see yourself in sin, my friend, repent. Jesus' salvation is for you. Some wonder if a truly saved person can be lost; this passage isn't designed to answer that question. It is a metaphor.[53]

---

[51] Ephesians 5:25b-27; John 17:17; 1 Peter 1:22-23; James 1:18.

[52] "Withers" is *xērainō*, "to stop a flow (such as sap or other liquid) in something and so cause dryness, to dry, dry up." It also can refer to paralysis, "to become dry to the point of being immobilized, be paralyzed," (BDAG 684, 1).

[53] To explore the question of "the eternal security of the believer" in greater depth, see "A Brief Look at TULIP Calvinism," an appendix to my study, *Grace: Favor for the Undeserving* (JesusWalk Publications, 2023). www.jesuswalk.com/grace/tulip-calvinism.htm

Q43. (John 15:1-3) How does skillful pruning increase the fruitfulness of a grapevine? How are we pruned or cleansed by exposure and obedience to Jesus' words? According to John 8:31-32, *how* does obeying Jesus' teaching bring cleansing and freedom from sin?
https://www.joyfulheart.com/forums/topic/2217-q43-pruning/

Remaining, Abiding in the Vine (John 15:4-5)

Jesus has explained the metaphor of pruning the vine. Now he looks at the metaphor of abiding in the vine in verses 4 and 5. I am using the ESV translation here.

> "⁴ Abide *(menō)* in me, and I in you. As the branch cannot bear fruit by itself, unless it abides *(menō)* in the vine, neither can you, unless you abide *(menō)* in me. ⁵ I am the vine; you are the branches. Whoever abides *(menō)* in me and I in him, he it is that bears much fruit, for apart from me you can do nothing." (John 15:4-5, ESV)

The key word here is "remain" (NIV), "abide" (NRSV, ESV, KJV), the Greek verb *menō*, "remain, stay," occurring three times in these two verses. It means "stay," often in the special sense of "to live, dwell, lodge." Here, it is in the transferred sense of someone who does not leave a certain realm or sphere: "remain, continue, abide."[54] We just saw *menō* in John 8:31.

When you think about it, the most natural thing a "branch" can do is to continue being a branch, connected to the sap that flows from the vine. To do anything else is unnatural! To "abide" means that we "hold to" (NIV) or "continue in" (NRSV, KJV) Jesus' teaching.[55] Jesus taught that the elect will continue in the faith.[56] The Apostle Paul also taught that salvation is contingent upon believers continuing or persevering in their faith.[57]

I. Howard Marshall says:

> "The element of trust and commitment in faith is particularly emphasized and expressed in John by the use of the verb 'to abide' *(menō)*, which might almost be said to be the Johannine equivalent for 'to persevere.'"[58]

---

[54] *Menō*, BDAG 631, 1bβ.
[55] John 5:38; 8:31; 2 John 9.
[56] Matthew 24:13; Mark 13:3; Luke 8:15.
[57] Colossians 1:23, *epimenō*, 1 Corinthians 15:2, *katechō*, 2 Timothy 3:14, *menō*; see Hebrews 3:6; cf. 10:39.
[58] I. Howard Marshall, *Kept by the Power of God* (Bethany Fellowship, 1969), p. 183. See my study of *Grace: God's Undeserved Favor* (JesusWalk Publications, 2023), Appendix 2. A Brief Look at TULIP Calvinism. www.jesuswalk.com/grace/tulip-calvinism.htm

9. Parables about Disciple Character 217

But "abiding" extends beyond continuing in faith. In this metaphor of the vine and the branches, "abiding" refers to being intimately connected to and receiving nourishment from the vine. Look at the passage again, this time in the NIV

> "⁴ Remain in me, and I will remain in you. No branch can bear fruit by itself; it must remain in the vine. Neither can you bear fruit unless you remain in me. ⁵ I am the vine; you are the branches. If a man remains in me and I in him, he will bear much fruit; apart from me you can do nothing." (John 15:4-5)

What does this "remaining" or "abiding" entail? To start with, believing. But we're not talking about belief as intellectual assent here, but believing as embracing, clinging to, and continuing to receive spiritual sustenance from.

Mutual Indwelling (John 15:5b)

Abiding also involves a person who
> "... **remains** (*menō*) **in me and I in him.**" (John 15:5b)

This phrase intrigues me, we see it elsewhere in John, such as:

> "Whoever eats my flesh and drinks my blood **remains** (*menō*) **in me, and I in him.**" (John 6:56)

> "Believe the miracles, that you may know and understand that **the Father is in me, and I in the Father.**" (John 10:38)[59]

This mutual indwelling is part of the Father's relationship with the Son. The Father and Son are the exemplars of what our relationship is to be with Jesus – constant living together, sharing a deepening relationship of love and (on our part) obedience. This is abiding.

Apart from Me You Can Do Nothing (John 15:4-6)

> "⁴ᵇ No branch can bear fruit by itself; it must remain in the vine. Neither can you bear fruit unless you remain in me. ⁵ ... If a man remains in me and I in him, he will bear much fruit; apart[60] from me you can do nothing. ⁶ If anyone does not remain in me, he is like a branch that is thrown away and withers; such branches are picked up, thrown into the fire and burned." (John 15:4-6)

Abiding also involves utter dependence upon Jesus the Vine. If we branches don't continue intimately connected to the vine, our "sap" is cut off. We wither and whatever fruit might have been in the process of ripening becomes like dry raisins rather than like lush grapes

---

[59] See also John 14:10, 20, 23; 17:21-23, 26.
[60] "Apart from" (NIV, NRSV, ESV), "without" (KJV) is *chōris*, an adverb, here used as a preposition, "pertaining to the absence or lack of something, without, apart from, independent(ly of)" (BDAG 1095, 2aα).

bursting with juice. Not only we can "do nothing" by ourselves, we see the same language from Jesus about himself and the Father. For example,

> "I tell you the truth, the Son can do nothing by himself; he can do only what he sees his Father doing, because whatever the Father does the Son also does." (John 5:19)[61]

Sometimes we resent *dependence*. Something in us longs for utter *independence*. Part of our old nature loves the lines in William Ernest Henley's poem "Invictus" (1875) that read:

> "I am the master of my fate,
> I am the captain of my soul."[62]

But the path of the Master is a different path than self-determination. It is a path of listening and obeying, of observing and following. Jesus walked this path before us, doing exactly what he saw the Father doing. Now he beckons us to follow him in this same way. It is the path of a disciple following a Master, a Son following a Father. And it requires from us a humility that fully believes that apart from him we can do nothing.

Oh, we can do things by ourselves. God has naturally gifted us. But Jesus is talking about the things that last, that count for eternity. These we cannot do without his leading and his power. The older and wiser man or woman knows something that the young do not always grasp. Paul put it this way:

> "His work will be shown for what it is, because the Day will bring it to light. It will be revealed with fire, and the fire will test the quality of each man's work. If what he has built survives, he will receive his reward. If it is burned up, he will suffer loss; he himself will be saved, but only as one escaping through the flames." (1 Corinthians 3:13-15)

Do you want your life to count for something? Then live your life abiding with Jesus, and then with his direction and power accomplish something that lasts.

C.T. Studd (1860-1931) was a British missionary, one of the "Cambridge Seven" who went to evangelize China with Hudson Taylor. Later, he served in India and the Congo. But perhaps he is best known today for a poem with this memorable refrain:

> "Only one life, 'twill soon be past,
> Only what's done for Christ will last."

Bearing Much Fruit (John 15:7-8)

Now Jesus points to the positive benefits of abiding (verses 7 and 8).

---

[61] See also John 5:30; 8:28b; 12:49; 14:10b; cf. 9:33.
[62] Published in William Ernest Henley, *Book of Verses* (1888).

9. Parables about Disciple Character

> "⁷ If you remain (*menō*) in me and my words remain (*menō*) in you, ask whatever you wish, and it will be given you. ⁸ This is to my Father's glory, that you bear much fruit, showing[63] yourselves to be my disciples." (John 15:7-8)

"My words abide in you" means that we continue to obey his teachings and therefore receive Christ's wisdom (John 8:31b-32). If we abide in Christ in obedience to his teachings, then we can ask anything in prayer and he'll give it to us. Why? Because we'll be praying according to his will and leading! We'll be requesting things that will expand his kingdom, not just selfish requests.

What exactly does Jesus mean by "bear much fruit"?[64] A brief survey of *karpos* in the New Testament indicates that "fruit" refers to a new way of life, one's actions, to a way of living.[65] Abiding in Christ produces the fruit of righteous character – especially of love – and influence of this character upon others that brings glory to God.

We would like to bear memorable fruit, achievements that we can point to and say, "I did that – oh, with God's help." A good bit of that is pride and a desire for some kind of self-worth. But for most of us, fruitfulness consists in day-by-day faithfulness and obedience, of touching lives that God is working with, long forgotten but important to God's work. We may not be remembered a decade or two beyond our death, but God knows and remembers. And I pray that he will say of us, "Well done, good and faithful servant. Enter into the joy of your Master."

> **Q44. (John 15:4-5) What does it mean "to abide"? What does abiding have to do with "mutual indwelling"? With a "personal relationship"? What does Jesus mean when he says, "Apart from me you can do nothing"? What is the value of things done without Christ? What is the final end of things done without Christ?**
> **https://www.joyfulheart.com/forums/topic/2218-q44-abiding/**

---

[63] "Showing yourself" (NIV) and "so prove" (ESV) is not in the actual Greek text, which is more literally, "that you bear much fruit and be my disciples" (NRSV margin).

[64] The word *karpos* means "fruit," then, "result, outcome, product" (BDAG 510, 1b).

[65] Fruit can be positive or negative (Romans 6:21-22). False prophets can be identified by their "fruit" (Matthew 7:15b-16a). Both Jesus and John the Baptist demanded repentance. John the Baptist commanded the Pharisees and Sadducees who came to his meetings, "Produce fruit in keeping with repentance" (Matthew 3:8). Concerning the whole Jewish nation that rejected him, Jesus said, "I tell you that the kingdom of God will be taken away from you and given to a people who will produce its fruit" (Matthew 21:43). A number of verses identify fruit with righteous living (Philippians 1:11; James 3:18; Hebrews 12:11). Some passages spell out what this kind of living looks like (Ephesians 5:8b-9; Galatians 5:22-23a; James 3:17). This kind of righteous living is what grows in a person watered by the Holy Spirit. In addition to speaking of the fruit of righteousness, Paul speaks of fruit as people won to Christ on his mission (Romans 1:13; 15:28; Philippians 1:22).

Parable of Eating Jesus' Flesh (John 6:53-58)

Closely related to the idea of abiding in Christ are Analogies of the Bread of Life (Lesson 6.1) and the Parable of Eating Jesus' Flesh.

The context of these metaphors is Jesus speaking to an unbelieving crowd in what is called the Bread of Life Discourse. The crowds want Jesus to prove by a sign that they should put their faith in him. Moses fed us manna, "bread from heaven," they say. What will you do to prove yourself? (John 6:30-31). Jesus identifies himself as the Bread of Life (John 6:35, 48) which we examined in Lesson 6.1. Now he shifts the metaphor from feeding on the Bread of Life to eating his flesh:

"This bread is my flesh, which I will give for the life of the world." (John 6:51b)

The concept smacked of cannibalism and was repugnant to the unbelieving Jews as well as many of Jesus' disciples. Jesus explains in gross physical terms:

"⁵³ I tell you the truth, unless you **eat the flesh** of the Son of Man and **drink his blood**, you have no life in you. ⁵⁴ Whoever **eats my flesh and drinks my blood has eternal life**, and I will raise him up at the last day. ⁵⁵ For my flesh is real food and my blood is real drink. ⁵⁶ Whoever **eats my flesh and drinks my blood remains** (*menō*) **in me**, and I in him. ⁵⁷ Just as the living Father sent me and I live because of the Father, so the one who **feeds on me** will live because of me. ⁵⁸ This is the bread that came down from heaven. Your forefathers ate manna and died, but he who feeds on this bread will **live forever**." (John 6:53-58)

It is a difficult passage to understand – even today! Is Jesus speaking about the Lord's Supper in this passage? Jesus' initial audience wouldn't have made that association, though after Jesus' crucifixion and resurrection, his readers surely would!

I think the key to what he means is found in verse 51: " the one who **feeds on me** will live because of me." Notice that this is in the present tense, suggesting ongoing feeding, not just a one-time bite. What does it mean to "feed on Jesus"? It is metaphorical language.

- verse 47: He who **believes** has eternal life
- verse 51a: If anyone **eats** of this (living) bread, he will live forever
- verse 56: Whoever **eats** my flesh and **drinks** my blood remains (*menō*) in me, and I in him.
- verse 57. The one who **feeds on me** will live because of me.

It is quite clear that believing in Jesus corresponds to eating the Bread of Life *and* eating Jesus' flesh, since these are used as parallel statements in the same context and with the same result – everlasting life. This is a strong, even *extreme*, metaphor for faith that continues. After Jesus said this, many of his disciples were offended and left him.

"⁶⁷ 'You do not want to leave too, do you?' Jesus asked the Twelve.

9. Parables about Disciple Character   221

> [68] Simon Peter answered him, 'Lord, to whom shall we go? You have the words of eternal life. [69] We believe and know that you are the Holy One of God.'" (John 6:67-68)

Perhaps using such an offensive metaphor for believing and abiding was Jesus' way of sorting out the true believers from the hangers-on.

Feeding on these words of eternal life is what the disciples longed for and could not do without. St. Augustine summarized it this way:

> "For to believe on Him is to eat the living bread. He that believes eats; he is sated invisibly...."[66]

F.F. Bruce concludes:

> "To believe in Christ is not only to give credence to what he says; it is to be united to him by faith, to participate in his life."[67]

I see feeding on Jesus as a metaphor similar to abiding in Jesus (John 15:1-9). Both passages (1) use the verb *menō*, "remain, abide" and (2) employ the present tense, which suggests an ongoing, continuous relationship. We remain in him, meditate on him, ponder and hold fast his words, and find our spiritual nourishment in this living relationship.

> **Q45. (John 6:53-58)** What does the metaphor of "eat the flesh of the Son of Man and drink his blood," mean in practical terms? To extend the same metaphor, what do you think might be the difference between nibbling the Bread of Life rather than actually making a meal of it? How does "eating his flesh" relate to abiding in Jesus? Why do you think Jesus uses this offensive analogy that resulted in many disciples leaving him?
> https://www.joyfulheart.com/forums/topic/2219-q45-eating-his-flesh/

The Analogy of the Yoke (Matthew 11:28-30, §68)

A final analogy for abiding can be found in the Analogy of the Yoke. One figure for being a disciple who abides in Jesus is taking on his "yoke."

---

[66] Augustine, *Homilies on John*, 26, 1.
[67] F.F. Bruce, *The Hard Sayings of Jesus* (InterVarsity Press, 1983), p. 21.

"²⁸ Come to me, all you who are weary[68] and burdened,[69] and I will give you rest. ²⁹ Take my yoke upon you and learn from me, for I am gentle and humble in heart, and you will find rest[70] for your souls. ³⁰ For my yoke is easy and my burden is light." (Matthew 11:28-30)

To carry heavy loads more efficiently, humans invented yokes – wooden devices that enable men or beasts to carry weight across their shoulders.[71] A yoke joins a pair of oxen so they can pull a load together. But here, I think Jesus has in mind a human yoke that helps distribute the weight over the shoulders. Such yokes have been used to carry a pair of buckets, for example; a backpack is a kind of modern-day yoke.

In Jesus' day, the expression, the "yoke of the law" was common among rabbis to describe taking upon oneself an obligation to obey the law. But the Pharisees' expression of law-keeping was oppressive.

Chongqing, China (1941). Photo: Harrison Forman, University of Milwaukee Libraries.

> "They tie up heavy burdens, hard to bear, and lay them on people's shoulders, but they themselves are not willing to move them with their finger." (Matthew 23:4)

The Pharisees taught a strict legalism – a heavy, joy-less, legalistic religion. Jesus offers his alternative. "I will give you rest"[72] (Matthew 11:28). Jesus offers relief from toil, rest, a refreshing, a reviving of spirit. He offers an alternative "yoke" to the yoke of the Pharisees.

> "Take my yoke upon you and learn from me, for I am gentle and humble in heart, and you will find rest for your souls." (Matthew 11:29a)

The people had been absorbing the exhausting values of the Pharisees – or perhaps the corrupting values of the world. Now Jesus calls them to "*learn* from me."[73] The Greek noun

---

[68] "Labor" (ESV, KJV), "are weary" (NIV, NRSV) is *kopiaō*, "become weary/tired" or, perhaps, "to exert oneself physically, mentally, or spiritually, work hard, toil, strive, struggle" (BDAG 558, 1).

[69] "Heavy laden" (ESV, KJV), "burdened" (NIV), "are carrying heavy burdens" (NRSV) is the perfect passive participle of *phortizō*, "to load/burden" someone with something, more exactly, "cause someone to carry something," in imagery, of the burden of keeping the law (BDAG 1064).

[70] "Rest" in verses 28 and 29 is the noun *anapausis*, "cessation from wearisome activity for the sake of rest, rest, relief" (BDAG 69, 2).

[71] "Yoke" is *zygos*, "a frame used to control working animals or, in the case of humans, to expedite the bearing of burdens, yoke," in our literature only figurative, of any burden (BDAG 429, 1). Galatians 5:1; Acts 15:10.

[72] "Rest" is *anapauō*, "to cause someone to gain relief from toil, cause to rest, give (someone) rest, refresh, revive" (BDAG 69, 1).

[73] "Learn from" (ESV, NIV, NRSV), "learn of" (KJV) is the aorist imperative of *manthanō* with the preposition *apo*, "from." The verb means, "to gain knowledge and skill by instruction, learn" (BDAG 615, 1).

9. Parables about Disciple Character

"disciple" is formed from the same root. Disciples are those eager to learn from Jesus. Become a disciple of Jesus, take his "yoke" on you.

Jesus gives three reasons we should come to him. (1) He is "gentle."[74] The word suggests humility, consideration of others, not being impressed with one's own importance. (2) He is "humble in heart." This is a similar word: unpretentious, humble – unlike the Pharisees.[75] And (3) he offers "rest for your souls."[76] He shows you how to unwind and relax in a joyful faith – something you learn as you walk with him.

He does have a yoke, a device to help carry the burdens of life along his path, and a discipline of life for you to follow him in. But his yoke has two characteristics: It is "easy," that is, it doesn't cause discomfort; it is easy to wear.[77] Jesus' yoke is formed especially for you, to fit your shoulders, to help you live your life. And it is "light." Yes, there is a burden,[78] but it is light. Jesus doesn't overload you, nor is he a slavedriver. We are assured that Jesus' burden will be light in weight.[79]

We've been examining what the character of a Christian disciple should be like. In the next lesson we'll turn to the values that Jesus desires his disciple hold dear.

Prayer

Lord Jesus, we long for the character you taught your disciples about. We long to walk in the light, to be people of humility, to be transparent rather than hypocritical. Lord, we want to abide in You. Help us! We pray in your holy name. Amen.

---

[74] "Gentle" (NIV, ESV, NRSV), "meek" (KJV) is the adjective *praus*, "pertaining to not being overly impressed by a sense of one's self-importance, gentle, humble, considerate, meek in the older favorable sense" (BDAG 861).

[75] "Lowly" (ESV, KJV), "humble" (NIV, NRSV) is the adjective *tapeinos*, "pertaining to being unpretentious, humble" (BDAG 989, 3).

[76] "Souls" is the plural of the noun *psychē*, "seat and center of the inner human life in its many and varied aspects, soul," here, "as the seat and center of life that transcends the earthly" (BDAG 1099, 2d).

[77] "Easy" is the adjective *chrēstos*, "pertaining to that which causes no discomfort, easy," here, "easy to wear" (BDAG 1090, 1).

[78] "Burden" is the noun *phortion* (diminutive of *phortos*, "cargo"), "that which constitutes a load for transport, load," here, figuratively, "burden" (BDAG 1064, 2).

[79] "Light" is the adjective *elaphros*, "having little weight, light" in weight. Figurative, "easy to bear, insignificant" (BDAG 314, 1), 2 Corinthians 4:17.

10. Parables about Disciple Values

We've considered parables that talk about the character traits of Jesus' disciples – righteousness, humility, abiding in Christ. Now we'll examine parables about what a disciple's values should look like when he or she begins to seriously follow the Master.

10.1 Careful Discernment

- Analogy of the Wolf in Sheep's Clothing (Matthew 7:15-16a)
- Analogy of the Tree and Fruit (Matthew 7:16-20; Luke 6:43-44; Matthew 12:33-35)
- Analogy of the Treasure Chest of the Heart (Luke 6:45)
- Parable of the Unjust Steward (Luke 16:1-13)

Gustave Doré, 'Little Red Riding Hood' (1862), oil on canvas, 65x81 cm, National Gallery of Victoria, Melbourne, Australia.

10.2 Trust and Money

- Parable of the Rich Fool (Luke 12:16-21)
- Parable of the Two Masters (Luke 16:13; Matthew 6:24)
- Parable of the Birds and the Lilies (Matthew 6:25-34)

10.3 Faithful Prayer

- Analogy of Asking a Father for Bread (Matthew 7:9-11; Luke 11:11-13)
- Parable of the Friend at Midnight (Luke 11:5-10)
- Parable of the Unjust Judge (Luke 18:1-8)
- Analogy of the Faith of a Mustard Seed (Matthew 17:19; Luke 17:6)

These parables clarify what disciple values look like in action.

10.1 Careful Discernment

To begin, we'll look at parables that Jesus uses to teach his disciples to have careful discernment about money and false prophets. He is training them to be leaders who can protect the flock from false prophets and others who would cause harm. He also seeks to keep them from becoming disillusioned and cynical when deceived by people they thought to be genuine believers. In addition to these, we have already seen other parables Jesus told about discerment of our own sins in the Parable of the Speck and the Beam (Lesson 3.4) and the Parable of the Good Eye (Lesson 3.4).

Analogy of the Wolf in Sheep's Clothing (Matthew 7:15-16a, §41)

The Analogy of the Wolf in Sheep's Clothing appears in the Sermon on the Mount and is found only in Matthew. It follows Jesus' warning that most take the wide path on the way to destruction.

> "[15] Watch out for false prophets. They come to you in sheep's clothing, but inwardly they are ferocious[1] wolves. [16] By their fruit you will recognize them." (Matthew 7:15-16a)

The command in this passage is to "watch out for" false prophets, with the verb *prosechō*, "be in a state of alert, be concerned about, care for, take care," here "beware of" something.[2]

When you think about it, Jesus' comparison, is kind of bizarre and funny if the subject weren't so serious – wolves dressed up as sheep. The sheep, of course, typifies a harmless animal, while the wolf represents a dangerous one.[3] I can't help but think of the fairy tale of the Little Red Riding Hood and the wolf dressed up as her grandmother. We're amused at how poor a disguise the wolf has! Jesus tells us to discern by looking at the results or the fruit of the person's life.

Analogy of the Tree and Fruit (Matthew 7:16-20, §41; Luke 6:43-44; §77; Matthew 12:33-35, §86)

Matthew moves immediately from the Analogy of the Wolf in Sheep's Clothing to the Analogy of the Tree and the Fruit. The topic is still being on one's guard for false prophets.

Karpos, "fruit," can refer to physical fruit, but here it is used more generally as "result, outcome, product,"[4] that is, actions and results of their lives, as we saw in the Parable of the Vine and the Branches (Lesson 9.3, on John 15:8). Jesus turns from one analogy to another on the word "fruit" (which is used figuratively in verse 16a, but of physical fruit in verses 16b-19). (In Luke, the parable appears in the Sermon on the Plain following Jesus' Parable of the Speck and the Beam, Lesson 3.4).

---

[1] "Ferocious" (NIV), "ravenous" (ESV, NRSV, cf. KJV) is the adjective *harpax*, "rapacious, ravenous." It is also used as a substantive for "robber" (BDAG 134, 1), from the verb *harpaxō*, "snatch, seize, that is, take suddenly and vehemently" (BDAG 134).

[2] *Prosechō*, BDAG 879-880, 1.

[3] A fable attributed to Aesop (sixth century BC) of the Wolf in Sheep's Clothing (Perry Index #451) may have been familiar around the Mediterranean at this time (France, *Matthew*, p. 290, fn. 20), though we don't know that. In this fable, a wolf found a sheep's pelt and wore it to blend in with the flock. It worked for a while until the shepherd noticed, then killed the wolf.

[4] *Karpos*, BDAG 510, 1b.

Let's explore Matthew's version of the parable, still in the context of false prophets.

> "¹⁶ By their fruit you will recognize them. Do people pick grapes from thornbushes, or figs from thistles? ¹⁷ Likewise every good tree bears good fruit, but a bad tree bears bad fruit. ¹⁸ A good tree cannot bear bad fruit, and a bad tree cannot bear good fruit. ¹⁹ Every tree that does not bear good fruit is cut down and thrown into the fire. ²⁰ Thus, by their fruit you will recognize them." (Matthew 7:16-20)

The twin analogies make the same point. You can tell the good from the bad by tasting its fruit. In the same way that you don't expect one kind of plant to bear the fruit of another kind of tree, Jesus is saying, false prophets will have different fruit than you'd expect. And that will indicate "bad fruit" rather than "good fruit."

Jesus oversimplifies here, using hyperbole to make his point. There are two kinds of trees, he says:

1. "Good," *kalos*, "beautiful" ... of quality, in accordance with the purpose of something or someone, "good, useful." In the physical sense, "free from defects, fine, precious ... morally good, noble, praiseworthy, contributing to salvation, etc."[5]
2. "Bad," *sapros*, "rotten, putrid," literally, of such poor quality as to be of little or no value, bad, not good," here, "bad, evil, unwholesome."[6]

It is in the character of the tree itself, Jesus says. A good tree can be counted on to bear good fruit consistently, year after year. On the other hand, a bad tree tends to bear scarcely edible fruit. It may be a beautifully formed tree with wonderful branches and cool shade. But when fruit-tasting time comes, its true nature is revealed. "By their fruit you shall know them," Jesus says.

Analogy of the Treasure Chest of the Heart (Luke 6:45, §77)

In Luke, Jesus shifts from the Parable of the Tree and Fruit to talking about the inner person, represented by "the heart."

> "The good person out of the good treasure of his heart produces good, and the evil person out of his evil treasure produces evil, for out of the abundance of the heart his mouth speaks." (Luke 6:45, ESV)

"Treasure" (ESV, NRSV, KJV), "stored up" (NIV) is *thēsaurus* (from which get our word, "thesaurus"). It can mean (1) "a place where something is kept for safekeeping, repository," such

---

[5] *Kalos*, BDAG 504.
[6] *Sapros*, BDAG 913, 2.

10. Parables about Disciple Values

as a treasure box or chest, or (2) "that which is stored up, treasure."[7] In our verse, it could bear either definition.[8] The New Jerusalem Bible puts it this way:

> "Good people draw what is good from the store of goodness in their hearts; bad people draw what is bad from the store of badness. For the words of the mouth flow out of what fills the heart." (Luke 6:45, NJB)

Here, Jesus turns from adjectives describing fruit (beautiful/spoiled), to moral words signifying moral goodness (*agathos*[9]) and moral evil (*ponēros*[10]). The corruption that is inside a person can't help but manifest itself in a person's words and deeds.[11]

At the end of verse 45, Jesus gives us a useful guideline for discerning false prophets. (The saying is also found in Matthew 12:34 in the context of good and bad fruit.)

> "Out of the **overflow** of his heart his mouth speaks. (NIV)

> "Out of the **abundance of the heart** his mouth speaks" (ESV, NRSV, KJV)

The key word here is *perisseuma*, "a condition of great plenty, abundance, fullness."[12]

In other words, Jesus is saying, listen carefully to what a person says. People (both good and evil) speak out of what they have tucked away or stored in their heart. It can't help but come out. Call it a "Freudian slip" or whatever. If we listen and ask for the Holy Spirit's help, God will enable us to discern what is in a person's heart from his or her words. Yes, people can speak deceptively, but it will slip out if we listen. And when a wise leader senses falsity in an influential person, he or she probes further to see what is actually in them.

To sum up, Jesus teaches his disciples that you can tell a false prophet by carefully examining both that persons':

1. Actions and outcomes (Analogy of the Tree and Fruit), and
2. Words (Analogy of the Treasure of the Heart).

Discerning a False Prophet

What do false prophets look like? How can you tell if someone is a false prophet? First, Jesus says that they look like everyone else. They come in "sheep's clothing," that is, they look

---

[7] *Thesaurus*, BDAG 456, 1b.
[8] We also see this word in the Parable of the Scribes of the Kingdom (Lesson 12.4).
[9] *Agathos*, "pertaining to a high standard of worth and merit, good" (BDAG 3, 2aα).
[10] *Ponēros*, "pertaining to being morally or socially worthless, wicked, evil, bad, base, worthless, vicious, degenerate" (BDAG 851, 1aα).
[11] Jesus uses an interesting word translated "stored up" (NIV) or "treasure" (ESV, NRSV, KJV). It is Greek *thesauros*, from which we get our English words "thesaurus" and "treasure." It means "a place where something is kept for safekeeping, repository" such as "a treasure box or chest" or "storehouse, storeroom" (BDAG 456, 1b).
[12] *Perisseuma*, BDAG 850, 1.

like other members of the flock – harmless, innocuous, friendly. But they're also "prophets," that is, they are active in the church, typically opinion leaders, influential, and vocal.

I've met a few of these false prophets in my day. To *outward* appearances they aren't particularly bad people. But Jesus says that their *inward* character is as ravenous wolves. They destroy the unity of the flock and pull away the sheep who are at the edges to fulfill their own personal agendas. Their lives may be corrupt, turning people to sin.

The danger of false prophets is one reason that Paul advises Timothy: "Do not be hasty in the laying on of hands." (1 Timothy 5:22a). Don't be quick to ordain someone into a church office. "They must first be tested; and then if there is nothing against them, let them serve as deacons" (1 Timothy 3:10).

The bad fruit Jesus tells us to look for might be:

- Strange or somewhat perverted teachings.
- Dominant character flaws.
- Actions and attitudes that don't conform to what you expect of a Christian leader.

We have an example from the Church at Thyatira in the Book of Revelation:

> "You tolerate that woman Jezebel, who calls herself a prophetess. By her teaching she misleads my servants into sexual immorality and the eating of food sacrificed to idols. I have given her time to repent of her immorality, but she is unwilling." (Revelation 2:20-21)

Jezebel is an influential woman in a congregation of Asia Minor who encourages members not to be worried about illicit sex and idol worship, and, as a result, many have entered into sin. She could have repented and been forgiven by the Lord, but she isn't willing. Scary!

False prophets ravage the flock and destroy sheep. I've seen pastors who teach one thing and then live another way. But when their lifestyle is exposed, it devastates the congregation who had been taken in by their hypocrisy. I've seen treasurers with the sin of greed who can control and turn a congregation away from God's will. I've seen power-hungry trustees who take godly pastors, chew them up and spit them out because the godly pastors tried to actually lead the congregation in God's ways.

I have also learned that a person, who at one point in time may be of strong character and healthy doctrine, can at a later time become compromised by sin or false doctrine (Hebrews 12:15). We are also to take heed to ourselves (Galatians 6:1; Luke 21:34).

I've tried very hard to learn from my experiences and not be bitter. There are some wrong lessons, such as: Never trust people again. Or: Hold all the power yourself.

But the lessons Jesus wants us to learn are: Watch out for false prophets and observe their fruits. Listen carefully to their words. Don't ignore or quickly pass over things that strike you

10. Parables about Disciple Values 229

as wrong. Jesus teaches us that there *will* be false prophets, that our congregations will not be immune from them.

False Prophets vs. Imperfect Leaders

Having said that, we shouldn't expect perfection in our leaders. None of us is perfect. We all have weaknesses and flaws. We must be gracious towards one another and bear with each other's weaknesses. Though we do expect Christian leaders to quickly repent of sin.

We aren't to go on a crusade that condemns innocent people like the Salem witch trials by the Puritans of the Massachusetts Bay Colony in 1692. (Look that up and study it for lessons to learn.) Don't let your corrupt heart take a person's minor flaw turn it into them being a false prophet!

Nevertheless, when you find a person in the congregation who is setting himself or herself up as a competing leader and pulling people's allegiance away to him or her, go to the leaders. They must be called on to expose the person formally (1 Timothy 5:19-20). Of course it is messy! Very messy! People take sides. Confrontation can harm the body. But the congregation is harmed much more, if it allows false prophets to ruin Christ's flock.

Paul solemnly warns the Ephesian elders:

> "[29] I know that after I leave, savage wolves will come in among you and will not spare the flock. [30] Even from your own number men will arise and distort the truth in order to draw away disciples after them. [31] So be on your guard! " (Acts 20:29-31a)

We've spent quite a bit of time on these very short analogies, but Jesus' teaching is so important for us today! Spotting false prophets, false leaders, requires careful discernment from disciples, but also great courage!

> **Q46. (Matthew 7:15-20; Luke 6:43-45) From Jesus' images of wolves in sheep's clothing, good and bad fruit, and the treasure chest of the heart, how does he teach us to discern false leaders? Why is this so important in our churches? Why must we distinguish flawed Christian leaders from dangerous false prophets?**
> https://www.joyfulheart.com/forums/topic/2220-q46-false-prophets/

Parable of the Unjust Steward (Luke 16:1-13; §174)
(Also known as the Parable of the Dishonest Manager or Penitent Steward)

Now we consider another of Jesus' parables about discernment. It will be confusing, especially since we've just been talking about false prophets. It is a notoriously difficult parable to interpret. The problem is because that Jesus uses dishonest deeds to teach a spiritual truth and we find that troubling. The overall theme of the parable, however, is the need for careful discernment by disciples, but this one has its own twist. Let's look at it in some detail.

Wasting the Master's Possessions (Luke 16:1)

The Parable of the Unjust Steward, found only in Luke, follows the Parable of the Prodigal Son (Lesson 1.1). Luke seems to include it here because it is another parable Jesus told, not because it has a similar theme to the preceding parables.

> "There was a rich man whose manager was accused of wasting his possessions."[13] (Luke 16:1)

The main character in the story is an estate manager.[14] He has been accused of "wasting" or "squandering"[15] his master's possessions. It is the same verb that described how the Prodigal Son, "*squandered* his wealth in wild living" (Luke 15:13).

Someone has warned[16] the master that his estate manager is wasteful. The man has been a trusted employee (not a slave, since he would soon be unemployed), but the administrator has betrayed the trust he has been given. His job has been to work for his master's best interests, but instead he has been sloppy and his master's fortune is being scattered, squandered on frivolous pursuits. We aren't told that he was embezzling money from his employer, but his subsequent actions indicate that he isn't beyond that kind of behavior.

Turn in Your Accounting Books (Luke 16:2)

> "So he called him in and asked him, 'What is this I hear about you? Give an account of your management, because you cannot be manager any longer.'" (Luke 16:2)

The rich man calls the steward in for a meeting. "Give an account of your management," means to give a final report of where things stand and then turn over the accounting books to

---

[13] "Possessions" (NIV), "property" (ESV, NRSV), "goods" (KJV) is *hyparchō*, "be present, be at one's disposal," here a substantive, "what belongs to someone, someone's property, possessions, means" (BDAG 1029, 1).

[14] "Manager" (NIV, NRSV, ESV), "steward" (KJV) is *oikonomos*, "manager of a household or estate, (house) steward, manager" (BDAG 698, 1).

[15] "Wasting" (NIV, ESV, KJV), "squandering" (NRSV) is *diaskorpizō*, "scatter, disperse," of a flock or seeds. Here it means, figuratively, "waste, squander" (BDAG 236, 2).

[16] "Accused" (NIV, KJV), "charges were brought" (ESV, NRSV) is *diaballō*, "to make a complaint about a person to a third party, bring charges, inform," either justly or falsely (BDAG 226).

10. Parables about Disciple Values

the master.[17] The same verb "account" is also used of each person having to appear before God's throne to give an account of their lives.[18]

The steward is being fired. But until he actually turns in the accounting books he is still officially the steward, and thus can still act in an official and legal capacity on behalf of his master. No wonder the modern practice is to have a fired employee clear out his desk immediately, turn in his keys, and leave the building under the watchful eye of a security guard.

Ingratiating Himself to the Debtors (Luke 16:3-4)

The man's time as manager is short.

> "The manager said to himself, 'What shall I do now? My master is taking away my job. I'm not strong enough to dig, and I'm ashamed to beg – I know what I'll do so that, when I lose my job[19] here, people will welcome me into their houses.'" (Luke 16:3-4)

He is desperate – and unscrupulous. The key phrase to remember is, "people will welcome[20] me into their houses," since Jesus repeats this phrase later in the parable and it relates to the point he is making.

> "So he called in each one of his master's debtors. He asked the first, 'How much do you owe my master?'
> 'Eight hundred gallons of olive oil,' he replied.
> The manager told him, 'Take your bill, sit down quickly, and make it four hundred.'
> Then he asked the second, 'And how much do you owe?'
> 'A thousand bushels of wheat,' he replied.
> He told him, 'Take your bill and make it eight hundred.'" (Luke 16:5-8)

The master's debtors are obviously well-to-do farmers in their own right. Those who deal in 800 gallons of olive oil and 1,000 bushels of wheat own much more than a small family farm.

The dishonest steward, in the waning hours of his employment, brings in his master's debtors one-by-one, and instructs them to change the records from the full amount owed to a lower

---

[17] "Give an account" (NIV, NRSV, KJV), "turn in the account" is two words: *apodidōmi*, "give, give up", here, "to meet a contractual or other obligation, pay, pay out, fulfill" (BDAG 109, 2c). "Account" is the common Greek word *logos*, "word." Here it means "computation, reckoning." This is a formal accounting, especially of one's actions, and frequently with figurative extension of commercial terminology, "account, accounts, reckoning" BDAG 600, 2a).

[18] Matthew 12:36; Acts 19:40; Hebrews 13:17; 1 Peter 4:5.

[19] "Lose my job" (NIV, "removed" (ESV), "dismissed" (NRSV), "put out of" (KJV) uses the verb *methistēmi*, "remove, depose" (BDAG 625, 1b).

[20] "Welcome" (NIV, NRSV), "receive" (ESV, KJV) is *dechomai*, "take, receive," here, "to be receptive of someone, receive, welcome," especially of hospitality (BDAG 221, 3).

amount – to replace or alter the bills or IOUs that they had previously written in their own hand. This has several implications:

1. The steward has the legal power to act for his master, and thus what he has done – though dishonest – is yet perhaps legal.
2. The steward is now seen as a friend and patron by the wealthy debtors. Not as a *trusted* friend, but a friend.
3. It seems to me possible that the steward could now blackmail the debtors concerning the changed bill.

In some ways, it is the perfect crime. The debtors that have made the changes in their own hand – the manager hasn't falsified the records personally. The debtors have profited from the change; he hasn't profited directly. There is nothing to prove any wrongdoing on his part; it is his word against theirs, and they had the most to gain from it. If the steward were to claim that this had been done without his authorization, at the very least the debtors' reputations might be ruined and perhaps they could be prosecuted under law for fraud. The debtors, therefore, may be inviting the ex-steward into their homes out of goodwill – and fear.[21]

Jesus refers to the steward as "dishonest," Greek *adikia*, "unrighteousness, wickedness, injustice."[22] Jesus doesn't justify his action, but calls it what it is – wickedness (verse 8).[23]

Commended for Acting Shrewdly (Luke 16:8)

When the master recovered the accounting books and receipts he could see what his ex-steward had done. Suddenly his accounts receivable were 30% lower than the previous week. But he couldn't take either his steward or his debtors to court.

> "The master commended the dishonest manager because he had acted shrewdly."
> (Luke 16:8a)

Instead, as one shrewd man to a shrewder[24] one, the master grudgingly commends the dishonest steward.

---

[21] There are many interpretations of the steward's actions. One is that the steward only reduced the amount of the bill by the excessive and illegal interest (usury) – making him in fact righteous compared to his blood-sucking master. But that doesn't fit the story as Jesus told it, nor would it be obvious to the hearers of the story.

[22] *Adikia*, BDAG 20, 2.

[23] Marshall (*Luke*, pp. 614-617) cites J.D.M. Derrett ("The Parable of the Unjust Steward," *New Testament Studies* 7, 1961, pp. 198-219), concluding that "Derrett's interpretation has the most to be said for it." So Morris, *Luke*, pp. 245-249. I think they're wrong for the reasons stated above. Green, *Luke*, pp. 591-592, fn. 272, also disputes Derrett's interpretation.

[24] "Shrewdly" (NIV, NRSV), "shrewdness" (ESV), or "wisely" (KJV) in verse 8 translate the Greek adverb and adjectives *phronimōs*, "prudently, shrewdly," from the root *phronis*, "prudence."

10. Parables about Disciple Values

Using Worldly Wealth to Gain Friends (Luke 16:8b-9)

Now to the application of the parable. Jesus doesn't applaud dishonesty, but he notes that "the people of the light" aren't as smart as worldly people when it comes to securing their future.

> "For the people of this world are more shrewd in dealing with their own kind than are the people of the light. I tell you, use worldly wealth[25] to gain friends for yourselves, so that when it is gone, you will be welcomed into eternal dwellings." (Luke 16:8b-9)

This is a hard verse to understand: How can you create eternal friends with money?

Rewards in Heaven

Many Christians minimize the idea of rewards in heaven given in return for faithful service here on earth. For many it probably it smacks too much of "works righteousness" that Luther so strongly and rightly opposed during the Reformation. But the Jews believed – and Jesus seems to endorse – that giving alms to the poor is rewarded by God, and is a way of laying up treasure in heaven.[26] There is also the idea in the Old Testament that you should give to the poor or the poor will curse you and God will give heed to the poor person's protest.[27]

Thus, Jesus is saying that Christians ought to help the poor, realizing that God will bless them for it. Not only will the poor in heaven remember their kindness, but so will God. See, for example, the Parable of the Rich Man and Lazarus (Luke 16:19-31, Lesson 4.1) that follows closely after this parable in Luke and explores a similar theme. The Parable of the Sheep and the Goats (Lesson 4.2) also indicates that Jesus rewards those who care for "the lease of these."

There is a wonderful verse in Proverbs:

> "He who is kind to the poor lends to the Lord,
> and he will reward him for what he has done." (Proverbs 19:17)[28]

What is it like to have God as a "debtor"? It is an oxymoron. But it gives credence to the popular saying, "You can't out-give God."

---

[25] "Worldly wealth" (NIV), "unrighteous wealth" (ESV), "dishonest wealth" (NRSV), "the mammon of unrighteousness" (KJV) is two words: *adikia*, "the quality of injustice, unrighteousness, wickedness, injustice" (BDAG 20, 2); and *mamōnos*, "wealth, property" (BDAG 614), the same word for Mammon used in the Analogy of the Two Masters that we'll see later in this Lesson 10.2. The noun, *mamōnas*, is a transliteration of an Aramaic word which means "wealth, property." and most likely derives from the root *aman*, "that in which one trusts." Though the word *mamōnas* carried the negative connotation of tainted wealth or dishonest gain, the rabbis did make a distinction between tainted mammon and property or wealth which is free from ethical objection (*Mamōnas*, BDAG 614-615. Hauck, *mamōnas*, TDNT 4:388-400).

[26] Matthew 19:21; Mark 10:21; Luke 12:33; 18:22.

[27] Psalm 140:12; Proverbs 19:17; 21:13; 22:22-23; 28:27.

[28] See also Proverbs 11:24-25; 28:27a.

We are not saved by giving to the poor (though a saved person will certainly have compassion on the poor), but we are rewarded on earth and in heaven for it. Jesus wonders in this parable, however, why most believers aren't smart enough to figure this out.

Honest with Little, Honest with Much (Luke 16:10)

Now Jesus shifts from telling this story to reflecting on being a manager of someone else's money.

> "Whoever can be trusted[29] with very little can also be trusted with much, and whoever is dishonest[30] with very little will also be dishonest with much." (Luke 16:10)

First, Jesus makes the observation that those who are honest in the little details of inconsequential things can be trusted to be honest with large responsibilities and large amounts of money. It raises an important question for you and me: Can we be trusted with the trivial? With small amounts?

Are you honest with the small responsibilities God gives you? With the small income or the small tithe you owe? If you are, God knows he can trust you with really large responsibilities and considerable wealth. If you are seeking to find who in your church you can trust with an important ministry to, watch carefully to see who has fulfilled the tiny responsibilities given them. If a people are sloppy with a small responsibility, they won't be any more careful with the big responsibility. It is a matter of character. Paul advises such a method for selecting deacons for the church (1 Timothy 3:10).

The True Riches (Luke 16:11-12)

> "So if you have not been trustworthy in handling worldly wealth, who will trust you with true riches? And if you have not been trustworthy with someone else's property, who will give you property of your own?" (Luke 16:11-12)

Jesus contrasts worldly wealth with the true spiritual riches. If you can't be trusted to handle materialistic wealth, how much less will God trust you with the true spiritual wealth.

Of course, there is a very real sense in which everything we own is God's – not just 10%, but everything. The phrase "someone else's property"[31] in verse 12 suggests that how we handle God's money relates directly to what he will entrust us with.

Here we are taught that we are stewards of God's property, managers of God's resources – our finances, our time, our talents and abilities, our position in society, all of it.

---

[29] "Trusted/trustworthy" (NIV), "faithful" (ESV, NRSV, KJV) is the adjective *pistos*, "pertaining to being worthy of belief or trust, trustworthy, faithful, dependable, inspiring trust/faith" (BDAG 820-21, 1aα).

[30] "Dishonest" (NIV, ESV, NRSV), "unjust" the adjective *adikos*, "unjust, pertaining to acting in a way contrary to what is right, unjust, crooked," here, "dishonest, untrustworthy" (BDAG 21, 1).

[31] "Someone else's property" (NIV), "that which is another's" (ESV), "what belongs to another" (NRSV), "that which is another man's" (KJV) is *allotrios*, "pertaining to what belongs to another" (BDAG 47).

10. Parables about Disciple Values

Q47. (Luke 6:1-13) In what way is the dishonest steward supposed to be a positive example to disciples? How does one "lay up treasures in heaven"? Why is the quality of our work of very small things so important to God? What is he waiting to see in us? What happens to people in the church who are promoted beyond their spiritual growth?
https://www.joyfulheart.com/forums/topic/2221-q47-unjust-steward/

10.2 Trust and Money

Since money has such a potential to corrupt, disciples must not wiggle out of facing the next principle that Jesus teaches in the Parable of the Rich Fool.

Parable of the Rich Fool (Luke 12:16-21, §156)

Greed has been an ongoing theme in Jesus' training of his disciples. Sometimes it is implied, other times it is out in the open.[32] The Parable of the Rich Fool is a longer parable, found only in Luke focuses directly on the sin of greed, as Jesus teaches his disciples about this hard-to-discern spiritual killer, a sin that tempted Judas to betray Jesus.[33]

The parable is given on the occasion of someone asking Jesus to adjudicate an inheritance dispute between brothers (Luke 12:13-14). Jesus refuses to get into it; rather he warns them about greed. Jesus uses the occasion as a "teachable moment."

Eugene Burnand, 'The Rich Fool' (1909), in *The Parables* (France, 1909), Conté crayon and charcoal.

> "Watch out! Be on your guard against all kinds of greed; a man's life does not consist in the abundance of his possessions." (Luke 12:15)

"Greed" (NIV, NRSV), "covetousness" (ESV, KJV) is *pleonexia*, "the state of desiring to have more than one's due, greediness, insatiableness, avarice, covetousness," literally, "a desire to

---

[32] Greed as a common theme in Jesus' teaching: calling Levi the tax collector (Luke 5:27-32); the Parable of the Sower, about thorns of riches that choke spiritual life (Lesson 8.1); Pharisees who inside are full of greed (Lesson 3.1); giving a party in order to be reciprocated by one's "rich friends" (Luke 14:12); the Parable of the Prodigal Son who squanders his wealth on wild living (Lesson 1.1); the Parable of the Unjust Servant (Lesson 10.1); the Parable of the Two Masters (Lesson 10.2); the Parable of the Rich Man and Lazarus (Lesson 4.1); the incident of the Rich Young Ruler; the saying about the impossibility of a rich person to enter the Kingdom in the Analogy of the Camel and the Needle (Lesson 6.1); and the story of wealthy Zacchaeus' generosity (Luke 19:1-10).

[33] John 12:6; Matthew 26:15.

have more."[34] Our English word "greed" is defined as "excessive or reprehensible acquisitiveness, avarice."[35] Notice that Jesus warns not just against greed, but against "all kinds of greed," greed in all its hidden forms. The temptation to greed requires vigilance since it is often subtle. "Watch out!" and "be on your guard,"[36] he says. The Tenth Commandment warns against coveting (Exodus 20:17). Covetousness is the desire for something that one doesn't have a legitimate right to, something that belongs to someone else.

Jesus gives the reason for his warning: "because a man's life does not consist in the abundance[37] of his possessions" (Luke 12:15), similar to, "Man does not live by bread alone" (Luke 4:4; Deuteronomy 8:3).

The Rich Man's Good Crop (Luke 12:16 -21)

Jesus tells a parable to illustrate his teaching on greed.

"¹⁶ The ground of a certain rich man produced a good crop. ¹⁷ He thought to himself, 'What shall I do? I have no place to store my crops.'

¹⁸ Then he said, 'This is what I'll do. I will tear down my barns[38] and build bigger ones, and there I will store all my grain and my goods. ¹⁹ And I'll say to myself, "You have plenty of good things laid up for many years. Take life easy; eat, drink and be merry."'

²⁰ But God said to him, 'You fool! This very night your life will be demanded from you. Then who will get what you have prepared for yourself?'

²¹ This is how it will be with anyone who stores up things for himself but is not rich toward God." (Luke 12:16-21)

The generous harvest has created a problem – lack of storage.[39] The most common type of above-ground granary unearthed in Palestine is circular, with openings below the almost flat

---

[34] *Pleonexia*, BDAG 824. This is a different word from *harpagē*, "robbery, plunder, greediness," used to describe the Pharisees' heart in Luke 11:39. In that context greed involved taking away what belonged to others; here it is a desire for more.

[35] *Merriam-Webster*, p. 511. "Avarice" means "excessive or insatiable desire for wealth or gain; greediness, cupidity," from the word "avid" (Latin *avidus*), "desirous to the point of greed; urgently eager; greedy" (*Merriam-Webster*, pp. 79, 30).

[36] *Phylassō*, "watch, guard," here, "to be on one's guard against, look out for, avoid" (BDAG 1068, 3).

[37] "Abundance" is the present active infinitive of *perisseuō*, "to be in abundance, abound" (BDAG 805, 1a).

[38] *Apothēkē*, BDAG 110. The word translated "barn" is Greek *apothēkē*, "storehouse, barn," a place in which anything is laid by or up, from which we get our English word "apothecary."

[39] "Store" (NIV, ESV, NRSV), "bestow" (KJV) *synagō*, "to cause to come together, gather (in)" It can be used broadly, of fish, crops, people, etc. (BDAG 962, 1a).

10. Parables about Disciple Values

roof so that air could circulate. Stairs on the outside formed a kind of ramp to carry the sacks of grain and then pour the grain in at the top.[40]

In the parable, the farmer's abundance is far greater than what he needs for his own household. So instead of dumping his grain onto the market during a good harvest year, he plans to hold the grain for the future, when he can get higher prices. He is a shrewd agribusinessman. Jesus doesn't fault him for his business acumen, but for his self-centered attitude. The rich man says to himself:

> "You have plenty of good things laid up for many years. Take life easy; eat, drink and be merry." (Luke 12:19)

The man actually believes that his riches will now insulate his life from hardship. God isn't in the equation at all. The man's focus is squarely on goods rather than God.

> "20 But God said to him, 'You fool![41] This very night your life will be demanded[42] from you. Then who will get what you have prepared[43] for yourself?'" (Luke 12:20)

Our life is not ours to control, but God's. He is in charge and can call due the loan of our lives at any moment he chooses. A radio commentator used to talk about "talent on loan from God." Yes, God will hold us accountable for how we used our lives and the gifts are God's. And we cannot take credit for what is God's.

Unfortunately, the rich man's focus is on himself – "what you have prepared for yourself" – not on God. And so God chooses to take back that night what belonged to God in the first place.

Not Rich toward God (Luke 12:21)

Jesus concludes the parable with these words:

> "This is how it will be with anyone who stores up[44] things for himself but is not rich[45] toward God." (Luke 12:21)

---

[40] Avraham Negev (Luke ed.), *The Archaeological Encyclopedia of the Holy Land* (Revised Edition; Thomas Nelson, 1986), p. 357; Edward M. Blaiklock, "Storehouses," *The New International Dictionary of Biblical Archaeology* (Edward M. Blaiklock and R.K. Harrison, general editors; Zondervan, 1983), p. 424.

[41] "Fool" is *aphron*, "pertaining to lack of prudence or good judgment, foolish, ignorant" (BDAG 159).

[42] "Demanded" (NIV, NRSV), "required" (ESV, KJV) is *apaiteō*, "to demand something back or as due, ask for, demand" (BDAG 96, 1).

[43] "Prepared" (NIV, NRSV, ESV), "provided" (KJV) is *hetoimazō*, to cause to be ready, put/keep in readiness, prepare" (BDAG 400, a).

[44] "Stores up" (NIV, NRSV), "lays up" (ESV, KJV) is *thēsaurizō* (from which we get our word "thesaurus"), "to keep some material thing safe by storing it, lay up, store up, gather, save" (BDAG 456, 1).

[45] "Is rich" is the present active participle of *plouteō*, "to be plentifully supplied with something, be rich" (BDAG 831, 2).

What does it mean to "be rich toward God?" A few verses after this, Jesus tells his followers to hold material things lightly. Rather,

> "Provide purses for yourselves that will not wear out, a treasure in heaven that will not be exhausted, where no thief comes near and no moth destroys. For where your treasure is, there your heart will be also." (Luke 12:32-34; cf. Matthew 6:1-18; 1 Timothy 6:17-19)

As you may recall, we explored "treasures in heaven" in the Parable of the Unjust Steward above (Lesson 10.1). We lay up treasures for heaven by humbly living for him now – giving to the needy, praying, fasting, doing good deeds. Such humble deeds contrast with selfish actions that accrue to our earthly wealth. Greed will not get us to heaven, but it may well hinder us from ever arriving there.

We're not so immune from greed ourselves. As I write, the news is that the Mega Millions jackpot is up to $1.35 billion USD. Such news will drive ticket sales even higher. What is behind it? Greed. Greed is not just a rich man's sin; you also see it among the very poor of the world also. The writer of Proverbs recognizes its dangers as he prays,

> "Give me neither poverty nor riches, but give me only my daily bread.
> Otherwise, I may have too much and disown you and say, 'Who is the Lord?'
> Or I may become poor and steal, and so dishonor the name of my God."
> (Proverbs 30:8-9)

Q48. (Luke 12:16-21) Is being wealthy a sin for a Christian? What was the rich man's actual sin or sinful attitude? How do you sometimes see greed in the people in your neighborhood or social circle? Christians aren't immune. In what ways might greed influence a Christian's behaviors and values?
https://www.joyfulheart.com/forums/topic/2222-q48-rich-fool/

Evelyn de Morgan (Pre-Raphaelite painter), 'The Worship of Mammon' (1909), oil on canvas, 24 x 21 inches, De Morgan Galleries at Cannon Hall, Barnsley, UK.

Parable of the Two Masters (Luke 16:13, §174; Matthew 6:24, §34)
(Also known as the Parable of the Wicked Mammon)

Jesus finishes teaching his disciples about money in Luke's account with the Parable of the Two Masters. In Matthew, this saying appears in the Sermon on the Mount (Matthew 6:24) where Jesus is teaching

10. Parables about Disciple Values

his disciples not to worry about clothing and food in the Parable of the Birds and the Lilies (that we'll consider next). In Luke, the Parable of the Two Masters follows the Parable of the Rich Fool that we just looked at.

> "No servant can serve two masters. Either he will hate the one and love the other, or he will be devoted to the one and despise the other. You cannot serve both God and Money." (Luke 16:13)

Jesus' short parable in Luke introduces the characters. First, a slave, specifically (in Luke) a house slave.[46] The translation "servant" may blunt the affront of slavery, but these are slaves, not domestic employees. The second character is a master (*kyrios*), one who is in charge by virtue of possession, owner."[47] The word can be used of "one who is in a position of authority, lord, master," but the context in Luke requires this to be a slave owner.[48] For more on this see Appendix 6. Slavery in Jesus' Day.

Probably only a few in Jesus' audience were actual slaves, but many of his hearers had the experience in a business of trying to please two bosses who had contrary ideas. Unless these bosses were always of the same mind and temperament, it would be impossible not to prefer one over the other.

> "Either he will hate the one and love the other, or he will be devoted to the one and despise the other." (Luke 16:13b = Matthew 6:24)

Jesus states the contrast twice in characteristic Hebrew parallelism:

Hate	Love
Devoted	Despised

Now that Jesus has set the stage, he makes his comparison.

> "You cannot serve both God and Money." (Luke 16:13c = Matthew 6:24)

The NIV capitalizes Money to indicate that Jesus personifies Money/Mammon as a competing god. "Money" (NIV, ESV), "wealth" (NRSV), "mammon" (KJV) is *mamōnas*, "wealth, property."[49] Jesus' point is that a man cannot render the exclusive loyalty and service inherent in the concept of slave to more than one master.

---

[46] The word "servant" here is *oiketēs*, literally, "member of the household," then specifically, "house slave, domestic," and "slave" generally (BDAG 694).

[47] *Kyrios*, BDAG 577, 1b.

[48] In Jesus' day a slave might work for two or more persons in partnership (Acts 16:16, 19) or for two different masters (*Pesachim* 8:1). A slave might even have been freed by one master, while still a slave to another (Marshall, *Luke,* p. 624, citing Strack and Billerbeck I, 433f.).

[49] *Mamōnas*, BDAG 614.

Oh, I don't serve Money, says the social climbing church board member or tight-fisted church treasurer. I don't serve Money, says the churchgoer who spends more on recreation and "toys" each month than he would ever consider giving to God's work.

The truth is that many, many would-be disciples *are* trying to serve both God and Money, and one or the other will come out on top. Look at how a person/church/company spends money, says one consultant, and I'll tell you what their values are. How we spend or allocate our money tells the story.

The question a disciple must ask is: God, how would You have us spend our money. That places Him in the position as the Lord of our life decisions, not we ourselves. Money decisions are either spiritual decisions or self-serving decisions. Making a contract has spiritual implications. Taking out a loan has spiritual implications. Buying on credit has spiritual implications. Writing a will has spiritual implications.

How we relate the Lordship of Jesus to our use of money is one of the core issues Jesus seeks to teach us disciples. *Failure to make Jesus Lord of your money* is to allow by default the money itself to influence your decisions.

Turning Worldly Values Upside Down (Luke 16:14-15)

Luke concludes the teaching with an observation about a portion of his audience.

> "¹⁴ The Pharisees, who loved money, heard all this and were sneering at Jesus. ¹⁵ He said to them, 'You are the ones who justify yourselves in the eyes of men, but God knows your hearts. What is highly valued among men is detestable in God's sight.'" (Luke 16:14-15)

The wealth that impresses people doesn't impress God at all. The Apostle John, who had internalized Jesus' teaching, wrote these words to his own disciples near the end of his life:

> "For everything in the world – the cravings of sinful man, the lust of his eyes and the boasting of what he has and does – comes not from the Father but from the world" (1 John 2:16).

At the root of discipleship is adopting the values of the One we are following and learning from. His values will either displace that which is evil and selfish within us, or we will resist His values to the end.

> **Q49. (Luke 16:13) What are the very subtle ways that we can begin to serve Money rather than God? How can we detect these temptations in our hearts? Why did Jesus tell his disciples the Parable of the Two Masters?**
> https://www.joyfulheart.com/forums/topic/2223-q49-god-and-mammon/

10. Parables about Disciple Values

Parable of the Birds and the Lilies (Matthew 6:25-34, §35; Luke 12:22-31, §157)

I won't spend much time on this familiar parable, except to point out that Jesus uses analogies of birds and lilies to teach his disciples about worry over material things. As you read this, remember from the Parable of the Sower (Lesson 8.1) that "the worries of this life and the deceitfulness of wealth" (Matthew 13:22) are specific "thorns" that choke out the fruitfulness of the Word.

> "25 Therefore I tell you, do not **worry** about your life, what you will eat or drink; or about your body, what you will wear. Is not life more important than food, and the body more important than clothes? 26 Look at the **birds of the air**; they do not sow or reap or store away in barns, and yet your heavenly Father feeds them. Are you not much more valuable than they? 27 Who of you by **worrying** can add a single hour to his life?
>
> 28 And why do you **worry** about clothes? See how **the lilies of the field** grow. They do not labor or spin. 29 Yet I tell you that not even Solomon in all his splendor was dressed like one of these. 30 If that is how God clothes the grass of the field, which is here today and tomorrow is thrown into the fire, will he not much more clothe you, O you of little faith? 31 So **do not worry**, saying, 'What shall we eat?' or 'What shall we drink?' or 'What shall we wear?' 32 For the pagans run after all these things, and your heavenly Father knows that you need them." (Matthew 6:25-32)

'Field of Lilies' (1910), stained glass window by Tiffany Studio, in Tiffany Gallery at the Smith Museum of Stained Glass Windows, Navy Pier, Chicago.

Jesus has pointed his disciples away from worry about material things. Instead, he points them to what is most important:

> "33 But **seek first** his kingdom and his righteousness, and all these things will be given to you as well. 34 Therefore do not worry about tomorrow, for tomorrow will **worry** about itself. Each day has enough trouble of its own." (Matthew 6:33-34)

For an exposition of this passage, see *The Jesus Manifesto: Sermon on the Mount* (JesusWalk Publications, 2011), Lesson 10. www.jesuswalk.com/manifesto/10_worry.htm

Q50. (Matthew 6:25-34) How does the Parable of the Birds and the Lilies teach us not to worry? What does Jesus teach about worrying about the future? Rather than worrying, what does Jesus instruct his disciples to do? What does obeying verse 33 look like in

your life?
https://www.joyfulheart.com/forums/topic/2224-q50-birds-and-lilies/

10.3 Faithful Prayer

Jesus tells several parables to teach his disciples about the power of prayer – and the nature of God.

Analogy of Asking a Father for Bread (Matthew 7:9-11, §38; Luke 11:11-13, §148)

Jesus' first parable about prayer is found in Matthew's Sermon on the Mount and in Luke's Sermon on the Plain. Jesus is comparing how human fathers respond to their son's requests to how our Heavenly Father will respond to our requests.

Matthew's version of the parable has the son asking for food: a loaf of bread, a fish. It begins with a rhetorical question.

> "⁹ Which of you, if his son asks for bread, will give him a stone? ¹⁰ Or if he asks for a fish, will give him a snake?" (Matthew 7:9-10)

Luke's version – no doubt given in a different time and context – adds a third request: for an egg.

> "... Or if he asks for an egg, will give him a scorpion? (Luke 11:12)

The answer to Jesus' questions is obvious. No good father will give his children a cynical or harmful gift. Matthew sums up Jesus' conclusion to this analogy:

> "¹¹ If you, then, though you are evil, know how to give good gifts to your children, how much more will your Father in heaven give good gifts to those who ask him!" (Matthew 7:9-11)

Notice that Jesus characterizes us human fathers as "evil" (*ponēros*). He doesn't assume the basic goodness of man, but the basic evil. But even so, human fathers still try to respond positively to their children's requests when they can. They don't trick them by giving them dangerous things that will hurt them. If human fathers don't return evil for good, Jesus is saying, how much more your heavenly Father. He is not peevish or petulant. He loves you.

Luke's version is similar.

> "How much more will your Father in heaven give the Holy Spirit to those who ask him!" (Luke 11:13b)

The Holy Spirit is the best gift God could ever give us!

I've heard people say, "Be careful what you pray for...." with the idea that the Father will give you what you ask for, even if it will hurt you. No! That is the world's cynicism. Jesus' teaching is opposite.

We can trust in our heavenly Father's basic goodness – even when we might be praying amiss or immaturely or selfishly. Jesus is saying: Don't ever, ever fear to pray to your Father. You can trust him to do you good and not evil, even if you don't know how to pray.

> Q51. (Matthew 7:9-11; Luke 11:11-13) Why did Jesus give his disciples the Parable of Asking a Father for Bread? What misconception was he seeking to correct?
> https://www.joyfulheart.com/forums/topic/2225-q51-confident-asking/

Parable of the Friend at Midnight (Luke 11:5-10, §147)
(Also known as the Parable of the Importunate Neighbor)

Our next parable on prayer is found in Luke's Sermon on the Plain, sandwiched between Jesus' teaching on the Lord's Prayer and asking a father for a fish (which we just looked at above).

> "⁵ Suppose one of you has a friend, and he goes to him at midnight and says, 'Friend, lend me three loaves of bread, ⁶ because a friend of mine on a journey has come to me, and I have nothing to set before him.'" (Luke 11:5-6)

The Obligations of Hospitality

Jesus has just set up his hearers for a jolt, a shock. They are expecting him to tell a story about legendary Middle Eastern hospitality, a value that was bred into the very fiber of each son and daughter of Israel.[50] In the Middle East, hospitality is more than the courteous thing to do; it is a moral obligation. To neglect hospitality to a guest is unthinkably insulting and rude. Notice that the word "friend" (*philos*[51]) occurs four times in as many verses. Hebrews weren't obligated to entertain enemies, but required to entertain friends.

William Holman Hunt, detail of 'Importunate Neighbor' (1895), oil on canvas, 36 x 53 cm, National Gallery of Victoria, Melbourne, Australia.

---

[50] For example, Abraham prepares a meal for his three (angel) visitors (Genesis 18:3-8). Lot perceives his obligation towards his (angel) guests was even greater than his responsibility for the welfare of his own daughters (Genesis 19:2-8). You can also find examples in the stories of Laban, Jethro, Manoah, Gideon, Samuel, David, Barzillai, the Shunamite woman, and others all offered hospitality to guests, even to strangers.

[51] *Philos*, "one who is on intimate terms or in close association with another, friend" (BDAG 1059, 2aα).

Now the shocker – the refusal of hospitality.

> "Then the one inside answers, 'Don't bother me. The door is already locked, and my children are with me in bed. I can't get up and give you anything.'" (Luke 11:7)

The typical poor Israelite family lived in a one-room house. In many poorer homes, the house also served as a part-time stable for the family's few sheep, goats, and chickens. Family members would sleep in the same room, sometimes on a raised platform, perhaps 18 inches (about 46 cm.) higher than the floor of the rest of the house, so the family could eat and sleep without constant intrusions by their animals. Family members usually slept with their clothes on, covering themselves with the cloaks they had worn during the day. They would bed down side-by-side on straw mats rolled out at night.[52]

Getting a whole family to bed is a considerable undertaking, as all parents know. Once children are asleep, parents work hard to keep them asleep. Once the chickens are settled down, parents don't want to wake them either.

The door is locked for the night.[53] The poorest homes would have a bar across the door to prevent the leather-hinged wood door from opening.[54] The friend couldn't just let himself in and get the bread. The father would have to get up ever-so-quietly from the sleeping area, find the bread in the food storage area, and cross the area where the animals were near the door, unlock the door, and give the bread to his neighbor. There would be no way to keep the entire household from waking up.

The plot introduces cognitive dissonance, breaking of a social obligation. Jesus' audience is troubled.

Shameless, Persistent Knocking

Verse 8 give us the resolution of the story.

> "I tell you, though he will not get up and give him the bread because he is his friend, yet because of the man's boldness he will get up and give him as much as he needs." (Luke 11:8)

As strong as his friendship with the neighbor is, it isn't strong enough for him to wake up his whole family. But the neighbor's "boldness" (NIV), "impudence" (ESV), "persistence" (NRSV), "importunity" (KJV) motivates the father to take action. The Greek noun is *anaideia*, "lack of sensitivity to what is proper, carelessness about the good opinion of others,

---

[52] Madeleine S. and J. Lane Miller, *Harper's Encyclopedia of Bible Life* (Third Revised Edition; Harper & Row, 1978), pp. 35-37.

[53] The Greek verb is *kleiō*, "shut, lock, bar" (BDAG 547, 1a).

[54] Wealthier homes might have been equipped with a primitive wooden lock using two- or three-pegged keys that would allow a bar to be lifted from its socket from the outside (William Sanford LaSor, "Locks and Keys," ISBE 3:149; *Harper's Encyclopedia of Bible Life*, p. 34).

10. Parables about Disciple Values

shamelessness, impertinence, impudence, ignoring of convention."[55] There is a Yiddish term that describes it: *chutzpah* – "supreme self-confidence, nerve, gall, audacity."

The point of the parable, of course, is the importance of persistence, of never giving up. Jesus' word to express this is remarkable: "because of the man's *shamelessness*." The friend has no sense of decency to wait until morning, of not disturbing his sleeping neighbor. He goes at midnight and knocks! And he shamelessly keeps on knocking until his neighbor gets up and shoves a loaf of bread through the door at him just to shut him up.

Asking, Seeking, Knocking (Luke 11:9-10 = Matthew 7:7-8)

The following verses are found in both Luke's Sermon on the Plain and in Matthew's Sermon on the Mount. We'll follow Luke's version where Jesus follows up the Parable of the Friend at Midnight with a three-fold exhortation.

> [9] "So I say to you:
> Ask and it will be given to you;
> seek and you will find;
> knock and the door will be opened to you.
> [10] For everyone who asks receives;
> he who seeks finds;
> and to him who knocks, the door will be opened." (Luke 11:9-10)

Ask is *aiteō*, "ask, ask for, demand."[56] In the case of a superior speaking to an inferior it can carry the idea "demand," as in an accounting. But here the idea is "ask for, petition."

Seek is *zēteō*, "try to find something, seek, look for' in order to find.[57] The corresponding result ("you will find") is expressed by Greek *euriskō*, "find, discover, come upon."[58] "Seek and you will find!"

Knock is *krouō*, expressing the figure of seeking by knocking on a door until it is opened, just like in Jesus' Parable of the Friend at Midnight. "Knock and the door will be opened to you."

Each of these verbs is in the present tense, with the sense of continued action.

> Ask – and keep on asking!
> Seek – and keep on seeking!
> Knock – and keep on knocking!

Of course, God can answer our asking with "No!" or "Later!" -- and sometimes does. The Apostle Paul had a "thorn in the flesh," some kind of affliction from Satan, whether physical

---

[55] *Anaideuomai*, "be unabashed, bold," literally "shameless" (BDAG 63).
[56] *Aiteō*, BDAG 30.
[57] *Zēteō*, BDAG 428, 1b.
[58] *Euriskō*, BDAG 411, 1a.

or mental or external opposition we do not know. Paul pleads with the Lord three times to take it away, but then receives the answer, "My grace is sufficient for you, for my power is made perfect in weakness" (2 Corinthians 12:9). Paul accepts this answer, and now begins to glory in his weaknesses that Christ's power may rest on him.

Parable of the Unjust Judge (Luke 18:1-8, §185)
(Also known as the Parable of the Importunate Widow, or Persistent Woman)

We've just examined Jesus' Parable of the Friend at Midnight, followed by his teaching to ask, seek, and knock. Luke includes another parable on prayer several chapters later that begins a new block of teaching on faith and the quality of those disciples who please God.

> "Then Jesus told his disciples a parable to show them that they should always[59] pray[60] and not give up." (Luke 18:1)

Jesus is teaching repeated prayer – praying again and again. When Paul exhorts us to "pray without ceasing"[61] (1 Thessalonians 5:17), he means to pray repeatedly, time and again. He's not talking about non-stop prayer, but repeated prayer.

I've heard Bible teachers say that once you've asked God for something, it displays lack of faith to ask for it again, since you ought to believe you already have received it (Mark 11:24). It sounds spiritual. But Jesus clearly teaches us here that we are to continue to pray until we receive the answer. Continued prayer is not a sign of little faith, but of persistent faith.

The danger is that we "give up,"[62] get discouraged, and quit praying. Jesus tells the parable to encourage his disciples to pray constantly, without getting discouraged.

The Unjust Judge (Luke 18:2)

Now Jesus tells a story to make his point.

> "In a certain town there was a judge who neither feared God nor cared about men." (Luke 18:2)

The judge is a law unto himself. He is neither devout nor a man-pleaser.[63] He is basically selfish. He doesn't respect the special needs of the poor and oppressed. He isn't overly concerned

---

[59] "Always" is the adverb *pantote*, "always, at all times" (BDAG 755).
[60] "Pray" is the common Greek word *proscheuomai*, "to petition deity, pray" (BDAG 879).
[61] 1 Thessalonians 1:3; 2:13; and 5:17 use the adverb *adialeiptōs*, "constantly, unceasingly" (BDAG 20). 2 Timothy 1:3 uses the related adjective *adialeiptos*, "unceasing, constant" (BDAG 20).
[62] "Give up" (NIV), "lose heart" (ESV, NRSV), "faint" (KJV) is *enkakeō*, "to lose one's motivation in continuing a desirable pattern of conduct or activity, lose enthusiasm, be discouraged" (BDAG 272, 1).
[63] The phrase "feared God" refers to piety, faith in God, and recognition that God will judge humans. The judge had no regard for God's justice. The phrase "cared about" (NIV) or "respected" (KJV, ESV, NRSV) is *entrepō*, "to show deference to a person in recognition of special status, 'turn toward something/someone, have regard for, respect,'" in this context, "who showed deference to no human" (BDAG 341).

10. Parables about Disciple Values

about public opinion. He is independent or imagines himself to be, concerned with himself – his own opinions, his own comfort, his own income, his own reputation.

In verse 6, Jesus calls him "unjust."[64] Though Jesus doesn't spell it out, there may have been a reason why the judge doesn't give the widow justice. The judge is either taking bribes to fatten his purse or has an "arrangement" with a wealthy citizen who stands to lose if the widow wins her case. We don't know.

The Persistent Widow (Luke 18:3)

> "And there was a widow in that town who kept coming to him with the plea, 'Grant me justice[65] against my adversary.'" (Luke 18:3)

Widows had a difficult place in Palestine – indeed, around the world to this day! In Israel, the wife of a deceased husband would normally have no legal right to inherit her husband's estate, so when her husband died, she couldn't take for granted living in his house or on his land. If her deceased husband had no children, the estate would revert to her husband's male relatives on his father's side – his brothers, his father's brothers, and then the nearest family kinsman. If she had grown children, things might be easier; they would take care of their mother. But a widow with small children might just as well have to contend for property rights with her in-laws, and if they didn't happen to like her, things could be difficult.[66]

We don't know how the widow is being cheated, but the judge is on her opponent's side. She doesn't have money for lawyers – or bribes. She is probably just keeping her head above water financially. But there is one thing we know about her – she is persistent.

The phrase "kept coming" reflects the imperfect tense of *erchomai*, "come." The imperfect tense indicates repeated or continued action in the past. She hasn't come just once, but time after time.

She doesn't take "no" for an answer. Instead, every time court is in session, here comes the widow, asking for – no, demanding – the justice to which she is entitled. Everyone in town knows about her case. If she had kept quiet, things would have died down. But since she keeps on demanding justice – vocally, publicly, time after time – the inevitable questions begin to circulate. "Maybe she *is* being cheated." "Maybe she *does* have a case." The judge's credibility is being called into question. She is a squeaky wheel demanding oil.

---

[64] *Adikia*, BDAG 20-21.

[65] The word translated "grant me justice" (NIV, ESV, NRSV) or "avenge me" (KJV), here and in verse 5, is *ekdikeō*, "to procure justice for someone, grant justice" (BDAG 300, 1).

[66] Gerhard F. Hasel, "Heir," ISBE 2:673-676. In some cases, she might manage to have the estate inherited by her young children as a trustee, but that was by no means a sure thing.

The Value of Persistence (Luke 18:4-5)

> "⁴ For some time he refused. But finally he said to himself, 'Even though I don't fear God or care about men, ⁵ yet because this widow keeps bothering[67] me, I will see that she gets justice, so that she won't eventually wear me out[68] with her coming!'" (Luke 18:4-5)

This weak little widow is starting to make the powerful judge uncomfortable. Her constant appeals are eroding his reputation. Whatever bribe he had been paid isn't worth the hassle she is causing. He decides to grant her justice solely to get rid of her.

Jesus' hearers had met widows like her and had experience with judges like him. The story is true-to-life.

Now that Jesus has his audience with him, he brings the application:

> "⁶ Listen to what the unjust judge says. ⁷ And will not God bring about justice for his chosen ones, who cry out to him day and night? Will he keep putting them off? ⁸ I tell you, he will see that they get justice, and quickly. However, when the Son of Man comes, will he find faith on the earth?" (Luke 18:6-8)

For the unjust judge and the widow, Jesus substitutes God and his elect (*eklektos*, "chosen ones"). Wait a minute, you say. God isn't unjust! No, and that's just the point. Jesus' argument is from the lesser to the greater: If an unjust, selfish judge will see that justice is done in response to persistent requests, how much more will the just God bring justice to his own beloved people who pray constantly for relief.

Sometimes we cry, "How long, Lord?" (Revelation 6:10). Sometimes it seems that God will never answer, that he delays[69] answering. Jesus' answer is firm: "He will see that they get justice, and quickly"[70] (Luke 18:8).

---

[67] The phrase "keeps bothering" (NIV, ESV, NRSV), "troubleth" (KJV) translates two Greek words. *Parechō*, "to cause to happen or be brought about, cause, make happen" (BDAG 776, 3a) is in the present tense, which here indicates continued action in the present. The second word is noun *kopos*, "a state of discomfort or distress, trouble, difficulty," originally "a beating". The idea here is "cause trouble for someone, bother someone" (BDAG 558, 1).

[68] The phrase "wear me out" (NIV, NRSV, KJV) "beat me down" (ESV) is *hypopiazō*, literally, "give a black eye to, strike in the face." The judge may have been speaking in hyperbole or exaggeration – she wasn't threatening him with bodily harm. But a figurative meaning of the word is "to bring someone to submission by constant annoyance, wear down, browbeat," or perhaps "slander, besmirch" (BDAG 1043, 2).

[69] In the sentence, "Will he keep putting them off? I tell you, he will see that they get justice, and quickly" (Luke 18:7), the phrase "keep putting them off" (NIV), "delay long" (ESV, NRSV), "bear long" (KJV) is Greek *makrothumeō*, "delay." This is the only place in the New Testament where this meaning occurs. Usually it is translated "have patience" or "be patient" (BDAG 612, 3).

[70] "Quickly" (NIV, NRSV), "speedily" (ESV, KJV) is Greek *tachos*, "speed, quickness, swiftness, haste." With the preposition *en* as an adverbial unit, "soon, in a short time" (BDAG 994, 2). Our word "tachometer" (measuring speed of rotation) comes from this Greek word.

10. Parables about Disciple Values

Will He Find Faith on the Earth? (Luke 18:8b)

"However, when the Son of Man comes, will he find faith on the earth?" (Luke 18:8b)

Jesus has told a parable of persistence, of a widow – weak in the world's estimation – who has won a real victory because she doesn't give up hope, doesn't give up her plea, and finally wins the day. But what about you and me? We sometimes become so worn down and discouraged that we stop praying, stop hoping, stop expecting God to intervene. Jesus wonders.

"When the Son of Man comes, will he find faith on the earth?" (Luke 18:8b)

We must continue our persistent faith and faithful prayers up to his Coming!

Jesus told this story to us disciples so that we might be encouraged to continue in prayer. None of you is weaker than the widow. But because of her persistence and faith, even the unjust judge gave her what was hers by right. We must not quit. We must not give up praying.

> "Therefore, my beloved brethren, be steadfast, immovable, always abounding in the work of the Lord, knowing that in the Lord your labor is not in vain." (1 Corinthians 15:58, RSV)

Q52. (Luke 11:5-10; 18:1-8) What is the similarity between Jesus' Parables of the Friend at Midnight and the Unjust Judge? What does this persistence look like in your life? What will persistence in prayer do to develop you as a disciple?
https://www.joyfulheart.com/forums/topic/2226-q52-persistence/

Analogy of the Faith of a Mustard Seed (Matthew 17:19, §127; Luke 17:6, §180)

Finally, Jesus taught his disciples the power of faith in prayer with a simple analogy – a grain of mustard seed vs. a mountain. In Matthew, Jesus is away on the mountain of transfiguration with Peter, James, and John. A man brings his demon-possessed boy to the disciples to cast it out. They fail. When Jesus returns, he casts out the spirit quickly. Jesus attributes their failure to lack of faith.[71]

> "I tell you the truth, if you have faith as small as a mustard seed, you can say to this mountain, 'Move from here to there' and it will move. Nothing will be impossible for you." (Matthew 17:20)

In Luke, the saying is somewhat different, given when Jesus is telling his disciples they must keep forgiving someone who sins and then repents – and does it again and again. The disciples are beyond themselves, and say, "Increase our faith." Jesus responds:

---

[71] Mark 9:29 attributes their failure to lack of prayer, and, in some texts, fasting.

"If you have faith as small as a mustard seed, you can say to this mulberry tree, 'Be uprooted and planted in the sea,' and it will obey you." (Luke 17:6)

The point of these parables is that even a tiny bit of genuine faith is extremely powerful.

Through these parables, Jesus challenges us to discern carefully, to not be deceived by the lures of money, and to pray faithfully and persistently. Let us do so!

Prayer

Father, you know our weakness and fears. But Jesus came to redeem us, to teach us, and to make us fully his disciples. Please refocus our faith and strengthen it. Where our knees are weak, strengthen us that we might serve you well all our days as your faithful servants. In Jesus' name, we pray. Amen.

11. Parables about Disciple Practices

In previous lessons we have considered a number of parables and analogies designed to train disciples in both character and values. Here we continue with practices that Jesus sought to embed in his disciples' lives.

11.1 Humble Service

- Acted Parable of Washing the Disciples' Feet (John 13:4-17)
- Parable of the Dutiful Servant (Luke 17:7-10)

11.2 Service in the Kingdom

- Parable of the Talents (Matthew 25:14-30)
- Parable of the Minas or Pounds (Luke 19:12-27)

11.3 Showing Love and Mercy

- Parable of the Good Samaritan (Luke 10:30-37)

Ford Madox Brown (British Pre-Raphaelite painter, (1821-93), 'Jesus Washing Peter's Feet' (1852-56), oil on canvas, 1167 x 133 mm, Tate Gallery, London.

11.1 Humble Service

We'll begin with parables about disciples as servants – humble servants. We discussed several parables about humility in Lesson 9.1 – the Parables of the Pharisee and Tax Collector, Becoming Like Little Children, Welcoming Little Children, and Places at the Table. Here, we'll consider two additional parables that add the idea of *service* with humility – the Acted Parable of Washing the Disciples' Feet and the Parable of the Dutiful Servant.

Acted Parable of Washing the Disciples' Feet (John 13:4-17)

Most studies of Jesus' parables don't include Jesus washing his disciples' feet. But I feel I must include it, since Jesus obviously intended it as an acted parable, a visual example of what humble service looks like, with the purpose of teaching his disciples to be humble servants of one another.

The Setting of the Last Supper

At the Last Supper, the disciples are arranged around a very low table, reclining on their left arms and supported by divans or cushions, leaving their right hands free to feed themselves, as was the custom of the day. Their feet, sandals removed, are splayed out behind them, with some space between their feet and the walls so those serving the meal can bring the various dishes to the table.

We know from Luke's Gospel that even at this holy meal there is an undercurrent of unrest among the disciples, an argument that had come up again and again over the course of Jesus' ministry.

> "A dispute arose among them as to which of them was considered to be greatest." (Luke 22:24)

Jesus uses this dispute as a "teachable moment."

Washing the Disciples' Feet (John 13:4-5)

Since sweaty feet clad only in sandals get grimy on unpaved roads and streets, it was customary for a host to provide a basin of water so guests could wash their own feet upon entering.[1] Washing *someone else's feet* was a task reserved for the most menial of servants. A Jewish commentary on the Book of Exodus suggests that Jewish slaves could not be required to wash the feet of others, that this task was so demeaning that it should be reserved for Gentile slaves or for women, children, or pupils.[2] A wife might wash a husband's feet; a child might wash a parent's feet. Rarely, a disciple might honor a distinguished rabbi by washing his feet. But for a superior to wash an inferior's feet was never ever done! Except by Jesus.

> "⁴ He got up from the meal, took off his outer clothing[3] and wrapped[4] a towel[5] around his waist.[6] ⁵ After that, he poured water into a basin and began to wash his disciples' feet, drying[7] them with the towel that was wrapped around him." (John 13:4-5)

But Jesus goes further. He pours some water into a basin[8] and proceeds to gently wash the feet of the disciples. If you've ever participated in a foot washing service, you know that most

---

[1] Brown, *John* 2:564.
[2] *Mekhilta* §1 on Exodus 21:2.
[3] "Outer clothing/garments" (NIV, ESV), "outer robe" (NRSV), "garments" is *himation*, "a piece of clothing," here, of outer clothing, "cloak, robe" (BDAG 475, 2).
[4] "Wrapped around ... waist" (NIV), "girded" (KJV) is *diazōnnymi*, "tie around" (BDAG 228), from *dia* + *zōnnymi*, "gird," in verses 4 and 5.
[5] "Towel" is *lention*, "linen cloth, towel" (BDAG 592), in verses 4 and 5.
[6] Luke 12:37; 17:8. In both these verses the servant "girds himself" as Jesus did.
[7] "Dry" (NIV), "wipe" (NRSV, ESV, KJV) is *ekmasso*, "to cause to become dry by wiping with a substance, wipe" (BDAG 306).
[8] "Basin" is *niptēr*, "(wash) basin" (BDAG 674), from the verb *niptō*, "to wash," used in this verse.

people's feet aren't soft and pretty – especially older people whose toes have been broken numerous times and whose feet are often bony and calloused. These disciples are relatively young, but have spent their lives in sandals or bare feet and have suffered many injuries – not to mention the dust of the day.

Jesus takes the feet of each disciple in his hands, washes them gently, then dries them with the towel that is around his waist. He goes to the next disciple and to the next. I imagine that the room is absolutely still, except for softly spoken encouragements of love from the Master. His disciples don't know what to say. It is painful for them to see him like this. To submit to this intimate service from him is awkward in the extreme!

Simon Peter's Objection (John 13:6-9)

The bold fisherman can't stop himself from protesting.

> "⁶ He came to Simon Peter, who said to him, 'Lord, are you going to wash my feet?'
> ⁷ Jesus replied, 'You do not realize[9] now what I am doing, but later you will understand.[10]'" (John 13:6-7)

Peter loves this man and he can't stand this, so he blurts out, "Lord, are you going to wash my feet?" I can't stand seeing you like a menial servant! It offends my sense of rightness and order! And I don't deserve it from you!

Jesus gently replies that later he'll understand why this is necessary. But Peter will have none of it.

> " 'No,' said Peter, 'you shall never wash my feet.'" (John 13:8a)

The Greek here is extremely strong, literally, "not ever unto the age."[11]

Washed by Jesus (John 13:8b-11)

Jesus' response is equally strong:

> "⁸ᵇ Jesus answered, 'Unless I wash[12] you, you have no part[13] with me.'
> ⁹ 'Then, Lord,' Simon Peter replied, 'not just my feet but my hands and my head as well!'" (John 13:8-9)

---

[9] "Realize" (NIV), "know" (NRSV, KJV), "understand" (ESV) in verse 7a is *eidō*, here in the sense of, "to grasp the meaning of something, understand, recognize, come to know, experience" (BDAG 694, 4).

[10] "Understand" (NIV, ESV, NRSV), "know" (KJV) in verse 7b is *ginōskō*, "know," here, "to grasp the significance or meaning of something, understand, comprehend" (BDAG 200, 3).

[11] The Greek uses the double negative *ou mē*, with the idea of "to eternity, eternally, in perpetuity" (*aiōn*, BDAG 32, 1b).

[12] "Wash" is *niptō*, "to cleanse with use of water, wash" (BDAG 674, 1a).

[13] "Part" (NIV, KJV), "share" (NRSV, ESV) is *meros*, "share," here, "have a place with someone" (BDAG 634, 2).

Jesus insists that he must wash Peter. But here, Jesus moves in meaning from physical foot washing to spiritual cleansing from sin that is absolutely necessary for any person to have fellowship with Christ the Lord, symbolized here by foot washing and elsewhere by baptism.[14]

Peter's response is immediate: Then wash me from head to toe!

> "Jesus answered, 'A person who has had a bath[15] needs only to wash his feet[16]; his whole body is clean.'"[17] (John 13:10a)

What does Jesus mean by this? Jesus is using the analogy of taking a bath vs. footwashing. It is necessary for every believer to experience full salvation and cleansing from sin (depicted by taking a bath). After that, all that is necessary is washing away the occasional dust of the road, the sins that we commit day by day (1 John 1:8-9; 2:1-2).

Sometimes, like Peter, we resist this frequent need for cleansing – whether out of false pride or a sense of unworthiness or vulnerability We don't want to let the Holy One this close, this intimate. And so we resist him. How foolish of us! He knows us and our sins and wants to restore to us his full cleansing and fellowship. And we must let him!

Now, on this night in which he was betrayed, Jesus extends this teaching to inform his disciples that he knows Judas will betray him. Judas is the exception in this band of cleansed men.

> "'And you are clean[18], though not every one of you.' [11] For he knew who was going to betray[19] him, and that was why he said not every one was clean." (John 13:10-11)

A Parable of Humble Service (John 13:14-17)

The acted parable is over. Now Jesus takes a few minutes to explain part of its meaning to the disciples.

---

[14] Acts 22:16; Titus 3:5; 1 Corinthians 6:11; Ephesians 5:26.

[15] "Had a bath/has bathed" (NIV, NRSV, ESV), "is washed" (KJV) is *louō*, "to use water to cleanse a body of physical impurity, wash, as a rule of the whole body, bathe" (BDAG 603, 1b).

[16] There is some confusion with John 13:10a in the manuscripts. A number of manuscripts omit the words "except for his feet," but Metzger (*Textual Commentary*, p. 240) concludes that these words "may have been omitted accidentally (or even deliberately because of the difficulty of reconciling them with the following declaration, 'his whole body is clean'), a majority of the committee considered it safer to retain them on the basis of the preponderant weight of external attestation," giving it a {B} "some degree of doubt" confidence level.

[17] "His whole body is clean" (NIV) is more literally, "entirely/completely clean" (NRSV, ESV), "clean every whit" (KJV). There are two words, the adjective *katharos*, "pertaining to being clean or free of adulterating matter, clean, pure" (BDAG 489, 1); and *holos*, "pertaining to being complete in extent, whole, entire, complete" (BDAG 704, 1bγ).

[18] *Katharos*, "clean," here in the sense of, "pertaining to being free from moral guilt, pure, free from sin" (BDAG 489, 3a).

[19] "Betray" is *paradidōmi*, "hand over, turn over, give up a person," as a technical term of police and courts hand over into [the] custody [of]" (BDAG 762, 1b).

"[12] When he had finished washing their feet, he put on his clothes and returned[20] to his place. 'Do you understand what I have done for you?' he asked them. [13] 'You call me "Teacher" and "Lord," and rightly so, for that is what I am.'" (John 13:12-13)

Jesus has a right to be served by virtue of being Rabbi and Lord. In this parable, he takes that right to be served and turns it on its head. He serves; they must serve each other.

"[14] Now that I, your Lord and Teacher, have washed your feet, you also should wash one another's feet. [15] I have set you an example[21] that you should do as I have done for you. [16] I tell you the truth, no servant[22] is greater than his master,[23] nor is a messenger[24] greater than the one who sent him. [17] Now that you know these things, you will be blessed[25] if you do them." (John 13:14-17)

Remember the context of his acted parable: Jesus' disciples arguing about who is greatest (Luke 22:24). If Jesus the Lord and Rabbi sets an example of humbling himself to serve, how much more should we, his disciples, serve one another and the hurting of this world, rather than tout our own self-importance. In Mark's Gospel, Jesus taught his disciples:

"Whoever wants to become great among you must be your servant, and whoever wants to be first must be slave of all. For even the Son of Man **did not come to be served, but to serve**, and to give his life as a ransom for many." (Mark 10:43-45)

Jesus washing the disciples' feet is indeed a parable. Jesus is saying, like I am a servant to you, so you must be a servant to one another. It is an acted parable, summarized with a clear comparison.

I am sure that Jesus' disciples talked over his precious parables for the rest of their lives. But this Acted Parable of Washing the Disciples' Feet was one they never, ever forgot, for he had acted it out in their midst.

Q53. (John 13:4-17) In what way is Jesus washing the disciples' feet a parable? Why did this act of washing their feet feel so shocking to the disciples? In what sense is this a parable of cleansing? In what way is it a rebuke of pride and competition? In what way is it a parable of humble service? In what areas of your life do you need to implement

---

[20] "Returned to his place" (NIV) is *anapiptō*, "to recline on a couch to eat, lie down, recline" (BDAG 70, 1).
[21] "Example" is *hypodeigma*, "an example of behavior used for purposes of moral instruction, example, model, pattern" (BDAG 1037, 1).
[22] "Servant" is *doulos*, "male slave as an entity in a socioeconomic context, slave" (BDAG 259, 1).
[23] "Master" (NIV, NRSV, ESV), "lord" (KJV) is *kyrios*, "one who is in charge by virtue of possession, owner (BDAG 572, II, 1b).
[24] "Messenger" (NIV, NRSV, ESV), "he that is sent" (KJV) is the noun *apostolos*, "of messengers without extraordinary status, delegate, envoy, messenger" (BDAG 122, 1).
[25] "Blessed" (NIV, NRSV, ESV), "happy" (KJV) is *makarios*, "pertaining to being especially favored, blessed, fortunate, happy, privileged," here, "privileged recipient of divine favor" (BDAG 611, 2a).

its teaching?
https://www.joyfulheart.com/forums/topic/2227-q53-footwashing/

Parable of the Dutiful Servant (Luke 17:7-10, §181)
(Also known as the Parable of the Master and Servant)

Our next parable also talks about humble service.

> "⁷ Suppose one of you had a servant plowing or looking after the sheep. Would he say to the servant when he comes in from the field, 'Come along now and sit down to eat'?[26] ⁸ Would he not rather say, 'Prepare my supper, get yourself ready and wait on me while I eat and drink; after that you may eat and drink'?" (Luke 17:7-8)

The slave that Jesus describes in this brief parable seems to be the only slave in this household, used mostly for farm labor – plowing, looking after livestock – but also responsible for cooking and household chores. The slave would live with the family as a part of the household, but his was a pretty hard existence. (For more, see Appendix 6. Slavery in Jesus' Day.)

Being Served or Serving (Luke 17:7-8)

Jesus invites his hearers to imagine that they had such a slave to work around their house and farm. Then he asks a rhetorical question: Does the master offer to fix dinner for the slave or the other way around? Of course, the slave has to prepare the meal *and* serve the master and his family before he can eat himself – all that after a hard day in the fields!

That isn't fair! we retort. Of course, many people in our own culture work two or three jobs because they *have to*. Is it fair? No. But it is required by the responsibilities they have. The point here is that, fair or not, the slave is expected to work in the fields *and* fix the food. That is his duty. The master isn't there to serve the slave, but the slave to serve the master.

Thanking the Servant (Luke 17:9)

In the culture of Jesus' day the master wouldn't "owe" the servant a reward for his hard work.

> "Would he thank the servant because he did what he was told to do?" (Luke 17:9)

---

[26] In Jesus' Parable of the Watching Servants (Luke 12:35-39, Lesson 5.2), we see a role reversal. When the master returns from his trip, he will serve his servants at the table (Luke 12:37). This is a hint of the coming Great Banquet at the End of the Age. See Appendix 5. The Great Messianic Banquet.

We might expect a "thank you."[27] But in that culture, the idea of a debt of gratitude that must be offered to even the score would be seen as placing the master in debt to the slave.[28] If you've watched British period shows on television, you observe that the lords and ladies of the manor never call the serving staff by their first names, nor are they thanked each time they perform a service. That has some similarities to our parable.

A Servant's Duty (Luke 17:9-10)

> "⁹ Would he thank the servant because he did what he was told[29] to do? ¹⁰ So you also, when you have done everything you were told to do, should say, 'We are unworthy servants; we have only done our duty.'"[30] (Luke 17:9-10)

"Duty" and "order" and "command" aren't very popular concepts in current American culture. In the first half of the twentieth century the concept of duty was widely accepted. But by the mid-1960s, authority was the target of widespread protest. The society shifted. To be real disciples, we must be obedient to God's word and do our duty as followers of Jesus in a fallen world.

Unworthy Servants (Luke 17:10)

Now Jesus brings the parable to the point of application.

> "So you also, when you have done everything you were told to do, should say, 'We are unworthy servants; we have only done our duty.'" (Luke 17:10)

Do we expect some reward from God when we obey his commands and do what he says? Are we like the Pharisees who expect that our piety will earn us some special treatment? To be true disciples we must forsake an attitude of entitlement and instead see ourselves as "unworthy slaves." The adjective is *achreios*, "pertaining to being unworthy of any praise, unworthy."[31]

The New Testament is quite clear about the difference between merit and grace (Romans 4:4-5; Ephesians 2:8-10). The blessings of God are ours because of our adoption as "sons," but that adoption itself is by grace. God doesn't owe us anything – he *gives* it freely. We owe him an unpayable debt.

---

[27] The phrase literally is: "He will not be grateful (*charis*) to the slave...." Here the phrase, literally "have gratitude" is used in the sense of "to be grateful" (Hans Conzelmann, *charis, ktl.*, TDNT 9:391-402).
[28] Green, *Luke*, p. 614.
[29] In both verses 9 and 10 in the NIV we see the word "told." It renders the Greek verb *diatassō*, "to give (detailed) instructions as to what must be done, order." Here the verb is in the form of a participle meaning "the things ordered or commanded," in other words, "duty" (BDAG 237-238).
[30] "Duty" (NIV, ESV, KJV), "what we ought to have done" (NRSV) is *opheilō*, "be obligated," with a verbal infinitive that means, "one must, one ought" (BDAG 743).
[31] *Achreios*, BDAG 160.

Who Is the Servant?

It is easy for us to get grace backwards. Our prayers tend to be "gimme" prayers, not servant prayers.

- Help my business succeed.
- Help my children to be safe at school.
- Heal my mother's cancer.
- Protect the widows and orphans.
- Provide food to those experiencing a famine.
  And – while you're at it, God, -
- Work in my boss's heart to give me a raise.

Too often we pray in the way you might command a genie who has granted us ten wishes. Is this any way to address God to whom you owe your allegiance and life and salvation? You are *his* servant, not the other way around!

Our prayers should rather be servant's prayers:

- Father, what do you want me to do today?
- How can I help Johnny learn to be more polite to his friends?
- Give me strength and boldness to witness for you in this situation.

We are not to command God, but he is to command us![32]

The Parable of the Dutiful Servant is has a two-fold lesson for us disciples:
1. We are not to allow ourselves to be soft and pampered, so as to excuse ourselves from hard labor and hard hours in serving the Lord.
2. We are not to presume upon God and expect his thanks. Instead we are to serve him dutifully without any expectation of reward.

Anything he bestows upon us – and those blessings are *very* great – is not because of any obligation God has toward us, but come to us fully and completely at his gracious pleasure. We are his servants, his slaves *first*. And afterward, *after* we have learned that lesson of obedience well – oh, what joy! – he condescends to call us his "friends"

> "¹⁴ You are my friends if you do what I command you. ¹⁵ **I no longer call you servants**, because a servant does not know his master's business. Instead, **I have called you**

---

[32] I remember listening to Pentecostal healer-evangelist A.A. Allen on the radio in the 1960s. Allen would quote the Bible: "Thus saith the Lord, the Holy One of Israel, and his Maker, Ask me of things to come concerning my sons, and concerning the work of my hands *command ye me*" (Isaiah 45:11, King James Version). A more accurate translation of this verse, reflected in the NIV, NRSV, RSV, and Amplified Bible, renders this as a question: "Concerning things to come, do you question me about my children, or give me orders about the work of my hands?" (Isaiah 45:11, NIV).

11. Parables about Disciple Practices

friends, for everything that I learned from my Father I have made known to you." (John 15:14-15)

11.2 Service in the Kingdom

Jesus tells two similar parables about assignment of responsibilities to servants. The more familiar to us is the Parable of the Talents (Matthew 25:14-30). It has a great deal in common with The Parable of the Minas or Pounds (Luke 19:11-27).

Parable of the Talents (Matthew 25:14-30, §228)

Parable of the Minas or Pounds (Luke 19:12-27; §195)

Both parables are in the context of a delay in Christ's return. Both parables involve giving servants money to invest in various enterprises, so the master's total capital will be increased by the time he returns. Both teach that Christ's servants are expected to use what they have in Christ's work until he returns.

But these are different parables. Jesus, who repeated his teachings constantly in town after town, obviously told this basic parable in two different ways, depending upon what he was seeking to emphasize, even though the primary point of each form of this parable is nearly the same.

The best approach is for us to study them together, noting the differences as we go, and then drawing together the lessons designed for disciples to grasp. These parables are tricky to interpret, so I'll delay interpretation until we've assessed all the details.

Eugene Burnand, 'Parable of the Talents' (1909), illustration in *The Parables* (France, 1909).

Context of the Parables

Matthew's Parable of the Talents is included in a block of parables about the End Time. Jesus begins with the words:

> "It will be like a man going on a journey, who called his servants and entrusted his property to them." (Matthew 25:14)

"It" refers to "at that time the kingdom of heaven will be like..." (verse 1), referring to the time of Christ's Second Coming. Luke's Parable of the Minas or Pounds follows immediately after Jesus' encounter with Zacchaeus in Jericho, which is just a few miles from Jerusalem.

"He went on to tell them a parable, because he was near Jerusalem and the people thought that the kingdom of God was going to appear at once." (Luke 19:11)

Luke tells us something of the purpose of the Parable of the Minas – and both parables, for that matter -- to convey to his disciples that there will be a delay in the coming of the Kingdom.

A Wealthy Man / Nobleman Going on a Journey (Matthew 25:14)

Each parable begins with a man preparing to go on an extended journey. In Matthew, the man is a wealthy slave owner. In Luke, the man is a nobleman on the verge of being crowned a king.

"A man of noble birth[33] went to a distant country to have himself appointed king and then to return." (Luke 19:12)

Jesus' hearers in Jericho would have immediately thought of Herod the Great's son and heir Herod Archelaus (reigned 4 BC to 6 AD), who had been both feared and despised by his subjects.[34] He had gone to Rome to be made king over his father's domains, but was later deposed for misgovernment.

"[14] His subjects hated him and sent a delegation after him to say, 'We don't want this man to be our king.' [15] He was made king, however, and returned home." (Luke 19:14-15)

Jesus is providing a bit of local color for his hearers in Jericho, since Archelaus's former palace was in Jericho.[35]

Entrusting His Property to His Servants (Matthew 25:14; Luke 19:13)

Both parables have a powerful man going on a journey, and both have the man dividing up his wealth among his servants, so that his household and business enterprises continue to run smoothly and profitably in his absence, resulting in an increase in his overall wealth.

---

[33] "Noble birth" (NIV), "nobleman" (ESV, NRSV), "noble" (KJV) is *eugenēs*, "pertaining to being of high status, well-born, high-born" (BDAG 404).

[34] Just after the death of Herod the Great in 4 BC – before his son had been made king by Rome – Archelaus turned the army loose on the people of Jerusalem and slaughtered 3,000. Immediately, Archelaus went to Rome to defend himself from complaints – from a delegation of his subjects and as well as from his brothers, who still hoped to be declared king by Emperor Caesar Augustus. Caesar declared Archelaus an ethnarch (a ruler of an ethnic group), with control over the bulk of his father's kingdom. However, in 6 AD Caesar deposed him for misgovernment and exiled him to Vienna. Archelaus' cruelty is reflected in the Parable of the Minas where the king has his enemies slain before him (verse 27). Sources: "Archelaus," ISBE 1:235-Wikipedia article, "Herod Archelaus"; L.I. Levine, "Herod the Great," *Anchor Bible Dictionary* (Doubleday, 1992) 3:169; Morris, *Luke*, p. 274; Josephus, *Wars*, 2.10-13; *Antiquities* 17:188-90 (17.11); 17.340 (17.13.1).

[35] Snodgrass, *Stories*, p. 537.

11. Parables about Disciple Practices

Talents: "It will be like a man going on a journey, who called his servants and *entrusted* his property to them." (Matthew 25:14)

Minas: "He called ten of his servants and gave them ten minas. '*Put this money to work,*' he said, '*until I come back.*'" (Luke 19:13)

In ancient times, a businessman had several options to protect his capital when he must be gone for an extended period. He could bury his money, but he probably couldn't keep his household going at the same time. He could deposit his money with a banker for passive growth of interest on the funds. But for the best yield, he would find competent people who could invest his money wisely and then actively manage the investment so that when he returns, the money will have been at work and earned a handsome profit. Of course, there is some risk involved, but a businessman could minimize his risk in two ways:

1. Diversify by dividing the capital into several different investment pools.
2. Give the most capital to the most competent managers and less to those who have yet to prove themselves.

In the Parable of the Talents, the wealthy man uses both techniques. In the Parable of the Minas, only the first strategy is used.

The servants[36] are gathered into the master's office where he explains exactly what he wants them to do. Then he distributes his funds among them. In Matthew he "entrusted[37] his property[38] to them." Luke's version of the parable employs the phrase, "put this money to work" (NIV). The word is *pragmateuomai*, "do business, trade,"[39] variously translated:

"Put this money to work" (NIV).

"Engage in business" (ESV).

"Do business" (NRSV).

"Occupy" (KJV).

---

[36] The "servants" here could very well be house slaves, rather than paid employees. That is the basic meaning of the Greek word *doulos* (BDAG 260, 1a). Being slaves doesn't mean they were ignorant. In ancient times it was common for wealthy people to own slaves who were well-educated and very skilled at business. On the other hand, in Luke's parable, when the nobleman arrives home as king, *doulos* could mean "subject" in a positive sense, of a servant in relation to a superior human being such as a king (*doulos*, BDAG 260, 2bα). Servants rewarded with cities to rule (Luke 19:15-19) aren't likely to be slaves. (For more see Appendix 6. Slavery in Jesus' Day.)

[37] "Entrusted" (NIV, NRSV), "delivered" (KJV) is *paradidōmi*, "to convey something in which one has a relatively strong personal interest, hand over, give (over), deliver, entrust" (BDAG 763, 1a).

[38] "Property" (NIV, NRSV), "goods" (KJV) is a participle of *hyparchō*, "exist, be at one's disposal," here as a substantive, "what belongs to someone, someone's property, possessions, means" (BDAG 102, 1).

[39] *Pragmateuomai*, BDAG 859.

Each According to His Ability vs. Equal Investments (Matthew 25:15; Luke 19:13)

> **Minas**: "He called ten of his servants and gave them ten minas. 'Put this money to work,' he said, 'until I come back.'" (Luke 19:13)

In the Luke's Parable of the Minas or Pounds, each of ten servants gets one mina each to put to work.

"Mina" (ESV, NIV) or "pound" (NRSV, KJV) is Greek *mna*, a Greek monetary unit equal to 100 drachmas in Greek money.[40] A Greek drachma was worth approximately the same as a Roman denarius, or the average daily wage for a laborer. If we were to calculate a laborer's wages at $150 to $200 per day for 100 days, then a Mina might be worth perhaps $15,000 to $20,000 dollars USD in today's money.[41] While this isn't a fortune in Western cities, it could provide the beginnings for a profitable small business in the hands of a bold and skillful person.

> **Talents**: "To one he gave five talents of money, to another two talents, and to another one talent, *each according to his ability*." (Matthew 25:15)

In the Parable of the Talents only three servants are selected. Each servant gets an amount of capital commensurate with his potential – "each according to his ability."[42] The most promising servant gets the most, while the least promising servant gets the least.

As we saw in the Parable of the Unmerciful Servant (Lesson 1.2), a "talent" (*talanton*) was first a weight, then a unit of coinage. In general, one Tyrian talent would be worth about 6,000 denarii,[43] a denarius being the average amount that a laborer might earn for one day's work. If you calculate that a day laborer might earn $150 to $200 USD working six days per week, you could calculate a talent in today's currency to be about $900,000 to $1.2 million USD.

Servant 1	5 talents	$4.5 to $6 million
Servant 2	2 talents	$1.8 to $2.4 million
Servant 3	1 talent	$900,000 to $1.2 million

This is indeed a sizeable fortune entrusted to each of the servants.

Putting the Money to Work (Matthew 25:16-18)

Now the master leaves town and the servants get to work. In the Parable of the Talents we read:

---

[40] *Mna*, BDAG 654; H. W. Perkin, "Money," ISBE 3:409.
[41] $150 or $200 x 100 days = $15,000 to $20,000.
[42] "Ability" is *dynamis*, "power," in the sense of, "ability to carry out something, ability, capability" (BDAG 263, 2).
[43] *Talanton*, BDAG 988.

11. Parables about Disciple Practices

"¹⁶ The man who had received the five talents went at once and put his money to work and gained⁴⁴ five more. ¹⁷ So also, the one with the two talents gained two more. ¹⁸ But the man who had received the one talent went off, dug a hole in the ground and hid his master's money." (Matthew 25:16-18)

Notice that the first servant "went off at once" (NRSV, cf. NIV).[45] He was eager and motivated. He "put his money to work" (NIV) or "traded" (ESV, NRSV, KJV) with it.[46] We don't know what kind of businesses these were. But "trading" could have been purchasing goods at wholesale and selling at retail, investing in a mine, investing in a ship or caravan bringing goods from another area, etc. It would need to be relatively short-term, since the servants didn't know when their master would return.

The Master Returns and Settles Accounts (Matthew 25:19-23; Luke 19:15-19)

Now, at length, the master returns.

"After a long time the master of those servants returned and settled accounts[47] with them." (Matthew 25:19)

"He sent for the servants to whom he had given the money, in order to find out what they had gained[48] with it." (Luke 19:15)

The servants troop into the master's office one by one to report

The first two servants in Matthew have both doubled their money – an outstanding achievement! The master is pleased with each of them, rewards them accordingly, and praises their character.

Talents. "Well done,[49] good and faithful[50] servant! You have been faithful with a few things; I will put you in charge of many things. Come and share your master's happiness!" (Matthew 25:21)

---

[44] "Gained" is *kerdainō*, "to acquire by effort or investment, to gain" (BDAG 542, 1a).
[45] This idea of immediacy comes from the Aorist tense of the participle *poreuomai*, "go, proceed, travel" (BDAG 853, 1).
[46] *Ergazomai*, "work," here in the specific sense of a financial enterprise, "do business/trade with" (BDAG 389, 1).
[47] The verb "settle" is *synairō*, used here in a commercial sense of "settle accounts, cast up accounts" (BDAG 964.) The word "accounts" is the common noun *logos*, used in a special sense here as "computation, reckoning" (BDAG 603, 2b).
[48] "Gained" (NIV), "gained by doing business" (ESV), "gained by trading" (NRSV, KJV) is Greek *diapragmateuomai*, "gain by trading, earn" (BDAG 235).
[49] "Well done" is Greek *eu*, an interjection that pertains to meeting a standard of performance, "well done! excellent!" (BDAG 402, 2).
[50] "Faithful" (NIV, KJV), "trustworthy" (NRSV) is the common Greek word *pistos*, "worthy of belief or trust, trustworthy, faithful, dependable" (BDAG 820, 1aα).

Minas. "Well done, my good servant!' his master replied. 'Because you have been trustworthy in a very small matter, take charge[51] of ten cities.'" (Luke 19:17)

Notice that each servant is referred to as "good" in both Matthew and Luke. "Good" is used in the sense of "pertaining to meeting a high standard of worth and merit, good,"[52] but it can also contain a hint of moral goodness as well (Matthew 19:17).

These faithful servants are rewarded with greater responsibilities that will mean a higher position and a better life.

The servant who took one mina ($15,000 to $20,000) and traded it to be ten times as much ($150,000 to $200,000) is rewarded with control of ten cities in the newly-crowned king's realm – he now is a governor! Likewise, the servant who earned five times as much is given control over five cities. Governors were seen to be fabulously wealthy! Their nobleman master has now been made a king with a kingdom to govern so he is looking for tried and true people he can trust.

Beyond the rewards, in the Parable of the Talents the faithful servants can bask in the master's "happiness." They are invited to "enter into the joy of your master." The word *chara*, "joy," used here can have the sense of something that *causes* joy, such as "a festive dinner or banquet."[53]

The Wicked Servant (Matthew 21:24-35; Luke 19:20-27)

The third servant in both parables, however, is not nearly so eager to please. Burying something was considered a secure way of protecting one's treasure,[54] but that only protected the capital; it did not increase it, as the master had specifically ordered. We'll look at Matthew's account; Luke is similar.

> "²⁴ Then the man who had received the one talent came. 'Master,' he said, 'I knew that you are a hard man, harvesting where you have not sown and gathering where you have not scattered seed. ²⁵ So I was afraid and went out and hid your talent in the ground. See, here is what belongs to you.'" (Matthew 25:24-25)

The unproductive servant is bold in his excuse. He sounds almost like he is accusing his master of being an evil capitalist,

---

[51] "Take charge of" (NIV, NRSV) or "have authority over" (ESV, KJV) in Luke 19:17 centers on the Greek word *exousia*, "the right to control or command, authority, absolute power, warrant" (BDAG 352-353, 3).

[52] *Agathos*, BDAG 2aα.

[53] *Chara*, BDAG 107, 2c. Enter into" (NRSV, KJV), "share" is *eiserchomai*, "to enter into an event or state, come into something = share in something, come to enjoy something" (BDAG 294, 2 and 4a).

[54] Jeremias (*Parables*, p. 61, fn. 51) notes that according with rabbinical law, anyone who buried a pledge or deposit immediately upon receipt of it, was free from liability if it went missing (*b.B.M.* 42a). In Luke 19:29, "laid away" (NIV, ESV), "wrapped up" (NRSV), "laid up" (KJV) is *apokeimai*, "to put away for safekeeping" (BDAG 113, 1).

11. Parables about Disciple Practices

> "... Harvesting where you have not sown and gathering where you have not scattered seed." (Matthew 25:24)

What an outrageous thing to say to someone in power over you!

The servant claims to have acted out of fear. In Matthew, the servant accuses his master of being a "hard" (NIV, ESV, KJV) or "harsh" (NRSV) man, one who is "unyielding in behavior or attitude" in dealing with others, "hard, strict, harsh, cruel, merciless."[55] In Luke he is accused of being strict, uncompromising, tough.[56]

The truth is, that this servant hates his master. He will return to the master what is his, but he certainly won't help him increase it! Bitterness is apparent in the servant's answer, along with his self-justification.

The Judgment on the Wicked Servant (Matthew 25:26-27; Luke 19:22-23)

The master hears out the disobedient and insolent servant and then lambastes him. In Matthew, he is called a "wicked, lazy servant."

- **"Wicked"** is *ponēros*, "morally or socially worthless, wicked, evil, bad, base, vicious, degenerate."[57] This is in contrast to the "good" servants.
- **"Lazy"** (NIV, NRSV), **"slothful"** (ESV, KJV) is *oknēros*, "idle, lazy, indolent."[58]

In Luke, the master replies to the wicked servant's excuses rather sharply and destroys the servant's so-called logic.

> "²² I will judge you by your own words, you wicked servant! You knew, did you, that I am a hard man, taking out what I did not put in, and reaping what I did not sow?" (Luke 19:22)

In other words, since you knew I expected results from others, that is no excuse to refuse to produce results. Now the master suggests a painless way that even a lazy servant could have got an increase on his investment – let someone else do the work, in this case a banker.

---

[55] *Sklēros*, with the basic meaning of "rough, hard to the touch." Here, used figuratively (BDAG 930, 4a).

[56] "Severe" (ESV), "hard" (NIV), "harsh" (NRSV), "austere" is *austēros* (from which we get our word "austere"), "pertaining to being strict in requirement, punctilious, strict," used especially of persons who practice rigid personal disciple or are strict in the supervision of others, here imagery of a tough, uncompromising punctilious financier (BDAG 151-152).

[57] *Ponēros*, BDAG 851, 1aα.

[58] *Oknēros*, BDAG 702, 1.

"You should have put my money on deposit[59] with the bankers,[60] so that when I returned I would have received it back with interest." (Matthew 25:27)

Modern bank institutions don't appear until sixteenth century Europe. But in ancient times, some banking functions were available through business people, such as keeping money safe, coining money, money changing, and money lending.[61] If you had money to loan, you could deposit it with a money lender who would do the work and pay you for the use of your money.

Though Jews were forbidden in the Torah from receiving interest on money loaned to poor countrymen,[62] some other kinds of business loans were legal for them, such as loans to foreigners.[63] In fact, it may be that no prohibition whatsoever on business loans was in effect in the first century.[64] There is a considerable difference between loaning money to a poor person to buy food so his family doesn't starve and loaning money to a businessman so he can expand his business.

The Faithful Will Receive More (Matthew 25:28-29; Luke 19:24-26)

The wicked servant has not been merely lazy, but has deliberately refused to do anything that will benefit his master. There is no second chance for deliberate rebelliousness.

"[28] Take the talent from him and give it to the one who has the ten talents. [29] For everyone who has will be given more, and he will have an abundance. Whoever does not have, even what he has will be taken from him." (Matthew 25:28-29)

Luke's parable is similar. In Luke, one servant protests about the first servant getting more minas: "He already has ten" (Luke 19:25) But now, the king isn't distributing money on a trial, as he did before he left. Now he knows who is faithful, capable, and productive, so he gives more to those who he knows will *use* his investment to best advantage.

We see this kind of reward for the faithful and discerning, and punishment for the faithless and rebellious elsewhere. It seems to be a Kingdom principle.

"Whoever has will be given more, and he will have an abundance. Whoever does not have, even what he has will be taken from him." (Matthew 13:12 = Mark 4:29)

---

[59] "Put on deposit" (NIV), "invested" (ESV, NRSV), "put" (KJV) is *ballō*, "throw," here, "to entrust money to a banker for interest, deposit money" (BDAG 163, 5).

[60] "Bankers" (NIV, ESV, NRSV), "exchangers" (KJV) is *trapezitēs*, money changer, banker" (BDAG 1013), from *trapeza* (from which we get "trapezoid"), "table," specifically the table on which the money changers display their coins, hence simply "bank" (BDAG 1013).

[61] M. W. Call, "Bank, Banking," ISBE 1:408.

[62] Exodus 22:25; Deuteronomy 23:19; Ezekiel 18:18.

[63] R. J. Ray, "Interest," ISBE 2:860.

[64] Snodgrass, *Stories*, p. 538, cites John Nolland, *Luke* (Word Biblical Commentary; Word, 1993), Vol. 35B (2), p. 798.

11. Parables about Disciple Practices

"Therefore consider carefully how you listen. Whoever has will be given more; whoever does not have, even what he thinks he has will be taken from him." (Luke 8:18)

Punishment for the Wicked

The wicked and lazy servant, however, gets more than a tongue lashing and loss of the talent he had been given to invest. He is punished.

"And throw that worthless servant outside, into the darkness, where there will be weeping and gnashing of teeth." (Matthew 25:30)

This last verse in Matthew's account seems to shift from a parable about a wealthy slave owner punishing a recalcitrant slave, to punishment of the wicked at the Last Judgment. Elsewhere in Matthew, "weeping and gnashing of teeth" (Matthew 8:12) are identified with outer darkness (Matthew 8:12; 22:13) a fiery furnace (Matthew 13:42, 50); and being cut in pieces (Matthew 24:51), all terrible symbols of an even more terrible spiritual fate.

In Luke's account, remember that the nobleman's subjects hated him (Luke 19:14). Now as king, he acts decisively to protect his kingdom from future rebellion.

"Those enemies of mine who did not want me to be king over them — bring them here and kill them in front of me." (Luke 19:27)

While this seems harsh to us, to first-century ears a newly crowned king could be expected to shore up the his claim to the throne, and wipe out those who threaten his reign.

Interpreting the Parable of the Talents

I have deliberately resisted the temptation to jump too soon into these parable with interpretations and applications, but now is the time to apply this rather scary parable to ourselves.

Ultimately, this parable is not about the present. It is eschatological and applies to the time of Christ's Return. If you sense in yourself laziness or rebelliousness against God, there is still time to repent and change your heart – but you can only count on "today" in which to do that.

Now let's ask some questions that guide us in applying this parable.

What Do the Talents and Minas represent?

A talent and a mina, we determined, is each a denomination of money, currency. In the case of these parables, money is the basic resource that the master gives his servants to advance his business interests in his absence. But money by itself is useless; it must be invested in the business to grow!

What does the money represent? I believe it represents the spiritual gifts, abilities, "talents," resources, family position, knowledge, etc. that Jesus bestows on his disciples – to you and to me. What we have to "invest" in Kingdom work includes our station in life, our wealth (if we have any), our houses, our cars, our job, our network of contacts, and our personal friends. Clearly, these parables are about being stewards of what God gives us!

Each According to His Ability (Matthew 25:15)

In the Parable of the Minas or Pounds, the master initially gives each servant an equal amount – one mina. But in the Parable of the Talents, the master gives different amounts.

> "To one he gave five talents of money, to another two talents, and to another one talent, each according to his ability." (Matthew 25:15)

This is complex. "Ability" (*dynamis*) here means "ability to carry out something, ability, capability."[65] One's ability to carry out something is based on a number of things:

1. Raw talent
2. Drive, willingness to focus time to the task
3. Faithfulness
4. Moral character
5. Resources at one's disposal.

When the master returns, those who had shown faithfulness and ability he rewards with greater responsibility.

In the Parable of the Talents, Jesus answers the excuse, "I am not as talented as so-and-so." Jesus is saying in this parable that you are only responsible for what I give you. But you are fully responsible for that.

Many multi-talented people are extremely gifted, but selfish. They use their tremendous gifts to advance themselves and their family, but employ little or nothing to advance the Kingdom. They will be held responsible. Yes, they have been given much, but they also bear much greater responsibility. As Jesus taught his disciples in the Parable of the Wise and Faithful Steward (Lesson 5.3):

> "From everyone who has been given much, much will be demanded; and from the one who has been entrusted with much, much more will be asked." (Luke 12:48)

This is sort of like the idea expressed in the French phrase, *noblesse oblige* (literally, "nobility obliges"), "the obligation of honorable, generous, and responsible behavior associated with high rank or birth."[66] Except that in Christ's Kingdom, we are *all* brothers and sisters of the King. We *all* have responsibility.

---

[65] *Dynamis*, BDAG 263, 2.
[66] *Merriam-Webster 11th Collegiate Dictionary.*

11. Parables about Disciple Practices

How Will God Reward Us for Using our Talents?

One of the haunting lessons of these parables is the attitude – and fate – of the servant who had been given one talent and buries it in the ground, ostensibly for safekeeping.

I wonder how many of us "bury our talent" and do not use it or develop it? You can be an extremely gifted violinist, but if you do not practice, you won't improve. If you don't play regularly, you'll get rusty. If you aren't in the habit of both practicing regularly and playing often for others, you will have wasted a tremendous natural ability that can have powerful spiritual implications as well.

On Judgment Day, you and I will not be justified or condemned based on our works. Salvation is all by grace. But we will be judged – held accountable – for what we have done with our talents to build his Kingdom. Paul teaches:

> "If any man builds on this foundation using gold, silver, costly stones, wood, hay or straw, his work will be shown for what it is, because the Day will bring it to light. It will be revealed with fire, and the fire will test the quality of each man's work. If what he has built survives, he will receive his reward. If it is burned up, he will suffer loss; *he himself will be saved*, but only as one escaping through the flames." (1 Corinthians 3:12-15)

We are justified by faith in the grace and mercy of God through Jesus Christ. However, the scripture is very clear:

> "We must all appear before the judgment seat of Christ, that each one may receive what is due him for the things done while in the body, whether good or bad." (2 Corinthians 5:10)

This judgment is about rewarding Christ's servants for their faithfulness and obedience while here on earth. There are many verses that promise heavenly rewards for faithfulness.[67]

As mentioned, the reward does not consist in salvation. The reward for faithful labor is something else entirely. I wish I could tell you exactly what it is. I can't, but I know it will be wonderful when all is said and done. I expect that it is related to us ruling and reigning with Christ in the Kingdom of God, whatever that means.[68]

Q54. (Matthew 25:14-30; Luke 19:12-27) Why did Jesus give his disciples the Parables of the Talents and Minas? How are you using the "talents" Jesus has given you? What causes people to "bury" the talents they once used for the Lord? If it is not salvation itself, what is the reward for faithfulness? Why does God expect more of greatly gifted

---

[67] Ephesians 6:8; Matthew 6:4; 10:42; 16:27; Luke 14:14b.
[68] 2 Timothy 2:11-12a; 1 Corinthians 6:3; Revelation 1:6; 5:10; 20:4, 6; 22:5; Romans 8:17.

people?
https://www.joyfulheart.com/forums/topic/2228-q54-talents-and-minas/

11.3 Showing Love and Mercy

Jesus taught his disciples love and mercy. Several parables bear on these themes – the Parable of the Prodigal Son (Lesson 1.1) and the Parable of the Unmerciful Servant (Lesson 1.2), which we've already considered. But here we'll examine another – the Parable of the Good Samaritan.

Parable of the Good Samaritan (Luke 10:30-37; §144)

Of all Jesus' parables, none has worked its way deeper into Western consciousness than the Parable of the Good Samaritan, with possible exception of the Parable of the Prodigal Son. The name "good Samaritan" is popularly used to describe any person who goes out of his way to help another.

Vincent Van Gogh, 'The Good Samaritan (after Delacroix)' (1890), oil on canvas, 29 x 24 in., Kröller-Müller Museum, Otterlo, Netherlands.

But the Parable of the Good Samaritan says more than "It is good to help people in need." The parable is also about excuses. About self-justification. About racial prejudices. About letting oneself off the hook. It is also about love that goes far beyond the call of duty.

Testing Jesus

Somewhere in Judea, Jesus encounters a lawyer, Greek *nomikos*, "legal expert, jurist, lawyer,"[69] a man skilled in interpreting the Jewish Torah (i.e., the first five books of the Old Testament, also called the Pentateuch). He and Jesus have had a dialogue about the greatest commandments, and the lawyer answers correctly, that the great commandments are loving God and loving your neighbor as yourself. But the man's motive is flawed.

His goal is to expose Jesus' naiveté in contrast to his own sophistication and intellectual prowess. So he asks Jesus a "technical question" related to the command to love one's neighbor (Leviticus 19:18).[70]

---

[69] *Nomikos*, BDAG 676, 2.
[70] "One of your people" (NIV, cf. NRSV), "sons of your own people" (ESV), "children of your own people" (KJV) in verse 18a is parallel to "neighbor" in verse 18b. "Neighbor" is *rēaʿ*, "comrade, companion, friend, fellow" (Holladay, 342, 1).

11. Parables about Disciple Practices

"And who is my neighbor?" (Luke 10:29b)

It is a picky philosophical question, a field in which the lawyer intends to exhibit his superiority. In general, Jews limited the application of this law to fellow Jews only.[71] Love your own race and faith community and you have fulfilled the law. The lawyer's first motive is to "test"[72] Jesus (verse 25). His second motive is to "justify himself,"[73] to defend his own limited interpretation of the Torah (verse 29).

Dangers of the Jericho Road (Luke 10:30)

Jesus doesn't quibble about definitions, as philosophers often do. Instead, he answers by telling a story, a parable.

> "In reply Jesus said: 'A man was going down from Jerusalem to Jericho....'" (Luke 10:30a)

Jesus calls on his hearers' awareness of the dangers of traveling alone on the Jericho-Jerusalem road. The road is very real, of

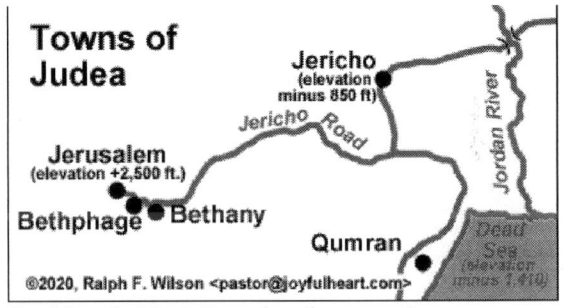

Road from Jericho to Jerusalem (larger map)

course, but the man is a fictional character, a hypothetical person whom Jesus employs to build his story.

> "A man was going down from Jerusalem to Jericho, when he fell into the hands of robbers. They stripped him of his clothes, beat him and went away, leaving him half dead." (Luke 10:30b)

Jerusalem is located along the ridge of coastal mountains running north and south in Palestine. Jericho, on the other hand, is located in the plain of the Jordan River, a geological rift zone hundreds of feet below sea level. The 17-mile (27-kilometer) road that connects these two cities climbs some 3,300 feet (1,000 meters) in elevation through desert and rocky country with

---

[71] The Jews typically interpreted "neighbor," meaning "one who is near," in terms of members of the same people and religious community, that is, fellow Jews (as in Matthew 5:43-48). The Pharisees tended to exclude "ordinary people" from their definition. The Qumran community excluded "the sons of darkness" from their definition of neighbors (Marshall, *Luke*, p. 444). Marshall cites 1QS 1:10; 9:21 for the Qumran sect's interpretation and Strack and Billerbeck I, 353-364 for common Jewish interpretations.

[72] Test" (NIV, NRSV), "put to the test" (ESV), "tempted" (KJV) is *ekpeirazō*, "to subject to test or proof, tempt," here, "to entrap someone into giving information that will jeopardize the person, entrap" (BDAG 307, 2).

[73] "Justify" is *dikaioō*, "show justice," here, "justify, vindicate" (BDAG 249, 2a), to show that his opinion was the correct one.

steep canyons that could easily hide brigands or bandits. Josephus notes that Pompey destroyed a group of brigands here and Jerome spoke of Arab robbers in his time.[74]

The robbers on the Jericho Road were desperate men. They would attack a man for the value of his clothing alone. Here they strip this man and then beat him, probably with wood staffs, to keep him from following them or perhaps to intimidate him from trying to identify them. They don't kill him, but he is severely wounded, "half-dead," as Jesus describes him.

Priests and Levites (Luke 10:31-32)

Jesus continues.

> "[31] A priest happened to be going down the same road, and when he saw the man, he passed by on the other side. [32] So too, a Levite, when he came to the place and saw him, passed by on the other side." (Luke 10:31-32)

The priest was perhaps going from Jericho to Jerusalem for service in the temple. Jericho was known as a principal residence for priests.[75] In New Testament times, Levites were an order of cultic officials, inferior to the priests, but still a privileged group in society, responsible for the liturgy and policing in the Temple.[76]

In Jesus' story, both priest and Levite see the wounded man and pass by on the other side of the road. They see the man's need, but choose not to help.

Perhaps they were concerned about ritual purity. They wouldn't be able to serve in the temple without repurification if they touched a corpse.[77] What if the man lying beaten by the side of the road were dead? One can't be too careful, you know. On the other hand, the law is crystal clear about helping those who are in need, both man and beast, friend and foe – even if he is your enemy.[78]

Placing religious purity over helping an injured person is, of course, gross hard-heartedness and selfishness. And walking on the other side of the road displays a deliberate "I-don't-want-to-know" attitude. The less they saw of the man's condition, the less they would feel obligated to help him. I don't want to get involved, they tell themselves.

---

[74] Marshall, *Luke*, p. 447, cites Josephus, *Wars of the Jews* 4:474, Strabo 16:2:41; and Jerome, *in Jerem.* 3:2. Joachim Jeremias (*Jerusalem in the Time of Jesus* (Fortress Press/SCM Press 1969), p. 52) discusses additional incidents, including whole villages around Jerusalem known to be nests of thieves.

[75] Marshall, *Luke*, p. 448, cites Strack and Billerbeck II, 66, 180.

[76] Marshall, *Luke*, p. 448.

[77] The Mosaic law stated that the high priest "must not enter a place where there is a dead body. He must not make himself unclean, even for his father or mother" (Leviticus 21:11). Even a regular priest "will also be unclean if he touches something defiled by a corpse" (Leviticus 22:4; Ezekiel 24:25).

[78] Exodus 23:4-5; Proverbs 24:17-18; 25:21-22.

11. Parables about Disciple Practices

Samaritans, the Hated Step-Brothers

Three people or situations are often found in stories of that period[79] *and* our own.[80] And so Jesus introduces his third and climatic character, but this character comes as a shock. The third man is a Samaritan.

The Samaritans were particularly hated in Jesus' day. They lived in an area south of Galilee and north of Judea, part of the old Northern Kingdom of Israel. In 721 BC Israel was conquered by Assyria, and Sargon II conducted a mass deportation of the entire region, carrying off some 27,270 captives and resettling the area with non-Jewish colonists from other parts of the Assyrian empire (2 Kings 17:24).[81] Their descendants were looked upon as half-breeds and heretics by the Jews of Jerusalem. Though Samaritans believed in the Torah, they worshiped on Mt. Gerizim, rather than Jerusalem (John 4:20-22) and built their own temple there about 450 BC.

However, Maccabees fighters came to Samaria in bold raid in 110 BC and destroyed the Samaritan's temple. The Samaritans' rage at this affront was predictable. Sometime between 6 and 9 AD at midnight during a Passover, some Samaritans deliberately scattered bones in the Jerusalem Temple in order to desecrate it.[82] The Jews were outraged! What remained now was disdain and hatred, as John observed: "Jews do not associate with Samaritans" (John 4:9b).

For Jesus to introduce the Samaritan as the caring person, after a priest and a Levite had neglected mercy, must have been intended as an especially biting commentary on what passed for "mercy" among the pillars of Judaism.

Taking Pity upon the Man (Luke 10:33-35)

> "But a Samaritan, as he traveled, came where the man was; and when he saw him, he took pity[83] on him." (Luke 10:33)

Love, sympathy, and mercy are each motivated by the need of another. Withholding mercy is essentially an act of selfishness, of self-protection.

> "He went to him and bandaged his wounds, pouring on oil and wine." (Luke 10:34a)

The Samaritan binds up the wounds (Greek *trauma*) of the injured man, perhaps with his own head covering or by tearing strips from his garment. The Samaritan also pours on oil and wine

---

[79] Matthew 25:14-30; Luke 19:11-27; 14:18-20; 20:10-12.
[80] Three Blind Mice, Goldilocks and the Three Bears, Three Billy Goats Gruff.
[81] D.J. Wiseman, "Samaria," NBD, p. 1061-1062.
[82] Josephus, *Antiquities*, 18.2.2.
[83] "Took pity" (NIV), "had compassion" (ESV, KJV), "was moved with pity" (NRSV) is *splanchizomai*, "have pity, feel sympathy with or for someone" (BDAG 938), from *splanchnon*, literally, "inward parts, entrails," figuratively of the seat of the emotions, in our usage "heart." In verse 17, "Has no pity" (NIV), "closes his heart" (ESV), "refuses help" (NRSV), "shutteth up his bowls of compassion" (KJV), is literally, "shuts his *splanchnon*."

as healing agents. Olive oil was widely employed to keep exposed parts of the skin supple, to relieve chafing, to soften wounds, and to heal bruises and lacerations (Isaiah 1:6).[84] Wine, perhaps, was poured on for cleansing.[85] Wine (typically 10% to 12% alcohol) would have had some disinfectant properties.

> "[34b] Then he put the man on his own donkey, took him to an inn and took care of him. [35] The next day he took out two silver coins and gave them to the innkeeper. 'Look after him,' he said, 'and when I return, I will reimburse you for any extra expense you may have.'" (Luke 10:34b-35)

The Samaritan used his own supplies to cleanse and soothe the man's wounds, his own clothing to bandage him, his own animal to carry him while the Samaritan himself walked, his own money to pay for his care, and his own reputation and credit to promise payment for any further expenses the man's care would require. Love can be costly. But if we have the means to help, we are to extend ourselves.

> "If anyone has material possessions and sees his brother in need but has no pity on him, how can the love of God be in him? Dear children, let us not love with words or tongue but with actions and in truth" (1 John 3:17-18).

There wasn't an emergency room where the Samaritan can take the man. Instead, he brings him to an inn, a hotel, and cares for the man himself that night. Edersheim sees the inn as a khan or hostelry, found by the side of roads, providing free lodging to the traveler. Such a hostelry would also provide food for both man and beast, for which they would charge.[86] "Silver coins" (NIV), "denarii" (ESV, NRSV), "pence" (KJV) is *dēnarion*, "denarius," a Roman silver coin that represented about one day's average wage. Two denarii, perhaps $300 to $400 USD in our currency, would probably provide for food and care for several days.

It seems likely that the Samaritan is a merchant who frequently traveled this way and had stayed at this inn before. He trusts the innkeeper enough to advance him money to care for the wounded man. And he promises the innkeeper – who also seems to trust the Samaritan – to reimburse him for any additional costs when he returns from his trip. The Samaritan's mercy is a generous mercy. A mercy that doesn't just keep the letter of the law, but its spirit as well. The Samaritan pledges "whatever he needs" – a blank check.

---

[84] Roland K. Harrison, "Heal," ISBE 2:640-647.
[85] Edersheim (*Life and Times* 2:238) cites *Jer. Ber.* 3a and *Shabb.* 134a as indicating that oil and wine were the common dressing for wounds. N. Angelotti and P. Martini ("Treatment of skin ulcers and wounds through the centuries," *Minerva Med.* 1997 Jan-Feb 88(1-2):49-55) note that Hippocrates washed ulcers with wine and after having softened them by oil, he dressed them with fig leaves. Marshall, *Luke,* p. 449, affirms that the use of wine and oil as healing agents is well-attested, citing *Shab.* 14:2; 19;4; Strack and Billerbeck I, 428; and Theophrastus, *Hist. Plant* 9:11:1.
[86] Edersheim, *Life and Times* 2:239.

Who Was Neighbor to the Man? (Luke 10:36-37)

Now Jesus asks the expert in the law about the story.

> "³⁶ 'Which of these three do you think was a neighbor to the man who fell into the hands of robbers?'
>
> ³⁷ The expert in the law replied, 'The one who had mercy on him.'
>
> Jesus told him, 'Go and do likewise.'" (Luke 10:36-37)

Who is my neighbor? By this parable Jesus is saying that my neighbor is not just "my kind of people," but anyone who has a need. Jews are not to love just Jews. White people are not to love only white people. We are to love everyone! Powerful!

Jesus' story is loaded with all sorts of religious, cultural, and historical baggage (priests, Levites, and a Samaritan). But the merciful response to need is so compelling that the lawyer is forced to admit that "the one who had mercy[87] on him" is the neighbor.

One summary of godly piety is found in Micah 6:8:

> "He has shown you, O man, what is good.
> And what does the Lord require of you?
> To act justly and to love mercy,[88]
> and to walk humbly with your God."

Mercy is required of us (Isaiah 58:6-7; Hosea 6:6). Jesus commands his disciples very specifically: "Be merciful, just as your Father is merciful" (Luke 6:36).

Q55. (Luke 10:30-37) Why does Jesus contrast a Jewish priest and Levite with a hated Samaritan? According to the parable, how do you think Jesus would define "neighbor," that is, someone we have a responsibility toward? How much does compassion move you to go out of your way and comfort zone to care for those in need?
https://www.joyfulheart.com/forums/topic/2229-q55-good-samaritan/

The parables we've studied in this lesson reflect Jesus' training his disciples into serving humbly and showing mercy. God help us!

---

[87] The Greek word used is *eleos*. In classical Greek *eleos* is the emotion roused by contact with an affliction which comes undeservedly on someone else. The New Testament meaning of *eleos* draws on the Hebrew concept of *hesed*, faithfulness between individuals that results in human kindness, mercy, and pity (Rudolf Bultmann, *oleos, ktl.*, TDNT 2:477-487).

[88] Hebrew *hesed*, Greek Septuagint *eleos*.

Prayer

Father, I find it so easy to let my own concerns get in the way of yours. To value my own time and priorities more than the "coincidences" that bring me face to face with need and the opportunity to serve and show mercy. Help me to learn these lessons well! In Jesus' name, I pray. Amen.

12. Parables about Caring for the Lost

We conclude our study of Jesus' parables with a set of parables closely related to Jesus' core mission, "to seek and to save the lost" (Luke 19:10). Jesus doesn't just want the disciples who follow him adopt his values, to become like him. He is also training his disciples to carry on his mission on earth.

Sickles were used to harvest gain as far back as the Neolithic era. Illustrator unknown.

12.1 A Heart for the Lost
- Analogy of the Doctor and the Sick (Matthew 9:12; Mark 2:17; Luke 5:31)
- Analogies of the Lost Sheep (Matthew 9:36; 10:5-6; 15:24; John 10:16)

12.2 Workers in the Harvest
- Analogy of the Harvest and the Laborers (Matthew 9:37-38; Luke 10:2)
- Analogy of the Sowers and Reapers (John 4:35-38)
- Analogies of the Sheep and Wolves, Serpents and Doves (Matthew 10:16; Luke 10:3)

12.3 Witnessing to the Lost
- Saying: "Fishers of Men" (Matthew 4:18-20; Mark 1:16-18; Luke 5:10-11)
- Analogy of the Savorless Salt (Matthew 5:13; Mark 9:50; Luke 14:34-35)
- Analogy of the City on a Hill (Matthew 5:14)
- Analogy of the Lamp under a Bushel (Matthew 5:15; Mark 4:21; Luke 8:16-17; Luke 11:33)

12.4 Teaching the Kingdom
- Parable of the Scribes of the Kingdom (Matthew 13:51-52)

12.1 A Heart for the Lost

Jesus provides a number of analogies and comparisons that teach us to love lost people like he does.

Analogy of the Doctor and the Sick (Matthew 9:12; Mark 2:17; Luke 5:31; §53)
(Also called the Parable of the Great Physician)

The first we'll consider is the Analogy of the Doctor and the Sick. The context of this gem is the occasion of the conversion of Levi/Matthew, a tax collector who becomes a disciple of Jesus, one of the Twelve. Luke lays the scene for us.

> "Then Levi held a great banquet for Jesus at his house, and a large crowd of tax collectors and others were eating with them." (Luke 5:29)

Tax Collectors and Sinners

As we learned when we studied the Parable of the Pharisee and Tax Collector (Lesson 9.1), tax collectors were hated. They collected taxes for the Romans and had a reputation for overcharging and cheating. Levi is wealthy, so he can afford to put on a "great banquet" for Jesus at his rather large home. He invites "a large crowd" of his friends. Since no self-respecting Jew would befriend a tax collector, his friends are other tax collectors, and those in town of questionable morals and character, the outcasts of reputable society.

Jesus is severely criticized by the strict, proud Pharisees for eating with such a collection of "sinners." To associate with them, they thought, was a sign that Jesus approved of their lifestyle. Matthew continues the story:

> "When the Pharisees saw this, they asked his disciples, 'Why does your teacher eat with tax collectors and sinners?'" (Matthew 9:11)

Similarly, when Zacchaeus the "chief tax collector" of Jericho invites him to a meal, Jesus enemies mutter, "He has gone to be the guest of a 'sinner.'" On that occasion, Jesus responded, "The Son of Man came to seek and to save what was lost" (Luke 19:7, 10).

Healing the Sin-Sick Soul

Jesus turns to the scribes and Pharisees and responds to their criticism:

> "[12] It is not the healthy who need a doctor, but the sick. [13] But go and learn what this means: 'I desire mercy, not sacrifice.' For I have not come to call the righteous, but sinners."[1] (Matthew 9:12-13)

The Analogy of the Doctor and the Sick is a simple metaphor. Jesus doesn't come for those who see themselves as righteous. As an African-American spiritual puts it, he comes to "heal the sin-sick soul."[2]

If all were righteous, spiritually healthy, Doctor Jesus would have no necessity to pay a house call. But because we are not so righteous after all, because our souls are troubled and

---

[1] Luke adds the words "to repentance."
[2] The phrase is from a wonderful African-American spiritual, "There Is a Balm in Gilead."

12. Parables about Caring for the Lost

besmirched by compromise – because of all this, we desperately need Jesus to come and call us to something better than the filth we may be living in. We need him to call us to our best.

Mercy, not Sacrifice (Matthew 9:13)

Look at verse 13 again.

> "Go and learn what this means: 'I desire mercy, not sacrifice.' For I have not come to call the righteous, but sinners." (Matthew 9:13)

Jesus is quoting the Old Testament prophet Hosea:

> "For I desire mercy,
> not sacrifice,
> and acknowledgment of God
> rather than burnt offerings." (Hosea 6:6)

The prophet speaks out God's frustration with both the northern and southern kingdoms (Ephraim and Judah), who claim that they loved God and go through the motions of religious observance, but have actually broken God's covenant and are unfaithful. They had kept the religious observances, but had lost the moral basis of a loving God.[3] David and the prophets say much the same thing.[4] As Tasker puts it, "It was mercy that found favor with God, not sacrifices offered by those who felt themselves to be morally superior."[5]

Jesus is saying that the Pharisees think they know the law, but they do not know God or God's heart of compassion for the lost. They honor God with their lips, Jesus says, "but their hearts are far from me."[6] Jesus desires "mercy, not sacrifice" – grace, not a sense of religious superiority over the lost.

> **Q56. (Matthew 9:13; Hosea 6:6) What does Jesus mean when he tells his disciples, "I desire mercy, not sacrifice"? What attitude did the Pharisees have towards sinners? What attitude did Jesus have toward sinners? What attitude do you have toward sinners?**

---

[3] "For I desire mercy, not sacrifice, and acknowledgment of God rather than burnt offerings" (Hosea 6:6, NIV). "Steadfast love" (ESV, NRSV), "mercy" (NIV, KJV) is the Hebrew noun *hesed*, is one of the words God uses to describe his steadfast love, mercy, and lovingkindness. This is parallel to "Acknowledgement of God" (NIV), "knowledge" (ESV, NRSV, KJV) using the noun *da'at*, "knowledge," from the very broadly used noun *yāda'*, "to know" in every sense. I believe that the NIV's "acknowledge" is a poor translation in this context. Rather the word means here "knowledge of = acquaintance with God" (Holladay 73, I, 3a). "Sacrifice" and "burnt offerings" are clearly used in parallel.
[4] Psalm 51:16-17; 40:6; 58:7-14; Proverbs 15:8; 21:27; Isaiah 1:11-15; Jeremiah 7:22-23; Amos 5:21-23; Mark 12:33; Romans 12:1; Hebrews 13:16.
[5] R.V.G. Tasker, *The Gospel According to St. Matthew* (Tyndale New Testament Commentaries; Eerdmans, 1961), p. 97.
[6] Matthew 15:8, quoting Isaiah 29:13.

What is the role of a spiritual doctor?
https://www.joyfulheart.com/forums/topic/2230-q56-mercy-not-sacrifice/

Analogies of the Lost Sheep (Matthew 9:36; 10:5-6; 15:24; John 10:16)

Jesus' Analogies of the Lost Sheep also show us his heart. We began our study with the Parable of the Lost Sheep (Lesson 1.1) and later studied Parables of the Good Shepherd and the Sheep Gate (Lesson 7.4). In these we see the affection and sense of responsibility that a good shepherd has for his sheep. Beyond these, however, Jesus offers a number of analogies of "lost sheep," an analogy with deep roots in the Prophets.

We all, like sheep, have gone astray...." (Isaiah 53:6)

"My people have been lost sheep;
their shepherds have led them astray.... " (Jeremiah 50:6)

"They were scattered because there was no shepherd, and when they were scattered they became food for all the wild animals." (Ezekiel 34:5)

Like Sheep without a Shepherd (Matthew 9:36)

Jesus' analogy is similar.

"When he saw the crowds, he had compassion on them, because they were harassed and helpless, like **sheep without a shepherd**." (Matthew 9:36)

They are lost because their leaders, their shepherds, have failed them. The Jewish leaders have not guided them well or cared for them as we saw in Jesus' Parables of the Good Shepherd and the Sheep Gate (Lesson 7.4).

The people are harassed or dejected. "Harassed" can mean "weary" as well as "maltreated, molested, troubled."[7] And they are also "helpless." This is from a word that means "to lie down," used of animals lying on the ground, perhaps "dejected."[8] Jesus sees them like a herd of sheep in bad condition. His heart bleeds for them. The KJV catches the idea when it says, "He was moved with compassion."[9]

---

[7] "Harassed" (NIV, ESV, NRSV), "fainted" (KJV) is *skyllō*, originally, "flay, skin," then "weary, harass," here in the passive, "dejected" (BDAG 933, 1). In classical Greek it can mean "maltreat, molest" as well as "trouble, annoy" (Liddell-Scott 1617, meanings 2 and 3).

[8] "Helpless" (NIV, ESV, NRSV), "scattered abroad" (KJV) is *rhiptō*, here, with no connotation of violence, "put/lay something down." It can be used of an animal lying on the ground. Here, "they were distressed and dejected" (BDAG 906, 2).

[9] "Had compassion" (NIV, ESV, NRSV), "moved with compassion" (KJV) is *splanchnizomai*, "have pity, feel sympathy" (BDAG 938), from *splanchnon*, "inward parts, entrails," seen in the ancient world as the seat of the emotions.

Peter picks up on this theme in his First Epistle:

> "For you were like sheep going astray,
> but now you have returned
> to the Shepherd and Overseer of your souls." (1 Peter 2:25)

There is no startling lesson, since this isn't a parable-story with a point. It is, however, a powerful analogy that explains Jesus' view of his mission and the state of the people he is seeking to bring to his Father.

The Lost Sheep of the House of Israel (Matthew 10:6; 15:24)

On two occasions the phrase, "the lost sheep of the house[10] of Israel" differentiates Israelites from other ethnic groups.[11]

> Upon sending out the Twelve: "⁵ᵇ Do not go among the Gentiles or enter any town of the Samaritans. ⁶ Go rather to the lost sheep of the house of Israel." (Matthew 10:5b-6, ESV)

> To the Syrophoenician Woman: "I was sent only to the lost sheep of the house of Israel." (Matthew 15:24, ESV).

In these two verses, Jesus seems to be referring to the Jewish people as a whole.[12] Jesus is the Jews' Messiah first, sent to them in fulfillment of promises made to David a thousand years before. Only when the Jewish leaders reject their Messiah does the door of salvation open to the Gentiles (see the Parable of the Wicked Tenants, Lesson 2.3), as Paul puts it, "first for the Jew, then for the Gentile" (Romans 1:16).

Sheep of another Sheep Fold (John 10:16)

Notice that Jesus anticipates his flock expanding in the future.

> "I have other sheep that are not of this sheep pen. I must bring[13] them also. They too will listen to my voice, and there shall be one flock and one shepherd." (John 10:16)

Who are the "other sheep that are not of this sheep pen"? Clearly, these are sheep that are not found in Judaism, but Gentiles who will come to faith in the future. Jesus' heart goes out to "lost sheep."

---

[10] The NIV excludes the words "the house of," presuming that the term Israel conveys the idea well enough by itself. In the New Testament outside of the Gospels, the term "house of Israel" appears also in Acts 2:36; 7:42; Hebrews 8:8, 10, mostly in quotations of Old Testament texts.

[11] "The lost sheep of the house of Israel" is used only in Matthew, a gospel intended for Jewish readers.

[12] "The lost sheep of the house of Israel" doesn't seem to refer to Jewish sinners in particular, as when he uses the phrase, "to seek and to save the lost" with regard to tax collectors and sinners (Luke 19:10), in the Analogy of the Doctor and Sick (Lesson 12.1), and in the Parable of the Lost Sheep (Lesson 1.1).

[13] "Bring" is *agō*, "lead, bring, lead off, lead away" (BDAG 16, 1a).

Q57. (Matthew 9:36) Why is Jesus' heartbroken over lost sheep? Who are the lost sheep of your community? Of the mission fields that you know about? What is your attitude toward them?
https://www.joyfulheart.com/forums/topic/2231-q57-lost-sheep/

12.2 Workers in the Harvest

Now let's examine a series of parables and analogies having to do with outreach that use the agricultural images of sowing and harvest. We've already seen such images in the Parable of the Sower (Lesson 8.1), the Parable of the Weeds or Tares (Lesson 4.2), and the Parable of the Seed Growing by Itself (Lesson 7.1). Now let's consider some additional uses of these images.

Sickles were used to harvest gain as far back as the Neolithic era. Illustrator unknown.

Analogy of the Harvest and the Laborers (Matthew 9:37-38, §58; Luke 10:2, §139)

Jesus' metaphor of the Harvest and the Laborers is given in two different contexts, indicating to me that he probably said these words on a number of occasions. In Luke, Jesus says this when sending out the Seventy two-by-two on a preaching mission to the villages and towns he would later visit himself.

The Harvest Is Plentiful (Matthew 9:37; Luke 10:2)

But I want us to consider these words in Matthew's context, since it gives us a glimpse into Jesus' broken heart for the lost. We just looked at this passage above with the phrase "sheep without a shepherd" (Matthew 9:36). Jesus sees the masses of people in town after town that are in such desperate spiritual need. He continues:

> "[37] The harvest is plentiful but the workers are few. [38] Ask the Lord of the harvest, therefore, to send out workers into his harvest field." (Matthew 9:37-38)

In the agrarian economy of Palestine, harvest was an ever-present reality. It isn't surprising that the idea of harvest is used not only for bringing men and women to faith in Christ, but also for a final gathering of God's people at the end of the age (See Appendix 5. The Great Messianic Banquet).[14] But here, Jesus has in mind an immediate harvest.

---

[14] Matthew 13:39; Revelation 14:15.

12. Parables about Caring for the Lost

Fields are typically planted so that the whole field will become ripe about the same time. Seldom would you go into a field or orchard for selective picking. Rather, when the field is ripe you'd hire a number of harvesters and reap the whole field at one time.

Having too few workers at harvest time can be a disaster. The crop can rot in the field unless workers are available at the right time in sufficient numbers, and are willing to work very hard for this concentrated harvest season. Farmers get some rest in the winter, but the long summer harvest season often sees them working night and day. It is hot, sweaty, muscle-aching work.

Jesus' own workforce of sowers and harvesters has grown from 12 to now 70. (As mentioned above, Jesus also said these words at the sending out of the Seventy.)

Ask the Lord of the Harvest to Send Out Workers (Matthew 9:38)

It is hard to find committed workers.

"The harvest is plentiful but the workers are few." (Matthew 9:37)

Immediately, Jesus gives his answer to the problem of too few workers

"Ask the Lord of the harvest, therefore, to send out[15] workers into his harvest field." (Matthew 9:38)

Jesus is teaching his disciples to pray to God, the Lord of the Harvest, for workers. Why? Because soon, Jesus will be in heaven and the apostles and their associates will be the harvest foremen in need of workers.

How does this process of recruiting harvesters work? Men can recruit workers, the best workers respond to an inner call from God, an inner sense that God himself wants them to be involved in an aspect of his work. Those who continue as workers are the ones who do so from a sense of calling, rather than having their arm twisted or doing a favor to me or to another leader.

Prayer must be our prime recruitment technique, preceding any other invitation to the work. That is Jesus' pattern. Before he appoints the Twelve Apostles, he spends the night in prayer (Luke 6:12). Human leaders may be the instruments in God's hands, but God is the moving force. Ultimately, it is the Lord of the harvest who sends out men and women as workers, not the foreman. The foreman merely directs the workers that the master hires and sends.

---

[15] "Send out" is *ekballō*. At the root level, the word means "to throw out," then, "force to leave, drive out, expel," literally, "'throw out' more or less forcibly." Here it has the idea, "to cause to go or remove from a position (without force), send out/away, release, bring out" (BDAG 299, 2).

Analogy of Fields White for Harvest (John 4:35)

We see a similar figure of speech referring to spiritually needy people who are clearly *not* of "the house of Israel" to whom Jesus has been specifically sent (Matthew 10:6; 15:24). They are Samaritans.

John's Analogy of Fields White for Harvest is similar to the Synoptics' Analogy of the Harvest and the Laborers. As we saw in the Parable of the Good Samaritan (Lesson 11.3), the Jews hated the Samaritans and the Samaritans hated the Jews with equal enmity.

Jesus and his band of disciples are traveling through Samaria and have stopped at Jacob's well. The disciples go into the nearby village of Sychar to get food, while Jesus has an encounter with a Samaritan woman at the well, leading her to faith (John 4:1-30).

When the disciples return, Jesus isn't interested in eating. Rather, he says:

> "My food is to do the will of him who sent me and to finish his work." (John 4:34)

Jesus sees the tremendous spiritual needs of Samaria itself, so he shares this passion with his disciples.

> "Do you not say, 'Four months more and then the harvest'? I tell you, open your eyes and look at the fields! They are ripe for harvest." (John 4:34)

It isn't yet the season of harvest; harvest is still four months off. But Jesus asks his disciples to look beyond the natural harvest that isn't ready, to the spiritual harvest that is indeed ripe! He has just brought a Samaritan woman to faith, and knows that she will bring the whole town, many of whom will become believers as well (John 4:39-42). Jesus tells his disciples, "Open your eyes" (NIV), "look around you" (NRSV), "lift up your eyes" (ESV, KJV). So often we are blind to the spiritual state of others, such as their state of readiness to receive Christ. Jesus tells his disciples to become alert to the readiness of the harvest. When Jesus speaks of "harvesting the crop for eternal life" (verse 30), he is talking about bringing people from unbelief to faith and from sin and destruction to eternal life.[16]

Analogy of the Sowers and Reapers (John 4:36-38)

Jesus continues the harvest analogy by focusing on the importance of all the jobs related to the harvest – and the disciples' part in it.

> "[36] Even now the reaper draws his wages, even now he harvests the crop for eternal life, so that the sower and the reaper may be glad together. [37] Thus the saying 'One sows and another reaps' is true. [38] I sent you to reap what you have not worked for.

---

[16] A number of Christian hymns use this kind of language, such as "Bringing in the Sheaves" and "Come Ye Thankful People Come."

12. Parables about Caring for the Lost

Others have done the hard work, and you have reaped the benefits of their labor." (John 4:36-38)

Jesus refers to a popular proverb of the day: "One sows and another reaps."

In Jesus' analogy, both sower and reaper are glad, because when the harvest comes in the workers get paid! – the sower (usually the farmer himself) and the reapers (often temporary workers hired to bring in the harvest quickly). Who sowed the seed that resulted in the spiritual harvest of this Samaritan town? Perhaps the Old Testament prophets or the Father, who prepared them for this hour.

To the Corinthian church that was tearing down one preacher to exalt another, the Apostle Paul used a similar analogy:

> "What, after all, is Apollos? And what is Paul? Only servants, through whom you came to believe – as the Lord has assigned to each his task. I planted the seed, Apollos watered it, but God made it grow. So neither he who plants nor he who waters is anything, but only God, who makes things grow. The man who plants and the man who waters have one purpose, and each will be rewarded according to his own labor." (1 Corinthians 3:5-8)

Whether your ministry is primarily to sow (share your faith, testify, preach), to water (encourage people on their faith journey), or to reap (lead people to Christ), all are important – and when the harvest comes in, everyone will "get paid," that is, receive our reward.

Q58. (Matthew 9:37-38; John 4:35-38) Where in your region does the harvest seem most ripe, that is, where people are most receptive to the gospel? Do you see yourself mainly as a sower or a reaper? Why is there such a shortage of reapers? Would you be willing to be a reaper, if Jesus helps you?
https://www.joyfulheart.com/forums/topic/2232-q58-sowers-and-reapers/

Analogies of the Sheep and Wolves, Serpents and Doves (Matthew 10:16, §58; Luke 10:3, §139)

As Jesus sends out his laborers into the harvest, he uses analogies of sheep and wolves, serpents and doves. Matthew's citation is at the sending out of the Twelve. Luke's is at the sending out of the Seventy.

"I am sending[17] you out like sheep among wolves.
Therefore be as shrewd as snakes and as innocent as doves." (Matthew 10:16)

"Go! I am sending you out like lambs among wolves." (Luke 10:3)

Sheep, of course, are vulnerable animals that are often prey to wolves.[18] Jesus knows that the preaching of his message will bring his disciples ferocious attacks from enemies who will seek to silence them by any means.

"'No servant is greater than his master.' If they persecuted me, they will persecute you also." (John 15:20)

He tells his followers to expect persecution and not be intimidated by it.[19] Sheep among wolves.

Because he knows this is coming, he switches to another pair of analogies.

"Therefore be as shrewd as snakes and as innocent as doves." (Matthew 10:16b)

Snakes[20] are sometimes symbols of deceit and lurking danger. Their venom is deadly. Satan is identified as a serpent,[21] as are the Pharisees and Sadducees.[22] The disciples, however, are to take on a serpent's legendary craftiness, cleverness, and shrewdness,[23] not the serpent's threat of attack. Rather, they are to be as harmless as doves.[24] They are not to win people over by force, but by truth and love.

We will not survive long as Christian workers unless we stay very close to the Shepherd for our protection and strength. We are not supermen. We are very vulnerable to Satan's attack and therefore we must continually rely upon Jesus' strength rather than our own.

---

[17] "Sending" (Matthew 10:16; Luke 10:3) is *apostellō*, "to dispatch someone for the achievement of some objective, send away/out" (BDAG 120, 1bβ).

[18] "Sheep" is the plural of *probaton*, "sheep" (BDAG 866). "Lambs" is the plural of *arēn*, "lamb" as an animal for slaughter, here as a type of weakness (BDAG 130). Used only in this passage in the New Testament. "Wolves" is the plural *lukos*, "wolf" (BDAG 604, 1).

[19] Matthew 10:22–25; 24:9; Luke 21:12–19; John 16:2.

[20] "Serpents" (NIV, ESV, KJV), "snakes" (NRSV) is the plural of *ophis*, "a limbless reptile, snake, serpent," here as a symbol of cleverness (BDAG 744, 1).

[21] Genesis 3; Revelation 12:9; 20:2.

[22] Matthew 3:7; 12:34; 23:33; Luke 3:7.

[23] "Wise" (ESV, NRSV, KJV), "shrewd" (NIV) is *phronimos*, "pertaining to understanding associated with insight and wisdom, sensible, thoughtful, prudent, wise" (BDAG 1063).

[24] "Innocent" (NIV, ESV, NRSV), "harmless" (KJV) is *akeraios*, "unmixed," figuratively, "pure, innocent" (BDAG 35). The KJV follows the Western Text (D) in using instead the adjective *aplous*, "single, without guile, sincere, straightforward," that is, without a hidden agenda (BDAG 104). "Doves" is the plural of *peristera*, "pigeon, dove" (BDAG 806).

12.3 Witnessing to the Lost

We have been examining Jesus' parables and analogies about caring for the lost. Now let's look at his parables concerning a disciple's witness.

Analogy of Sparrows (Matthew 10:29-30, §60; Luke 12:6-7, §155)

One fear we have of witnessing is the adverse reaction of the people we are witnessing to. Indeed, the disciples had reason to fear physical violence against them or even death. They refuse to accept it, but Jesus knows he will soon be crucified. Jesus seeks to allay their fears.

Your opponents can only kill the body, he tells them. Don't fear men; rather, fear God who is the final Judge (Matthew 10:26-28). And, of course, he can usher you into his Kingdom!

Now he gives a brief comparison, an analogy, to help his disciples understand God's love and care for them.

> "29 Are not two sparrows sold for a penny?[25] And not one of them will fall to the ground apart from[26] your Father. 30 But even the hairs of your head are all numbered. 31 Fear not, therefore; you are of more value than many sparrows." (Matthew 10:29-31, ESV)

Jesus refers to sparrows, but not just regular sparrows – "little sparrows."[27] Sparrows and other wild birds were sold in the marketplace for food.[28] There isn't much meat on a little sparrow, of course – that is why the price is so very low. Nevertheless, for the very poorest person, it provided a bit of protein.

But small as these little birds are, not one falls to the ground without your Father knowing. He knows and cares for them! To underscore his point, Jesus says, "Indeed, the very hairs of your head are all numbered." Jesus wants us to know that God knows us intimately. We are not identified in his records merely as a "soul registration number," but as a person who is distinct and about which he knows every minute detail – and still loves us!

Jesus uses the argument of the smaller to the greater here. If the cheapest little sparrows are not forgotten by God, how much more he remembers you, who "are of more value than many sparrows" (Matthew 10:31). We are to speak the word of God fearlessly, knowing that God values us greatly and will take care of us forever!

---

[25] "Penny" is *assarion*, "a Roman copper coin worth about one-sixteenth of a denarius," here "be sold for a paltry sum" (BDAG 145). Luke has five sparrows for two pennies – a bargain!

[26] "Apart from" (ESV, NRSV), "without" (KJV). NIV renders this "apart from the will of your Father." But "will" is not in the text. This is the preposition *aneu*, "without," here, with the sense, "without the knowledge and consent of" (BDAG 78, a). So Liddell-Scott, p. 135. "Without one's will or intervention" (Thayer, p. 44).

[27] *Strouthion*, a diminutive form of *strouthos*, "sparrow" (BDAG 949; Marshall, *Luke*, p. 514).

[28] Marshall (*Luke*, p. 514) claims that "sparrows were not in fact eaten." However, Moulton and Milligan (p. 593) cite evidence of the sale of sparrows for food in antiquity. So also Morris, *Matthew*, p. 263, fn. 66; and Otto Bauernfeind, *strouthion*, TDNT 7:730-732.

Analogy of Fishers of Men (Matthew 4:18-20; Mark 1:16-18; §11; Luke 5:10-11, §17)

Stories of the call of Peter and the disciples are very familiar to us.

> "[18b] They were casting a net into the lake, for they were fishermen (*halieus*). [19] 'Come, follow me,' Jesus said, 'and I will make you fishers (*halieus*) of men.' [20] At once they left their nets and followed him." (Matthew 4:18-20)

The phrase "fishers[29] of men" is a simple comparison. In the same way that they used to catch fish, now they will catch men.

Luke has a wonderful turn of phrase that follows the miraculous catch of fish.

> "From now on you will be catching men." (Luke 5:10b)

The verb used here is nearly unique in the New Testament: *zōgreō*, "to capture alive" or "to spare life," and it builds on the idea of fish being taken alive in the nets.[30] Peter had been catching fish to kill and sell them. But now he will be taking men alive to give them liberty.[31] Catch and release to freedom in Christ!

Analogy of the Savorless Salt (Matthew 5:13, §20; Mark 9:50; Luke 14:34-35, §171)

In the Sermon on the Mount, Matthew groups together three parables on witness. For this reason, we'll follow Matthew's order as we study them. They occur immediately after the Beatitudes that end with predictions of persecution for those who stand up for Jesus, no doubt as an encouragement to witness no matter what the threat.

> "You are the salt of the earth. But if the salt loses its saltiness, how can it be made salty again? It is no longer good for anything, except to be thrown out and trampled by men." (Matthew 5:13)

A proper amount of salt (sodium chloride, NaCl) is essential to sustain life, so ancient peoples traded whatever was required to obtain it. In Palestine, most salt was mined from salt caves around the Dead Sea. Both ancient and modern peoples have used salt as both (1) a food preservative and (2) to bring out the flavor of foods.

---

[29] "Fishers" is the plural of *halieus*, "one whose occupation is catching fish, fisher" (BDAG 44), from *hals, halos*, "the sea." The word is used in the Septuagint and in Greek literature in the vocabulary of war and hunting.

[30] *Zōgreō*, BDAG 430; Green, *Luke*, pp. 234-235. The word also forms the title of a book on soul-winning by Charles Gallaudet Trumbull, *Taking Men Alive* (Revell, 1938, reprint of 1907 YMCA edition).

[31] The only other time the word is used in the New Testament is regarding helping people escape from "trap of the devil, who has taken them captive (*zōgreō*) to do his will" (2 Timothy 2:25-26). Men can either be live captives of Satan or freed servants of Jesus. Jesus "captures" men to free them.

Preservative or Seasoning?

What does it mean to be "the salt of the earth"?

Preservative. If we use the preservative analogy, we would say that Christians by their very presence help preserve the world and hold back the wrath of God against it. We think of Abraham arguing with God over the fate of Sodom and Gomorrah (Genesis 18:25, 23, 32) and God's quest for a man to "stand before me in the gap on behalf of the land" (Ezekiel 22:30).

But our presence is not only a shield against the wrath of God upon the earth. We also serve as those who by their wholesome presence bring about change and healing in a corrupt society. For example, historians credit the fearless preaching of John and Charles Wesley and George Whitefield for saving England from its drunkenness and sin. This awakened conscience was responsible for the final prohibition of the slave trade in England.

Seasoning. While it is true that ancient peoples used salt as a preservative, a search of the Bible for this use of salt comes up nearly empty.[32] There is much more mention of salt being used as seasoning, and in the parable we are studying, Jesus seems to be referring more to salt's taste than its effects.

Salt was used with sacrifices as a way of honoring the King to whom the sacrifices were made.[33] Salt was also used in the making of covenants.[34] We read of its ability to add flavor to food.[35] Paul writes,

> "Let your conversation be always full of grace, seasoned[36] with salt, so that you may know how to answer everyone" (Colossians 4:6).

Here, as in Jesus' parable of Christians being the salt of the earth, salt has to do with witness and conversation.

I believe that the primary meaning of "You are the salt of the earth" has to do with a willingness to live our lives with the "tang" of our faith intact. We are under so much pressure to soft-pedal our distinct faith in Christ in order to blend in with society. Believers are to be "tangy," yet gracious, rather than bland and insipid.

---

[32] The apocryphal *Epistle of Jeremiah* speaks of women who preserve some of the meat sacrificed to idols: "As for the things that are sacrificed unto them, their priests sell and abuse; in like manner their wives lay up part thereof in salt; but unto the poor and impotent they give nothing of it" (part of *Baruch* 6:28). In the canonical scriptures we see salt to render land unusable (Judges 9:45), the rubbing of newborns with salt (to purify them? Ezekiel 16:4), Elisha's use of salt to sweeten or purify a spring and remove its poison (2 Kings 2:20-21).

[33] Leviticus 2:13; Ezra 6:9; Ezekiel 43:24.

[34] Numbers 18:19.

[35] Job 6:6.

[36] "Seasoned" is *artuō*, "to add condiments to something, to season, to salt" (BDAG 137).

Impurities in Salt

The salt the Israelites obtained was often impure, mixed with alkali salts from around the Dead Sea. Water could leach out the sodium chloride, leaving the other salts intact. It still looked like salt, but tasted insipid. This seems to be the basis of Jesus' warning about salt losing its saltiness. The essential Christ-inspired difference in our lives can be leached out by the constant flow of the world's values through our lives.[37]

If we no longer stand boldly and faithfully for Christ and Christian values, we become worthless to him as disciples. Less than worthless, in fact, since by our mild claims of our Christianity, we act as a counterfeit of the real salt. Worthless, insipid, tangy-less salt is good for nothing except for throwing on the pathway to keep the grass from growing on it. Would you rather be a grass killer or a food enhancer?

Analogy of the City on a Hill (Matthew 5:14; §20)

The next parables in this series on the Sermon on the Mount involve visibility. Jesus says:

"You are the light of the world. A city on a hill cannot be hidden." (Matthew 5:14)

Cities were usually situated on hilltops for protection against attack. It is much more difficult to storm a walled city while attacking uphill. Defenders have always known that victory is achieved by capturing and holding the high ground. Jesus' point, however, is not a city's defense, but its visibility. You can't hide a city built on a hilltop, though you can certainly defend it.

At first glance, Jesus' saying about, "You are the light of the world," doesn't seem to go with his short analogy of a city on a hill. Before electricity, cities weren't lit up at night, except perhaps by some torches or small flickering lamps behind the city walls. But what connects "the light of the world" and the city set on a hill is *visibility*. These are both images of visibility. Christians are not to be hidden away. They are to be visible, not blending in, but distinct from the world. This and the next parable are to be metaphors of uncompromising witness.

Analogy of the Lamp under a Bushel (Matthew 5:15, §20; Mark 4:21; Luke 8:16-17, §94; Luke 11:33; §153)
(Also known as the Parable of the Lamp under a Bowl)

Jesus told the Analogy of the Lamp under a Bushel in various contexts, as we'll see. The Gospels show us at least three distinct lessons that Jesus taught from it.

---

[37] Friedrich Hauck, *halas*, TDNT 1:228-229; William Barclay, *The Gospel of Matthew* (Daily Study Bible; Edinburgh: St. Andrews Press, 1956, 1958), volume 1, p. 115.

12. Parables about Caring for the Lost

The Light of the World

Jesus tells his disciples (in Matthew only), "You are the light[38] of the world" (Matthew 5:14) – a simple metaphor. The concept of light and darkness are often used in the Bible to contrast righteousness vs. wickedness, life vs. death, truth vs. lies.[39] We explore this theme further in Analogies of Walking in Light and Darkness (Appendix 4.1). But here, by declaring the disciples "the light of the world," Jesus is saying that by your presence and witness and deeds people will see truth that can set them free.

True Israel was designed to display God's truth and goodness throughout the whole world, to be "a light for the Gentiles" (Isaiah 49:6b). Whereas this commission had once been given to the nation of Israel, it is now passed on to the people of the Messiah, the citizens of the Kingdom of God. It is our commission!

> "**Arise, shine**, for your light has come,
> and the glory of the Lord rises upon you." (Isaiah 60:1)

We are to be salt for the world and light for the world – to the glory of God!

Placement of a Lamp

Now that Jesus has established the disciples' importance as witnesses of Jesus' Kingdom, he carries the image further to the placement of a lamp.

> "You are the light of the world. A city on a hill cannot be hidden. Neither do people light a lamp and put it under a bowl. Instead they put it on its stand, and it gives light to everyone in the house." (Matthew 5:14-15)

Byzantine period oil lamp, found in tomb in Samaria, village of Fandaqomiya (Pentacomia). Photo: Thameen Darby.

In Jesus' day, homes were commonly lit by small clay lamps that could be held in the palm of the hand. The most primitive consisted of a saucer to hold the olive oil, in which was immersed one end of a wick that lay in an indentation or spout in the rim. Later, clay lamps were sometimes covered, with a hole in the top in which to pour the oil, and a hole at one side for the wick. (Incidentally, don't be confused by the KJV translation of Greek *lychnos*, "lamp," as "candle." The word is best translated "lamp.")

Now Jesus contrasts the way that the lamp might be displayed once you've lighted it.

---

[38] "Light" is *phōs*, from which we get word "phosphorescent." *Phōs* is the generic word for "light" in contrast to darkness.

[39] God lives in "unapproachable light" and glory (1 Timothy 6:16). In John's Gospel, Jesus proclaims himself as "the Light of the world" (John 8:12).

Do not put a lamp	Do put a lamp ...
Under a bushel basket[40] (Matthew 5:14-15; Mark 4:21; Luke 11:33)	On a stand[41] (Matthew 5:14-15; Mark 4:21; Luke 8:16; 11:33)
Under a vessel[42] (Luke 8:16)	
Under a bed[43] (Mark 4:21; Luke 8:16)	
In a cellar[44] (Luke 11:33)	

You don't put a lamp under something to hide its light. That is silly! Rather you elevate it on a lamp stand or perhaps hang it from the ceiling rafters so that it provides the greatest possible illumination within a room.

1. Live Open, Righteous Lives that Give Glory to God (Matthew 5:16)

"In the same way, let your light shine before men, that they may see your good deeds and praise your Father in heaven." (Matthew 5:16)

Sometimes people place a false dichotomy between words and deeds. "I testify to my faith in God by the way I live," some say defiantly. "I don't have to say anything."

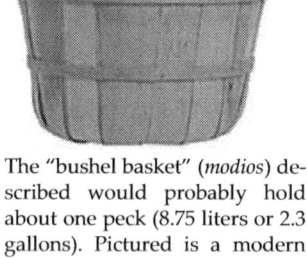

The "bushel basket" (*modios*) described would probably hold about one peck (8.75 liters or 2.3 gallons). Pictured is a modern peck basket, about 11 inches (28 cm.) in diameter and about 12 inches (30 cm.) height.

I agree that we *must* live lives that bring credit upon Jesus or our words won't be taken seriously. They will be laughed at as hypocrisy, thrown back in our face, and become a cause of greater unbelief on the part of those who watch us.

---

[40] "Basket" (ESV), "bowl" (NIV), "bushel basket" (NRSV), "bushel" (KJV) is *modios*, a grain measure containing 16 *sextarii* = about 8.75 liters about 2.3 gallons, almost one peck, 'a peck measure' (Matthew 5:15; Mark 4:21; Luke 11:33) (BDAG 656). Also "a vessel of this capacity" (Liddell-Scott 1140, 2). ISBE (1:562) sees this as "perhaps a tub or bowl such as are used to measure grain," but if it were pottery, it would be quite heavy and bulky. I think this must be a basket. A modern peck basket is about 11 inches (28 cm.) in diameter and about 12 inches (30 cm.) high.

[41] "Stand" (NIV, ESV), "lampstand" (NRSV), "candlestick" (KJV) is *luxnia*, "lampstand" upon which lamps were placed or hung (BDAG 606).

[42] "Jar" (NIV, ESV, NRSV), "vessel" (KJV) is *skeuos*, "A container of any kind, "vessel, jar, dish" (BDAG 927, 2).

[43] "Bed" is *klinē*, "bed, couch" (BDAG 549, 1).

[44] "Cellar" (ESV, NRSV), "a place where it will be hidden" (NIV), "in a secret place" (KJV) is *kruptē*, "a place for hiding or storing something, a dark and hidden place, a cellar" (BDAG 570).

12. Parables about Caring for the Lost

But deeds without words tell only half the story. Our witness must consist of both deeds *and* words that point to God the Father and bring glory to him. What a privilege we have to be the agents of evoking praise to our Father in heaven!

2. Truth Cannot Ultimately Be Hidden (Mark 4:22-25; Luke 8:16-18)

Jesus teaches a second truth from the image of the lamp out in the open rather than being hidden.

> "¹⁶ No one lights a lamp and hides it in a jar or puts it under a bed. Instead, he puts it on a stand, so that those who come in can see the light. ¹⁷ For there is nothing hidden that will not be disclosed, and nothing concealed that will not be known or brought out into the open. ¹⁸ Therefore consider carefully how you listen. Whoever has will be given more; whoever does not have, even what he thinks he has will be taken from him." (Luke 8:16-18)

This is a simple comparison. Just as you put a lamp in the open to shed its light to all, so nothing will be hidden on Judgment Day. As a result, listen carefully and put what you know into practice. Those who do, will understand more; those who don't, will lose what they think they have. We cannot live double lives; we must live the truths we know!

> **Q59. (Matthew 5:13-14) Why is a sharp and tasty witness so important? What is a bland witness to Jesus? How do we stay "salty"? Why are people tempted to hide their "light" or witness? What does Jesus say about that?**
> **https://www.joyfulheart.com/forums/topic/2233-q59-witness/**

12.4 Teaching the Kingdom

Parable of the Scribes of the Kingdom (Matthew 13:51-52, §103)
(Also known as the Parable of the Householder)

We conclude our study of Jesus' parables with a parable placed by Matthew at the end his "parables chapter." Jesus has just explained to his disciples the meaning of the Parable of the Net (Matthew 13:47-50).

> "⁵¹ 'Have you understood all these things?' Jesus asked.
>
> 'Yes,' they replied.
>
> ⁵² He said to them, 'Therefore every teacher of the law who has been instructed about the kingdom of heaven is like the owner of a house who brings out of his storeroom new treasures as well as old.'" (Matthew 13:51-52)

The term "teacher of the law" (NIV), "scribe" (ESV, NRSV, KJV) is unexpected, since in Jesus' day, the scribes were Jesus' enemies, though the word "scribe" itself didn't have negative connotations. In secular Greek *grammateus* is the title of a high official. In Judaism it usually refers to "specialists in the law of Moses: experts in the law, scholars versed in the law, scribes," here by extension, "an interpreter of teaching, scribe, instructor."[45] Scribes in Judaism were "responsible for making decisions in courts of law; they taught the Torah to their students; and they expounded the meaning and application of the Torah."[46]

The great post-exilic reformer Ezra is described as "the priest, the scribe, a man learned in matters of the commandments of the Lord and his statutes for Israel" (Ezra 7:11). Like Nicodemus and the Apostle Paul, scribes were trained by being disciples of leading rabbis for several years. Then they were qualified as Torah scholars, trained in the application of the Torah (the first five books of the Bible) to everyday life.

Later in Matthew's Gospel, the word "scribe" is applied to Jesus' disciples themselves. To the leaders of the Jews, who have made themselves enemies of the Messiah, Jesus says:

> "I send you prophets and wise men and **scribes**, some of whom you will kill and crucify, and some you will flog in your synagogues and persecute from town to town." (Matthew 23:34, ESV)

Cross-Trained Disciples

Jesus uses a curious phrase that could be translated, "a scribe **discipled** for the kingdom of heaven." The word translated "instructed" or "trained" is the verb form of the common noun translated "disciples."[47] In Matthew 13, Jesus has been training or discipling his disciples by telling parables and then explaining parables to his disciples. He asks them, "Do you understand what I've been teaching you?" and they respond positively.

Only then he says to them,

> "Therefore every **scribe** who has been **trained** for the kingdom of heaven is like a master of a house, who brings out of his treasure what is new and what is old." (Matthew 13:42, ESV)

A regular scribe in Jesus' day was trained to interpret the Torah. But the disciples are "scribes trained for the Kingdom," equipped to interpret the Torah *correctly*, as tutored by the Messiah himself.

---

[45] *Grammateus*, BDAG 206, 2b.
[46] D. A. Hagner, "Scribes," ISBE 4:360.
[47] "Instructed" (NIV, KJV), "trained" (ESV, NRSV) is *mathēteuō*, "to be a pupil," with implication of being an adherent of the teacher, here, "become a disciple" (BDAG 609, 1b). The verb is used three times in the New Testament. Much more common is the noun form, *mathētēs*, "disciple," used 260 times.

12. Parables about Caring for the Lost

"Cross-training" began as a term used of military special forces members who might be trained in several different disciplines so they become proficient in each – weapons, medic, and explosives, or weapons, sniper, communications. In sports, cross-training is athletic training in sports other than one's usual sport. In fitness, cross training is employing fitness practices from several disciplines. CrossFit gyms, for example, train members in Olympic weight training, rope climbing, running, rowing, as well as normal push-ups, pull-ups, jumping jacks, and burpees.

Both Old and New

Jesus cross-trains his disciples with a knowledge of both the Old Testament Scriptures *and* how to walk in the Spirit, preach, heal, witness, and teach the "new wine" of the gospel. A kingdom-trained scribe is:

> "... Like the owner of a house who brings out of his storeroom new treasures as well as old." (verse 52)

Imagine a wealthy farmer whose household consists of his immediate family as well as several servants.[48] Every wealthy man would have a secure storeroom kept locked at all times. Or a chest-type lock box where valuables could be secured.[49] (Today, we would call it a "safe.") To show off to his guest, he brings out of his storeroom some old family heirlooms handed down from his grandfather's time, as well as a few of his new acquisitions, such as a beautiful gold broach studded with emeralds imported from Corinth for his wife to wear on special occasions. Some old treasures, and some new ones also.

The Kingdom-trained scribe isn't just able to expound on and apply the Torah. He or she also is able to listen for God's voice, heal the sick, explain the gospel of salvation in simple terms, and comfort the hurting.

My friend, Jesus has you in training to be a scribe of the Kingdom, competent in the Scriptures as well as in sharing the Good News and ministering to the needy. Don't skip his training, or just rush through it. He wants you to be well-equipped to represent his Kingdom.

---

[48] "Owner of a house" (NIV), "master of a house/household" (ESV, NRSV), "householder" (KJV) is *oikodespotēs*, "master of the house, householder" (BDAG 695). *Despotēs* means "owner, master." We usually use the derived word "despot" in a negative sense, but the Greek didn't carry a negative implication.

[49] "Storeroom" (NIV), "treasure" (ESV, NRSV, KJV) is *thēsauros* (from which we get our word "thesaurus"), "a place where something is kept for safekeeping, repository," here, "storehouse, storeroom" (BDAG 456, 1aβ), from *thēsaurizō*, "lay up, store up, gather, save." We also see this word in the Analogy of the Treasure Chest of the Heart, Lesson 10.1.

"Do your best to present yourself to God as one approved, a workman who does not need to be ashamed and who correctly handles[50] the word of truth." (2 Timothy 2:15)

Aspire to teach the Scriptures carefully and accurately.

Q60. (Matthew 13:51-52) What is the "old" that the householder brings out of his treasure box? What is the "new." In what way must we disciples be "cross-trained" as scribes of the Kingdom?
https://www.joyfulheart.com/forums/topic/2234-q60-scribes-of-the-kingdom/

This concludes our study of Jesus' parables. There are a few more in Appendix 4 that you might consider as well. I encourage you – don't leave these parables behind, but ponder them, talk about them with your Christian friends, extract from them all the juice of Jesus' disciple-forming teaching. Turn them over in your mind, seek not only to understand them, but to walk in their truths, that you might be a well-equipped disciple, a "scribe trained for the Kingdom."

Prayer

Father, we know that Jesus has a passionate heart for the harvest. Too often we are complacent about reaching others for Christ. Rather than being disciples who follow Jesus in this, we ignore his teaching and leading. Renew in us a zeal for you and your work, for the lost and for the harvest for which Jesus died. In His holy name, we pray. Amen.

---

[50] "Handles/handling" (ESV, NIV), "explaining" (NRSV), "dividing" (KJV) is *orthotomeō*, "to cut straight," from *ortho-*, "straight" + *temnō*, "to cut." Here it would probably mean "to guide the word of truth along a straight path (like a road that goes straight to its goal)," without being turned aside by wordy debates or impious talk (BDAG 722). Moulton and Milligan discuss other meanings such as, "teach the word aright, expound (it) soundly, shape rightly, and preach fearlessly" (cited in BDAG 722).

Appendix 1. Participant Handouts

If you are working with a class or small group, feel free to duplicate the handouts at no additional charge. If you'd like to print 8-1/2" x 11" or A4 size pages, you can download the free Participant Guide handout sheets at:

www.jesuswalk.com/parables/parables-lesson-handouts.pdf

Discussion Questions

You'll typically find 3 to 7 questions for each lesson. Each question may include several sub-questions. These are designed to get group members engaged in discussion of the key points of the passage. If you are running short of time, feel free to skip questions or portions of questions.

Suggestions for Classes and Groups

Individuals who are studying online can probably complete one full lesson per week, though they'll need to be diligent to do so. But some of the chapters just have too much material for a one-hour class discussion. You may want to be selective, or to extend your class session beyond twelve weeks.

Feel free to arrange the lessons any way that works best for your group. Because of the length of these handouts – and to keep down the page count so we can keep the book price lower – they are being made available at no cost online.

www.jesuswalk.com/parables/parables-lesson-handouts.pdf

Appendix 2. List of Jesus' Parables and Analogies

In this list you'll find Jesus' teaching parables, some allegories, some analogies Jesus used as brief illustrations, and a few sayings. Parables in John's Gospel take a somewhat different form than most of the parables in the Synoptic Gospels, but I have included them in this study. I've tried to be inclusive, if not exhaustive. Some will disagree whether something is a parable or an analogy or a saying. That's okay. On a few occasions I have lumped several mini-parables into one.

1. Asking a Father for Bread (Matthew 7:9-11; Luke 11:11-13; Lesson 10.3)
2. Baptism (Mark 1:4-8; Matthew 28:19-20; Mark 16:15-16; Lesson 6.2)
3. Barren Fig Tree (Luke 13:6-9; Lesson 2.1)
4. Becoming Like Little Children (Matthew 18:3-4; Lesson 9.1)
5. Birds and the Lilies (Matthew 6:25-34, Lesson 10.2)
6. Binding the Strong Man (Matthew 12:29; Mark 3:27; Luke 11:21-22; Lesson 6.3)
7. Blind Leading the Blind (Matthew 15:14; Luke 6:39; Appendix 4.3)
8. Bread and the Wine (Matthew 26:26-29; Mark 14:22-25; Luke 22:15-20; Lesson 6.2)
9. Bread of Life (John 6:35, Lesson 6.1)
10. Bridegroom's Guests (Matthew 9:14-15; Mark 2:18-20; Luke 5:33-35; Lesson 7.2)
11. Bridegroom's Friend (John the Baptist, John 3:29-30; Appendix 4.2)
12. Brood of Vipers (Matthew 12:34; 23:33; Appendix 4.3)
13. Budding Fig Tree (Matthew 24:32-33; Mark 13:28-29; Luke 21:29-31; Lesson 5.1)
14. Burglar (Luke 12:39-40; Matthew 24:43-44; Lesson 5.2)
15. Camel and the Needle (Matthew 19:23-24; Mark 10:24-25; Luke 18:24-25; Lesson 6.1)
16. Children in the Marketplace (Matthew 11:16-19; Luke 7:31-32; Appendix 4.3)
17. City on a Hill (Matthew 5:14; Lesson 12.3)
18. Cleansing the Cup (Matthew 23:25-26; Luke 11:39-41; Lesson 3.1)
19. Dead Burying the Dead (Matthew 18:21-22; Luke 9:59-60; Lesson 8.3)
20. Den of Robbers (Matthew 21:13; Luke 19:46; John 2:16; Appendix 4.3)
21. Defiling Heart of Man (Mark 7:14-23; Matthew 15:10-11, 15-20; Lesson 3.1)
22. Doctor and Sick People (Matthew 9:12; Mark 2:17; Luke 5:31; Lesson 12.1)
23. Dutiful Servant (Luke 17:7-10; Lesson 11.1)
24. Eating Jesus' Flesh (John 6:53-58, Lesson 9.3)
25. Empty House (Matthew 12:43-45; Luke 11:23-26; Lesson 6.3)
26. Faith of a Mustard Seed (Matthew 17:19; Luke 17:6; Lesson 10.4)
27. Fields White for Harvest (John 4:35)

Appendix 3. A Vocabulary for Parables and Analogies 299

28. Fishers of Men (Matthew 4:18-20; Mark 1:16-18; Luke 5:10-11; Lesson 12:3)
29. Foxholes and Nests (Matthew 18:19-20; Luke 5:57-58; Lesson 8.3)
30. Friend at Midnight (Luke 11:5-10; Lesson 10.3)
31. Good Eye (Matthew 6:22-23; Luke 11:34-36; Lesson 3.4)
32. Good Samaritan (Luke 10:30-37; Lesson 11.3)
33. Good Shepherd and the Sheep Gate (John 10:1-18; Lesson 7.4)
34. Great Banquet (Luke 14:15-24; Matthew 22:2-10; Lesson 2.2)
35. Guilty Defendant (Matthew 5:25-26; Luke 12:57-59; Lesson 3.2)
36. Harvest and the Laborers (Matthew 9:37-38; Luke 10:2; Lesson 12.2)
37. Hen and Chickens (Matthew 23:37; Luke 13:34; Lesson 2.2)
38. Hidden Treasure (Matthew 13:44; Lesson 8.5)
39. House Divided (Matthew 12:25-26; Mark 3:24-26; Luke 11:17-18; Lesson 6.3)
40. Kernel of Wheat (John 12:24; Lesson 6.2)
41. Keys of the Kingdom (Matthew 16:19; Appendix 4.4)
42. Laborers in Vineyard (Matthew 20:1-16; Lesson 4.3)
43. Lamp under a Bushel (Matthew 5:15; Mark 4:21; Luke 8:16-17; 11:33; Lesson 12.3)
44. Lifting the Bronze Serpent (John 3:14, Lesson 6.1)
45. Light of the World (John 8:12; 9:5; 1:4-9, Appendix 4.1)
46. Lightning (Luke 17:24; Matthew 24:27; Lesson 5.1)
47. Looking Back from the Plow (Luke 9:61-62; Lesson 8.3)
48. Lost Coin (Luke 15:8-10; Lesson 1.1)
49. Lost Sheep, Parable of (Luke 15:3-6a; Matthew 18:12-14; Lesson 1.1)
50. Lost Sheep, Analogies of (Matthew 9:36; 10:5-6; 15:24; John 10:16; Lesson 12.1)
51. Lost Son or the Prodigal Son (Luke 15:11-32; Lesson 1.1)
52. Minas or Pounds (Luke 19:12-27: Lesson 11.2)
53. Mustard Seed (Matthew 13:31-32; Mark 4:30-32; Luke 13:18-19; Lesson 7.1)
54. Narrow Door (Luke 13:23-27; Lesson 8.2)
55. Narrow and Wide Gates (Matthew 7:13-14; Lesson 3.2)
56. Net (Matthew 13:47-50; Lesson 4.2)
57. Ox and the Son (Luke 14:2-5, Appendix 4.2)
58. Pearl of Great Price (Matthew 13:45-46; Lesson 8.5)
59. Pearls before Swine (Matthew 7:6; Lesson 8.1)
60. Peter the Rock (Matthew 16:18; John 1:42, Appendix 4.4)
61. Pharisee and Tax Collector (Luke 18:9-14; Lesson 9.1)
62. Physician, Heal Yourself (Luke 4:23-24; Appendix 4.2)
63. Places at the Table (Luke 14:7-11; Lesson 9.1)
64. Rich Fool (Luke 12:16-21; Lesson 10.2)

65. Rich Man and Lazarus (Luke 16:19-31; Lesson 4.1)
66. Rooms in the Father's House (John 14:2-4; Lesson 6.2)
67. Savorless Salt (Matthew 5:13; Mark 9:50; Luke 14:34-35; Lesson 12.3)
68. Scribes of the Kingdom (Matthew 13:51-52; Lesson 12.4)
69. Seed Growing by Itself (Mark 4:26-29; Lesson 7.1)
70. Sheep and the Goats (Matthew 25:31-46; Lesson 4.2)
71. Sheep and Wolves, Serpents and Doves (Matthew 10:16; Luke 10:3; Lesson 12.2)
72. Sign of Jonah (Matthew 12:38-42; Luke 11:29-32; Appendix 4.2)
73. Slave and the Son (John 8:34-36; Appendix 4.2)
74. Sower (Matthew 13:1-9, 18-23; Mark 4:3-9, 13-20; Luke 8:4-8, 11-15; Lesson 8.1)
75. Sowers and Reapers (John 4:35-38; Lesson 12.2)
76. Sparrows (Matthew 10:29-30; Luke 12:6-7; Lesson 12.3)
77. Speck and the Beam (Matthew 7:3-5; Luke 6:41-42; Lesson 3.4)
78. Spiritual Birth (John 3:3-7; Lesson 6.1)
79. Streams of Living Water (John 7:37-39, Lesson 6.1)
80. Taking Up One's Cross (Matthew 16:24-25; Mark 8:34-35; Luke 9:23-24; Matthew 10:37-39; Luke 14:25-27; Lesson 8.4)
81. Talents (Matthew 25:14-30; Lesson 11.2)
82. Temple of Jesus' Body (John 2:18-22, Appendix 4.2)
83. Tower-Builder (Luke 14:28-30; Lesson 8.4)
84. Treasure Chest of the Heart (Luke 6:45, Lesson 10.1)
85. Tree and Fruit (Matthew 7:16-20; Luke 6:43-45; Lesson 10.1)
86. Two Cancelled Debts (Luke 7:41-43, 47; Lesson 1.2)
87. Two Masters (Luke 16:13; Matthew 6:24; Lesson 10.2)
88. Two Sons (Matthew 21:28-31; Lesson 3.3)
89. Unjust Judge (Luke 18:1-8; Lesson 10.3)
90. Unjust Steward (Luke 16:1-13; Lesson 10.1)
91. Unmerciful Servant (Matthew 18:23-35; Lesson 1.2)
92. Unshrunk Cloth (Matthew 9:16; Mark 2:21; Luke 5:36; Lesson 7.3)
93. Vine and the Branches (John 15:1-8; Lesson 9.3)
94. Vultures Gathering (Luke 17:37; Matthew 24:38; Lesson 5.1)
95. Walking in Light and Darkness (John 9:4; 11:9-10; 12:35-36a; Appendix 4.1)
96. Warring King (Luke 14:31-32; Lesson 8.4)
97. Washing the Disciples' Feet (John 13:4-17; Lesson 11.1)
98. Watching Servants (Mark 13:34-37; Luke 12:35-38; Lesson 5.2)
99. Water for Eternal Life (John 4:13-14; Lesson 6.1)
100. Weather Signs (Luke 12:54-56; Lesson 5.1)

Appendix 3. A Vocabulary for Parables and Analogies

101. Wedding Banquet (Matthew 22:1-10; Lesson 2.2)
102. Weeds or Tares (Matthew 13:24-30; 36-43; Lesson 4.2)
103. Welcoming Little Children (Matthew 19:13-15; Mark 10:13-14; Luke 18:16-17; Lesson 9.1)
104. Whitewashed Tombs (Matthew 23:27-28; Lesson 3.1)
105. Wicked Tenants (Matthew 21:33-46; Mark 12:1-12; Luke 20:9-19; Lesson 2.3)
106. Wind of the Spirit (John 3:8; Lesson 6.1)
107. Wineskins (Matthew 9:17; Mark 2:22; Luke 5:37-39; Lesson 7.3)
108. Wise and Faithful Steward (Matthew 24:45-51; Luke 12:42-46; Lesson 5.3)
109. Wise and Foolish Builders (Matthew 7:24-27; Luke 6:47-49; Lesson 3.2)
110. Wise and Foolish Virgins (Matthew 25:1-13; Lesson 5.2)
111. Wolf in Sheep's Clothing (Matthew 7:15-16a; Lesson 10.1)
112. Woman in Childbirth (John 16:21; Lesson 6.2)
113. Yeast of the Pharisees (Matthew 16:5-12; Mark 8:15; Luke 12:1; Lesson 9.2)
114. Yeast or Leaven (Matthew 13:33; Luke 13:20-21; Lesson 7.1)
115. Yoke (Matthew 11:28-30, Lesson 9.3)

Appendix 3. A Vocabulary for Parables and Analogies

Hebrew and Greek Words for Parable

The word that underlies the Hebrew understanding of parables is the Hebrew noun *mashal* (*māšāl*). It covers a wide territory, from pithy proverbs and parables, allegories, sayings and riddles, to bywords, taunts, and discourses, even a developed comparison or similitude.[1] When *māšāl* was translated into the Greek Septuagint in the second century BC, it was translated by *parabolē*, "parable," and, in a very few instances, as *paroimia*.

The Greek word *parabolē* is compounded from two words, the preposition *para* ("beside") + the noun *bolē* (from the verb *ballō*, "to cast"). The image is of something cast beside something else, a comparison. In John's Gospel we don't see the word *parabolē*, but rather *paroimia*, "veiled saying, figure" of speech.[2] In the Synoptic Gospels, *parabolē* is defined as:

> "A narrative or saying of varying length, designed to illustrate a truth especially through comparison or simile, comparison, illustration, parable, proverb, maxim."

In the Synoptics Gospels, the word refers to a wide variety of illustrative formulations in the teaching of Jesus.[3]

An English Vocabulary for Parables

A.M. Hunter writes helpfully,

> "In germ, a parable is a figurative saying: sometimes a simile ('Be wise as serpents'), sometimes a metaphor ('Beware of the leaven of the Pharisees'). What we call parables are simply expansions of these. 'All we like sheep have gone astray' is a simile. Expand it into a picture and you get a similitude like the Lost Sheep. Expand it into a story by using past tenses and circumstantial details, and you get a story-parable like The Prodigal Son. The difference between a similitude and a story-parable is this: whereas the similitude bases itself on some familiar truth or process (like putting a patch on a garment or leaven into meal), the story parable describes not what men

---

[1] Victor P. Hamilton, *māšāl*, TWOT #1258a; Holladay 219. Friedrich Hauck, *parabolē*, TDNT 5:741-761, especially pp. 747-749.

[2] *Paroimia*, BDAG 779, 2. It seems to be compounded from two words, the preposition *para* ("beside, aside") + *oumos*, "way," which may amount to "a saying out of the usual course or deviating from the usual manner of speaking, here, "a symbolic or figurative saying" (Thayer 490, 2), "figure, comparison" (Liddell-Scott 1342, 2). Hauck sees John's use "in the sense of "obscure speech" that needs interpretation (Friedrich Hauck, TDNT 6:854-856). Used of a proverb in 2 Peter 2:22 and of figurative speech in John 10:6; 16:25, 29.

[3] *Parabolē*, BDAG 759, 2a.

Appendix 3. A Vocabulary for Parables and Analogies

commonly do but what one man did. 'A sower went out to sow.' 'A certain man made a Great Banquet.'"[4]

We have a rich English vocabulary to describe all kinds of sayings, comparisons, and stories. In the text of the study, I'll mainly use "parable," "analogy," and "saying" to differentiate different parables. I've grouped some of the English words below with their dictionary definitions to help you understand the precise meaning of each.[5]

Sayings

Adage, "a saying often in metaphorical form that embodies a common observation."

Aphorism, "a concise statement of a principle," "a terse formulation of a truth or sentiment, adage."

Epigram, "a terse, sage, or witty and often paradoxical saying."

Maxim, "a general truth, fundamental principle, or rule of conduct;" "a proverbial saying."

Proverb, "a brief popular epigram or maxim, adage.

Saying, "something said, especially adage."

Comparisons

Analogy, "resemblance in some particulars between things otherwise unlike, similarity, then comparison based on such resemblance." This is an umbrella term that would include both metaphor and simile.

Figure of speech, "a form of expression (such as a simile or metaphor) used to convey meaning or heighten effect often by comparing or identifying one thing with another that has a meaning or connotation familiar to the reader or listener."

Metaphor, "a figure of speech in which a word or phrase literally denoting one kind of object or idea is used in place of another to suggest a likeness or analogy between them" (as in "drowning in money").

Simile, "a figure of speech comparing two unlike things that is often introduced by 'like' or 'as'" (as in "cheeks like roses"). In Matthew 13 we often see the phrase, "The kingdom of heaven is like...."

Similitude, "an imaginative comparison."

Word picture, "a graphic or vivid description in words."

---

[4] Hunter, *Parables*, p. 9.
[5] English definitions from *Merriam-Webster 11th Collegiate Dictionary*.

Stories

Story, "an account of incidents or events ... anecdote."

Narrative, "something that is narrated, story, account."

Parable, "a usually short fictitious story that illustrates a moral attitude or a religious principle." [Note: this is the *English* definition of "parable," but doesn't include the wide range denoted by Hebrew *mashal* and Greek *parabolē*.]

Allegory, "the expression by means of symbolic fictional figures and actions of truths or generalizations about human existence." Especially parables in which characters in the story are meant to be seen as real figures.

Appendix 4. Miscellaneous Parables, Analogies, and Sayings

In an attempt to be fairly comprehensive, I have placed 14 parables and analogies in this appendix, rather than include them in the twelve lessons of the study. Trying to keep the word count of each of the lessons under control and maintaining unity of lessons requires a bit of picking and choosing. In general, I have judged these are less important in training disciples for the Kingdom.

Some of these are brief sayings and simple analogies. Others are more obscure analogies that don't have as much relevance today as they might have had in the first century. Others are figures of speech included for the vivid word pictures they create.

1. Light and Darkness
- Analogies of Walking in Light and Darkness (John 9:4; 11:9-10; 12:35-36a)
- Analogy of the Light of the World (John 8:12; 9:5; 1:4-9)

2. Jesus
- Saying: Physician, Heal Yourself (Luke 4:23-24)
- Analogy of the Temple of Jesus' Body (John 2:18-22)
- The Parable of the Sign of Jonah (Matthew 12:38-42; Luke 11:29-32)
- Analogy of the Slave and the Son (John 8:34-36)
- Analogy of the Bridegroom's Friend (John the Baptist, John 3:29-30)

3. Jesus' Enemies
- Analogy of the Children in the Marketplace (Matthew 11:16-19, Luke 7:31-32)
- Analogy of Rescuing from a Well (Matthew 12:9-14; Luke 14:2-5)
- Saying of the Blind Leading the Blind (Matthew 15:14; Luke 6:39)
- Analogy of the Brood of Vipers (Matthew 12:34; 23:33)
- Analogy of the Den of Robbers (Matthew 21:13; Luke 19:46; John 2:16)

4. The Kingdom
- Analogy of Peter the Rock (Matthew 16:18; John 1:42)
- Analogy of the Keys of the Kingdom (Matthew 16:19)

1. Light and Darkness

Analogies of Walking in Light and Darkness (John 9:4; 11:9-10; 12:35-36a)

Based on himself as the Light of the World, Jesus discusses how disciples must learn to walk in the light rather than to walk in the darkness, particularly to take advantage of Jesus' presence with them while he is still present in the flesh. John's Gospel records several instances where Jesus speaks about walking by daylight vs. walking in darkness.

1. Context: the man born blind

"⁴ As long as it is day, we must do the work of him who sent me. Night is coming, when no one can work. ⁵ While I am in the world, I am the light of the world." (John 9:4-5)

We see the theme of working while you have daylight, as well as the metaphors of light vs. darkness, evil, death.

2. Context: Going to Visit Lazarus

"⁹ Are there not twelve hours of daylight? A man who walks by day will not stumble, for he sees by this world's light.[1] ¹⁰ It is when he walks by night that he stumbles, for he has no light."[2] (John 11:9-10)

Twelve hours were thought of as the length of a day. In other words, Jesus is saying: So long as I am still alive and it is "day," we must do what we are called to do while we are still able (cf. Jeremiah 13:15b-16a).

3. Context: Will the Christ Remain Forever?[3]

"³⁵ You are going to have the light just a little while longer. Walk while you have the light, before darkness overtakes you. The man who walks in the dark does not know where he is going. ³⁶ Put your trust in the light while you have it, so that you may become sons of light."[4] (John 12:35-36a)

In other words, you will have the light of my presence only a bit longer, before I am killed. Take advantage of that. Jesus' disciples who trust in the light and follow Jesus will take on the characteristic of light in themselves as "children of light" (Luke 16:8). In Lesson 12.3 we see

---

[1] "This world's light" (NIV) doesn't refer here to Jesus' title as "the Light of the World" (John 8:12), but to the sun's light during the day.

[2] Verse 10, "for he has not light" (NIV), is literally, "the light is not in him" (ESV, NRSV).

[3] They are using "law" in a general sense as the Scripture as a whole. While the Christ remaining forever isn't in the Pentateuch, it was widely held in Judaism in Jesus' day (Morris, *John*, p. 599, fn. 88).

[4] "Sons of light" carries the idea of sharing in light. *Huios*, "son," with the genitive of thing denotes "one who shares in it or who is worthy of it, or who stands in some other close relation to it," often made clear by the context (BDAG 1025, 2cb).

Appendix 4. Miscellaneous Analogies and Sayings

the Analogies of the City on a Hill and of the Lamp and the Bushel, where light becomes a metaphor of witness and visibility.

Analogy of the Light of the World (John 8:12; 9:5; 1:4-9)

Light and darkness are themes throughout the Bible, beginning at creation (Genesis 1:2-4). Light is often used as a symbol of goodness, uprightness, or blessing, while darkness is linked with disaster and wickedness.

Light is a metaphor of both righteousness and enlightenment found in Christ (Proverbs 13:9; 1 John 1:5). The opposites of light are darkness and blindness. John begins his Gospel with the idea that Jesus is the Light.

> "⁴ In him was life, and that life was **the light of men**. ⁵ The light shines in the darkness, but the darkness has not understood it. ... ⁹ **The true light** that gives light to every man was coming into the world." (John 1:4-5, 9)

> "I have come into the world as a **light**, so that no one who believes in me should stay in darkness." (John 12:46)

It is not surprising that Jesus uses light and darkness in his teachings. The Parables of the Wise and Foolish Virgins (Lesson 5.2), the Lamp under a Bushel (Lesson 12.3), the City on a Hill (Lesson 12.3), the Good Eye (Lesson 3.4), and the Lost Coin (Lesson 1.1) all employ light.

One of the seven "I AM" statements of Jesus in John's Gospel is: "I am the Light of the World," found twice in John (John 8:12; 9:5). Light is an ongoing theme in John's Gospel (e.g., John 3:19). Indeed, several Messianic prophecies contain the promise of light (Isaiah 9:2, 6; Malachi 4:2a; Luke 2:30-32).

2. Jesus

Several parables tell us something about Jesus and his understanding of his ministry. We see him as the Great Physician, the Son, and the Bridegroom. And we observe cryptic references to his death and resurrection on the third day.

Saying: Physician, Heal Yourself (Luke 4:23-24, §10)

Jesus is in his hometown of Nazareth, asked to read the Scriptures in the synagogue on the Sabbath. He opens the scroll to Isaiah 61 ("the Spirit of the Lord is upon me, because he has anointed me ...."). He finishes, then says, "Today this scripture has been fulfilled in your hearing." The people say nice things about their native son, but Jesus knows that in their hearts there is unbelief. They know him as Joseph's son, not as a prophet of God.

> "²³ Jesus said to them, 'Surely you will quote this proverb to me: "Physician, heal yourself! Do here in your hometown what we have heard that you did in

Capernaum." I tell you the truth,' he continued, 'no prophet is accepted in his hometown.'" (Luke 4:23-24)

"Physician, heal yourself," seems to be a popular saying, what we might call an aphorism or maxim.[5] It is short, only three words, found only in Luke.

In English, we have an old proverb that dates back at least to the sixteenth century: "The cobbler's children go barefoot."[6] The cobbler makes shoes for everyone except his own family. Here, Jesus sees in their hearts the thought: You have been performing miracles everywhere else. Do some miracles here in your hometown also.[7]

Jesus' short saying, "Physician, heal yourself," reminds us that we can't expect all to accept us, even if they think they know us. Elsewhere, Jesus refers to himself as a physician in the saying, 'It is not the healthy who need a doctor, but the sick" (Matthew 9:12). See the Analogy of the Doctor and the Sick (Lesson 12.1).

Analogy of the Temple of Jesus' Body (John 2:18-22)

On at least one occasion, Jesus gives a kind of cryptic statement that alludes to his resurrection. The audience isn't solely his disciples, but includes Jewish leaders who are his opponents.

"[18] Then the Jews demanded of him, 'What miraculous sign can you show us to prove your authority to do all this?'

[19] Jesus answered them, 'Destroy this temple, and I will raise it again in three days.'

[20] The Jews replied, 'It has taken forty-six years to build this temple, and you are going to raise it in three days?' [21] But the temple he had spoken of was his body. [22] After he was raised from the dead, his disciples recalled what he had said. Then they believed the Scripture and the words that Jesus had spoken." (John 2:18-22)

The essence of a temple is that inside lives the deity. In Jesus' body is God himself. Thus, Jesus is the true temple in their midst, not the temple in Jerusalem made by hands. His body that they will kill will be raised from the dead on the third day. As we note in the Parable of the Sign of Jonah below, the Hebrews counted parts of days as full days, so for them, three days and the third day meant essentially the same thing.

---

[5] The Greek word is *parabolē*, "a narrative saying of varying length, designed to illustrate a truth especially through comparison or simile, comparison, illustration, parable, proverb, maxim."[5]

[6] John Haywood, *Proverbes* (1538), Part I, chapter XI, page 147.

[7] Marshall, *Luke*, p. 187 cites three similar references including "Physician, heal your own limp" (Gn. R 23 (15c), in Strack and Billerbeck II, 156); Euripides, *Frg.* 1071; and an Arabic proverb, "A doctor who cures other people and is himself ill" (Bultmann, *Die Geschichte der synoptischen Tradition* (Göttigen, 1958), p. 112n).

Appendix 4. Miscellaneous Analogies and Sayings

Later, at his trial before the Sanhedrin, the Jewish leaders use this cryptic analogy against him, and secure two people to testify that he said it (in Matthew's and Mark's accounts). Of course, they misunderstood the analogy of Jesus' body being the temple.

"⁶⁰ They did not find any [witnesses], though many false witnesses came forward.

Finally two came forward ⁶¹ and declared, 'This fellow said, "I am able to destroy the temple of God and rebuild it in three days."'

⁶² Then the high priest stood up and said to Jesus, 'Are you not going to answer? What is this testimony that these men are bringing against you?' ⁶³ But Jesus remained silent. (Matthew 26:60-63a; cf. Mark 14:57-59)

To Jesus' group of disciples, his saying was a confirmation to them after the resurrection on the third day. I don't think that disciples today have something in particular to learn here, except perhaps that our bodies are a temple (1 Corinthians 6:19-20), because of the Holy Spirit living within us (Romans 8:9-11).

The Parable of the Sign of Jonah (Matthew 12:38-42, §87; Luke 11:29-32, §152)

When the Pharisees and scribes demanded a sign to prove Jesus' authenticity, he responded with a reference to the story of Jonah.

"³⁹ A wicked and adulterous generation asks for a miraculous sign! But none will be given it except the sign of the prophet Jonah. ⁴⁰ For as Jonah was three days and three nights in the belly of a huge fish, so the Son of Man will be three days and three nights in the heart of the earth. ⁴¹ The men of Nineveh will stand up at the judgment with this generation and condemn it; for they repented at the preaching of Jonah, and now one greater than Jonah is here." (Matthew 12:38-41)

The comparison is: between Jonah and the Son of Man.

"**As** Jonah was three days and three nights in the belly of a huge fish,
so the Son of Man will be three days and three nights in the heart of the earth."
(Matthew 12:40)

The sign, of course, involves his resurrection from the tomb on the third day. As mentioned in the Analogy of the Temple of Jesus' Body above, Jews counted as a day any part of a day. To get picky that three days and three nights don't equal three 24-hour days introduces a problem that first century believers didn't see, because of how they counted time in their culture. The sign of Jonah is the sign of Jesus' death, burial, and resurrection.

Analogy of the Slave and the Son (John 8:34-36)

Jesus has just said to some Jewish leaders that his true disciples who hold to his word will be free.

> "Then you will know the truth, and the truth will set you free." (John 8:32)

Jesus' hearers took "set free" to mean emancipation from slavery, as the word is often used.[8] Some of them took offense. Though politically under Roman rule, Jews still maintained some freedom under their own kings (Herod's sons), the Sanhedrin, and the high priests (appointed by Herod's family). They insist that they are not *slaves*! (For more see, Appendix 6. Slavery in Jesus' Day.)

Jesus responds by explaining that he is not talking about political or social slavery, but spiritual slavery.

> "*34 I tell you the truth, everyone who sins[9] is a slave[10] to sin. 35 Now a slave has no permanent place in the family, but a son belongs to it forever. 36 So if the Son sets you free, you will be free indeed.*" (John 8:34-36)

Slavery to sin is a difficult concept for us – mainly because we usually don't understand how trapped we can become by our habits, core beliefs, thought patterns, desires, passions, and lifestyles (Ephesians 2:1-3). We imagine that we act of our own free will, but our will can easily become ensnared, trapped in our sin. The sin we may have once committed out of our own (relatively) free will, now enslaves us, making us unable to stop.[11]

The analogy of the slave and the son seems like an observation on the difference between a slave and a son.

> "Now a slave has no permanent place in the family, but a son belongs to it forever." (John 8:35)

Jesus' Jewish hearers imagine themselves "sons of Abraham" in a genealogical sense, but Jesus says they are not really spiritual sons of Abraham, but rather slaves to sin. Verse 35 simply states that the difference between a slave and a son is that a slave is temporary – he can be sold at any time. But a son is always a son by right, even if he is estranged or far away. The unbelieving Jews are not permanent members of the household; they need freedom.

> "So if the Son sets you free, you will be free indeed." (John 8:36)

---

[8] "Set free" is *eleutheroō*, "to cause someone to be freed from domination, free, set free" (BDAG 317).

[9] "Sins" (NIV), "commits sin" (NRSV, KJV), "practices sin" (ESV) is two words: *harmartia*, "sin"; and the present tense of *poieō*, "to do, make," here, "do, commit, be guilty of" sins and vices (BDAG 840, 3c). The present tense suggests continued activity, not just a past event.

[10] "Slave" is *doulos*, "slave" (BDAG 260, 2a).

[11] Paul speaks clearly of this slavery to sin (Romans 6:17-18, 22; 8:2).

Appendix 4. Miscellaneous Analogies and Sayings

Only the Son, the Heir, a true member of the family, can manumit a slave and set him free. And then adopt him, so that he becomes a permanent member of the family.

The simple analogy of the slave and the son reminds us that we aren't automatically saved or part of God's family, though we are his creation. We need to be freed from spiritually slavery – saved – by the Son of God himself!

Analogy of the Bridegroom's Friend (John the Baptist, John 3:29-30)

Now we examine a parable that John the Baptist used – even though it is strictly speaking beyond the scope of our study of Jesus' own parables.

In the Parable of the Bridegroom's Guests (Lesson 7.2), Jesus has identified himself using the figure of a bridegroom. John the Baptist comes at this from a whole different point of view, but still refers to Jesus as the bridegroom.

A report comes to John the Baptist about Jesus baptizing and attracting large crowds – even exceeding in size the crowds John used to attract. You can sense a bit of resentment in John's disciples who bring the report. John is the original baptizer, but this upstart is upstaging him and "everyone is going to him."[12] John's reply is remarkable in its humility.

> "27 A man can receive only what is given him from heaven. 28 You yourselves can testify that I said, 'I am not the Christ but am sent ahead of him.' 29 The bride belongs to the bridegroom. The friend who attends the bridegroom waits and listens for him, and is full of joy when he hears the bridegroom's voice. That joy is mine, and it is now complete. 30 He must become greater; I must become less." (John 3:27-30)

John makes four points:
1. God directs our lives, not ambition.
2. I am not the Christ.
3. I find fulfillment in the bridegroom's joy.
4. He must increase, I must decrease.

In verse 29, John compares his role to that of a friend of the actual bridegroom, who takes joy in his friend's joy. The "friend of the bridegroom" – we would say, the "best man" – is the traditional Jewish *shoshᵉbin* who acts as an agent for the groom and takes care of arranging for the wedding. He works behind the scenes to prepare for the celebration, but he isn't the focus of the day. The focus, of course, is on the bridegroom and his bride. The best man receives his joy when he hears the groom conversing with the bride. "It is not about me," John insists. "It is about the Messiah."

---

[12] John 4:2 explains that Jesus wasn't baptizing people himself; he had delegated this ministry to his disciples.

3. Jesus' Enemies

Analogy of the Children in the Marketplace (Matthew 11:16-19, §65; Luke 7:31-32, §82)

The Analogy of the Children in the Marketplace is a short parable, a simple comparison. Jesus has been praising John the Baptist to the crowds, and bemoaning the fact that the Pharisees and other Jewish leaders had "rejected God's purpose for themselves" (Luke 7:30) by rejecting John's message. Both Jesus and his cousin John have been criticized – but for opposite reasons. Their opponents are arbitrary, fickle, like children.

> "¹⁶ To what can I compare this generation? They are like children sitting in the marketplaces and calling out to others:
>
> ¹⁷ 'We played the flute for you,
> and you did not dance;
> we sang a dirge,
> and you did not mourn.'
>
> ¹⁸ For John came neither eating nor drinking, and they say, 'He has a demon.' ¹⁹ The Son of Man came eating and drinking, and they say, 'Here is a glutton and a drunkard, a friend of tax collectors and "sinners." 'But wisdom is proved right by her actions.'" (Matthew 11:16-19)

Jesus seems to be picturing children playing, where one group complains that the other group will never go along with what they want. They won't dance to the fast tunes of the pipe, nor will they mourn to the sad harmonies of a funeral. They won't go along. Neither John the Baptist nor Jesus had gone along with what the leaders wanted.

But notice the saying has two parts: dancing and mourning, perhaps intended to correspond to the differences between John and Jesus. John is the mourner who would not dance, while Jesus is the dancer who would not mourn. They criticized John for his asceticism and Jesus for his refusal to fast and for going to parties thrown by tax collectors and sinners. Like children, you couldn't please his opponents.

The cryptic phrase, "Wisdom is proved right by her actions" (verse 19b) seems to suggest that "both Jesus and John in their different ways have displayed ... practical wisdom, which is thus 'justified' over the criticism of those who represent a more conventional lifestyle."[13]

---

[13] France, *Matthew*, p. 435

Appendix 4. Miscellaneous Analogies and Sayings

The message of this parable is simple. Jesus is explaining why he ignores his critics. Don't listen to criticism, he is saying, listen to God and what he wants you to do. Only that, in the end, will justify your actions no matter what your critics say.

Parable of Rescuing from a Well (Matthew 12:9-14, §70; Luke 14:2-5, §168)

Jesus was notorious for healing on the Sabbath. The Jews objected to healing on the Sabbath as "work," the work of a physician. Jesus uses a similar comparison or analogy to show their hypocrisy on two different occasions when he is about to heal an afflicted person on the Sabbath.

Luke's account finds him invited for dinner at the home of a prominent – and skeptical – Pharisee where one of the guests has dropsy or edema, a condition where the tissues swell because of fluid retention, particularly visible in the legs and feet. Jesus challenges his critics:

> "⁵ If one of you has a son[14] or an ox that falls into a well on the Sabbath day, will you not immediately pull him out?' ⁶ And they had nothing to say." (Luke 14:5-6)

Matthew's account has Jesus healing a man with a withered hand in the synagogue.

> "¹¹ If any of you has a sheep and it falls into a pit on the Sabbath, will you not take hold of it and lift it out? ¹² How much more valuable is a man than a sheep! Therefore it is lawful to do good on the Sabbath." (Matthew 12:11-12)

Rabbis of the day had ruled that rescuing an animal was permissible on the Sabbath. So Jesus argues from the lesser (the animal) to the greater (the human sufferer) to permit healing on the Sabbath. There wasn't much that Jesus' enemies could say, but it angered them.

Saying of the Blind Leading the Blind (Matthew 15:14, §115; Luke 6:39, §76)

In Luke's Gospel, the Parable of the Blind Leading the Blind is connected with the Parable of the Speck and the Beam (Lesson 3.4), immediately preceding it. It is a brief parable, an illustration of the ridiculousness of following people who are spiritually blind.

Pieter Bruegel the Elder, 'The Blind Leading the Blind' (1568), distemper on linen canvas, 34 x 61 in., Museo di Capodimonte, Naples, Italy.

---

[14] "Son" (NIV, ESV), "child" (NRSV), "ass" (KJV) reflects a textual variant in the Greek manuscripts. Metzger (*Textual Commentary*, p. 138) says that the oldest reading preserved in the manuscripts seems to be "son" (P[45, 75] (A) B W). "Because the collocation of the two words appeared to be somewhat incongruous, copyists altered "son" to either "donkey" (as in Luke 13:15) or "sheep" as in Matthew 12:11. The Committee gives it a {B}, "some degree of doubt" confidence rating.

"He also told them this parable: 'Can a blind man lead a blind man? Will they not both fall into a pit?'" (Luke 6:39)

In another instance, Jesus has referred to the Pharisees concerning their criticism of eating with hands that haven't first been ritually washed.

"Leave them; they are blind guides. If a blind man leads a blind man, both will fall into a pit." (Matthew 15:14)

It almost sounds as if the blind leading the blind were a common proverb in Jesus' culture.

Analogy of the Brood of Vipers (Matthew 12:34, §85; 23:33, §210)

Jesus had some harsh comparisons of his critics, calling them snakes – vipers, whose bite was capable of poisoning and sometimes killing.

"You brood of vipers, how can you who are evil say anything good? For out of the overflow of the heart the mouth speaks." (Matthew 12:34)

"You snakes! You brood of vipers! How will you escape being condemned to hell?" (Matthew 23:33)

John the Baptist had also used this comparison (Matthew 3:7 = Luke 3:7).

Analogy of the Den of Robbers (Matthew 21:13; Luke 19:46, §198; John 2:16)

The temple was to be a holy place, but the religious leaders – particularly the high priest – had licensed franchises for merchants to sell certified sacrificial animals and exchange money at exorbitant rates, right within the temple walls. Jesus didn't spare them when he cleansed the temple.

"'It is written,' he said to them, '"My house will be called a house of prayer," but you are making it a "den of robbers."'" (Matthew 21:13)

"To those who sold doves he said, 'Get these out of here! How dare you turn my Father's house into a market!'" (John 2:16)

4. The Kingdom

Finally, we see two parables that tell us something about the Kingdom. I didn't include them in the text because they are the focus of much controversy between Catholics, Orthodox, and Protestant scholars. Whole books have been written about this, but we'll examine them very briefly here.

Analogy of Peter the Rock (Matthew 16:18, §122; John 1:42)

We almost miss the fact that Peter's nickname, given by Jesus, is a metaphor itself. Andrew brings his brother Simon to meet Jesus.

> "He brought him to Jesus. Jesus looked at him and said, 'You are Simon son of John. You will be called Cephas (which, when translated, is Peter).'" (John 1:42)

Jesus sees something in Simon and prophetically calls him Peter (Greek *petros*, "stone, rock") – in Aramaic, *Cephas*, which is what Paul calls him.

Later, at Caesarea Philippi, Peter declares, "You are the Christ, the Son of the Living God!" (Matthew 16:15). Jesus, excited at Peter's discernment and faith in what the Father revealed to him, responds:

> "And I tell you that you are Peter, and on this **rock** I will build my church, and the gates of Hades will not overcome it." (Matthew 16:18)

Peter has said: You are the Messiah. Jesus responds: You are the Rock. Roman Catholics see verse 18 as granting Peter himself primacy as the first Pope and Bishop of Rome. Protestants tend to see this as Christ founding his church on the solid rock of faith illustrated by Peter's confession of Jesus the Messiah. No matter how you see it, Simon Peter is a pillar apostle and a foundation stone in the Church (Galatians 2:9; Ephesians 2:20).

Analogy of the Keys of the Kingdom (Matthew 16:19, §122)

In Peter's faith declaration that Jesus is the Messiah at Caesarea Philippi we see an additional analogy:

> "I will give you **the keys of the kingdom of heaven**; whatever you bind on earth will be bound in heaven, and whatever you loose on earth will be loosed in heaven." (Matthew 16:19)

Keys are used in the Bible figuratively to indicate authority over a household or domain (Isaiah 22:22; Revelation 1:18; 3:7; 9:1; 20:1).

There is much debate about the exact meaning of the "power of the keys." Roman Catholics connect the keys with Jesus' statement to his apostles after his resurrection:

> "[21b] 'As the Father has sent me, I am sending you.' [22] And with that he breathed on them and said, 'Receive the Holy Spirit. [23] If you forgive anyone his sins, they are forgiven; if you do not forgive them, they are not forgiven.'" (John 20:21-23)

Thus, Catholics believe that Peter and his successors have the authority to grant absolution and salvation, or to deny it.

Protestants, on the other hand, see Peter as representing the apostles. That the keys refer to the total apostolic mission of bringing the message of remission of sins to those who believe.

Appendix 5. The Great Messianic Banquet

To understand some of Jesus' Parables we must consider Jewish expectations of the afterlife and of the Last Days. They conceived of blessedness in the afterlife as being in Abraham's Bosom. This was connected with an idea of being seated around a table feasting with the Patriarchs and the Messiah when the Kingdom of God finally came.

The Bosom of Abraham

In Jesus' Parable of the Rich Man and Lazarus (Lesson 4.1), Jesus tells of Lazarus's place of bliss in the afterlife.

> "The time came when the beggar died and the angels carried him to Abraham's side." (Luke 16:22a)

"Side" (NIV, ESV, NRSV), "bosom" (KJV) is *kolpos*, "bosom, breast, chest."[1] When people would recline around a table, they would rest on their left elbows and eat with their right hands. Thus, you would lean close to the chest of the person to your left. You would be on their right side, considered the place of honor. So, in Jesus' parable, Lazarus is seated at table to the right hand of Abraham (cf. John 13:23; 21:20).[2] The image of the Bosom of Abraham was parallel to and coexisted with the image of the great Messianic Feast in the Kingdom of God.

The Feast in the Kingdom of God

In the Historical Books you sometimes see references to having a place at the king's table, in other words, being fed at the expense of the king as part of his royal court.[3] In Isaiah we see this celebration of a meal at Yahweh's table, where Isaiah looks beyond the embarrassment of the Exile.

> "On this mountain the Lord Almighty will prepare
> **a feast of rich food for all peoples**,
> a banquet of aged wine –
> the best of meats and the finest of wines.
> On this mountain he will ... swallow up death forever.
> The Sovereign Lord will wipe away the tears from all faces;
> he will remove the disgrace of his people from all the earth." (Isaiah 25:6-8a)

---

[1] *Kolpos*, BDAG 556, 1.
[2] James Orr, "Abraham's Bosom," ISBE 1:18.
[3] 2 Samuel 9:7, 10, 13; 19:28, 33; 1 Kings 2:7.

Appendix 5. The Great Messianic Banquet

It will be a time when God will "remove the disgrace of his people," interpreted by the Jews as God sending his Messiah at the End of the Age.[4]

Among the Dead Sea Scrolls from the Qumran community is a document known as the "Rule of the Congregation" (1QSa) dating from about 100 BC. It pictures a feast at a common table.

> "The Messiah of Israel shall extend his hand over the bread, [and] all the congregation of the Community [shall utter a] blessing, [each man in the order] of his dignity" (1QSa 2).

It is this End Time Messianic Banquet that a guest speaks about in Luke's account of a feast at the home of a prominent Pharisee.

> "Blessed is the man who will eat at the feast in the kingdom of God." (Luke 14:15)

The Last Supper

We see this feast referred to at the Lord's Supper. In celebrating Passover in Jesus' time, the Jews set aside a cup for the Messiah in case he were to come that very night to deliver them and fulfill the promise of the Messianic Banquet.[5] At Jesus' Last Supper with his disciples, he refers to this banquet:

> "16 For I tell you, I will not eat [this Passover] again until it finds fulfillment in the kingdom of God. 17 After taking the cup, he gave thanks and said, 'Take this and divide it among you. 18 For I tell you I will not drink again of the fruit of the vine until the kingdom of God comes.'" (Luke 22:16-18)

Other References to the Messianic Banquet

Jesus refers to this Messianic Banquet a number of times:

To his disciples at the Last Supper:

> "29 And I confer on you a kingdom, just as my Father conferred one on me, 30 so that you may eat and drink at my table in my kingdom and sit on thrones, judging the twelve tribes of Israel." (Luke 22:29-30)

In the Parable of the Narrow Door (Lesson 8.2):

> "People will come from east and west and north and south, and will take their places at the feast in the kingdom of God." (Luke 13:29)

About the centurion who believed that Jesus could heal his servant:

---

[4] R.K. Harrison, "Meals," ISBE 3:292.
[5] R. S. Wallace, "Lord's Supper (Eucharist)," ISBE 3:165. B.L. Bandstra, "Wine," ISBE 4:1071; M.R. Wilson, "Passover," ISBE 3:678.

"¹⁰ I tell you the truth, I have not found anyone in Israel with such great faith. ¹¹ I say to you that many will come from the east and the west, and will take their places at the feast with Abraham, Isaac and Jacob in the kingdom of heaven. ¹² But the subjects of the kingdom will be thrown outside, into the darkness, where there will be weeping and gnashing of teeth." (Matthew 8:10-12)

At a banquet to which Jesus was invited, he offered this advice:

"¹³ But when you give a banquet, invite the poor, the crippled, the lame, the blind, ¹⁴ and you will be blessed. Although they cannot repay you, you will be repaid at the resurrection of the righteous." (Luke 14:13-14)

In other words, they will be repaid at the great Messianic Banquet to which God will invite you at the End Time. This may be the idea of one of the Beatitudes in Luke, where the poor will enjoy sumptuous food in the Kingdom.

"Blessed are you who hunger now,
for you will be satisfied.' (Luke 6:21)

We see hints of the Messianic Banquet in Jesus' Parable of the Wedding Banquet and the Parable of the Great Banquet (Lesson 2.2).

"The kingdom of heaven is like a king who prepared a wedding banquet for his son." (Matthew 22:2)

In Luke's version of the Parable of the Watching Servants (Lesson 5.2), we see a hint of this when the faithful servants are surprised to be served by their master when he returns from being away:

"It will be good for those servants whose master finds them watching when he comes. I tell you the truth, he will dress himself to serve, will have them recline at the table and will come and wait on them." (Luke 12:37)

Finally, in the Book of Revelation we see this great Messianic Banquet at the End of the Age described in terms of the Marriage Supper of the Lamb.

"⁷ 'Let us rejoice and be glad and give him glory!
For the wedding of the Lamb has come,
and his bride has made herself ready.
⁸ Fine linen, bright and clean, was given her to wear.'
(Fine linen stands for the righteous acts of the saints.) ⁹ Then the angel said to me, 'Write: "Blessed are those who are invited to the wedding supper of the Lamb!"'" (Revelation 19:7-9)

Perhaps there is also a hint of this marriage supper when Jesus refers to himself as the bridegroom in the Parable of the Bridegroom's Guests (Lesson 7.2).

Appendix 6. Slavery in Jesus' Day

Several of Jesus' parables picture "servants" in first century Palestine. Our English Bibles usually translate Greek *doulos* as "servant," though the word actually describes a slave in most cases. Bartchy says,

> "In contrast to the practice of the [King James Version], *doulos* should be translated 'slave' instead of 'servant' in order to point to the legal subordination of the 'slave' as property of the owner."[1]

The standard New Testament Greek lexicon defines *doulos* as:

> "Male slave as an entity in a socioeconomic context, slave. ('Servant' for 'slave' is largely confined to Biblical translations and early American times.)"[2]

In addition, a few other words are used in the Gospels for slaves as opposed to servants.[3]

Slavery as Involuntary Servitude

One way to define slavery is involuntary servitude, subjecting one person to the power of another. Most slaves were considered chattel, that is, property that can be bought or sold.

In America, we still haven't recovered from 400 years of slavery. Blame, victim mentality, economic disadvantage, and racism continue to plague our society. But slavery is repugnant to us – so repugnant, in fact, that it is difficult for Americans to read about slavery in the Bible without loading the subject with a great deal of emotional and historical baggage that relate to the treatment of plantation slaves in the South.

But to Jews in the first century Roman empire, slavery was just a fact of life. Rome's wars to subjugate the Mediterranean world, much of Europe, and the British Isles had resulted in taking hundreds of thousands of slaves captive, and selling them in the slave markets of Rome and other Italian cities. This is how soldiers – and especially the officers – were paid!

---

[1] S. Scott Bartchy, "Servant; Slave," ISBE 4:420.
[2] *Doulos*, BDAG 260, 1a.
[3] *Misthios*, "day laborer, hired man" (BDAG 653) distinguished hired workers from slaves (Luke 15:17, 19, 21). Another term we find is *pais*, "child," is commonly used in the sense, "one who is committed in total obedience to another, slave, servant," used of slaves and personal attendants (BDAG 750, 3a), such as in Matthew 8:6, 8, 13; Luke 7:7; 15:26. *Oikétēs*, "house slave, domestic, and "slave" generally (BDAG 694; Luke 16:13). *Syndoulos*, "one who, along with others, is in a relationship of total obedience to one master or owner, fellow-slave" (Matthew 24:49), or "a subordinate in total obedience to a ruler, slave" (Matthew 18:49; BDAG 966, meanings 1 and 2a).

Slavery came about through warfare, piracy, brigandage, the international slave trade, kidnapping, infant exposure, failure to pay a debt, forced labor of alien populations, natural reproduction of the existing slave population, and the punishment of criminals to the mines or gladiatorial combat.

Of these, warfare seems to be the main source of slaves as Roman armies expanded the Empire and carried out wars to reinforce their control. In urban areas of Roman imperial society, the slave population was considerable – perhaps between 17% and 33%.[4] For example, we know that after Roman general Pompey conquered Judea and Jerusalem in 63 BC, many thousands of Jews were enslaved and transported to Rome.

By New Testament times, however, most of the Roman world was at peace, reducing the numbers of prisoners of war sold on the slave market, though there were still many, many slaves remaining, and their children and children's children.

Though it might seem strange to us, a number of people would sell themselves into slavery, principally "to enter a life that was easier and more secure than existence as a poor, freeborn person." Slaves sometimes received an education at their owner's expense, and, if they sold themselves to a Roman citizen, when manumitted they might expect to become Roman citizens themselves. According to the Torah, thieves could be sold as slaves if they were unable to make restitution (Exodus 22:3).

While the Greeks considered slaves to be sub-human, Hebrew history in Egypt taught Jews to show respect to their slaves. And Romans, as mentioned, might manumit a slave and make him a citizen. Nor did slaves just have servile duties. Some might be tutors, physicians, companions, household managers, sales agents, and administrators.[5]

Slavery in Jesus' Parables

The average person in Jesus' culture didn't own slaves, but many villages would have a wealthier person who owned one or more slaves. A farmer might have a single slave to help with farming, as well as around the house (as in the Parable of the Dutiful Servant, Lesson 11.1). But many of Jesus' parables talk about household slaves of a wealthy person, as well as a manager or steward to direct them.

Slaves and slavery figure into a number of parables.

- Parables of the Talents and of the Minas (Lesson 11.2)
- Parable of the Prodigal Son (Lesson 1.1)
- Parable of the Wise and Faithful Steward (Lesson 5.3)

---

[4] J. Albert Harrill, "Slavery," in Craig A. Evans and Stanley E. Porter (eds.), *Dictionary of New Testament Background* (Intervarsity Press, 2000), pp. 1124-1127.
[5] S. Scott Bartchy, "Slavery," ISBE 4:539-546; S. Scott Bartchy, "Servant," ISBE 4:419-421.

Appendix 6. Slavery in Jesus' Day

- Analogy of the Slave and the Son (Lesson 4.2)
- Parable of the Two Masters (Lesson 10.2)
- Parable of the Unmerciful Servant (Lesson 1.2)
- Parable of the Dutiful Servant (Lesson 11:1)
- Acted Parable of Washing the Disciples' Feet (Lesson 11.3)

Printed in Great Britain
by Amazon